Making and Remaking
Asian America
Through Immigration Policy
1850–1990

# ASIAN AMERICA

*A series edited by Gordon H. Chang*

The increasing size and diversity of the Asian American population, its growing significance in American society and culture, and the expanded appreciation, both popular and scholarly, of the importance of Asian Americans in the country's present and past—all these developments have converged to stimulate wide interest in scholarly work on topics related to the Asian American experience. The general recognition of the pivotal role that race and ethnicity have played in American life, and in relations between the United States and other countries, has also fostered this heightened attention.

Although Asian Americans were a subject of serious inquiry in the late nineteenth and early twentieth centuries, they were subsequently ignored by the mainstream scholarly community for several decades. In recent years, however, this neglect has ended, with an increasing number of writers examining a good many aspects of Asian American life and culture. Moreover, many students of American society are recognizing that the study of issues related to Asian America speaks to, and may be essential for, many current discussions on the part of the informed public and various scholarly communities.

The Stanford series on Asian America seeks to address these interests. The series will include work from the humanities and social sciences, including history, anthropology, political science, American studies, law, literary criticism, sociology, and interdisciplinary and policy studies.

# Making and Remaking
# Asian America
# Through Immigration Policy
# 1850–1990

Bill Ong Hing

STANFORD UNIVERSITY PRESS
STANFORD, CALIFORNIA

Stanford University Press
Stanford, California
©1993 by the Board of Trustees
of the Leland Stanford Junior University
Printed in the United States of America

CIP data are at the end of the book

Original printing 1993
Last figure below indicates date of this printing:
03   02   01

*To my big brothers and sisters—*
*Lilly, Minnie, Ally, Holy, Bob,*
*Mary, Grace, Joyce, and Johnny—*
*for their inspiration, challenges, support, and love*

# Acknowledgments

Over the many years that it took me to research and write this book, dozens of friends, students, colleagues, and relatives contributed to the work. Some of the students that helped me with research and editing were Tom Boasberg, Susan Bowyer, Dorianne Davidson, Lindsay Harris, Katie Ho, Sallie Kim, Amanda Lehman, Katharine Lewis, Dorothy Liu, Roslyn Powell-Lima, Amy Reid, Caitlin Schneider, Clarence Wong, May Woo, and John Young. Several members of the Stanford Law School support staff worked on the manuscript at various stages: Kathleen Ansari, Elaine Anderson, Ann Babb, Louisa Clemens, Heather Haven, and particularly Yvonne Yazzie Nakahigashi, my phenomenal clinical assistant who is also a miracle worker. I had the help of many brilliant colleagues at the law school who took the time to read drafts of the manuscript and provide insightful critique: Barbara Babcock, Lawrence Friedman, Tom Grey, Bob Gordon, Mark Kelman, Michael Piore, Bill Simon, and especially Michael Wald. Gordon Chang in the history department also gave me excellent advice.

Gary Peck, a graduate of Stanford, was incredibly helpful to me in framing Chapter 5, counseling me on its approach, and reviewing several drafts. An Asian American reading group on campus read and critiqued my section on Asian American identity. The group included Diana Akiyama, Rudy Bustos, Michael Chan, David Palumbo-Liu, Ron Nakao, Masao Suzuki, Sylvia Yanagisako, Alice Yang-Murray, Nancy Youn, Rick Yuen, and Judy Yung. My sister Joyce gave me some good leads on unusual historical notes, and my brothers-in-law Bill McGowan and Herb Yee read early drafts and provided me with good feedback as well. I am sincerely grateful to the excellent Stanford Law School library staff, including Paul Lomio and Iris Wildman, but especially Arline "Andy" Eisenberg. Muriel Bell at Stanford University Press was also quite helpful. And throughout the project, two deans, John Hart Ely and Paul Brest, provided me with full support and encouragement. Much of the research was supported by a bequest from the Claire and Michael Brown Estate.

A project of this nature and size preys heavily upon one's mental health. Thankfully, at various times I was able to rely upon a good group of friends to keep me going (some for all too brief visits): Regina Austin, Sally Dickson, Ed Epstein, Bill Gould, Char Hamada, Maya Harris, Alex Johnson, Chuck Lawrence, Mari Matsuda, Miguel Méndez, Rose Ochi, Dru Ramey, Maria Rodriguez, Blanca Silvestrini, Kim Taylor, Patricia Williams, and Jackson Wong. And the staff attorneys at the Immigrant Legal Resource Center—Kathy Brady, Eric Cohen, Susan Lydon, Mark Silverman, Juliette Steadman, and Susan Woolley—kept me involved in real-life issues that also helped me maintain balance in my life.

My wife, Lenora, and children—Eric, Sharon, and Julianne—deserve high praise for putting up with me during this enterprise. I was able to salvage the delight of a family life with them often, but certainly not as much as they deserve. Their patience, direction, tolerance, love, and especially their sense of humor make me quite the lucky guy.

My greatest expression of thanks must be reserved for my colleague at Stanford, Jerry López. He guided me through several stages of the project's development, pushing me to strive for high scholarly goals while standing by me as a friend. For that I shall forever be grateful.

B. O. H.

# Contents

REFERENCE MATTER

# Tables and Figure

FIGURE

# Making and Remaking
# Asian America
# Through Immigration Policy
# 1850–1990

# Introduction

In 1882 Congress enacted immigration legislation excluding "idiots," "lunatics," and "Chinese laborers." Eventually, a range of policies and laws restricted the entry of every Asian group—including Filipinos, who began the twentieth century as U.S. nationals and hence were not subject to immigration laws. The number of immigrants from China, Japan, the Philippines, and India dropped sharply as a result.

These policies and their subsequent repeal shaped and reshaped Asian American communities. Beyond cutting back on new immigrants, they manipulated gender ratios that influenced population growth. The Chinese American population, for example, decreased from 1890 to 1920, and the Filipino American population began to decline by 1940; but the Japanese American population grew steadily because a higher proportion of Japanese laborers were able to send for spouses and children. By the end of World War II, exclusionary policies eased, more women were able to join their husbands, and the population of each group rose.

Changes to the immigration selection system in 1965 caused the most dramatic increase in Asian Americans—from 1 million in 1965 to over 7 million in 1990. Table 1 compares immigration rates for several Asian groups before and after 1965. Currently Asians are increasing faster than any other racial or ethnic minority in the United States. Between 1931 and 1965, however, they were a mere 5 percent of all those who entered the country legally. The accompanying figure illustrates that by the late 1980's and early 1990's, they were nearly half (48 percent) of all legal entries, with Latin Americans (35 percent) and Europeans (12 percent) accounting for most of the rest. Even so, Asian Americans are less than 3 percent of the entire U.S. population (see Table 2). Since

TABLE 1

*Comparison of Asian Immigration Rates, 1959–1989*

| Country | Total immigrants |
|---------|------------------|
| **1959** | |
| China[a] | 5,722 |
| Hong Kong | 844 |
| India | 506 |
| Japan | 5,851 |
| Korea | 1,720 |
| Philippines | 3,963 |
| **1970** | |
| China[a] | 14,093 |
| Hong Kong | 3,863 |
| India | 10,114 |
| Japan | 4,485 |
| Korea | 9,314 |
| Philippines | 31,203 |
| Vietnam | 1,450 |
| **1978** | |
| China[a] | 21,315 |
| Hong Kong | 5,158 |
| India | 20,753 |
| Japan | 4,010 |
| Korea | 29,288 |
| Philippines | 37,216 |
| Vietnam | 2,758  (and 85,000 refugees) |
| **1989** | |
| China, Mainland | 27,394  (plus 4,878 amnesty recipients) |
| Taiwan | 12,457  (plus 1,517 amnesty recipients) |
| Hong Kong | 8,624  (plus 1,116 amnesty recipients) |
| India | 28,498  (plus 2,677 amnesty recipients) |
| Japan | 4,401  (plus 448 amnesty recipients) |
| Korea | 32,204  (plus 2,018 amnesty recipients) |
| Philippines | 49,535  (plus 7,499 amnesty recipients) |
| Vietnam | 7,148  (plus 168 amnesty recipients, 8,540 Amerasians, and 20,000+ refugees) |

SOURCES: 1959 *INS Annual Report*, table 6, p. 17; 1970 *INS Annual Report*, table 6, p. 40; 1978 *INS Statistical Yearbook*, table 6, p. 8; 1989 *INS Advance Report*, table 4.
[a]Includes Taiwan

1965 Filipinos have become the second largest Asian American group, and discernible Korean and Asian Indian communities have developed, each approaching the size of the Japanese American community that had been the largest group as recently as 1970.

Immigration policies have also affected the demographic and social characteristics of Asian America. Though they continue to prefer the West Coast, more Asian Americans have settled in the East and South.

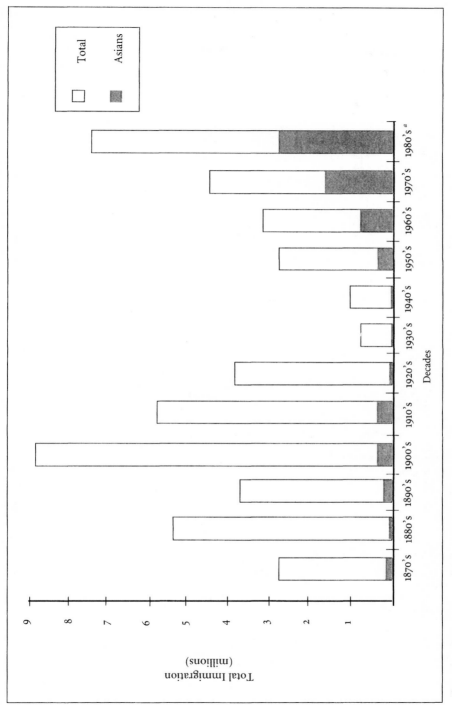

Change in Asian proportion of total immigration, 1871-1990.
SOURCES: *INS Statistical Yearbook* 1990; INS Statistical Branch, Advance INS Report, 1992.
[a] Includes almost 3 million aliens granted amnesty under 1986 legalization laws.

## TABLE 2
### U.S. Census Data: Race and Hispanic Origin, 1990 and 1980

| Race or Hispanic Origin | 1990 Census Number | 1990 Census Percent | 1980 Census Number | 1980 Census Percent | Increase Number | Increase Percent |
|---|---|---|---|---|---|---|
| All persons | 248,709,873 | 100.0 | 226,545,805 | 100.0 | 22,164,068 | 9.8 |
| White | 199,686,070 | 80.3 | 188,371,622 | 83.1 | 11,314,448 | 6.0 |
| Black | 29,986,060 | 12.1 | 26,495,025 | 11.7 | 3,491,035 | 13.2 |
| American Indian, Eskimo, or Aleut | 1,959,234 | 0.8 | 1,420,400 | 0.6 | 538,834 | 37.9 |
| American Indian | 1,878,285 | 0.8 | 1,364,033 | 0.6 | 514,252 | 37.7 |
| Eskimo | 57,152 | 0.0 | 42,162 | 0.0 | 14,990 | 35.6 |
| Aleut | 23,797 | 0.0 | 14,205 | 0.0 | 9,592 | 67.5 |
| Asian or Pacific Islander | 7,273,662 | 2.9 | 3,500,439[a] | 1.5 | 3,773,223 | 107.8 |
| Chinese | 1,645,472 | 0.7 | 806,040 | 0.4 | 839,432 | 104.1 |
| Filipino | 1,406,770 | 0.6 | 774,652 | 0.3 | 632,118 | 81.6 |
| Japanese | 847,562 | 0.3 | 700,974 | 0.3 | 146,588 | 20.9 |
| Asian Indian | 815,447 | 0.3 | 361,531 | 0.2 | 453,916 | 125.6 |
| Korean | 798,849 | 0.3 | 354,593 | 0.2 | 444,256 | 125.3 |
| Vietnamese | 614,547 | 0.2 | 261,729 | 0.1 | 352,818 | 134.8 |
| Hawaiian | 211,014 | 0.1 | 166,814 | 0.1 | 44,200 | 26.5 |
| Samoan | 62,964 | 0.0 | 41,948 | 0.0 | 21,016 | 50.1 |
| Guamanian | 49,345 | 0.0 | 32,158 | 0.0 | 17,187 | 53.4 |
| Other Asian or Pacific Islander | 821,692 | 0.3 | NA | NA | NA | NA |
| Other Race | 9,804,847 | 3.9 | 6,758,319 | 3.0 | 3,046,528 | 45.1 |
| Hispanic origin[b] | 22,354,059 | 9.0 | 14,608,673 | 6.4 | 7,745,386 | 53.0 |
| Mexican | 13,495,938 | 5.4 | 8,740,439 | 3.9 | 4,755,499 | 54.4 |
| Puerto Rican | 2,727,754 | 1.1 | 2,013,945 | 0.9 | 713,809 | 35.4 |
| Cuban | 1,043,932 | 0.4 | 803,226 | 0.4 | 240,706 | 30.0 |
| Other Hispanic | 5,086,435 | 2.0 | 3,051,063 | 1.3 | 2,035,372 | 66.7 |
| Not of Hispanic origin | 226,355,814 | 91.0 | 211,937,132 | 93.6 | 14,418,682 | 6.8 |

SOURCE: Release CB91-215, Bureau of Census, *U.S. Dept. of Commerce News*, June 12, 1991, table 1.

NA = Not Available from 1980 100-percent tabulations.

[a]The 1980 number for Asians or Pacific Islanders shown in this table is not entirely comparable with 1990 counts. The 1980 count includes only the nine specific groups. A 1980 total Asian or Pacific Islander population of 3,726,440 from sample tabulations is comparable to the 1990 count because it includes groups not listed on the 1980 census form.

[b]Persons of Hispanic origin may be of any race.

Some ghettos, such as the Chinatowns of the past, survive because refugees were admitted in the early 1960's and working-class relatives after 1965. Suburban residential enclaves (among Filipinos and Indians) as well as economic ones (among Koreans and Vietnamese) have evolved more recently.

Employment profiles have been impacted as well. Before 1950 Chinese, Japanese, Asian Indians, and Filipinos were primarily employed in rural, farm-worker, or service jobs. But the 1965 amendments infused every group with more professionals so that a significant portion of Asian America is now considered white-collar. United States refugee and resettlement policies have shaped the size, residential patterns, and economic profile of Vietnamese Americans. And Asian American academic performance, political participation, and personal identity all are linked to the effect of immigration policies on demographics.

As their numbers have grown, their visibility in the mainstream has caused a swirl of activity prompting policymakers, scholars, journalists, community and grassroots organizers, activists, and, of course, restrictionists to take Asian Americans more seriously. As they have become more involved in social, political, and economic life at both national and local levels, Asian Americans figure prominently on the agendas of lawmakers, social service providers, and those interested in fundamental social change. But at the same time they have become the target of racist hostilities, which are sometimes physical but more often sociopolitical and economic, such as the recent concerns about the disproportionate number being admitted to prestigious colleges and universities. That kind of nativist sentiment led to historical immigration restrictions meant to control an influx that seemed to be getting out of hand.

As a second-generation Chinese American immigration attorney and legal academic, I have been caught up in this swirl. For years I practiced law in San Francisco's Chinatown, where it seemed natural to work with immigrants and with grassroots and community organizations whose members included friends and relatives. When I took a faculty post in the mid-1970's, my experiences as a practitioner carried over to my teaching and my scholarship. I directed clinical programs and a legal services support center, where my colleagues and I strove to prepare future lawyers and paralegals for the special problems of immigrant clientele. When I wrote, I did so to facilitate better work in the field—the sort of lawyering that would prove enabling to immigrants themselves, hopefully helping them to better cope with life's challenges.

Because of my work in the community and in the academy, I gained a reputation as something of an expert on immigration law. I was enlisted to serve on the staff advisory group of the Select Commission on Immigration and Refugee Policy during the Carter administration. The commission, whose members included Senators Alan Simpson and Edward Kennedy, Representatives Peter Rodino, Elizabeth Holtzman, Hamilton Fish, and Romano Mazzoli, Attorneys General Griffin Bell and Benjamin Civiletti, Secretary of Labor Ray Marshall, Secretary of State Edmund Muskie, Secretary of Health and Human Services Patricia Harris, Justice Cruz Reynoso, community activist Rose Matsui Ochi, and labor leader Joaquin Otero, was prominent in the formation of national policy and law. More recently, I was appointed to the advisory committee of the Immigration Policy Project of the Carnegie Endowment for International Peace. I have often been asked to recommend, draft, and/or review various legislative proposals, and I have been called to testify before state and congressional committees on these subjects. I have appeared on local and national radio and television shows to discuss immigration, particularly Asian immigration.

In significant regards, these involvements and experiences have proven disconcerting. I came to appreciate how much we need to learn about Asian Americans before claiming to be experts. And I mean at a fundamental level. For all the differences that might exist between me and other policymakers, commentators, and "experts," we all shared the need for a basic description of Asian America. Most purported experts appeared to me to know little about, or to misunderstand, its demographics. They seemed not even to understand that there are several Asian American communities rather than some single, monolithic one. They were, moreover, both unaware of and seemingly uninterested in how demographics affect the experiences of Asian Americans and their place in society. Most just do not have a full sense of the history, nor have they made a careful study of Asian Americans as a people.

Worse still, they appear not to comprehend the degree to which Asian Americans have been affected by immigration policies and laws. Remarkably, in spite of the palpable consequences to these groups, the absence of reliable basic descriptions has been translated into misconceptions and generalizations—at times conflicting—about life in the communities. And this lack of knowledge is shared by policymakers, scholars, Asian American activists, and the popular media.

## Policymakers

Consider, for example, the conventional wisdom that the 1965 changes in the law were too generous toward Asians.[1] That Asians constitute almost half of the legal immigrants to the United States today and that European immigration has declined greatly are perceived as conclusive evidence that the design of the 1965 law gave too much to Asians while disadvantaging Europeans. The truth is that the 1965 amendments were intended not to encourage Asian immigration but to advance European immigration. Yet a section of the 1986 Immigration Reform and Control Act was deliberately designed to advantage non-Asians by adjusting quotas for two years.[2]

This program proved so popular with policymakers that it was extended first for two additional years and then more permanently in 1990. Liberals like Congressman Howard Berman and Senator Edward Kennedy were among its strongest supporters. At one point, Kennedy proposed the creation of a permanent point system that would help potential immigrants from certain non-Asian countries who are unable to take advantage of the family reunification provisions of the 1965 law.[3] Throughout, his actions have been motivated by a desire to assist Western European residents, particularly those from Ireland. After the Senate passed his bill in 1989, Kennedy said, "In effect, we will no longer be shortchanging people from countries who have not been able to come to this country in such great numbers."[4] Sections of the 1990 law continue to reflect these attitudes, providing extra independent and transition visas that are unavailable to Asians.

The more conservative Senator Alan Simpson, one of the chief architects of contemporary immigration law and co-sponsor of Kennedy's bill, is more blunt in expressing concerns that immigration patterns that include large numbers of Asians may produce insulated communities whose residents fail to assimilate:

> Assimilation to fundamental American public values and institutions may be of far more importance to the future of the United States. If immigration is continued at a high level and yet a substantial portion of the newcomers and their descendants do not assimilate, they may create in America some of the same social, political and economic problems which existed in the country which they have chosen to depart. Furthermore, as previously mentioned, a community with a large number of immigrants who do not assimilate will to some degree seem

unfamiliar to longtime residents. Finally, if linguistic and cultural separatism rise above a certain level, the unity and political stability of the nation will in time be seriously eroded.[5]

Senator Simpson's sentiments are echoed by other influential lawmakers like former Colorado Governor Richard Lamm:

> America can accept additional immigrants, but we must be sure they become American. We can be a Joseph's coat of many nations, but we must be unified. We must have English as one of the common glues that hold us together. We should be color blind but not linguistically deaf. ... We can teach English via bilingual education, but we should take great care not to become a bilingual society.[6]

These statements are void of any demographic or sociological data about Asian immigrants or any other group. They reflect little about the real impact of immigration laws on Asian America.

## Scholars

Although some have contributed to a better understanding of the composition of Asian American communities and of how demographics influence assimilation, the scholars who are taken most seriously have done nothing to quell policymakers' fears of "ghettoization" brought on by recent immigration patterns. A 1988 report by the Center for Immigration Studies conveyed the impression that immigration is at an all-time high, when in truth more immigrants entered between 1900 and 1910.[7] Some researchers predict that the rate of immigration will continue to rise throughout the current decade.[8] Such forecasts reinforce the conventional policy-making wisdom that unless something is done to stem the tide of non-European immigration, the assimilation of recent arrivals will be impeded. This position is stated succinctly by Bouvier and Gardner:

> There is another major difference between today's situation and that of immigrants arriving in the early decades of the 20th century. The quota laws of the 1920's, the depression, and World War II reduced immigration sharply until the 1960's. With few of their countrymen following them to the U.S., these immigrants and their children had time and incentive to assimilate into their new milieu. Such acculturation may take longer for today's immigrants with the continuing large additions of their numbers that are likely in future years, even if illegal immigration is curbed substantially.[9]

The idea that a drastic upsurge in immigration threatens to undermine the assimilability of non-English-speaking newcomers is coupled with the equally mistaken belief that the vast majority of Asians are economically advantaged and well educated. Rather than carefully examining differences in socioeconomic status and educational attainment among diverse Asian American groups, researchers often appear to base their conclusions on census-like data indicating simply that Asians have higher than average household incomes. And they seem to accept stereotypes regarding the academic prowess and accomplishments of Asians, particularly in comparison with other immigrants of color. Consistent with this, Bouvier and Gardner note that "Except for most post–Vietnam War Indochinese refugees, Asian immigrants in general . . . are much better educated than Latin American immigrants, occupy higher rungs on the occupational ladder, and earn more."[10]

These views frequently find expression in policy-making circles, where scholars are quick to tell lawmakers what they consider best for a country already overburdened by foreigners. Former Hoover Institution Fellow Otis Graham, for example, testified before the Joint Economic Committee of Congress that increased immigration restrictions were necessary to "give ourselves more breathing space" to perform the "task of assimilation." Graham, also a spokesman for the restrictionist Federation of Americans for Immigration Reform (FAIR), warned what type of nation ours would become unless we tighten entry requirements for those who lack the ability or the resources to succeed academically and economically:

> It would be a two-tiered society, the one young, overwhelmingly Hispanic and black and low income, the other largely older whites and Asians, affluent, with a woefully small intermixing of these categories. It is a segmented society, a nation within a nation, the rich who work in high-technology enterprises or who are retired in Palm Springs moving uneasily among a mass population with low educational attainments and income levels; those who own businesses communicate to the work force through foremen who translate from English into foreign languages. . . . That scenario in California may sound good to the people who live, retired, the white affluent or Asian affluent in Palm Springs.[11]

While not all scholars subscribe to Graham's stereotypic images of Asians as overachievers and Latinos and African Americans as underachievers, few descriptions of Asian Americans debunk the popular myths. Indeed, they often replace one stereotype with a more unflattering one—that Asian immigrants are actually ill prepared to compete in and are a drag on the American economy. They focus on the fact that most Asian immigration today occurs under the auspices of family reunification provisions in the law. Barry Chiswick, the dean of Economics and Business Administration at the University of Illinois in Chicago and a former fellow at the Center for Immigration Studies, for example, joined Graham in testifying before the Joint Economic Committee of Congress. He said:

> The earliest Asian immigrants came mainly under the occupational preferences and under the investor category. They were a very highly skilled group. But what we are seeing over time is that these individuals are now in the United States serving as sponsors of their less highly educated, less well-skilled relatives in the country of origin.[12]

Chiswick went on to argue that the family reunification categories make Asian immigration a matter of "nepotism" and selfishness where personal welfare and connections are more important than the overall health of our economy. The results, claimed Chiswick and his supporters, demand a shift from a family- to a skills-based immigration policy. Chiswick seems unaware of the actual increase in Asian professionals who have entered under a family system.

Even some good scholarly work on Asian American life contains images premised on little serious demographic knowledge. For example, the two seemingly contradictory views—that Asians are highly educated and economically advantaged or that they are undereducated and ill-equipped to function in our modern economy—become especially problematic when trying to square them with research that shows unusually low levels of political participation. This finding is vexing to those who believe that Asian Americans are comparatively well-to-do, since research reveals consistently that high levels of political participation are correlated with educational attainment and high socioeconomic status. To make sense of this paradox, one scholar has attributed low participation to the fact that most Asian immigrants are "from countries with a single dominant party where elections produce little [meaningful change]."[13] She argues that because these immigrants do not speak English, they do not understand the major issues in American politics. Besides, she concluded, immigrants continue to concern themselves principally with politics in their homelands.[14]

## Popular Media

Despite increased coverage portraying Asian immigrants as uneducated and unassimilable, print and broadcast journalists more typically focus upon immigrant successes and perpetuate the myth of Asians as a model minority.[15] Asian students in these stories are whiz kids who outshine their more advantaged peers, particularly in math, science, and related technical fields. By highlighting the disproportionate numbers of Asians admitted to elite colleges, the media create the impression that such successes are the norm. The media have, for example, reported extensively on the high percentages of Asian students at Harvard (14 percent), MIT (20 percent), and the University of California at Berkeley (25 percent) compared with their representation in the general population (2.9 percent). And journalists frequently profile individual academic stars who excel in the face of seemingly insurmountable odds.[16]

This type of reporting is dangerous. The prodigies featured in these stories are usually immigrants, as are the successful entrepreneurs featured in kindred stories about Asian Horatio Algers. This writing leaves the impression that Asians, at least those not born in the United States, can succeed where other minorities have failed. And even those born in this country are presumed to be more gifted intellectually and harder working than most other Americans and thus able to take advantage of an open system that rewards the truly deserving. Reports highlight the fact that the 1990 median annual income for Asian American households ($42,250) exceeded that of the white population ($36,920), glossing over the fact that there are more workers per Asian American household with lower per capita income.[17] This image raises a fear in the general population of unfair competition from these "superbeings" that is reminiscent of what led to the desire to control them historically. And nowhere, of course, is this image reconciled with the view that Asian immigrants are ill equipped to prosper in society. This is hardly surprising given the lack of coverage that might provide a nuanced depiction of Asian Americans in all their complexity.

Reporters are not alone in stereotyping Asian Americans and Asian immigrants. Bespectacled math whizzes and buck-toothed businessmen are standard characters on television and in the movies. Often these figures are depicted as fools whose conversation is filled with fortune cookie clichés.[18] Asian women frequently appear as exotic sex objects rather than as multidimensional characters.[19] Asian communities are "filled with thoroughly ruthless ganglords, evil drug rings, secret taverns, and hidden lairs behind neon lights."[20]

## Organizers and Activists

Asians do not even receive sustained attention and support from those who might be expected to be their natural allies. Political activists and community organizers, particularly those in immigration, seldom speak out on the problems faced by Asian Americans and Asian immigrants. Their silence bespeaks the belief that most Asians are, indeed, well off economically and reflects a preoccupation with Central American and Haitian refugees and Mexican immigrants, which is understandable given the political repression and economic deprivation to which they have been subjected. During debate regarding the plight of Chinese students in the United States who fear persecution upon return to their country after the Tiananmen Square massacre in 1989, immigration activists were more concerned about establishing a policy that would benefit Salvadoreans and Guatemalans fleeing political persecution than about the concerns of the Chinese students.

My experience as an activist, attorney, and professor has made clear to me how little attention is paid to Asians by advocates who work mainly with Latin Americans and Haitians. Their neglect troubles me because of the number of Asians who enter the United States for similar reasons and who face the same sorts of difficulties. Only a handful of activists have taken an interest in halting the deportation of elderly Asian immigrants on public assistance, in stopping illegal raids of Japantown workplaces by the Immigration and Naturalization Service (INS), or in organizing Asians in sewing factories and sweatshops. Students in my own immigration law classes seem oblivious to these battles. They do not draw what seems to me to be an obvious parallel between the plight of Asians and that of Latinos and other people of color. Not even the more dramatic and well-publicized cases have reordered their priorities. Neither the mass exodus of Filipinos from the repressive Marcos regime and their poor treatment by the INS nor the brutal suppression of the Chinese democracy movement has spurred much activism directed at improving conditions for Asian Americans or Asian immigrants at the local, regional, or national levels.[21]

This lack of attention to Asian issues and concerns is disturbing, especially since Asian American activists themselves seem not to appreciate how a diversity of Asian experiences and interests might impede political unity. They overlook the possibility that their constituencies may not comprise a single community with identical aspirations but a myriad of groups with agendas that sometimes conflict significantly. They assume that Asian Americans will eventually mobilize once their emerging political consciousness evolves beyond the "toddler stage."[22] They mistakenly assume that the growing numbers of Asian Americans and the revitalization of Asian neighborhoods will necessarily translate into increased political influence as residents come to recognize their "true" interests. Rarely do they acknowledge that the absence of a unified Asian front does not reflect false or undeveloped consciousness so much as carefully considered responses to a host of socioeconomical and political circumstances that discourage groups from forming alliances or involving themselves in political institutions. Still other Asian American activists bemoan what they perceive to be apathy and regard Asians as not important politically in part because they are not political.

## Rethinking Asian America

In short, serious gaps in fundamental information persist. Although some researchers and commentators have tried to correct the worst distortions, no one has provided a comprehensive demographic overview of Asian American communities or of how their composition might affect everyday life within their midst. Nor does there appear to be adequate appreciation of how U.S. immigration policy and law have been implicated in the making of Asian America.

Consequently, lawmakers often miscalculate or ignore completely the effects of their decisions on the groups they target, while others more removed from the political scene seem unaware that domestic policy actually influences Asian affairs. This is problematic. It is plainly naive to think that immigration laws have shaped every facet of Asian American experience. Yet it is equally misguided to discount the effects of such laws on the decision to immigrate and on what happened to people once they arrived. Careful attention must be paid to demographics, to the influence of law and policy on demographics, and the connection between demographics and how these groups live.

My book is intended to provide detailed information about Asian Americans and Asian immigrants that either was not previously available or was too scattered to be of much use. I will compare the development of immigration policies with the impact they had on the demographics of specific communities and consider their influence on certain aspects of Asian American life.

I do not pretend that my data are complete. Asian America comprises those people whose cultural and ethnic heritage is from Asia or the Pacific Islands, but I will examine only six communities: Filipinos, Chinese, Japanese, Koreans, Vietnamese, and Asian Indians. They are nearly 90 percent of the census classification of Asian and Pacific Islander. I have omitted Laotians, Cambodians, Thais, Pakistanis, Indonesians, Hmong, Samoans, and Tongans, who are also beginning to establish substantial communities in the United States. Their omission is noteworthy but does not negate the significance of my findings. My attention to Filipinos, Chinese, and Japanese is more comprehensive because of the scarcity of data on Asian Indians and Koreans. A discussion of Koreans, Asian Indians, and Vietnamese is, however, important because they represent a third of Asian America.

Some may take issue with my inclusion of Filipinos and Asian Indians because their unique racial features supposedly set them apart from Chinese, Japanese, and Vietnamese. These critics also note that the Philippines and India are geographically distanced from the rest of Asia and have distinctive cultures, and that Filipino and Asian Indian experience in the United States disassociates them from others.

I explore this issue more thoroughly in Chapter 5, but based on my experiences, I find such arguments unpersuasive. Growing up in a small, predominantly Mexican town in Arizona, where ours was one of only three Chinese families, I was constantly reminded of my own ethnicity and equated it with being "Oriental." My perceptions changed when a Chinese doctor and his Filipino wife moved to town when I was in high school. I was struck by the fact they were like me in some ways yet not in others. The food they ate, the way they related to their children, and the holidays they celebrated together underscored our similarities and differences. As a student at UC Berkeley, I was not surprised to find Chinese, Japanese, Korean, and Filipino students in the Asian American fraternity I joined. Nor was I surprised when, at a Carter administration gathering in 1979 to celebrate Asian and Pacific American Heritage Week, a group of Asian Indians who attended were concerned about the same issues as the rest of us—concern that seemed to be rooted in our common attitudes and values. The reaction to them was uniform—if they wanted to join our community because they experienced a certain bond with us, they should be welcomed.

This book is about how immigration laws and policies shaped Asian American communities. In the process of exploring this connection, a number of principal themes emerged: (1) To a surprising degree immigration policies have been and still are reflected in the population, gender ratios, and employment profiles of these communities. (2) Great diversity exists within and between the communities. (3) Policies and laws seem to be designed to control Asian Americans—of course I mean in the sense of excluding Asians and limiting their presence, but I even mean that there is evidence that plausibly makes the case that the efforts went further than that. Alien land laws and the prevention of family formation helped keep Asians in low-paid jobs. Asians were marginalized by the encouragement of enclaves in some quarters and were kept down politically by their migrant, noncitizen status, which kept them from establishing roots. (4) Agricultural interests in Hawaii and on the West Coast were behind much of the desire to allow each Asian group into the country. (5) A sense of family stands out. For all their hardships Asian Americans have shown a remarkable resourcefulness, perhaps best revealed through an extraordinary drive to reunite their families. (6) Who these people are, why they came, how they got here, and what they do here have been neglected.

Once I appreciated the relationship between law and policy and the demographics, I began wondering and speculating about the relationship between these policies and demographics with dimensions of social life. The first six themes emerge from my discussion in the first four chapters. In Chapter 5 I consider the impact immigration policies have had on academic performance, political participation, and identity.

While I have been able to collect historical information that is of great interest at least personally, my account should not be regarded as a complete history of Asian America.[23] The work is simply a detailed comparison of immigration policies, giving attention to their development and their impact.

Likewise I make no pretense to developing a comprehensive theory of the social, political, and cultural formation of Asian America. I do intend to take a first step toward better understanding the complex relationship between basic demographics and Asian American life. I will try to begin unraveling how both have been shaped and conditioned by U.S. immigration policies and laws, particularly by the persistent impulse to control the presence of Asians within our borders. I will not neglect the complex interplay between situations and events in both the sending and the receiving communities, but my treatment of this dynamic is not complete. My book will not outline more effective policies, although my findings will most assuredly contain policy implications. I intend simply to contribute to a better understanding of relationships and experiences that few have bothered to study.

\* \* \*

Since the first printing of this book, the spectacle—some might say specter—of boatloads of Chinese at America's shores has reignited the controversy over our refugee policies and helped fuel the debate over the impact of immigrants on our society. Arguing that our borders are far too porous, some policymakers have rushed to attack the refugee and asylum system under which an increasing number of émigrés are seeking admittance. Such proposals include summary screening, a higher burden of proof for asylum, and elimination of judicial review. Once again, not only are we confronted with proposals intended to control and shape the community, but Asian Americans are implicated in the making and remaking of U.S. immigration policy.

As the move to summarily exclude the influx of Chinese seeking refuge intensifies, we should recall our nation's experience not only with Jews in the 1930's (when we turned away thousands fleeing Nazi persecution), but also with Haitians, Guatemalans, and Salvadoreans in the 1980's. Recent revelations about the extent of murderous political repression in their countries suggests that we have repeated with these refugees the mistake we made in barring Jews seeking to escape Hitler. Do we really know enough about the situation in China to turn away Chinese fleeing Fujian province as obvious economic migrants? Why are they willing to endure such hazardous journeys, only to be subjected to reprehensible work environments in this country? Is arresting and deporting such desperate people a response we will look back on with pride? And do sporadic incidents involving Chinese refugees justify altering the entire asylum system? The lessons learned about the harsh impact of policies visited upon Asian immigrants in the past continue to be relevant. These experiences should remind us that when it comes to raising barriers—particularly for refugees—we must stop and consider the special values at play because what is at stake may be life itself.

—*January 1994*

# Two Contrasting Schemes: Understanding Immigration Policies Affecting Asians Before and After 1965

An understanding of the evolution of Asian America commences with an appreciation of the history of immigration policies and laws and of the social and political forces that motivated them. This chapter traces Asian arrival and cycles of acceptance (motivated primarily by the desire for cheap, rootless, and dependable labor) and rejection (fueled by racial prejudice and fear of economic competition); U.S. relationships with the countries of Asia; the specific laws that produced and reflected these cycles and how they related to general immigration policies; and how these laws ultimately became the framework of today's system.

The cycles of rejection and acceptance are represented by federal immigration laws and state and local policies. State and local leaders supported the recruitment of Asian immigrants for the fields, the mines, the railroads, or as domestic help as well as discriminatory rules on landownership, business operations, education, civil rights, and taxes.

California charged fees for arriving boat passengers who were "ineligible for citizenship," demanded bonds for "lewd and debauched women," and required evidence that any "Mongolian, Chinese or Japanese [woman] is a person of correct habits and good character" specifically to discourage Asian immigration into the state.[1] These offensive statutes and ordinances were ultimately repealed or declared unconstitutional, but an ubiquitous air of hostility before, during, and after their currency took its toll. The cumulative effect of state and local laws may have been as great as the federal exclusion laws, which could be viewed as the culmination of local sentiment.[2]

What emerges from examining the evolution of immigration policies are two quite intriguing schemes governing immigration and resettlement. Before 1965 the United States aimed to admit Asians only for specific purposes, exclude them altogether if necessary, and always to keep them in check. At first, policymakers only vaguely appreciated the many ways federal, state, and local laws might be instrumental in this. Early restrictions on land and business ownership, the 1870 refusal to extend naturalization rights, and the 1875 exclusion of Chinese prostitutes, for example, reveal a decidedly strong-willed inclination to explore the use of immigration laws to deal with Asians.

The United States discovered that immigration might shape a self-serving relationship with those Asians it decided to admit, and it used a range of techniques and related rationales that no doubt were familiar to law and policy-making in other domains. It learned to selectively ignore, rediscover, reinterpret, recombine, rewrite, and recycle laws, treaties, and agreements to respond to shifting and often conflicting views about Asians. And it did so with great flexibility and often seemingly on a moment's notice. It learned how to justify to itself—legally and morally—having to exclude first specific groups, then all Asians, as a necessary and perhaps vital aspect of the reassertion of a control otherwise in doubt.

In 1965 the United States fundamentally restructured its immigration scheme with little consideration as to the potential consequences on Asian America. It established a uniform framework for the admission of all people that, in large part, is still in operation today. These changes, modestly prefigured in wartime adjustments and in a 1952 Immigration and Nationality Act, aspired to a new global egalitarianism. They relaxed the nation's historical efforts to control Asian immigration, though perhaps only inadvertently. Whatever the impulses for enacting these new laws, politicians and legislators largely ignored, or at least failed to study carefully, their potential impact. Even when Asians apparently were being treated like other groups, it was not because they were at all understood, as the legislative history of the 1965 reforms will reveal.

Asians played a distinctive and seldom recognized role in the history of immigration policy and law. They were the first group whose presence prompted the passage of a federal immigration law. They were, moreover, the first group excluded by federal law. But they were not just targeted and ultimately excluded. Their very presence fostered a fundamental rethinking and reordering of the role that immigration law might play in the construction of the United States as a national community. In thinking about Asians, nativists and non-nativist employers, policymakers, and commentators for the first time began to appreciate how immigration laws might be used to advance certain industries and promote social welfare. Indeed, they would be used later to control Mexicans and southern and eastern Europeans.

Employers, policymakers, commentators, and many others also began to realize that immigration laws expressed both to themselves and to the rest of the world what they thought about their country and about those people who might want to become a part of it. They might portray themselves, for example, as nationalistically self-interested or as globally connected, as rabidly xenophobic or as generously egalitarian. Apart from any other impact they might have on the Western world, Asians made obvious the self-defining capacity of a nation's immigration law. Deciding whom to admit, exclude, and why is at the heart of a people's claim to form a distinctive and stable national community.

## Asians and Immigration Before 1965

For 350 years after Columbus, Asian immigration to America was virtually nonexistent. The United States imposed no restrictions, but Japan, Korea, and China beginning in the seventeenth century executed émigrés upon their return.[3] In other Asian countries, there appears to have been less desire, need, and ability to resettle in the United States. Few Asians did so before the mid-1800's,[4] even though the era was one of free and open immigration from the New World's perspective.[5]

Chinese were the first to enter in number. Driven by the rice shortage and the devastation of the Taiping Rebellion and drawn by the lure of gold, Chinese peasants and laborers began making the long journey in the 1840's. As the population of China increased dramatically from 275 million in 1779 to 430 million in 1850, rice became scarce, particularly in populous Guangdong and Fujian provinces.[6] The declining Qing dynasty government, severely weakened by the 1839–42 Opium War with Britain and the 1850–64 Taiping Rebellion, was unable to control its own borders, let alone enforce its emigration law. With the cession of Hong Kong to Britain at the conclusion of the war in 1842, southeastern China was for the first time open to travelers and trade with the West.[7]

Early on, the Chinese were officially welcomed. The simultaneous opening of both China and the American West, along with the discovery of gold in the late 1840's, led to a growing demand for and a ready supply of Chinese labor. Chinese were actively recruited to fill needs in railroad construction, laundries, and domestic service. In 1852 the governor of California recommended a system of land grants to induce the immigration and settlement of Chinese.[8] A decade later a select committee of the California legislature advocated continued support of Chinese immigration. It reported that the 50,000 Chinese in the state paid almost $14 million annually in taxes, licenses, duties, freights, and other charges, that their cheap labor would be of great value in developing the new industries of the state, and that trade with China should be fostered.[9] After the Civil War some Southern plantation owners seriously considered replacing their former slaves with Chinese labor.[10]

Drawing praise for their industry and abilities and for their willingness to accept lower wages, Chinese were considered almost indispensable. In 1857 at the Oregon constitutional convention, a nativist amendment to exclude Chinese failed principally because they made "good washers, good cooks, and good servants."[11] Chinese immigrants were regarded as less demanding and more dependable than other laborers. After all, they were escaping a rice shortage and the devastation of war, so they desperately needed work. Even the skeptical had their reasons for coming to see the usefulness of the Chinese. The Central Pacific Railroad, doubtful about Chinese ability to handle heavy construction but frustrated over the dependability of the native work force, decided nonetheless to hire them. They were available, placer mining was giving out, and they could be purchased for two-thirds the price of white workers. Eventually it was widely acknowledged that without the Chinese, it would have been impossible to complete the western portion of the transcontinental railroad in the time required by Congress.[12] By 1882 about 300,000 Chinese had entered and worked on the West Coast.[13]

Despite the official encouragement of importing Chinese labor, the Chinese who arrived soon encountered fierce racial animosity in the 1840's, as did miners from Mexico, South America, Hawaii, and even France.[14] Irish Roman Catholics in California, replicating the racial prejudice they had suffered on the East Coast, rallied against the brown, black, and yellow foreigners in the mines.[15] This racial prejudice, exacerbated by fear of competition from aliens, prompted calls for restrictive federal immigration laws.

In the meantime, control was also asserted over aliens by state and local laws. Responding to the demands of the Irish and German miners, California enacted a foreign miners' tax in 1850. The law, primarily directed at forcing Latinos out of the mines, required all persons who were not native-born (California Native Americans excepted) or who had not become citizens under the Treaty of Guadalupe Hidalgo to take out a license to mine at $20 per month.[16] The law accomplished its aim of forcing out Latino miners, who refused to pay the exorbitant tax.

With the expulsion of many Latinos, the Chinese stood out as the largest body of foreigners in California, and in the West the full weight of prejudice fell upon them.[17] A new foreign miners' tax, this time directed at the Chinese, was enacted in 1852.[18] "Anti-coolie" clubs surfaced in the early 1850's, and sporadic boycotts of Chinese-made goods soon followed.[19] By 1853 anti-Chinese editorials were common in San Francisco newspapers. Statutes and ordinances like the 1858 Oregon law that required Chinese miners and merchants to obtain monthly, four-dollar licenses were not unusual.[20]

For a time this sentiment gained powerful political backing from the newly formed Know-Nothing party. Organized in the 1850's to exclude all foreign-born citizens from office, to discourage immigration, and to "keep America pure," the Know-Nothing party demanded a 21-year naturalization period.[21] On the East Coast it fought against Irish Catholic immigration, while on the West Coast the target was usually the Chinese.[22] But the voluntary enlistment of hundreds of thousands of immigrants (principally on the East Coast) into the Union armies led to the demise of the Know-Nothing party by 1870; the Civil War "completed the ruin of organized nativism by absorbing xenophobes and immigrants in a common cause."[23]

The demise of the Know-Nothing party notwithstanding, by the late 1860's the Chinese question became a major issue in California and

Oregon politics. Many white workers felt threatened by the competition they perceived from the Chinese, while many employers continued to seek them as inexpensive laborers and subservient domestics. Employment of Chinese by the Central Pacific Railroad was by this time at its peak. Anti-coolie clubs increased in number, and mob attacks against Chinese became frequent.[24] Seldom outdone in such matters, many newly organized labor unions were by then demanding legislation against Chinese immigration. Chinese were at once resented for their resourcefulness in turning a profit on abandoned mines and for their reputed frugality.[25] Much of this resentment was transformed into or sustained by a need to preserve "racial purity" and "Western civilization."[26]

The tension between a desire for Chinese labor and nativist resentment of Chinese immigrants is best captured by the commotion surrounding the 1868 Burlingame Treaty. The treaty between the United States and Chinese governments represents the high-water mark of official Chinese acceptance. China agreed to end its strict control over emigration and recognized the "inherent and inalienable right of man to change his home and allegiance, and also the mutual advantage of the free migration and emigration of their citizens. . . ."[27]

The treaty was greeted with fanfare and delight. Enjoying the international prestige and eager for trade after the Civil War, Congress readily approved it. According to Secretary of State William Seward, the treaty would greatly benefit the United States: "The free emigration of the Chinese to the American [continent] is the essential element of trade and commerce [and] will tend to increase the wealth and strength of all Western nations; while at the same time, the removal of the surplus population of China will tend much to take away the obstructions which now impede the introduction into China of art, science [and] religion."[28]

In discussing the treaty many writers esteemed the cultural greatness of China. Some wrote of the "special destiny" connecting the United States, the youngest nation, with China, the most ancient one. Others stressed the cultural rewards that intermingling with the Middle Kingdom would bring, noting that at a time when our forebearers were "digging for roots in swamps and forests . . . , the Chinese were rich, civilized, fertile in poets, philosophers, economists, moralists, and statesmen."[29]

The salutary view toward China and its people reflected in the Burlingame Treaty, however, soon clashed head-on with rising anti-Chinese sentiment in California and the West. Eventually, the Sinophobic sentiment prevailed, and the treaty's provisions for free emigration were overrun by a series of laws that first limited and then entirely excluded Chinese from the United States.[30] Only two years after the passage of the treaty and just months after the enactment of civil rights legislation responding in part to Chinese grievances,[31] Chinese immigrants were judged unworthy of citizenship. In amending the Nationality Act of 1790, which had limited citizenship through naturalization to "free white persons" (specifically excluding African Americans and Native Americans[32]), Congress in 1870 extended the right to naturalize to aliens of African descent.[33] But it deliberately denied Chinese that right because of their "undesirable qualities."[34]

Histories of these policies generally begin with the Chinese Exclusion Act of 1882, to the neglect of earlier federal laws (as well as the effect of local efforts) that discouraged immigration. The 1870 denial of the opportunity to naturalize was the first congressional step toward excluding Chinese and the first such limitation based on national origin beyond the subordination of African Americans. Another far less prominent statute enacted five years later proved to be equally pivotal.

Responding to law-enforcement claims that Chinese women were being imported for prostitution, Congress in 1875 passed legislation prohibiting their importation for immoral purposes.[35] In one case 21 Chinese women were disallowed entry on the ground that they were "lewd," though this action was overturned by the Supreme Court.[36] But the overzealous enforcement of the statute, commonly referred to as the Page Law, effectively barred Chinese women and further worsened an already imbalanced sex ratio among Chinese.[37]

The exclusion of prostitutes marked the beginning of direct federal regulation of immigration, though it did little to stem nationwide pressure for further significant curbs on Chinese immigration. In 1879 a measure was placed on the California ballot to determine public sentiment: 900 favored the Chinese, while 150,000 were opposed.[38] During the 1881 session of Congress, 25 anti-Chinese petitions were presented by a number of civic groups, like the Methodist Church and the New York Union League Corps, and from many states, including Alabama, Ohio, West Virginia, and Wisconsin.[39] The California legislature declared a legal holiday to facilitate anti-Chinese public rallies that attracted thousands of demonstrators.[40]

Responding to this national clamor, the 47th Congress enacted the Chinese Exclusion Act on May 6, 1882.[41] The law excluded laborers for ten years, and effectively slammed the door on all Chinese immigration.[42] It did permit the entry of teachers, students, and merchants, but their quota was quite small. Immigrants were issued certificates of identity (issued under section 6 of the act) known as Section Six certificates.[43] Immigration officials tried to prohibit the reentry without such certificates of Chinese who were legal residents but who were out of the country temporarily at the time of the act's passage. The Supreme Court, however, ruled in *Chew Heong v. United States* (1884)[44] that a Chinese laborer not in possession of a certificate could reenter since he was lawfully in the country in 1880 when the United States and China modified the Burlingame Treaty.[45]

The act crippled the development of the Chinese American community because Chinese women were defined as laborers. Chinese laborers who had already immigrated therefore had no way to bring wives and families left behind. Chinese pleas for a different statutory interpretation were to no avail. Although men could reenter under *Chew Heong*, the Supreme Court denied laborers the right to have any spouse join them who had not been otherwise legally in the United States by 1880. As a result the only women permitted to enter were the wives of American-born Chinese and of a few merchants.[46] The ban on laborers' spouses effectively halted the immigration of Chinese women, thereby exacerbating the restraints imposed by the exclusion of women through expanded enforcement of the Page Law and preventing family formation for Chinese immigrants.[47]

Despite the pervasive anti-Chinese sentiment in the West that was heard and respected in the halls of Congress from 1875 to 1882, European immigration was encouraged. Except for the anti-Chinese legislation, exclusion laws focused on nonracial characteristics such as criminality, indigence, and mental disorders.[48] In spite of a depression from 1873 to 1877, Americans were confident in the country's ability to revive itself economically, and they "saw little reason to fear the influence of [European] foreigners."[49]

Leaders of the anti-Chinese movement, however, were not satisfied. They pressed for something beyond the ten-year exclusion period, using undisguisedly Sinophobic sentiments to protect white labor. They succeeded, over the next dozen years, through a series of treaties and new laws that led to an indefinite ban on Chinese immigration in 1904. Most notable among them for their increasingly clever techniques of and rationales for control were the Scott Act of 1888 and the Geary Act of 1892.

Overturning the Supreme Court's decision in *Chew Heong,* the Scott Act prohibited the entry of all Chinese laborers, including those who had left the United States temporarily with valid return certificates.[50] The constitutionality of the Scott Act was upheld in the Chinese Exclusion Case of 1889.[51] A Chinese lawful resident laborer had left the United States in 1887 to visit China holding a valid Section Six reentry certificate. While he was at sea, the Scott Act was passed; when his boat docked, the laborer was not permitted to reenter. The Supreme Court upheld his exclusion, ruling that Congress's power to regulate immigration was a matter of sovereignty. The Scott Act was held to be a constitutionally permissible protection against aggression by a foreign national.

Four years after the passage of the Scott Act, the exclusionists successfully pushed the Geary Act through Congress. Claiming that Chinese names and faces were all alike,[52] the nativists argued that a registration requirement was necessary to distinguish those legally in the United States prior to exclusion from those who might have been smuggled in afterward.[53] In the Geary Act, Congress readily acceded to the unprecedented demand for registration of all Chinese laborers with immigration officials, and the exclusion laws were extended for another ten years.[54] The Geary Act also denied bail to Chinese in habeas corpus proceedings and provided that, prior to deportation, any Chinese "not lawfully entitled to be or remain in the United States shall be imprisoned at hard labor" for up to a year.[55] This final provision, however, was declared unconstitutional by the Supreme Court because it imposed a criminal penalty without trial.[56]

According to the Geary Act, those failing to register within a year were deportable. Many Chinese resisted registration on the grounds that it was unconstitutionally selective. But in *Fong Yue Ting v. United States* (1892), the Supreme Court concluded that the statute was a necessary extension of the power to exclude and expel aliens.[57] Lawful residents who violated the act's provisions might be deported, the Court observed, since as aliens they were permitted to remain only on sufferance. After the Court upheld the constitutionality of registration, the period for it was extended for six months, and a majority of Chinese did register. If the extension had not been granted, a mass deportation of Chinese could have resulted—something that California agriculture wanted to avert because Chinese labor was necessary for the expanding fruit industry.[58]

Two years after the passage of the Geary Act, the United States concluded an 1894 treaty with the crumbling Qing government in which
China agreed to accept the act's provisions.[59] In exchange the United
States revised the Scott Act to permit the return of any lawful resident
laborer who had left temporarily, and who had a wife, child, or parent or
who had property valued at $1,000 in the United States.[60] But in 1904,
when China declined to renew the treaty, Congress reenacted the
Chinese exclusion laws indefinitely.[61]

The extension of the exclusion laws coincided with a shift in the
national mood against immigrants. After another depression from 1883
to 1886 threatened the livelihood of the working class, many workers
became convinced that immigration was a major problem, and they
successfully lobbied state legislatures to exclude immigrants from certain types of jobs.[62] By the late 1880's Congress enacted labor laws and
deportation provisions aimed at curtailing the practice of importing
cheap foreign labor under contracts that were believed to depress the
labor market.[63] Continued industrial depression in the 1890's fueled
nativist movements almost until the end of the century.[64]

The 1904 legislation extending Chinese exclusion indefinitely
marked the culmination of a thirty-year series of laws that, beginning
with the 1875 act barring Chinese prostitutes, limited and then excluded
Asian immigrants. Not until the alliance with China during World War
II would Congress reconsider any aspect of those barriers. And not until
1965 would it substantially alter nearly a century of laws aimed at keeping the Chinese in check. The effects of these laws on Chinese immigrants and their communities are examined in Chapters 2 and 3.

The early history of Japanese immigration differs considerably from
that of the Chinese mainly because of the strength of the restored Meiji
government.[65] Unlike the decaying Qing dynasty (which fell in 1911), the
Japanese government was able to negotiate mutually beneficial emigration treaties with the United States and to enforce its own emigration
laws. That kind of stature left its imprint on the lives of immigrants in
more than a few ways.

The Japanese opening to the West commenced with the arrival of
Commodore Matthew Perry and four U.S. naval ships in Tokyo Bay in
1854. Perry forced the Japanese to sign the Treaty of Peace and Amity,
in which Japan agreed to open its doors to foreign trade,[66] and which
helped bring about the Meiji Restoration of 1868. In the decades that followed Japan rapidly emerged from centuries of feudalism and isolation

into modern industrialization and international commerce.[67] Yet, for a decade and a half the Meiji government, which was very protective of its citizens' interests abroad, continued to strictly regulate travel by students, bureaucrats, and statesmen.[68] Between 1860 and 1880, when almost 200,000 Chinese laborers came to the United States, the Japanese permitted only 335 emigrants.[69]

Not coincidentally, the first appreciable numbers entered at the height of the Chinese exclusion movement. Agricultural labor demands, particularly in Hawaii and California, led to increased efforts to attract Japanese workers after the exclusion of the Chinese.[70] In 1884, two years after the Chinese Exclusion Act, the Japanese government yielded to internal pressures to permit laborers to emigrate to work on Hawaiian sugar plantations.[71] The next year, in the midst of Meiji Japan's new-found interest in foreign lands, the Japanese Diet passed the country's first modern emigration law, allowing government-sponsored contract laborers to travel to Hawaii.[72]

Like the initial wave of Chinese immigrants, Japanese laborers were at first warmly received by employers. These young and healthy men were needed to perform the strenuous work on Hawaiian sugar plantations. So many of them came that the Japanese became the largest group of foreigners on the islands. Few came to the mainland, so little effective political pressure was incited to exclude them. In San Francisco in 1869 the new immigrants were described as "gentlemen of refinement and culture . . . [who] have brought their wives, children, and . . . new industries among us."[73] By 1894, the same year China was forced to accept the exclusionary provisions of the Geary Act, Japan and the United States reaffirmed their commitment to open travel, each promising the other's citizens "liberty to enter, travel, and reside" in the receiving country.[74]

This treaty applied only to Japanese citizens until Korea became a Japanese protectorate in 1905. The United States and Korea had entered into a Treaty of Amity and Trade in 1882, ending Korea's self-imposed isolation as the Hermit Kingdom.[75] Nonetheless, for twenty years there was no recorded Korean emigration.[76] The earliest Korean immigrants were 7,500 laborers who came to Hawaii between 1902 and 1905; only a few hundred of these went on to the Pacific coast of the mainland.[77] But after Korea's protectorate status was formalized in 1905, Japan severely limited Korean emigration.[78]

By the turn of the century, unfavorable sentiment toward the Japanese grew as their laborers began to migrate to the western United States. After

Hawaii was annexed in 1898, the Japanese were able to use it as a stepping-stone to the mainland, where the majority engaged in agricultural work.[79] Economic competition with white farm workers soon erupted.[80]

Japanese agricultural workers were more financially independent than the Chinese. They were not fleeing abject poverty as much as deliberately pursuing alternative economic opportunities and higher wages.[81] They had survived a screening process in Japan required of prospective immigrants, which was aimed at ensuring that they were "healthy and literate."[82] They were determined not to submit to the constraints imposed by agricultural employers. Many intended to eventually become independent farmers, and menial work was regarded simply as a step toward something far better. They considered themselves the competent equals of white workers, with a right to make the most of their opportunities for success.[83]

The determination of the Japanese to secure their place in American society was greatly resented by a rising chorus of white workers. By the 1890's, when economic xenophobia was gaining greater acceptance on the East Coast, nativists with the backing of organized labor in California formed the Japanese and Korean Exclusion League (later renamed the Asiatic Exclusion League).[84] The league joined forces (and membership often overlapped) with smaller organizations such as the Anti-Jap Laundry League and the Anti-Japanese League of Alameda County.[85] In those California cities and agricultural communities where competition was most intense and conspicuous, immigrants encountered violence from whites who claimed that California would be "overrun" by Japanese.[86] Exclusion once again became a major political issue, only this time the Japanese were the target.[87]

After Japan's crushing victories over China in 1895 and Russia in 1905, policymakers viewed exclusion as a means of controlling a potential enemy. Many Americans had regarded Japan as an eager student at the knee of the United States.[88] But when the Japanese Navy defeated its Russian counterpart, American observers realized how much Japan had advanced since Commodore Perry's visit a half-century before and how powerful the "yellow" nation had become, signaling a turning point in relations between the United States and Japan.[89] America was so concerned about geo-political change that President Theodore Roosevelt helped negotiate the 1905 Treaty of Portsmouth which ended the Russo-Japanese War and ceded Korea to Japan as a protectorate. In 1910 Japan would possess Korea outright.[90]

In the wake of the 1906 San Francisco earthquake, fierce anti-Japanese rioting resulted in countless incidents of physical violence.[91] Japanese students in San Francisco were ordered to segregated schools—an act that incensed Japan and later proved to be a major stumbling block in negotiations over restrictions on Japanese laborers (the Gentlemen's Agreement).[92] Demands for limits on Japanese immigration resonated.

Japanese laborers were eventually restricted but not in conventional legislative fashion.[93] Japan's emergence as a major world power meant that the United States could not restrict Japanese immigration in the heavy-handed, self-serving fashion with which it had curtailed Chinese immigration. To do so would have offended an increasingly assertive Japan when the United States was concerned about keeping an open door to Japanese markets. To minimize potential disharmony between the two nations while retaining the initiative to control immigration, President Roosevelt negotiated an informal agreement with Japan.[94] Under the terms of the so-called Gentlemen's Agreement reached in 1907 and 1908, the Japanese government refrained from issuing travel documents to laborers destined for the United States.[95] In exchange for this severe but voluntary limitation, Japanese wives and children could be reunited with their husbands and fathers in the United States, and the San Francisco school board would be pressured into rescinding its segregation order.[96]

The reduction in Japanese immigration contrasted sharply with general immigration policies at the time. The first decade of the century actually witnessed expanded tolerance toward other immigrants because of the national economic recovery. This resulted in the largest influx ever, particularly of European immigrants (mostly southern and eastern).[97] (See the Figure in Introduction.) Exclusionists, of course, were not muzzled and the decade's record-setting influx was sufficient impetus for the convening of a special commission in 1907 to investigate the immigration system.[98]

Japan's growing military power in the Pacific tempered any congressional inclination to give in to calls for the total exclusion of Japanese immigrants. Concerned about its citizens abroad and now capable of demanding respect, Japan proved effective in countering the most zealous exclusionists' demands through vigorous efforts on behalf of Japanese Americans. Japan challenged the segregation in San Francisco and later complained formally to the federal government over the passage of alien land laws in state legislatures. Since the Japanese believed that their nation had made much progress in its relations with Westerners, they remained appalled that their emigrants were viewed as "undesirable Asiatics."[99] Though there is little evidence that mainstream social and racial attitudes were any more tolerant of the Japanese than the Chinese, Congress remained unable to enact a set of Japanese exclusion laws that paralleled those for Chinese.[100]

Unlike the Chinese, the Japanese were able to keep their families intact. Since the wives and children of Japanese men in the United States could continue to enter, Japanese immigrants could marry and form families. And Japan bitterly resented the restrictions and fought to keep open the few family reunification channels that the agreement provided.[101]

But exclusionists continued their attack and found alternative means of discouraging newcomers. In addition to continued racial animosity, a sense of economic competition persisted. By the 1910's, Japanese immigrants using intensive farming techniques produced more than 10 percent of California produce while owning only 1 percent of its farmland.[102] So in 1913 the California legislature passed the Alien Land Law (later mimicked by other states[103]), which provided that "All aliens eligible to citizenship may acquire, possess, enjoy, transmit and inherit real property or any interest therein."[104] Since the Naturalization Act of 1870 denied Asians the right to become citizens, the Land Law precluded Japanese (who unsuccessfully challenged the naturalization preclusion)[105] from owning property. If they could not halt all immigrants at the border, exclusionists at least hoped to make life so difficult in the United States that none would want to come.

At the turn of the century, the United States was beginning its relationship with the Philippines as it was changing its view toward Japan. After the victory over Spain in 1898 in the Spanish-American War, President McKinley concluded that the people of the Philippines, then a Spanish colony, were "unfit for self-government" and that "there was nothing left for [the United States] to do but to take them all, and to educate the Filipinos, and uplift and civilize and Christianize them."[106] The takeover met with violent resistance from many Filipinos who had yearned for independence from colonial domination.[107]

If becoming a United States colony had a positive side, it was that Filipinos automatically became noncitizen nationals of the United States. They could travel without regard to immigration laws, they were not subject to exclusion or deportation, and requirements for obtaining full citizenship were relaxed.[108] Yet fewer than three thousand Filipinos, most of them farm workers in Hawaii, had immigrated by 1910.[109] Not until appreciable numbers came in after World War I (when Chinese and Japanese workers could no longer be recruited) did exclusionary efforts against them begin.

The advent of the twentieth century witnessed the entry of other Asians, such as Asian Indians, but in even smaller numbers. Even though those seeking trade were among some of the earliest migrants to the United States, Indians had insignificant contacts with this country during the nineteenth century. The poorer workers among them found labor opportunities in British colonies.[110] Furthermore, the voyage to America from India was longer, more complicated, and more expensive.[111] The few thousand who immigrated, most of them men, settled primarily in California, and most of them found agricultural jobs.[112] Their families remained in India while husbands and fathers worked to earn money to send for them or to return. A small number of more educated Indians also entered, bringing the total number of arrivals from 1881 to 1917 to only about seven thousand.[113]

Even small numbers of Asian Indians managed to agitate the Asiatic Exclusion League, which had sprung up in response to Japanese and Korean immigration.[114] Racial and economic nativism was again at the core of the agitation.[115] Asian Indians competed for agricultural jobs and were willing to work for lower wages in other jobs,[116] so nativists used violence to force them out of local jobs.[117] Not satisfied with making life in the United States miserable and even dangerous, exclusionists also persuaded federal immigration authorities to block their entry. Although about two thousand Asian Indians immigrated from 1911 to 1917, more than seventeen hundred were denied entry during the same period, mostly on the grounds that they would need public assistance.[118] The California commissioner of state labor statistics concluded that the "Hindu is the most undesirable immigrant in the state. His lack of personal cleanliness, his low morals and his blind adherence to theories and teachings, so entirely repugnant to American principles, make him unfit for association with American people."[119]

Like the Chinese and Japanese before them, Indians sought to have laws discriminating against them overturned by the courts. Lower federal courts had granted them the right to naturalize on the grounds that they were Caucasians and thus eligible "white persons" under the naturalization legislation of 1790 and 1870.[120]

But in *United States v. Bhagat Singh Thind* (1923),[121] the Court reversed its racial stance, deciding that Indians, like Japanese, would no longer be considered white persons, and were therefore ineligible to become naturalized citizens. Naturalization certificates previously granted were subject to cancellation,[122] and Indians fell under the harsh Alien Land Laws.[123]

Strict control of Chinese and Japanese immigration had done little to satisfy the demands of American nativists. They insisted that Asians were racially inferior to whites and should be completely barred. One California legislator called for amending immigration laws so that instead of merely excluding all those "ineligible to citizenship," they would exclude "Hindus and all persons of the Mongolian or yellow race, the brown race or the African race." The United States Immigration Commission defined any native of India as Hindu, and the term was often misused to describe all Indians.[124]

Congress responded to this anti-Asian clamor and a renewed xenophobia aroused by the influx of southern and eastern Europeans by passing the Act of February 5, 1917. The constant flow of Italians, Russians, and Hungarians, which peaked in the first decade of the century, fueled racial nativism and anti-Catholicism, culminating in a controversial requirement that excluded aliens "who cannot read and understand some language or dialect."[125] But the act also created the "Asiatic barred zone" by extending the Chinese exclusion laws to all other Asians.[126] The zone covered South Asia from Arabia to Indochina, as well as the adjacent islands. It included India, Burma, Thailand, the Malay States, the East Indian Islands, Asiatic Russia, the Polynesian Islands, and parts of Arabia and Afghanistan. China and Japan did not have to be included because of the Chinese exclusion laws and the Gentlemen's Agreement. But together these provisions declared inadmissible all Asians except teachers, merchants, and students. Only Filipinos and Guamanians, under U.S. jurisdiction at the time, were not included.

The reactionary, isolationist political climate that followed World War I, manifested in the Red Scare of 1919–20, led to even greater exclusionist demands. The landmark Immigration Act of 1924,[127] opposed by only six senators, once again took direct aim at southern and eastern Europeans, whom the Protestant majority in the United States viewed with dogmatic disapproval.[128] The arguments advanced in support of the bill stressed recurring themes: the racial superiority of Anglo-Saxons, the fact that immigrants would cause the lowering of wages, and the unassimilability of foreigners, while citing the usual threats to the nation's social unity and order posed by immigration.[129]

The act restructured criteria for admission to respond to nativist demands and represented a general selection policy that remained in place until 1952. It provided that immigrants of any particular country be limited to 2 percent of their nationality in 1890. The law struck most deeply at Jews, Italians, Slavs, and Greeks, who had immigrated in great numbers after 1890, and who would be most disfavored by such a quota system.[130]

Though sponsors of the act were primarily concerned with limiting immigration from southern and eastern Europe, they simultaneously eliminated the few remaining categories for Asians. The act provided for the permanent exclusion of any "alien ineligible to citizenship."[131] Since Asians were barred from naturalization under the 1870 statute, the possibility of their entry was cut off indefinitely. The prohibition even included previously privileged merchants, teachers, and students. Asians were not allowed even under the 2 percent quota rule. The primary target were the Japanese, who, while subject to the Gentlemen's Agreement, had never been totally barred by federal immigration law until then.[132]

The only Asians not affected by the 1924 Act were Filipinos, who remained exempt as nationals and who by then had settled into a familiar pattern of migration. Before 1920 a few resided mostly in Hawaii; their presence on the islands helped establish conditions later conducive to a more substantial labor migration.[133] They became a convenient source of cheap labor after Japanese immigration was restricted in 1908.[134] Just as the Chinese exclusion law had encouraged employers to look to Japan, so the limitations on Japanese immigrants led to an intense recruitment, especially by the Hawaiian Sugar Planters' Association, of Filipino laborers because of their open travel status as noncitizen nationals.[135]

Growers thought Filipinos (like Mexicans on the mainland) were well-suited to "stoop" labor and were not as aggressive as Japanese or as enterprising as Chinese. They were praised as especially hardworking, submissive, and reliable—praise that ironically rooted itself in well-entrenched racist sentiment.[136] Despite the arduousness of the work in the sugar and pineapple industries, the steady pay lured many Filipino laborers (most of whom came from the Ilocos region and other economically underdeveloped areas of the Philippines populated by poor peasants and farm workers) who could not earn comparable wages in their home country.[137]

By the late 1920's, Filipino laborers began to look beyond Hawaii where the demand for their labor was shrinking to the mainland where the need for cheap labor, especially in agriculture, was growing.[138] Many left Hawaii partly in response to employers' recruitment efforts. Most Filipinos who had come to the mainland previously had been students.[139] But in the late 1920's, laborers came to California predominantly to work on citrus and vegetable farms.[140]

Filipino laborers differed significantly from those from Japan, China, and India. They were Catholics and had been exposed to American culture in their schooling.[141] They entered as wards of the United States and were free to come and go. Because of their special status, they often considered themselves American in important respects. Still, on their arrival familiar cycles of rejection quickly surfaced, much to their consternation. They were met with acceptance by eager employers and then, almost immediately, resentment from white workers, particularly as their numbers increased on the mainland in the late 1920's.[142]

One strain of American thought regarded Filipinos as "savages."[143] The 1904 St. Louis Exposition had featured certain Philippine tribes that practiced head-hunting. Returning American missionaries described "shocking" practices.[144] The paternalistic view was that Filipinos depended on the United States to help them develop socially and culturally; after all, they had "never produced a great teacher, priest, business man, or statesman."[145] Nevertheless, most white racism directed at Filipino laborers sprang, perhaps paradoxically, not so much from tabloid impressions but more from the immigrants' success at acculturation. They were resented largely for their ability to get jobs and even for their contact with white women.[146] In many respects they were perceived as a greater threat to white laborers than their Chinese and Japanese predecessors had been.

To white workers in California the privileged immigration status of Filipinos did not change the fact that they were an economic threat who had the physical characteristics of Asiatics. They were just another undesirable Asian race who seemed to be taking over white jobs and lowering standards for their wages and working conditions. As it had toward Chinese and Japanese, white resentment of Filipinos soon boiled over into violence, and numerous anti-Filipino outbursts erupted in California between 1929 and 1934.[147] Their strong concentration in agriculture made them visible and competitive (of the 45,000 reported on the mainland in 1930, about 82 percent were farm laborers[148]) especially during the severe unemployment of the Great Depression. Since Filipinos were often on the bottom of the economic ladder, the depression struck them particularly hard.[149] Exclusionists suggested that the United States ought to "repatriate" unemployed Filipino workers, for their own benefit as well as for that of the United States.[150]

Calls for the exclusion of Filipino workers were warmly received in Congress, which welcomed any seemingly uncomplicated proposal that promised relief for the depression's high unemployment.[151] For policymakers, however, dealing with anti-Filipino agitation was not as simple as responding to earlier anti-Chinese, anti-Asian Indian, and even anti-Japanese campaigns. They could travel legally, so until the Philippines was granted independence, Congress could not exclude Filipinos.

An unlikely coalition of exclusionists, anti-colonialists, and Filipino nationalists managed to band together to promote the passage of the Tydings-McDuffie Act in 1934.[152] Many of the exclusionists had initially wished to keep the Philippines, but they soon realized that to exclude Filipino laborers they had to support Filipino nationalists and anti-colonialists and grant the nation its freedom.[153] Independence and exclusion became so intertwined that the former was often used as a motive for the latter.[154]

Tydings-McDuffie was everything exclusionists could hope for. When their nation would become independent on July 4, 1946, Filipinos would lose their status as nationals of the United States, regardless of where they lived.[155] Those in the United States would be deported unless they became immigrants. Between 1934 and 1946, however, any Filipino who desired to immigrate became subject to the immigration acts of 1917 and 1924, and the Philippines was considered a separate country with an annual quota of only 50 visas.[156] This was an especially bitter pill for Filipinos to swallow. After first being stripped of their noncitizen national status, they now were given half the minimum quota that the 1924 act had established for all other non-Asian nationalities.[157] And the Supreme Court had made it clear in 1925 that, like Japanese and Asian Indians, Filipinos were not "free white persons" eligible for naturalization.[158]

The passage of Tydings-McDuffie, the last congressional act excluding immigration from Asia, signaled the formal end of an era. The refusal to extend Asians the right to naturalize, the laws against the Chinese, the Gentlemen's Agreement with Japan, the 1917 and 1924 immigration acts, and Tydings-McDuffie were the legacy of the schizophrenic attempt by Congress to satisfy economic ambitions and nativist demands. These exclusion laws remained in full force throughout the 1930's and much of the 1940's, and in many ways symbolized the peak of anti-immigrant power.

## Changes for World War II Allies and the Postwar Era

World War II brought about the first cracks in the wall of Asian exclusion. Although liberal congressional forces had for years advocated the repeal of Chinese exclusion on grounds of international equity,[159] not until the United States and China became allies against the Japanese during the war did Congress agree to repeal some aspects of the exclusion laws. Japan had been successfully exploiting Asian exclusion in its wartime propaganda, and Congress felt compelled to respond to the charges that it was discriminating against the citizens of an ally.[160] Despite stiff opposition from the American Federation of Labor and from some veterans' groups, Congress in 1943 passed the Chinese Repealer.[161] For the first time it allowed Chinese to naturalize and become American citizens; it also struck from the books most of the Chinese exclusion laws.[162] However, the Repealer by no means flung open the door to Chinese immigration since Chinese or "persons of Chinese descent" were allotted a yearly quota of only 105 immigrants under the law.[163]

Three years later, however, Congress extended nonquota immigration status to Chinese wives of citizens.[164] Admitting these Chinese women without regard to the annual quota of 105, while not resulting in a huge influx immediately, was important because it reversed the long-standing practice of excluding Chinese women. For 70 years after the 1875 Page Law excluding prostitutes, Chinese women had been systematically barred from entering and joining Chinese men to form families here. Now citizens could petition for their spouses to come join them and form families.

A month before, on July 2, 1946, two days before the Philippines regained independence under Tydings-McDuffie, Congress also extended naturalization rights to Filipinos and Indians.[165] It also established immigration quotas of 100 for each country and extended nonquota status to Filipino and Indian spouses and children of citizens. The legislation was actually introduced to strengthen ties with India, which during World War II the United States began to regard as a prominent political and military force and as a potentially valuable ally. Many Indian journalists, propagandists, and politicians came to the United States during and after the war to win American support for their independence movement. After India won independence in 1946 and the two countries grew closer, the relaxation of exclusion became important to their new alliance.[166] Although the legislation was originally intended to benefit only nationals of India, the Philippines were added at the last minute for similar political reasons.[167] In 1942 Filipinos who joined the armed forces in the Pacific were extended citizenship opportunities.[168]

Despite postwar liberalization and a growing antipathy toward quotas, Japan and Korea, which had gained its independence from Japan in 1945, remained subject to the 1924 limit. Anti-Asian sentiment lingered because the impetus for positive changes affecting Chinese, Filipinos, and Asian Indians had been largely political.[169] The nativist ideology of the 1924 law gave little ground in the 1940's. Exceptions were made only for unique, war-related legislation such as the War Brides Act[170] and the Fiancees Act[171] for relatives of U.S. servicemen and the humanitarian Displaced Persons Act for refugees.[172] But the biases of the 1924 act came under heavy fire after the war, especially when the United States assumed leadership at the United Nations and other international organizations. The ideological Cold War between capitalism and communism made the United States acutely conscious of how its domestic policies, including immigration, were perceived abroad.

Nine years after the Chinese Repealer, following considerable study,[173] Congress enacted the McCarran-Walter (Immigration and Nationality) Act of 1952.[174] But in spite of the increasing resistance in some quarters to the racist quota system, the quotas were retained. The sentiment that carried the day was riddled with postwar anxieties about enemy aliens and divided loyalties. The new law actually broadened the definition of subversives and expanded the categories of excludable and deportable aliens.[175]

Yet the new act also provided immigration rights for other Asian nationalities similar to those recently afforded the Chinese. Foremost for Asians, however, was the removal of the prohibition on their naturalization. This effectively eliminated the 1924 Act's "ineligible for citizenship" barrier and allowed Congress to have a positive impact on international relations in the Far East (including Japan).[176] But although it abolished the 1917 act's Asiatic barred zone, the law created a new restrictive zone—the Asia-Pacific triangle—that consisted of countries from India to Japan and all Pacific islands north of Australia and New Zealand. A maximum of two thousand Asians from this new triangle were allowed to immigrate annually.[177] Small quotas were set for each of the nineteen countries in the area.[178]

One feature of the Asia-Pacific triangle bears special mention, for it reveals how Congress, while ostensibly striving to eliminate racial exclusion from immigration laws, still inserted a provision prejudiced against aliens of Asian origin. Generally, under the 1952 act, a quota immigrant's visa was charged against the country of his or her place of birth regardless of ethnic background or citizenship.[179] A person born in Great Britain of a Russian father and a Norwegian mother, for example, would be charged to the quota for Great Britain. An important exception was made for persons at least half of whose ethnic ancestry could be traced to one of the nineteen nations arbitrarily placed in the triangle.[180] Such a person would have to come under the triangle quota regardless of birthplace. So, whether born in Great Britain to a British father and a Japanese mother, he or she would be charged to the quota for Japan even though his or her mother and family had resided in Britain for several generations and were all British citizens.[181]

The 1952 Immigration and Nationality Act thus ended the absolute exclusion of Asians, but retained control over how many might enter. Though it was symbolically important domestically and abroad, the act did little for Asian immigrants. It certainly provided no affirmative remedy for the decades of exclusion they suffered. Rather, the act demonstrated the consistent desire of Congress to keep Asian immigration tightly in check. Once again Congress proved schizophrenic. Foreign policy dictated an end to absolute exclusion, but exclusionist ideology at home would not permit immigration beyond the token quota of two thousand immigrants a year from the entire Asia-Pacific region.

## 1965: A Different Attitude and a New Order

The national-origins quota system continued to exasperate many observers, including President Truman, who vetoed the 1952 legislation largely due to its failure to repudiate the quota system.[182] Many felt the system perpetuated the philosophy that "some people are more equal than others," and they pointed to the creation of the Asia-Pacific trian-gle as evidence.[183] Congress, however, overrode Truman's veto,[184] and critics were resigned to cite the law as an embarrassment that was incon-sistent with our stature as leader of the free world.[185]

Truman and other critics did not relent. Soon after the enactment of the 1952 law, he appointed a special Commission on Immigration and Naturalization to study the system.[186] A 319-page report issued in 1953 strongly urged the abolition of the national-origins system and recom-mended quotas without regard to national origin, race, creed, or color.[187] President Eisenhower embraced the findings, but his push for corrective legislation failed.[188] Despite repeated attempts at new legislation, no major action was taken on any of the commission's recommendations until more than ten years later.[189]

After years of unsuccessful efforts by Truman and Eisenhower to eliminate the quota system, President Kennedy submitted a comprehen-sive program that provided the impetus for ultimate reform.[190] His pro-posals reflected his long-standing interest in immigration reform.[191] Kennedy called for the repeal of racial exclusion from the Asia-Pacific triangle,[192] and he assailed the nativism that led to the Chinese exclusion laws as well as the national-origins system of the 1924 law.[193]

President Kennedy envisioned a system governed by the skills of the immigrant and family reunification. For him, the proposed changes meant both an increase in fairness to applicants and in benefits to the United States. His approach recognized the interdependence among nations, making the old system appear anachronistic.[194]

Although Kennedy's global vision was not without its detractors,[195] it remained the driving theme for the proponents of reform for whom repeal of the Asia-Pacific triangle was only one aspect of the more open movement across international borders, in which the United States would stand both as a leader and as an example. Their high rhetoric was meant to evoke a romantic allegiance to the highest sort of aspirations. People were supposed to feel as if they could transcend the world in which they were living.

This vision was apparently so mesmerizing that little attention was paid to what, if any, impact the reforms might have on Asian American communities. Its proponents, who included President Johnson, simply did not expect that many Asians would actually take advantage of the reforms.[196] Attorney General Robert Kennedy estimated that perhaps only five thousand immigrants from the Asia-Pacific region might immigrate in the first year, but he expected no "great influx after that."[197] He thought that the most important impact would be on Greece, Italy, and Portugal.[198] His brother and Senate floor manager of the reforms, Senator Edward Kennedy, said "the ethnic mix of this country [would] not be upset" and that the reform would "not inundate America with immigrants from any one country or [from] the most populated and economically deprived nations of Africa and Asia."[199] Johnson, who was critical of the Asia-Pacific triangle in his 1964 State of the Union address, usually emphasized the corrective nature of the law for southern and eastern European immigrants without reference to Asian immigration.[200] Even Asian community leaders saw the reforms as more symbolic than remedial.[201] In fact, much of the critical support for the legislation came as much from those who perceived it as aiding the national economy because of the skills and training brought by immigrants as from those who sought the elimination of the racial discrimination that had burdened nonwhite immigrants for a century.[202] For the time being, however, nativism was quieted, since the legislation was debated at the height of congressional sensitivity over civil rights.

President Kennedy's hopes for abolishing the quota system were realized when the 1965 amendments were enacted. But his vision of visas on a first-come, first-served basis gave way to a narrower and more historically parochial framework that provided few, if any, obvious advantages for prospective Asian immigrants. The new law allowed twenty thousand immigrant visas for every country not in the Western Hemisphere.[203] The allotment was made regardless of the size of a country, so that mainland China had the same quota as Tunisia. Of the 170,000 visas set aside for the Eastern Hemisphere, 75 percent were for specified "preference" relatives of citizens and lawful permanent residents, and an unlimited number was available to immediate relatives of United States citizens.[204] (Appendix B explains the immediate-relative category and preference system.)

Except for a new refugee category that some Chinese might be able to use, the new provisions were not expected to bolster Asian immigration. Since most of the visas were reserved for family reunification, policymakers believed that countries of Asia (and Africa), with low rates of immigration prior to 1965, might in fact be handicapped, since their smaller numbers presumably meant there were fewer people here who had relatives there.[205]

Two occupational preference categories and a nonpreference cate-

gory were also established. The occupational categories helped professionals and other aliens who filled jobs for which qualified U.S. workers
were not available.[206] Under the nonpreference category,[207] an alien who
invested $40,000 in a business could qualify for immigration to the
United States.[208] While observers knew that these categories would open
the door for more professionals and investors,[209] Asians did not hold a
particular advantage over other nationalities.

A few Chinese were expected to take advantage of a new refugee category that reflected a sense of international responsibility by the United
States. The "seventh preference" favored persons fleeing a Communist
or Communist-dominated country.[210] The potential benefit of this provision to Chinese who had fled mainland China after 1949 was obvious,
but an annual worldwide limitation of 10,200 for the entire category
limited its usefulness. Large numbers from one particular country
would be unable to take advantage of this category because the annual
allotment had to be shared with nationals of other Communist-dominated, as well as Middle Eastern, countries.[211]

A colonial quota also limited potential Asian immigration, particularly for Chinese from Hong Kong. Although each sovereign country
had its own annual twenty thousand visas under the new system,
colonies or other dependent areas of a foreign state were provided individual allotments of only two hundred each year.[212] Hong Kong and
Macao were severely affected by this limitation.[213] Since visas would be
charged to the place of birth, anyone born in such an area would be subject to the colonial quota of two hundred.[214]

## Conclusion

Prior to the various exclusion laws, no federal statutes sought to bar
Asian immigration or to control Asian American communities. The
main impediments to the development of the communities had been
the emigration restrictions of certain Asian governments and the threat
of anti-Asian violence and local statutory discrimination in the United
States. As xenophobia and nativism heightened and as the control of
each particular group seemed inevitably to slip, federal legislators
responded with an ensemble of laws aimed fundamentally at keeping
Asian immigration in check. From 1875 to 1934 exclusionists were able to
wage successful attacks through immigration legislation on Chinese,

Japanese, Koreans, Asian Indians, and Filipinos. The attacks were mean-spirited, and the resulting laws were malevolent. The communities were expected to suffer. Only after wartime alliances had formed in the 1940's did the exclusionary policies even begin to erode.

When more global visions of international relations became popular in the 1960's, what remained of the Asian exclusion laws simply were eliminated as one aspect of a large makeover. The United States needed to repeal the pernicious national-origins quota system, which had tarnished its image in the eyes of the world. For a while at least, xenophobic impulses were suppressed. The potential effect of such reforms on Asian American communities, however, were either disregarded or underestimated.

## CHAPTER TWO

# The Communities' Responses:
# Asian America Prior to 1965

Immigration law took general aim at Asian social, economic, and political life in the United States, but no one ever knew precisely how demographics were being affected. The exclusion of Chinese women and the denial of the franchise were presumed to hit their mark, yet policymakers, scholars, journalists, and activists never bothered to examine any Asian American community in detail. If anyone ever realized just how little was understood, perhaps they took comfort in the belief that the United States could always exclude any Asians it could not otherwise control.

Today a close study reveals that, whether entirely anticipated or not, immigration laws and policies did play a highly influential role in the making and remaking of pre-1965 Chinese, Japanese, and Filipino American communities. In many ways, the United States drive to control proved to be as effective as it was ferocious. Family structure, vocational ambitions, economic achievements, residential patterns, political status, and community size all reflect the imprint of decades of strong

and usually high-handed rule. While each group's demographics impli-
cate distinctive historical patterns, cumulatively they disclose a powerful
connection between possibilities permitted and possibilities pursued—
along social, economic, and political dimensions.

Yet, in some respects this drive to control met its match in Asian
America's desire to endure. Each group managed somehow to weather
the most severe attacks, always making the most of what it had available,
and usually to heal itself. No doubt Asian America would have preferred
not to have been forced to exhibit such remarkable resilience. Perhaps,
too, each Asian American group now speculates about the effects of
those years. In any event, today's communities find their origins in the
demographic consequences of the drive to control them through policies and laws.

## The Chinese

### Population, Gender Ratio, and Family Formation

With no restrictions on their immigration in the mid-1800's, thousands
of Chinese laborers were able to emigrate to the West; that provided
them with an opportunity to seek their fortunes in the legendary Gold
Mountain of California, while they filled the need for an able and cheap
labor force.[1] Almost all of this first group were itinerant male laborers
who were unmarried or whose spouses had remained in China.
Disabled by bound feet and other cultural restrictions, few Chinese
women, even spouses, left their homes in China. Recruiters and
California growers sought men because of the rough conditions in the
fields.[2] Yet most men among this first group intended to return home to
their families after striking it rich. American employers valued the fact
that these workers were not burdened by families and could be called
upon to do migrant work. It was all the easier to establish the male-only
camps attached to railroads, farms, and mines, where hard work never
had to compete with the distractions of family life.

Employers felt that they could easily dominate their Chinese
employees, who, because they were unfamiliar with this country's language and customs and were striving to make as much money as quickly
as possible, could not resist the sometimes atrocious working conditions
they faced.[3] Chinese laborers did not have the mobility to seek other

forms of employment, and they were often barred by local laws from owning land or establishing businesses.[4] Most important perhaps, employers were confident that they could modulate the supply of Chinese laborers. When labor demands were high, Chinese could be recruited to come to California. When demands decreased, they would be expected, even compelled, to return to China.

That Congress too was fixated on controlling the aspirations of this migrant labor pool is confirmed in its 1870 refusal to extend naturalization rights to Chinese. That decision eliminated the chance for Chinese immigrants both to put down permanent roots and to gain the privileged responsibilities of full citizenship. Immigrant laborers would not be able to vote and become members of the body politic, but would remain sojourners subject to the dictates of their bosses. Their offspring could not derive citizenship because only Chinese born in the United States could claim it and given the obstacles to women immigrants, the odds against fathering children were considerable.

After the 1875 statute barring the entry of Chinese prostitutes, immigration authorities quite nearly treated all Chinese women as prostitutes. The Chinese Exclusion Act in 1882 made undeniably explicit the intent of Congress to keep a very tight rein on Chinese immigrants. Although the act formally barred laborers, most of whom had been men, immigration authorities acted, with the courts' approval, against all Chinese women as well, except for the wives of merchants. Beginning in 1907 U.S. women were divested of citizenship if they married an alien.[5] Thereafter, they would be regarded as nationals of their husbands' native country. Repealed in 1922, the act continued to apply to women who married an "alien ineligible to citizenship," in other words, any Asian immigrant.[6] Thus, until 1931 when expatriation of women married to Asian immigrants was rescinded, there was an added disincentive for women in America to marry them.

Combined with the antimiscegenation laws then in place in California and Oregon, the 1875 statute and the 1882 Exclusion Act deprived male laborers of the opportunity to marry and have children.[7] Congress now could dictate the size of the Chinese American population. More than ever before, it was understood that the isolated Chinese laborers were expected to lead lives revolving almost exclusively around their jobs. Employers would have less reason to worry about work hours and environments, and states would be under less pressure to accommodate Chinese American families and children.

Chinese American communities reflect decades of extreme numerical imbalance between men and women immigrants as a result. In 1882, for example, the last year before the Exclusion Act banned Chinese laborers, only 116 of the 39,579 Chinese immigrants were women.[8] The initial wave of immigrants was almost entirely men who intended to return home after a short period. But by the 1880's, four decades later, an ever-increasing number of Chinese intended to stay permanently in the United States.[9] Had the exclusion laws not gone into effect, a significant number of the men no doubt would have sent for their spouses and children. By 1890 men outnumbered women among Chinese Americans almost 27 to 1.[10]

Yet in drastically limiting the number of women immigrants, immigration law may have only fortified patterns that in Chinese culture kept women subordinate.[11] Sons were more highly prized than daughters, and married women became a part, and under the control, of the husband's family. Sons inherited land in equal parts and shared the formal financial responsibility for aging parents. A son would be counted upon to go to the United States if necessary to support his parents in China, while his wife would be expected to stay behind, care for the household, and distribute her husband's contributions.[12]

But Chinese American life may well have also been a response to a transitory, frontier life-style. Working conditions in the mines, on the railroads, and in agricultural projects were not seen by the Chinese as compatible with the needs of women and children, and employers were hardly eager to change these perceptions.

Where Chinese life was not so hard, women did migrate in larger numbers. A not insignificant percentage went to Hawaii, where contracts with plantation owners were better than with employers on the mainland and where the farm work was not as migratory. In Hawaii women were 13.5 percent of the Chinese population in the late 1800's,[13] but were less than 4 percent in California.[14]

Before the 1882 exclusion law the Chinese immigrant community continued to grow slowly in spite of the 1870 Nationality Act and the overreaching exclusion of prostitutes in 1875. Some Chinese returned to China, but the economic situation in southern China remained desultory, so many laborers remained in America. After major railroads were completed and placer mines exhausted, many turned to the cities in search of jobs.[15]

The 1882 Exclusion Act did more than bar Chinese laborers. The

United States also expected to constrain Chinese economic potential and to eliminate competition from foreign workers in periods of decreased labor demand. The act immediately influenced all Chinese immigration. In 1882 more than 39,000 Chinese entered the United States, but only 279 did so in 1884, and 10 entered in 1888.[16] By contrast, 82,394 immigrants entered from Great Britain in 1882, and 250,630 from Germany.[17] And from 1882 to 1890 the annual number of immigrants (mostly European, of course) averaged over half a million.[18] Chinese did not always dutifully accede to these systematic efforts to control their presence. Many who entered after the enactment of the exclusion laws did so under false citizenship claims.[19]

The precipitous decline in Chinese immigration registered, in part, the aftershocks of exclusion. Chinese merchants and students seriously questioned whether they should enter a country that was so hostile to their working-class compatriots. Many interpreted the exclusion law as an attack on all Chinese. After a while, however, a small but steady number began once again to enter, and from 1891 to 1920, about 56,000 arrived in the United States.[20] Yet even these numbers are deceptive, because more than ever large numbers of merchants and students entered with a "sojourner's intent" of returning to China.[21]

The exclusion laws resulted in a decline in Chinese American population from over 100,000 in 1882 to slightly more than 85,000 in 1920 (see Table 3). Further contributing to this decline was the Scott Act's (1888) cancellation of outstanding reentry certificates. About 20,000 Chinese laborers, many with families and property in the United States, were eventually barred from returning though they held initially valid reentry documents.[22]

The early 1920's witnessed the arrival of almost 20,000 immigrants. Many came because a loophole allowed those Asians who had resided for five years in a country in the Western Hemisphere to immigrate to the United States. Consistent with earlier patterns, most of these immigrants were men,[23] and their numbers swelled the Chinese American population from 85,202 in 1920 to 102,159 in 1930.

But after the passage of the 1924 Immigration Act, all Chinese (including students and merchants) became "ineligible to citizenship." The Great Depression and the Japanese invasion of China only stiffened the strict limits imposed by the act. As a result, between 1930 and 1940 fewer than 5,000 Chinese immigrated, and the Chinese American population increased only 4 percent to 106,334[24] (see Table 3).

TABLE 3

*Comparison of Chinese American Population with Immigration
by Decade and the Immigration Law in Effect, 1860–1990*

| Decade ending | Population | Immigration in prior decade[a] | Law in effect in prior decade |
|---|---|---|---|
| 1860 | 34,933[b] | 41,397 | Open |
| 1870 | 64,199[b] | 64,301 | Open until Burlingame Treaty in 1868 |
| 1880 | 105,465[b] | 123,201 | Burlingame Treaty |
| 1890 | 107,488[b] | 61,711 | Burlingame Treaty until 1882, then Chinese Exclusion Act |
| 1900 | 118,746 | 14,799 | Chinese Exclusion Act |
| 1910 | 94,414 | 20,605 | Chinese Exclusion Act |
| 1920 | 85,202 | 21,278 | Chinese Exclusion Act |
| 1930 | 102,159 | 29,907 | Chinese Exclusion Act and 1924 Act |
| 1940 | 106,334 | 4,928 | Chinese Exclusion Act and 1924 Act |
| 1950 | 150,005 | 16,709 | Chinese Exclusion Act, then Chinese Repealer in 1943 |
| 1960 | 237,292 | 25,201 | Chinese Repealer, then Asia-Pacific triangle in 1952 |
| 1970 | 436,062 | 109,771 | Asia-Pacific triangle, then 1965 amendments |
| 1980 | 812,178 | 237,793 | 1965 amendments |
| 1990 | 1,645,472 | 446,000 | 1965 amendments and separate Taiwan quota |

SOURCES: *INS Annual Reports and Statistical Yearbooks*; Gardner et al. 1985; R. H. Lee 1960; Sung 1967, 1978.

[a]The early immigration numbers may be misleading because immigration officials mixed reentries with new entries. These figures include mainland China, Taiwan, and Hong Kong. Taiwan was allocated its own quota in 1981.

[b]Mainland United States only.

The loosening of the exclusion laws during World War II eventually prompted significant changes in Chinese immigration patterns. Coupled with the extension of nonquota status to wives of citizens, the 1943 Chinese Repealer made family unification possible. Older laborers who had been separated from their families for generations were finally able to petition for their wives, as were merchants and students who had entered before 1924.[25] Perhaps not surprisingly, women were almost 90 percent of Chinese immigrants from 1946 to 1952.[26]

These reformed immigration patterns substantially remade Chinese communities. Men had outnumbered women 14 to 1 in 1910 and 7 to 1 in 1920. By 1950, however, the margin was under 2 to 1.[27] These changes reflect, in part, the deaths of earlier male immigrants. To a greater degree, however, they are evidence of both the postwar immigration of Chinese women and the birth of children to Chinese American families in the United States.

Because of World War II reforms, between 1946 and 1965 the Chinese American population, by a conservative estimate, nearly tripled in size, from about 125,000 to 360,000.[28] Most of the growth is attributable to births since only about 70,000 immigrated (15,000 of whom arrived in the early 1960's as refugees from the People's Republic).[29] In fact, by 1965, about 55 percent of the Chinese American population was American-born.[30]

## Geographic Distribution and Residential Patterns

Through 1965 the vast majority of Chinese were settled in California, in part because the majority of those who had worked in other states, such as on the railroads, moved there. The Northeast historically attracted Chinese diplomats, students, and merchants. New York had no antimiscegenation law and that no doubt added to its appeal.[31] In 1959, a typical year after the 1943 Chinese Repealer, 2,005 (35 percent) settled in California, and 1,574 (27.5 percent) went to New York.[32] By 1965 more than 15 percent of all Chinese Americans resided in New York.[33]

Many Chinese settled in rural areas, working in gold mines and on farms and starting up grocery stores, restaurants, laundries, and other small businesses. Those who settled in rural areas were characteristically from rural areas of southern China. They were willing to forgo the security of their numbers in urban settings to pursue other economic dreams and small-town life-styles, though that almost always meant long working hours.[34] Small mining, railroad, and farming communities developed in the late 1800's and continued through the early 1900's, but the numbers of Chinese Americans working in small businesses in the rural South, Midwest, and Southwest steadily dwindled in the middle of this century.[35] Many children of rural families went to college and later resettled in metropolitan areas, abandoning the labor-intensive businesses of their first-generation parents.

Ineligible for citizenship and the target of harsh social attitudes and an array of repressive state and local laws, Chinese found themselves segregated and excluded. Many laborers were forced to resettle in urban Chinatowns. Some needed jobs when gold mining waned and the transcontinental railroad was completed in 1885, but others had spent their lives working the land, and knew little about and even feared urban life.[36] To make matters worse, in 1879 the California legislature passed a law (later declared unconstitutional) requiring incorporated towns and cities to remove Chinese from city limits.[37] In Tucson in 1885 a petition was circulated urging that the Chinese be required to live in a Chinatown.[38] Landlords and realtors refused to rent and sell to Chinese outside of Chinatown, and some whites threatened physical violence to those who ventured beyond certain boundaries.[39]

This forced migration to Chinatowns seems to have been understood in two quite contrasting ways. The Chinese, who often suffered mob attacks during the anti-Chinese furor of the late nineteenth and early twentieth century, needed security and the chance to form much-needed social networks.[40] In the sanctity of their own enclaves, Chinese put together formal associations and confederations based on geographic origin and family clans that helped meet economic, social, religious, educational, and political needs.[41] These networks no doubt were particularly important to the men, serving as a substitute of sorts for the traditional family that they were denied.[42] For all Chinese they were a means of connection that was exceedingly important to and perhaps even necessary for social survival. As their numbers decreased after the exclusion laws, the impetus to congregate in Chinatowns proved even more compelling.[43]

For white mainstream citizens Chinatowns helped resolve the tension between needing the Chinese (or at least some foreign group like them) for certain dirty jobs and fearing their unknown Oriental powers. Chinatowns permitted everyone to keep an eye on the Chinese—check their wanderings, their aspirations, their capacity to infiltrate society, the economy, and politics—yet keep them at arm's length. If the Chinese found some odd comfort there, so much the better. No one imagined anything subversive could emerge from so tidy and convenient a quarantine.

For all their complex importance, the number of Chinatowns declined as immigrants decreased during the first half of the twentieth century (see Table 3). In the 1880's cities and towns with a Chinatown were scattered throughout the West, though the Chinatown might consist of only a street or a few stores and its inhabitants might number only a few hundred.[44] Eventually, these enclaves disappeared altogether. By 1940 only 28 cities with Chinatowns could be identified; by 1955, only 16.[45] As the older male laborers died, smaller enclaves broke up. Many of the second and third generations moved to larger, more viable Chinatowns or out of them altogether.

The surge in immigration after the war and the Chinese revolution (1949), however, especially from mainland China in the early 1960's, revitalized many Chinatowns. The more than fifteen thousand refugees who entered by 1965 needed affordable housing, the stability of an established community, and emotional support.[46] Much as before, Chinatowns in the larger cities met these needs, providing economic opportunities and help in adapting to life in the United States.

## Careers and Socioeconomic Status

The first Chinese who came to the vast, undeveloped regions of the western United States provided "the manpower to work the mines, drain the ditches, till the soil, harvest the seas, and build the net of railroads that would bind the nation together."[47] Their willingness to work long hours in the mines for low wages made their services desirable during the 1850's; thereafter, they contracted to plow fields and cultivate crops. Some helped in the first wine vineyards of California in Sonoma.[48] By the 1880's, a majority of the agricultural workers in California were Chinese.[49] Chinese immigrants—like the ten thousand who helped build the Central Pacific railroad—also did the heavy manual labor rejected by white settlers in the West.[50] They even transformed half-submerged marshes and swamps into the San Francisco peninsula.[51]

White workers, feeling threatened by the competition, sought to prevent more of them from entering the country and to exclude Chinese Americans already here from all but the lowest-paying jobs. When more Chinese moved to the cities in search of jobs, organized labor increasingly vilified them and pressured employers and businesses to favor white labor. The impact was soon apparent. In the shoe-making and cigar-rolling industries, hundreds were discharged and replaced by white workers. In many households white women servants displaced Chinese.[52]

It became more difficult for Chinese to earn a living. Organized labor's opposition, employment discrimination, anti-Chinese ordinances, and the rabid sentiment that led to the passage of the exclusion laws worked in tandem to force them out of the jobs that they had been recruited to fill. Turned away by white employers, they sought self-employment in laundries, where their resourcefulness still mattered, where expenses and rent were low, and where knowledge of English was unnecessary.[53] They were opposed here as well. White-labor laundries were established, and Chinese laundry workers in San Francisco were reduced by one-third.

Merchants admitted after 1882 had migrated from southern China and brought with them its millennia-old entrepreneurial tradition. They naturally gravitated toward self-employment in businesses in which they were experienced.[54] Self-reliance, notable among Chinese immigrants since the 1840's, especially marked the period between the passage of the first exclusion act and the Chinese Repealer of 1943. Small Chinese-run businesses—laundries, grocery stores, coffee shops—became common in cities and rural towns where they remained.

Small business was particularly prominent in the development of San Francisco's Chinatown. By the turn of the century, Chinese who made it the nation's largest were mostly male laborers or self-supporting students who intended to return home to help "modernize" China.[55] Some ventured outside of Chinatown to find jobs as manual laborers or domestics. Most, however, stayed to avoid racial animosity and violence. Their requirements were met, in time, by family-run enterprises that began to appear with the upsurge in merchant immigration before the 1924 Immigration Act.[56] Sequestered by racial and social barriers, the small businesses and the residents of Chinatowns satisfied one another's needs and helped make Chinatown self-sufficient.

China's alliance with the United States during World War II helped to precipitate socioeconomic changes in Chinese America. When wartime propaganda favorably depicted China as an ally, the stature of Chinese Americans suddenly rose.[57] The mainstream media instructed Americans on the art of distinguishing the Japanese from our "friends" the Chinese.[58] No longer the Yellow Peril, they were immigrants who traced their roots to the land of a close ally. Demand for Chinese men and women in the wartime industries was strong. Shipyards and aircraft factories began to employ both as engineers, technicians, and assembly-line workers, drawing, first, from the historically male-dominated Chinese American labor force and, then, from a pool of women who immigrated after the 1943 Chinese Repealer.[59]

These World War II changes in immigration policies, laws, and official attitudes helped to reconfigure occupational profiles. Chinese America, once almost exclusively merchant and laborer, saw the rise of a new professional class. In 1940 under 3 percent held professional and technical jobs; by 1950 more than 7 percent did.[60] As this trend continued, it was clear that some of these new professionals were either American-born children of earlier immigrants or foreign students who had never returned to war-torn China.[61] But others were in the United States because the Chinese Repealer and related immigration law reforms had made their migration possible. This expansion of the professional pool helped meet the demand for new, educated workers in technical and professional fields and developed a decidedly segmented labor market in Chinese America—a phenomenon that expanded after 1965 and is explored further in Chapter 3.

## The Japanese

### Population, Gender Ratio, and Family Formation

Barred by their own government from emigrating, only a few hundred Japanese immigrants were recorded before the 1880's. With the legalization of emigration in 1885, however, many responded to offers of work in the plantations of Hawaii. In the 1890's, almost 27,000 entered the United States, 12,635 in 1899 alone[62] (see Table 4). At the turn of the century recruitment of Japanese laborers became more organized, and 130,000 immigrated between 1901 and 1910 (when about 20,000 Chinese also entered).[63] Japanese immigration was still quite modest, however. From 1901 to 1910 Italy and Austria sent more than 2 million, 1.5 million came from Russia, 500,000 from the United Kingdom, and 300,000 from Ireland and Germany.[64]

The Gentlemen's Agreement of 1908 limited but did not totally bar Japanese laborers and permitted spouses and children as well. Compared to the 1882 Chinese Exclusion Law, it was something of a success for the Japanese government even though it cut back significantly on Japanese immigration. The 83,837 who immigrated between 1910 and 1920 represent a drop of almost 50,000 from the previous decade (see Table 4). And although 136,248 immigrated between 1908 and 1924,[65] about 38,000 went back to Japan for a net of less than 100,000.[66]

By the early 1920's, Japanese could do nothing to stem the strong post–World War I isolationist and exclusionist sentiment in Congress. With the passage of the Immigration Act of 1924, which excluded all Asians ineligible for citizenship, Japanese immigration declined precipitously. After the onset of the depression and then of World War II, it stopped almost completely. Between 1931 and 1950, only 3,503 Japanese

TABLE 4

Comparison of Japanese American Population with
Immigration by Decade and the Immigration Law in Effect, 1888–1985

| Decade ending | Population | Immigration in prior decade | Law in Effect in prior decade |
|---|---|---|---|
| 1890 | | 2,270 | Open immigration |
| 1900 | 85,716 | 25,942 | Open immigration |
| 1910 | 152,745 | 129,797 | Open immigration until Gentlemen's Agreement |
| 1920 | 220,596 | 83,837 | Gentlemen's Agreement |
| 1930 | 278,743 | 33,462 | Gentlemen's Agreement until 1924 Act |
| 1940 | 285,115 | 1,948 | 1924 Act |
| 1950 | 326,379 | 1,555 | 1924 Act |
| 1960 | 464,332 | 46,250 | 1924 Act until 1952 Act |
| 1970 | 591,290 | 39,988 | 1952 Act until 1965 amendments |
| 1980 | 716,331 | 49,775 | 1965 amendments |
| 1990 | 847,562 | 44,800 | 1965 amendments |

SOURCE: *INS Annual Reports* and *Statistical Yearbooks;* Gardner et al. 1985.

immigrants entered (see Table 4). Though immigration from all Asian countries dropped greatly during the depression and World War II, Japan's decrease was unmatched.

But the Japanese American population steadily increased during the first half of the twentieth century because the Gentlemen's Agreement allowed wives and children to enter.[67] The community was spared the extreme gender imbalance that had undermined Chinese America, which suffered a net population decrease during the same period. In 1910, for example, the ratio of Japanese men to women was 7 to 1; by 1920, however, it was less than 2 to 1.[68] (For Chinese Americans, the ratio was about 14 to 1 in 1910, and almost 7 to 1 in 1920, again almost entirely because during these years nearly five times more men entered.)[69]

A substantial share of the Japanese women immigrants during this period were "picture brides"—women whose prospective husbands had seen only a picture before the marriage.[70] Given antimiscegenation laws and the Japanese custom to arrange marriages, it is not surprising that many men sent back to Japan for brides. A Japanese immigrant who wished to marry but was unable to return to Japan had few other options.

Picture brides caused an outrage in the United States, and part of the impetus for Japanese exclusion grew out of an aversion to the practice.[71] The United States strongly protested Japan's issuing passports to the picture brides. Japan stopped the practice in 1920 and established a new policy that permitted marriages between Japanese women and émigrés who returned to Japan for as few as thirty days.[72] The new brides (called Kandodan brides, the Japanese word for excursion) were then issued passports. They were met with much the same outrage as their predecessors had been.[73]

The impact of picture brides and other Japanese wives on the Japanese American community during this era is clear. By 1920 approximately 30,000 American-born children of Japanese ancestry were counted compared to 4,500 in 1910; by 1930, they numbered 68,000.[74]

Though the Gentlemen's Agreement secured for Japanese women the right to immigrate, social, economic, and cultural conditions in their home country may have influenced their ability to leave as well. The Japanese government supervised emigration as a means of broadening the country's influence. Women would make "true settlement" through the establishment of families possible.[75] As a result of the modernization set in motion by the Meiji Restoration, Japan's economy was booming by the turn of the century. The country was still distinctly agrarian, but this modernization led to increased employment opportunities and greater economic independence for women. In 1911 they were more than half of the factory work force in Japan.[76] While little empirical evidence supports the claim that they wanted to leave as a result, the notion is hard to resist for some.[77] They had job experience, and Japanese women were certainly familiar with having to leave home.[78] By tradition only the oldest son inherited the parents' land. Apparently other sons were free to leave, and they often did, taking their wives with them (although many first sons also left).[79] These conditions prepared many Japanese women to accept jobs in Hawaii or the mainland United States.

For all its steady growth, Japanese America felt the impact of 30 years of exclusion. The 1924 act had blocked many relatives from joining those who had already immigrated. Less visibly, it generated related social problems within families. Tensions grew because second-generation Japanese were American citizens while their parents were still aliens, denied the right to naturalize.[80] In fact, the Japanese American Citizens League lobbied heavily for the passage of the 1952 McCarran-Walter Act largely so first-generation Japanese (Issei) could become eligible for citizenship.[81]

With the passage of McCarran-Walter, Japanese women continued to enter at a relatively high rate, and the community grew steadily.

Between 1952 and 1961 Japanese Americans were the largest group of Asian naturalization applicants.[82] Once they became citizens they were able to petition for their spouses on an unlimited, nonquota basis. In fact, between 1956 and 1965, the relatively large numbers of Japanese who immigrated were primarily these nonquota wives. In 1959, for example, 5,012 Japanese women immigrated, compared to 839 men;[83] in 1961, 3,665 women and only 648 men entered.[84] By 1965 the community consisted of more women than men (approximately 85 males for every 100 females)—the only Asian American group at the time with such a profile.[85] Between the 1952 and 1965 acts, far more Japanese immigrated than any other Asian nationality.[86] After overtaking Chinese Americans in 1910, they remained America's largest Asian group through 1970.[87]

## Geographic Distribution and Residential Patterns

In the late 1800's when the United States persuaded Japan to remove its emigration bars on laborers, recruiters attracted them primarily to Hawaii and the West Coast, and that trend was to continue. The first sizable group of Japanese in the 1880's worked on Hawaiian sugar plantations, with many remaining to establish what soon became a substantial population on the islands.[88] Those who went on to the mainland owned small businesses and worked as tenant farmers in the rural West. Initially, California, Washington, and Oregon afforded the Japanese opportunities to own their own farms and businesses.[89] By the time California's Alien Land Law was enacted in 1913, about 4,000 Japanese in California were agricultural landowners or lessees, and 20,000 Japanese were farm workers.[90] In response to the land laws more made their way to major cities. As early as 1910 Los Angeles was becoming the most popular urban area for Japanese, and by 1940 almost 37,000 lived there. About 11,000 lived in and around Seattle, while over 5,000 made San Francisco their home.[91]

Ironically, the 1924 cutoff of Japanese immigration appears to have ensured that they would remain concentrated in the West. Indeed, in many ways the xenophobic pressures behind the exclusion tied established families to Hawaii, California, and Washington. There they knew the rules, however harsh, and they knew how to survive, however uneasily. There friends and relatives offered at least the illusion of protection against a country now willing to wield any of several blunt instruments of control—exclusion provisions, citizenship ineligibility, and alien land laws. So there they remained.

If domestic land laws and the 1924 Immigration Act seemed unusually tough on Japanese Americans, the beginning of World War II brought a far more severe regime. After the bombing of Pearl Harbor, the bigotry and fear that had informed earlier anti-Japanese laws became a panic. Japanese Americans suddenly became suspected of acts of sabotage and treason. Though no such acts were ever proved, the civilian government acceded to unprecedented military orders that subjected all West Coast Japanese first to curfews and then to forced evacuation into detention camps.[92] Eventually, 120,000 Japanese Americans, most of them citizens by birth or lawful permanent resident aliens, were interned in camps scattered across the country.[93]

One of the most remarkable aspects of the internment was how easily most Americans accepted it. Nativists made Japanese Americans feel unwanted and insecure about whether they would be able to stay; many other Americans challenged their loyalty and commitment.[94] That the internment had little to do with the actual threat Japanese Americans supposedly presented seems clear because in Hawaii, the most vulnerable part of the United States and the site of the Pearl Harbor bombing, they were not subject to it. Instead, internment represented the culmination of many decades of harsh treatment of Asians on the West Coast, where they had never been accepted as equals or even as trustworthy. Even in the 1930's, the Japanese in particular had always aroused resentment for their upward mobility.[95] For a white majority that had long sought to keep a tight check on Asian immigration and had long refused to accord Asians the rights of other immigrant groups, internment did not seem an extreme measure.

Even the Supreme Court, which had often justified earlier restrictions on the grounds that those affected were not citizens, uncritically accepted the premises behind internment. Though the Court purported in *Korematsu v. United States* to apply "strict scrutiny" to the government's order, in reality it accepted at face value the military's fears and accusations that Japanese American citizens were all potential saboteurs—fears and accusations that were concocted, that were contradicted by official government reports, and that were later proved to be baseless.[96] Just as little scrutiny was given to racially based exclusionary laws and the denial of naturalization rights to Asian immigrants, so little inquiry was made of the pretexts by which the military supported its deportation order.

Internment, however, did not produce sweeping changes in Japanese settlement patterns, even though many second-generation Japanese Americans were bitter over the racial hostility on the West Coast. Most internment camps were in remote areas of the country, such as Louisiana, New Mexico, Oklahoma, Montana, and Texas.[97] Since areas surrounding the camps offered few economic opportunities, most of those who survived internment had little choice but to return to the West Coast.[98] A resentful few dispersed to major urban areas in the Midwest and East.[99] Since the internment order applied only to the West Coast, Japanese Americans in Hawaii had every incentive to remain there.

After the removal of the racial exclusion grounds from the 1952 Immigration Act, some Asians, including Japanese, migrated to New York, Texas, Pennsylvania, and Illinois. Encouraged by the growth in the domestic economy and accommodated by the new interstate highways, others were also among those willing in the 1950's to search out economic and social opportunities. But because Japanese Americans were still only a tiny percentage of the general population, those who settled in nonwestern states numbered only in the hundreds.[100]

From 1952 to 1965 Japanese immigrants continued principally to choose California (30 percent) and Hawaii (9 percent) as their homes.[101] From 1952 to 1965, only 5–6 percent settled in New York;[102] Illinois, Pennsylvania, and Texas each became home to 3–5 percent of the newcomers.[103] Since the number of new Japanese immigrants was small compared to the size of the predominantly American-born Japanese American community, the 1952 law did not significantly affect their geographic dispersion.

Though drawn to the familiarity of the western states, they did not often develop and sustain Japantowns. Although they were not shielded from racial and economic hostilities, their experience with immigration laws was different than those of other Asians who sought urban enclaves as homes. Perhaps the intervention of the Japanese government on their behalf afforded them some sense of being, at least on occasion, sufficiently well-protected. And certainly their ability to preserve and form families gave them economic and social networks that, in part, obviated one reason to escape to Japantowns. They could rely on members of their own families for companionship, help, comfort, and encouragement, making it easier to maintain rural jobs and life-styles.

Indeed, only the passage in 1913 of California's Alien Land Law prompted the development of the two most prominent Japantowns in San Francisco and in Los Angeles, though they would be stymied by internment. Deprived of the ability to own farms after 1913, Japanese were forced to move to towns and cities to find other jobs. For immigrants who had traditionally been farmers, this demanded considerable adjustment, and Japantowns buffered much of the transition.[104] But the four years of internment, during which many Japanese lost their property, essentially ended the Japantown phenomenon. Upon their release many internees, wary of racist sentiment, chose not to congregate in ethnically defined communities.[105] In 1940, there were 5,280 Japanese in San Francisco, almost all in Japantown; the postwar years, however, saw a much greater dispersion of the city's Japanese American residents.[106] Japantown had for a short time met some important needs, but the world had changed.

### Careers and Socioeconomic Status

Although some Japanese labored in mining camps and as maintenance workers for the railroads, agriculture became their mainstay during open immigration.[107] By the time California enacted alien land laws in 1913, about 30,000 were farmers or farm workers.[108] But many also found domestic service jobs, while others began developing small, family-run businesses (shops, cafes, laundries, barber shops) which became an important aspect of their economic life.[109] Still others worked in lumber mills, railroad yards, mines, meat-packing houses, and canneries.[110] Women were an integral part of this work force.[111]

While immigration and landownership restrictions gradually curbed the economic gains that Japanese Americans had made in agriculture, California's Alien Land Law furnished loopholes that allowed creative immigrants to retain land. The law did not prevent Japanese from leasing, for example, and landownership by corporations was permitted if corporate ownership was chiefly nonalien.[112] So long as they either used corporate forms ostensibly held by whites or transferred title to a citizen child born in the United States, they could continue to farm their land.[113] These loopholes annoyed white farmers and legislators alike. But active efforts to remove them stalled because the United States did not want to risk offending its World War I ally.

Soon after the war, however, anti-Japanese sentiment on the West

Coast quickly regained its prewar intensity. Washington legislated its own alien landownership restrictions. Hoping to close the loopholes of its 1913 statute, California enacted the Alien Land Law of 1920, which outlawed circuitous transfers, including those from alien parents to citizen children.[114] Attempts to avoid this new law through agricultural corporations and cropping contracts failed when the Supreme Court in *Webb v. O'Brien* (1923) ruled that the discriminatory impact of alien land laws did not violate equal protection guarantees of the constitution.[115] As a result, many Japanese farmers lost control of their land, moved to towns and cities, and began the search for viable occupations. For them it was too late when, in 1953, the alien land laws finally were declared unconstitutional because they were racially discriminatory.[116]

Japanese Americans adapted to urban life by redefining their vocation and their place in society. Those forced to the cities in 1924 worked in small shops and businesses. Many could take advantage of their opportunities because of their earlier successes in agriculture.[117] Often pooling resources, they were able to start restaurants, laundries, barber shops, and other service enterprises.[118] Others turned to gardening, the third most important occupation among prewar Japanese Americans after agriculture and small business.[119] Thus, by the 1930's, Japanese Americans who had started as laborers and service workers twenty years earlier had become managers or owners of small businesses.[120] Two-thirds of first-generation Japanese Americans in Seattle at the time were self-employed in trades or domestic and personal services such as hotels, groceries, restaurants, laundries, and produce houses.[121]

At about the same time, Japanese America was steadily developing a small professional class. The war and internment again disrupted this development for West Coast Japanese, making it difficult for them to reestablish an entrepreneurial character because of dislocation and job discrimination.[122] But in general, from 1924 to 1965, more and more second-generation Japanese Americans (ironically, many who were World War II veterans using the GI bill) were able to attend college, and many developed greater interests in science and technical fields.[123] They provided the nucleus for a middle class of doctors, dentists, lawyers, and engineers that drew exclusively from the American-born.[124] Statistics typical for the years after the 1952 Act (when Japanese immigration led other Asian nations) reveal that only about 2 percent of the entrants indicated prior employment as "professional, technical, and kindred workers."[125]

# The Filipinos

## Population, Gender Ratio, and Family Formation

Until the twentieth century few Filipinos immigrated. Small groups of sailors aboard Spanish galleons as early as 1565 jumped ship in Mexico and made their way to Louisiana to establish the first Filipino American community. But it would be three hundred years before many of their compatriots followed. By 1910, a dozen years after the United States annexed the Philippines and granted Filipinos special noncitizen national status, the reported Filipino American population stood at only 2,767 (see Table 5).[126] Lacking any particular social or economic incentive, the new nationals made little use of their newly acquired freedom to travel without restriction to the United States.

But after the Gentlemen's Agreement slowed Japanese immigration, employers in the United States (particularly Hawaii) began to recruit Filipinos, and the privileged travel status became a highly used commodity. By 1920, there were 26,634 Filipino Americans—a tenfold increase in ten years—counted in the census, virtually all of them working in the fields of Hawaii (see Table 5).[127]

The commencement of Filipino migration is significant, even

TABLE 5

*Comparison of Filipino American Population with Immigration*
*by Decade and the Immigration Law in Effect, 1910–1990*

| Decade ending | Population | Immigration in prior decade[a] | Law in effect in prior decade |
|---|---|---|---|
| 1910 | 2,767 | | U.S. possession |
| 1920 | 26,634 | | U.S. possession |
| 1930 | 108,424 | | U.S. possession |
| 1940 | 98,535 | 781[b] | 1917 and 1924 Acts beginning in 1934 |
| 1950 | 122,707 | 4,324[c] | Quota of 100 under 1924 Act beginning 1946 and eligible for citizenship |
| 1960 | 176,310 | 19,307 | 1952 Act |
| 1970 | 343,060 | 98,376 | 1952 Act, then 1965 amendments |
| 1980 | 781,894 | 354,987 | 1965 amendments |
| 1990 | 1,406,770 | 525,300 | 1965 amendments |

SOURCES: Gardner et. al. 1985: tables 1 & 2; 1988 *INS Statistical Yearbook*, table 2, p. 4; 1989 *INS Advance Report*, table 4; table 83 of 1931 *INS Annual Report*; table 64 of 1932 *INS Report*; 1937 *INS Annual Report*, p. 84; table 3 of 1940 *INS Annual Report*; 1959 *INS Annual Report*, tables 13 & 14, pp. 42–43.

[a]Does not include those who entered as noncitizen nationals prior to 1934 (see table 7).

[b]This does not include 1933. From 1934 to 1951 the Philippines were included in the Pacific Islands for INS statistical purposes. These figures are the totals for the Pacific Islands for these decades.

[c]Total for 1945 to 1950 only.

TABLE 6

Arrivals from the Philippines (Insular Travel), 1925–1931

| Year | Total | Men | Women |
|------|-------|-----|-------|
| 1925 | 26,601 | 21,577 | 5,024 |
| 1926 | 30,729 | 24,848 | 5,881 |
| 1927 | 33,541 | 27,329 | 6,212 |
| 1928 | 35,423 | 28,432 | 6,991 |
| 1929 | 37,620 | 30,120 | 7,500 |
| 1930 | 39,339 | 32,251 | 7,088 |
| 1931 | 36,535 | 29,419 | 7,116 |

SOURCES: 1925 INS Annual Report, table 73; 1926 INS Annual Report, table 66; 1927 INS Annual Report, table 69; 1928–31 INS Annual Reports, table 74.

though the 1920 figure is tiny compared to the approximately 5.5 million non-Asians who immigrated from 1911 to 1920.[128] The growing Filipino presence underscored a tradeoff heretofore largely unappreciated: when the United States brought the Philippines under its jurisdiction, it relinquished the capacity to control an Asian group through immigration policy.

From 1920 to 1934 Filipino students and farm workers entered in large numbers as nationals, the majority destined for the mainland. About 34,000 entered each year (see Table 6). This annual average is greater than the entire Filipino American population in 1920 because it includes both temporary entrants as well as long-term immigrants. Still, the 1930 census reported a quadrupling of the population to 108,424, with about 45,000 residing on the mainland and over 63,000 in Hawaii.[129] Though Filipino America remained quite small relative to the general population, its growth nevertheless convinced many exclusionists that control over Filipino immigration had been lost and somehow needed to be reasserted.

The majority of early Filipino immigrants were men, though not nearly to the same degree as were the Chinese. In this instance, however, the imbalance did not result from the legal exclusion of women, since noncitizen nationals both men and women could come to the United States. Instead, it owed more to economic and cultural dynamics. Hawaiian plantation owners and California farmers recruited primarily single Filipino men for the same reasons they preferred single Chinese men. They could move as the crops did, unencumbered by families and less likely to settle down and start competing farms. Women were less likely to come to the United States alone, especially since Spanish and Catholic tradition required that they travel with their fathers or husbands.[130] Moreover, many Filipino men married non-Filipino women, particularly Mexican women.[131] Antimiscegenation statutes then in place in many states prevented Asians and other people of color from marrying whites, but they could intermarry.

The Philippine Independence Act passed in 1934 ended the freedom to enter the United States and imposed an immigration quota of 50 per year. By the 1940 census the population had decreased by 10 percent to 98,376, about the size of Chinese America. Filipinos, whether here or abroad, remained ineligible for citizenship and were to lose their noncitizen national status in 1946. Rather than face forced repatriation or deportation then, many returned to the Philippines between 1934 and 1946.[132] The law managed at once to halt the growing numbers of Filipino immigrants and to discourage those who had entered from remaining.

A slightly more liberal attitude emerged during the Second World War, as the Philippines, like China, became a critical ally in the war against Japan. Almost ten thousand Filipinos took advantage of special citizenship opportunities extended to war veterans and others serving in the Armed Forces.[133] Congress presented a more significant opportunity in 1946 in its eleventh-hour suspension for Filipinos and Indians of the prohibition against Asian naturalization.[134] Several thousand were naturalized over the next two decades—3,257 in 1950 alone.[135]

Quota exemptions for family reunification after 1946 sharply increased immigration by women and children as newly naturalized husbands and fathers petitioned to reunify their families. (The quota had increased to a mere one hundred per year after Philippine independence.) In 1959 of the 2,633 immigrants admitted, 68.3 percent were women; in 1961, of 2,738 admitted, 65 percent were women.[136] In those years, 48.6 percent of Filipino immigrants were wives of U.S. citizens, including many servicemen.[137] The large proportion of women and the birth of citizen children virtually eradicated the gender imbalance by 1965. The 1940 ratio of about seven men for every woman dropped to less than 3 to 1 by 1950 and to about 1.25 to 1 in 1965.[138]

The reunification of families helped Filipino America grow. In spite of modest immigration figures before 1965 (20,000 in the 1950's and 1,500 from 1960 to 1965, most of them nonquota spouses and children),[139] the population increased to 122,707 in 1950 and to 176,310 in 1960, largely because of American births (see Table 5).

## Geographic Distribution and Residential Patterns

Filipinos, like the Japanese, were initially recruited to Hawaii and the rural areas of California, and through the 1960's, they continued to settle predominantly in those two states, though the proportion who lived in Hawaii gradually declined. In 1930 more than 58 percent resided in Hawaii; by 1960 less than 40 percent did.[140] Many of those who left Hawaii migrated to California.[141]

Recruited to agricultural areas, most Filipinos resided in rural areas through the 1930's. Though as noncitizen nationals Filipinos were not subject to the alien land laws, they never became tenant farmers and landowners as the Japanese did, largely because the predominantly single, male population was less inclined to settle down. Their family situation, however, was better than that of the early Chinese. But like the Chinese and Japanese, they faced increased racial violence and isolation, which was mainly the product of the same exclusion movement that led to the 1934 Independence Act.

In response to rural isolation and antagonism, Filipinos gradually moved to major urban areas in California, where Manilatowns or Little Manilas materialized in San Francisco, Los Angeles, Salinas, Stockton, and Fresno.[142] Six thousand resided in Los Angeles by 1933.[143] By 1950, 60 percent of all Filipinos were in cities, and by 1960, the figure increased to 80 percent.[144]

## Careers and Socioeconomic Status

Farm work dominated their employment profile for some time, even after 1920 when Filipinos looked to the West Coast rather than Hawaii for opportunity. From 1923 to 1929 about four thousand Filipino laborers entered annually to pick fruit and lettuce.[145] In the off-season they provided service labor for hotels, restaurants, and private homes as busboys, cooks, hotel chauffeurs, dishwashers, domestic help, and gardeners.[146] Some moved to Alaska and Washington to find jobs in the fishing and cannery industries.[147] And a few were able to open small businesses.[148] Although more students began traveling to the United States in the 1920's,[149] nearly 82 percent of the 45,000 Filipinos reported on the mainland in 1930 were farm laborers.[150]

After the extension of citizenship rights and nonquota status for spouses and children in 1946, the occupational profile of Filipino

America began to change. Young men were once again recruited to Hawaiian plantation work,[151] but more students began to enter. Some students and laborers began to find work in factories, retail sales, and certain trades. By 1950 the proportion of Filipino Americans employed in agricultural jobs dropped to 55 percent.[152]

Gradually a modestly sized class of professionals started to emerge. Before 1965 immigration law contained no special provision for Filipino professionals, and they were limited by the first-come, first-served quota of one hundred. Despite this queuing system the numbers of Filipino immigrants who designated their occupations as professionals, managers, or related workers steadily increased between 1946 and 1965. In 1959 the figure was 9.2 percent of all Filipino immigrants, in 1961 it was 12.3 percent, and in 1963 it was 18.1 percent.[153] Nearly 32 percent, however, were still employed as farmers or farm laborers in 1960.[154]

Through these years the Philippines experienced the somewhat predictable difficulties of new nationhood. While it enjoyed its constitutional independence, it remained highly dependent on the United States for trade.[155] Eventually production declined, and inflation and unemployment rose steadily. In spite of attempts at agrarian land reforms, economic instability plagued the new nation through the 1960's, and made Filipinos more willing to leave their home.[156]

## Koreans

### Population, Gender Ratio, and Family Formation

Prior to 1965 the Korean American population was quite small. About eleven thousand agricultural workers, predominantly men, were recruited for Hawaiian plantations before 1905. Most had been recruited by an American from Hawaii who had moved to Korea in 1902 and had been granted authority by the Korean government to arrange employment for laborers abroad. They were used primarily as strikebreakers when Japanese laborers challenged poor working conditions.[157] By and large they were recruited from an unemployed urban class, although many were illiterate farmers from northern Korea, which was suffering from drought and economic difficulties.[158] Because of the very limited nature of their immigration, after an initial surge from 1902–5 Koreans ceased to be perceived as a threat by most laborers on the West Coast.

TABLE 7

Comparison of Korean American Population with Immigration
by Decade and the Immigration Law in Effect, 1910–1990

| Decade ending | Population | Immigration in prior decade | Law in effect in prior decade |
|---|---|---|---|
| 1910 | 5,008 | | Gentlemen's Agreement |
| 1920 | 6,181 | | Gentlemen's Agreement |
| 1930 | 8,332 | | Gentlemen's Agreement and 1924 Act |
| 1940 | 8,568 | | 1924 Act |
| 1950 | 7,030[a] | [b] | 1924 Act |
| 1960 | 11,000[c] | 7,025[d] | 1924 Act, then Asian-Pacific triangle in 1952 |
| 1970 | 69,150 | 34,526 | 1952 Act, then 1965 amendments |
| 1980 | 357,393 | 267,638 | 1965 amendments |
| 1990 | 798,849 | 336,000 | 1965 amendments |

SOURCES: Knoll 1982: 138; Gardner et al. 1985: 8, table 2; Xenos et al. 1987: 252–53, table 11.1; 1959 and 1961 INS Annual Reports.

[a] Hawaii only.

[b] INS did not begin to count Koreans separately until 1948, when 39 entered each year until 1952.

[c] Foreign-born. This figure increased to 38,711 by 1970 (1975 census, p. 117). However, according to Hyung-Chan Kim, in 1965 there were 2,165 immigrants and 4,717 nonimmigrants of which 1,027 were naturalized (H. Kim 1974: 26, table 1).

[d] Calculated from table 14 of 1959 and 1961 INS Annual Reports.

When Korea was a protectorate and then a possession of Japan from 1905 to 1945, it was subject first to the restrictions of the Gentlemen's Agreement and then to the 1924 Act. These restrictions had little effect, however, because Japan refused to allow any significant Korean emigration. From 1910 to 1924 it permitted the same picture bride policy for Koreans as for Japanese, so that women could immigrate by marrying Korean immigrants already in the United States.[159] About 950 came to Hawaii, and 115 to the mainland.[160] Between 1910 and 1918, 541 refugee Korean students came without passports fleeing Japanese persecution. They campaigned against Japanese domination of their home country and became leaders in the Korean American community.[161] After 1924, however, further immigration was prohibited under the ineligible-to-citizenship bar. Until the Japanese defeat in 1945, when Korea was partitioned into two autonomous states, the only other Korean arrivals were several hundred who came via China, Europe, and Japan.[162]

Thus Korean immigration in the first half of the twentieth century never neared the numbers of the Chinese, Japanese, and Filipinos. The population, which stood at 5,008 in 1910, increased to only 8,332 in 1930 and to only 8,568 in 1940 (see Table 7). The overwhelming majority lived in Hawaii.[163]

Even after the partition of Korea in 1945, few were able to immigrate. North Koreans were immediately restrained by their military-dominated government. And South Koreans and other Asians continued to be excluded under the 1924 Act after the repeal of Chinese exclusion in 1943. From 1948 to 1951 the Immigration and Naturalization Service recorded a total of only 128 Korean immigrants.[164]

Between 1952 and 1965 South Koreans demonstrated an increasing interest in immigration to escape political unrest, social turmoil, and economic instability. The Korean War (1950–53) had caused great damage to the economy, and the failure to conclude a peace treaty left the threat of renewed confrontation with the North ever present.[165] South Korea relied heavily on U.S. aid to finance its postwar reconstruction. The lack of resources and the need to support a large army caused high inflation; by 1957 the economy was showing a net decline.[166] The lack of economic opportunity at home combined with the close American ties forged during and after the war caused many Koreans to view emigration to the United States as a desirable option. Many Americans felt sympathy for Koreans and their cause, although certainly some resented the idea of American soldiers dying over a Korean "problem."[167]

The Korean American population managed some impressive growth even before the 1965 reforms. The McCarran-Walter Act's repeal of racial exclusion and assignment of a minimum quota of one hundred[168] opened a small window of opportunity. Yet more Koreans—especially military wives and adopted orphans—were able to enter. Between 1952 and 1960, 6,993 Korean immigrants entered,[169] and 10,179, primarily nonquota immigrants, arrived from 1961 to 1965.[170] They and their children born in the United States pushed the population to about 45,000 by 1965,[171] a fivefold increase from the 1950 population of approximately 7,500 (see Table 7).

The ratio of men to women as of 1965 had become fairly even. Only 10 percent of the laborers who migrated to Hawaii from 1902 to 1905 were women, many of whom married non-Koreans.[172] The emigration of Korean picture brides between 1910 and 1924 helped provide some balance, yet by 1930 the population was still 66 percent male.[173] In the late 1950's and early 1960's, Korean immigration was increasingly dominated by women who entered through military marriages and adoptions under the 1952 nonquota provisions.[174] From 1959 to 1965, 70 percent were women, 40 percent of whom were 20 to 39.[175] Many were known as war brides because of their marriages to soldiers who fought in the

Korean War.[176] About 40 percent were girls under the age of 4, who were adopted by families moved by the huge number of orphans left after the Korean War.[177] Because the population was so small prior to 1952, a disproportionate number of women immigrants in the years following the 1952 Act accounted for the nearly balanced gender ratio by 1965.

## Geographic Distribution and Residential Patterns

Koreans were attracted to the West Coast soon after they were allowed to immigrate. Plantation representatives recruited them to work in Hawaii after Chinese exclusion. But eventually some of them were attracted to the West Coast after railway companies sent representatives to Hawaii. From there railroad workers were recruited to work in agriculture again. Two thousand Koreans had arrived in San Francisco by 1907, and by 1910 small groups of Korean farm laborers were scattered up and down the West Coast. Dinuba and Reedley in California's San Joaquin Valley became centers of small but flourishing communities. The expansion of agriculture in southern California created more jobs for Korean farm workers there.[178] In addition, Denver, Seattle, Salt Lake City, and Butte, Montana, had numbers of migratory Korean miners and railway workers who formed small, isolated farming communities. Like the Japanese, these farmers were able to sustain a rural life because within ten years they were able to form families with the thousand picture brides who arrived from Korea.[179]

In 1940 the population was predominantly rural, but like the rest of American society, became increasingly urbanized during and after World War II. As students and refugees entered in the 1920's and 1930's, small communities developed in New York, Chicago, Washington, D.C., and some college towns in the East and Midwest. By 1945, eight hundred Koreans lived in Los Angeles, three hundred in New York City, and three hundred in Chicago.[180]

Small residential and business areas emerged in these cities usually within or next to a larger Asian enclave, where certain needs, such as for specialized groceries, could be met.[181] Although supporting Korea's independence brought Koreans together as well,[182] establishing economic networks was a high priority. And though issues of race and a sense of comfort in numbers helped establish these enclaves, the intensity of the racial hostility that led to Chinatowns was not present. An emphasis on an economic impetus for the enclave would continue after 1965.

## Careers and Socioeconomic Status

Early Koreans were predominantly agricultural workers, but the arrival of students and political refugees resulted in some occupational variation. The students and refugees who entered between 1910 and 1940 struggled economically. Most students had to work in low-wage jobs as farm laborers, factory workers, cooks, waiters, chauffeurs, janitors, houseboys, stevedores, and dishwashers, while women worked mainly in sweatshops.[183] But some demonstrated a facility for small business. By 1920 they started laundries, restaurants, retail groceries, and shoe repair shops.[184] Korean-owned hotels also could be found throughout California and Washington.[185]

Especially early on, Korean laborers suffered from the same intense racial animosity that the Chinese and Japanese experienced. The mainstream often made little distinction between Chinese, Japanese, and Koreans. In one highly publicized event in 1913, Korean farm workers were attacked by an angry crowd of white workers and thrown on an outbound train because the crowd had mistaken them for Japanese.[186]

Of the men who entered after the 1952 Act, a noticeable proportion described themselves as professionals, managers, or the like. Without a doubt, the majority of those entering at the time were unskilled women and children. But 6 percent between 1959 and 1963 were classified as professionals and managers.[187] Thus the immigration laws facilitated the entry of some professionals from Korea even before the 1965 changes, although this effect was not as substantial as for Filipino immigrants.

# Asian Indians

## Population, Gender Ratio, and Family Formation

A few Asian Indians immigrated in the late nineteenth and early twentieth centuries. Unlike the other groups, Indian workers could explore prospects in British Empire colonies. They were a better option than the United States, which represented a longer, more arduous, and more expensive journey. The few laborers who took a chance on the United States, along with a small number of more educated Indians, accounted for a total from 1881 to 1917 of only about seven thousand.

India was ineffective in acquiring strong immigration rights for its

TABLE 8

*Comparison of Asian Indian American Population with Immigration by Decade and the Immigration Law in Effect, 1890–1990*

| Decade ending | Population | Immigration in prior decade | Law in effect in prior decade |
|---|---|---|---|
| | | 359[a] | Open |
| 1890 | | 269 | Open |
| 1900 | | 68 | Open |
| 1910 | 5,424 | 4,713 | Open |
| 1920 | | 2,082 | Asiatic barred zone of 1917 |
| 1930 | 3,130[b] | 1,886 | 1924 Act |
| 1940 | 2,405[b] | 496 | 1924 Act |
| 1950 | | 1,761 | 1924 Act, then limited quota beginning in 1946 |
| 1960 | 12,296[c] | 1,973 | 1946 quota, then 1952 Act |
| 1970 | 72,500 | 27,189 | 1952 Act, then 1965 amendments |
| 1980 | 387,223 | 164,134 | 1965 amendments |
| 1990 | 815,447 | 147,900 | 1965 amendments |

SOURCES: Hess 1976, 1986; Dutta 1982; Gardner et al. 1985; Census and INS reports; Kitano and Daniels 1988.
[a]Total from 1820 to 1880.
[b]In 1930, 1,873 were in California; 1,476 in 1940.
[c]Foreign-born. This figure increased to 51,000 by 1970 (1975 census p. 117).

émigrés. The first immigrants entered during a period of good relations between the United States and the British colonial government in India.[188] That relationship, however, was not strong enough to protect them as Japan could protect its nationals, or as India could help emigrants to South Africa. That country granted India's request to accept fixed numbers of women with men recruited as laborers. Therefore, although many of the men recruited to do agricultural work in the United States had families, those families remained while their husbands and fathers worked to earn money to send for them or to return to India.[189]

Educated Indians, dignitaries, and officials who entered before World War II did not need special protection, but they expected the same respect from Americans that upper-class Indians received in Great Britain.[190] Instead they were humiliated by racial prejudice.[191] And they were shocked by the deportation of seventeen hundred Indians between 1911 and 1920.[192]

The establishment of the Asiatic barred zone in 1917 put an abrupt end to Indian immigration (see Table 8). The exclusion was particularly untimely for Indians because their relations with Britain were growing very strained and many were looking to the United States as an alternative destination. The Supreme Court's 1923 decision that Indian Americans were Asians and thus ineligible for naturalization caused many to reassess their relationship with the United States. In the two decades after the decision three thousand returned to India.[193]

Because 80 percent of Asian Indian men married women of Mexican origins,[194] as had so many Filipino immigrants, some were able to enjoy a family life. Many farmers and farm workers were already married in India and intended to send for their wives, but were prevented from doing so after 1917. Mexican women offered love, an opportunity for children, domesticity, and housekeeping skills.[195] They were usually migrant laborers or displaced by the Mexican Revolution without any male relatives. The Indian American population, however, dropped between 1920 and 1940 as those leaving outnumbered new immigrants and American-born offspring combined (see Table 8).

Many Indian farming partners in California had known each other in India. The men would settle and work together; when one married, the Mexican wife would move into this joint household, and then the wife would introduce her relatives to her husband's friends or relatives. Many married sisters of friends or partners or sets of related women, reinforcing kinship and economic ties.[196] Some marriages ended in divorce, but the social networks that survived were based on the Asian Indian men's partnerships and the Mexican women's female kin.[197]

India-U.S. relations were not solidified until World War II. After World War I they were greatly strained when few American organizations supported Indian independence. The United States did not want to "displease the British government."[198] The prevalent British contention—that India was unfit for self-governance—seemed to be accepted in the United States. But as Gandhi's reputation spread, his movement attracted more and more supporters. By the time India attained independence in 1946, the United States had an important military ally.[199]

Although the increased international power of India (and its desirability as an ally) culminated in the 1946 repeal of immigration and naturalization restrictions, the quota established was the minimum of one hundred. In 1947, for example, only 375 were admitted; 109 of them (9 carryovers from 1946) were quota immigrants, and 236 were the wives of citizens.[200] The 1946 restrictions were perpetuated by the 1952 Act. Even after the United States removed its racial bar, large-scale immigration of poorer classes of Asian Indians was confined to Britain.[201]

Slowly but surely, however, immigration to the United States increased, as pressures within India escalated as well. In the 1950's about

2,000 entered, and 3,300 in the first half of the 1960's[202] (see Table 8). In 1930 there were 3,130 foreign-born Asian Indians counted in the United States, but by 1960 the figure increased to 12,296.[203] In the early 1950's pressure was mounting to adopt a more socialist path of development, which gave many the incentive to emigrate. Between 1947 and 1965 the number of Western-trained intellectuals exceeded India's capacity to place them, and political and economic instability heightened impulses to immigrate among those with money.[204] By 1965 approximately 50,000 Asian Indians resided in the United States.

## Geographic Distribution and Residential Patterns

Like Chinese, Koreans, and to a lesser extent Japanese and Filipinos, early Asian Indians settled primarily on the West Coast. Those who entered before 1917 as part of the first phase settled predominantly in the agricultural areas of California. They were primarily Sikhs from the Punjab region of north India.[205] Roughly 60 percent in 1930 and 1940 lived in California. A few who had been recruited to work in the lumber industry remained in Washington in spite of several outbreaks of violence directed at them. In 1907 a band of white workers raided a lumber camp in northern Washington and chased several hundred Indian workers across the Canadian border.[206] Still others, primarily Hindus, were attracted to New York, which was still the symbol of America for Asian Indians.[207]

To a degree they followed the same path as other early Asian immigrants who had been forced into ghettos. In the early 1900's, it was not uncommon for Indians in Western states to be the victims of restrictive racial covenants aimed at them as well as at African Americans and other Asians.[208] In 1913, the same year that California enacted its Alien Land Law, real estate brokers in Port Angeles, Washington, would not sell to "Hindoos and Negroes."[209] Because there were so few of them and because most worked in rural areas, Indian Americans did not form ethnic enclaves on the scale that they did in Britain and that other Asian immigrants in the United States did.[210]

## Careers and Socioeconomic Status

Before 1917 they were primarily agricultural workers, though some were initially recruited by Canadian railway agents. But after the Canadian government, yielding to anti-Asian sentiment, instituted an exclusion policy of its own, they were forced to move south. Some worked in the lumber mills of Washington, but racial violence there and the cold climate prompted many to move to California.[211] Most of these were agricultural workers from the Punjab who spoke little English and lacked other employment skills.[212]

Many of those who survived the hostilities demonstrated enterprising skills and goals reminiscent of Japanese immigrants. By 1920 Asian Indians leased and operated approximately 85,000 acres of farmland.[213] In spite of alien land laws many men and their Mexican wives entered into agricultural leasing and ownership arrangements in Imperial County in southern California until the 1930's.[214] But unlike the Japanese, Chinese, and Filipinos, few relied on domestic jobs to earn a living.[215]

The small Asian Indian population of the United States in 1940 continued to work predominantly in agriculture; only 3 percent were professionals. More than a third of the adults had attended less than one year of school, and the median amount of schooling was 3.4 years.[216] It was during the second phase of Indian immigration, between 1946 and 1965, that the profile of the Indian American community began to evolve into what it is today.

After independence, political and social instability in India created pressures to emigrate, and a professional class began to emerge in the United States. Indian and Western universities were graduating many intellectuals who were not able to obtain jobs in the Indian economy commensurate with their education.[217] They were attracted by employment opportunities in the United States, and their facility with English aided their transition into American society. During this period a high percentage of Indian immigrants were professionals and their families. In 1959, for example, 173 of 506 (34.2 percent) of the family heads were professionals and managers,[218] and in 1963, 613 of 1,173 (52.3 percent) listed such occupations.[219]

## Policy Enforcement and the Resulting Undocumented Population

Beyond their demographic and economic effects, restrictionist policies spawned another—but more difficult to measure—response. Asians did not always dutifully accede to the systematic efforts to control their presence in the United States. As a result, some were undocumented.

Resistance to restrictions was common among immigrants from Japan and India. Many Japanese evaded Japanese regulations on emigration, which were precursors to the Gentlemen's Agreement, by traveling to Hawaii and then on to the mainland.[220] As early as 1900, in what might be regarded as a major ring, labor brokers in Japan claimed that they procured the entry of as many as four thousand laborers by falsifying passports and other public documents.[221] While the Asian Indian population was declining between 1920 and 1940, an estimated three thousand Sikhs and Hindus crossed the Mexican border to work as farm laborers. At the same time many Muslims from Punjab and Bengal working as crewmen jumped ship on the eastern seaboard. Most were apprehended and deported.[222]

But because of their relatively larger numbers, longer stays in the United States, and the hardship of family separation and anti-miscegenation laws, Chinese were given to undocumented migration more than any other group. Their gambits were many. A legion entered after the enactment of the exclusion laws under false citizenship claims. A Chinese laborer might assert, for example, that he had been born in San Francisco and that his birth certificate had been destroyed in the 1906 earthquake. Then he would claim, after various trips to China, that his wife there had given birth to children (usually sons) who automatically derived citizenship. In fact, the children were often fictitious, and the few immigration slots were given or sold to others in China. They came to be known as "paper sons."[223] Some who had valid claims of entry would simply sell their identity to another.[224] Since merchants, students, and teachers were exempted from the first exclusion laws, laborers entered with falsified evidence of membership in one of those classes.[225] Thousands of others, including wives, sneaked across the Canadian or Mexican border.[226] In fact, the Border Patrol that today conjures up images of deportation of Mexicans was established in response to illegal entries of Chinese.[227] Any estimate of how many Chinese entered through any of these means would be speculative, but undocumented family members (living or deceased) are mentioned so often in casual conversation with Chinese Americans that the practice was undoubtedly widespread at one time.[228]

Immigration inspectors grew to distrust Chinese Americans.[229] Consequently, besides the Border Patrol, the government used other

enforcement tools against alleged offenders, such as the notorious holding camp on Angel Island in San Francisco Bay. Between 1910 and 1940,
about 50,000 Chinese were confined—often for months and years at a
time—in Angel Island's bleak wooden barracks, where inspectors would
conduct grueling interrogations.[230] The extensive carvings on the barracks' walls bear eloquent testimony both to the immigrants' determination and to the pain they endured.[231] Across the country, raids on private homes, restaurants, and other businesses were also favored by the
authorities.[232] Initiated at the turn of the century, raids were resurrected
in the 1950's to capture and deport supporters of the new Communist
regime in mainland China.[233]

Because many Chinese did have something to hide and because of
the intense level of deportation enforcement directed at them, many
Chinese Americans lived in constant fear of immigration authorities.[234]
Even those with nothing to hide were forced to constantly look over
their shoulder. A "confession program" offered by immigration authorities in the late 1950's for those Chinese desirous of clearing up their
immigration histories (since names and family trees had been confused
by earlier false claims) made matters worse. The program was purportedly a trade-off for the raids during the Red Scare and was promoted in
some quarters as an amnesty program. In fact, it offered only a weak
assurance that if a confessed Chinese was eligible for an existing statutory remedy, the paperwork would be processed. Some might now be
married to a citizen through whom immigration was possible, others
who had entered illegally prior to June 28, 1940, could be eligible for a
relief termed registry, and still others could apply for suspension of
deportation if extreme hardship and good moral character could be
demonstrated.[235] But many who admitted past fraud were not eligible
and were deported.[236] Because they feared immigration authorities, relatively few Chinese went through the confession program. In San
Francisco, the principal residence for most Chinese Americans at the
time, only about ten thousand Chinese came forward.[237]

## Conclusion

The Asian American communities that emerged by 1965 were dramatic
manifestations of the effects of the immigration laws and the social and
political forces driving them. Those forces complemented or competed

with one another to directly affect Asians and their communities once they were allowed to immigrate. The political and economic conditions in the sending country, relations with the United States, desire for cheap dependable labor, fear of competition by immigrants for jobs, and racial prejudice are among them. Racial prejudice remained constant, while international relations varied through time.

Largely because of the growth of its families, the Japanese American community was the largest in 1965. It grew steadily after the turn of the century, as the Chinese and Filipino communities declined. After postwar changes facilitated more family formation, they were able to grow again. Asian Indian and Filipino American communities, however, were quite small throughout the first half of the century and until 1965.

Asian immigration during the late 1800's and early 1900's was characterized by ambivalence and uncertainty. Many employers were eager to hire Asians, while white laborers wanted them deported. Asians were repelled by their mistreatment at the hands of nativists and attracted to the economic opportunities available in the United States. Each Asian group had to form communities within a hostile environment.

One of the most notable early trends was recruitment followed by repudiation. Chinese workers were initially attracted to gold mining and recruited to build the transcontinental railroad. When placer mining gave out and the railroad was completed, cities offered refuge. Others were employed in agriculture, which grew substantially with the advent of transnational transportation. Chinese were the first to be blamed for taking American jobs. They were subjected to legal controls and racial persecution, forced from rural to urban areas, and replaced in the fields by Japanese and, for a while, by Koreans. Although the early Japanese were not rejected as were Chinese or Filipinos because they were legally and economically able to settle down with their families intact, they also suffered from racial violence and isolation and were replaced in the fields by Filipinos. Filipinos became the target of racial violence in the late 1920's and early 1930's, and nativists pushed to revoke their national status in 1934. Asian Indians were similarly recruited and repudiated.

Most early Asian immigrants were men who arrived without their families often because of societal or cultural emigration conventions. The early Japanese, Filipino, Korean, and Asian Indian immigrants were mainly agricultural laborers; the first Chinese worked in the mines and on the railroad—work for which women were considered unsuitable. Sugar plantation jobs were available to those men and women who went to Hawaii first, although mostly men were recruited. Some of these were single, and some were sojourners. Many planned to send for their families when they had earned enough money. We shall never know how many intended to take root with families because the Chinese exclusion laws, the Asiatic barred zone of 1917, and the 1924 exclusion of those ineligible for citizenship prevented families from joining their husbands and fathers. Families would have undermined the design for a rootless class of cheap and dependable laborers. Japanese were the exception because under the Gentlemen's Agreement their families could immigrate intact. As a result, their population grew steadily prior to 1965, in spite of various restrictions.

Congress directed laws against the Chinese in 1870, 1875, and 1882; the Japanese in 1907 and 1924; the Filipinos in 1934; and the Asian Indians and other Asians in 1917. Chinese were subject to the first and the most legal restrictions, often affecting civil liberties and employment rights. Japanese, initially protected from the harshest immigration laws, were the first targets of California's alien land laws, and were interned during World War II. Filipinos, seemingly immune from immigration restrictions because of their status as nationals (except for Filipinos, most Asian immigration came to a halt in 1924), faced dramatic curtailment of their status and immigration rights after Philippine independence. Korean immigration was regulated by agreements restricting Japanese entries and by Japanese imperialism. Asian Indians simply fell prey to general restraints on Asian immigration and anti-Asian sentiment. All were subjected to anti-miscegenation laws in a number of states.

After being driven from rural and agricultural areas by job scarcity, landownership restrictions, and extralegal racial animus, each community responded, at least initially and in varying degrees, by forming close-knit enclaves in West Coast cities. Chinatowns provided jobs and social networks and served as refuges from racial hostility for the mostly male community. Manilatowns provided way stations, comradery, and services to new immigrants. Japanese Americans did not use enclaves as much as Chinese or Filipinos, because although some moved to urban areas after loopholes were eliminated in the alien land laws, their family formation was much further along. Koreans and Asian Indians formed enclaves, but their small populations could only support small, dispersed centers.

Most Asian immigrants settled primarily in Hawaii and California because they were recruited for agricultural work and other manual labor there. Some Chinese—students, merchants, and diplomats—were attracted to New York, Boston, and Chicago. The few but more wealthy and educated Asian Indians also were attracted to the Northeast.

After World War II resentment eased, at least officially. Limits began to be lifted, and in 1952 racial if not regional restrictions were eliminated. Gradually, local anti-immigrant laws were repealed or fell into disuse. The steady influx of new family members created fresh social and economic opportunities. During the postwar period the percentage from professional and managerial backgrounds steadily increased. The Japanese American community became the largest; most of its members were American-born. Chinese Americans more than tripled between 1940 and 1965 through immigration and new births. More Filipino Americans were born, but increases in the Asian Indian and Korean American populations resulted primarily from the immigration of family members, such as the wives of servicemen, many of whom were professionals. More women than men were immigrating in each community. These important postwar developments went largely unnoticed by policymakers. Had more attention been paid, perhaps the responses to the 1965 reforms covered in Chapter 3 would not have been so surprising.

Thus, if demographics tell a reliable story, immigration policies and laws powerfully influenced size, gender ratios, residential patterns, and occupational profiles in each community. Before World War II the nation's efforts to control Asian immigrants—to admit them only for specific purposes, to exclude them altogether if necessary, and always to keep them in check—proved reasonably effective. But the demands of war formally and informally loosened the reins on them, making social and economic possibilities long denied suddenly available, if sometimes only through inattention. In many ways Asian Americans had survived the worst, largely through what some might label a decidedly American ingenuity and resilience. In light of the long-standing consensus that they were not biologically suitable for membership in the national community, that was ironic indeed.

## CHAPTER THREE

# Social Forces Unleashed After 1965

In 1965, driven by its desire to be seen as the egalitarian champion of the "free world" and by a Kennedy-inspired sense of a single world, the United States changed the basic scheme of immigration law. Congress abolished the 1920's system that favored immigrants of Western European origins and established an open system premised on family reunification and designed to ensure that no country would have special preferences or quotas.

In considering and ultimately passing these reforms, policymakers did not pay careful attention to those Asian American and Asian social forces that Congress and state governments had previously endeavored to hold in check—Asian American family needs, economic ambitions, and residential patterns. Most policymakers did not understand how the political, economic, and social dynamics in Asian countries would influence immigration. They knew little about Asian American communities, Asian countries, and their relationship, and their analyses by and large were cursory and highly inaccurate. Asian immigration after 1965 took the United States by surprise.

The 1965 laws unleashed many of those social forces that national and local governments had effectively—and often cruelly—controlled but had never taken the time to understand. Families moved to "make themselves whole," and women joined their spouses. Workers, particularly in the secondary but also in the primary labor markets, immigrated to take advantage of new opportunities. Asian Americans multiplied, most often in regions and neighborhoods with the cultural and economic capacity to absorb newcomers.

All this activity might not have surprised anyone who had paid close attention before 1965 to the history and patterns of Asian American life. Certain possibilities created in 1965 had already been available in less generous and systematic terms, particularly after World War II. And Asian American and Asian dynamics already had begun to respond to the new possibilities. Patterns that were recognized for the first time in the late 1970's and early 1980's often found their origins in the years immediately preceding 1965.

Asian American gender ratios, labor markets, resettlement patterns, occupations, and income all responded rapidly and extensively to the newly possible. Communities that were already undergoing important changes as a result of post–World War II reforms were remade even more dramatically after the 1965 amendments. The character of each community reflected both the conditions in its home country and the constricted possibilities of resettlement before 1965. As a result, each community's political, social, and economic power varied considerably.

A quick reference to the immigration categories under the 1965 reforms and how various Asian groups were able to use them is available in Appendix B.

## Chinese Americans

The repeal of the Chinese exclusion laws in the 1940's had an immediate if limited impact on this community's profile. The entry of Chinese women and the forming of families, the reduction of the imbalanced gender ratio, the genesis of a professional class, and the shift in residential patterns all resulted in part from the liberation of social forces that policymakers had tried for decades to control. The overall size of the community, though, remained small, and demographic changes remained largely unappreciated in the debate over President Kennedy's global scheme of migration.

## Population and Gender Ratio

### Population

From 1965 to 1990 the Chinese American population increased from about 360,000 to 1,645,000.[1] Chinese Americans surpassed Japanese Americans, who had been the most populous group from 1910 to 1970.[2] The huge increase can be attributed to the 1965 amendments.

After the Chinese Repealer in 1943 and the establishment of the Asia-Pacific triangle in 1952, the Chinese increased annually by fewer than 2,000 until 1965. But after 1965 Chinese admissions grew dramatically, and today more than 40,000 immigrate each year from China, Taiwan, and Hong Kong.[3] Between 1965 and 1990 approximately 711,000 Chinese immigrants entered the United States.[4]

In 1965 Congress did not foresee this increase, although the conditions for it were in place. Immigrants came through Chinese American family networks whose gradual development might have been apparent. The entry of more than 14,000 refugees prior to 1978 under the category created for persons fleeing Communist countries was no less predictable.[5] Political instability in Taiwan and the development of a substantial professional class in Hong Kong were both apparent before 1965.

These developments, both in the United States and in Asia, enabled the Chinese American community to take advantage of the more open immigration scheme. Chinese American family networks formed by 1965 began using the new family-oriented system. Almost 61 percent in 1969 entered in the family categories, and 21 percent entered in the categories for professionals (see Table 9). Professionals could use the family categories to petition for spouses, children, parents, and siblings. By 1985, 81 percent of Chinese immigrants were entering in the family categories and only about 16 percent as professionals.[6]

Most strikingly, by 1980 the Chinese American population was once again mostly foreign-born (63.3 percent),[7] ending the predominance of the American-born that had lasted from 1940 to 1970.[8] A large proportion of foreign-born Chinese may be present for some time because as the population increased 104 percent between 1980 and 1990 (from 812,178 to 1,650,000), almost 446,000 Chinese immigrated.[9]

These numbers reflect basic changes in immigration law and international relations, such as the normalization of the relationship between the United States and the People's Republic of China in 1978, which

TABLE 9

*Comparison of Entrants in Family Reunification Categories with Those in Occupational and Investor Categories, 1969, 1985, and 1989*

| | Relatives | | Occupational | | Investors |
| Place of birth | 1969 | 1985 | 1969 | 1985 | 1969[a] |
| | (%) | | (%) | | (%) |
|---|---|---|---|---|---|
| China[b] | 60.9 | 80.9 | 20.8 | 15.8 | 4.5 |
| India | 27.0 | 85.9 | 45.0 | 12.6 | 26.8 |
| Japan | 74.5 | 59.4 | 17.6 | 33.1 | 6.1 |
| Korea | 64.0 | 89.2 | 23.2 | 7.6 | 11.6 |
| Philippines | 55.0 | 86.9 | 42.3 | 7.6 | 0.08 |
| Vietnam | 82.7 | 15.7 | 8.0 | 0.18 | 6.4 |

| | 1989[c] Relatives (%) | 1989 Occupational (%) |
|---|---|---|
| China, Mainland | 92.6 | 5.2 |
| Taiwan | 30.4 | 32.2 |
| Hong Kong | 90.3 | 1.1 |
| India | 85.1 | 1.4 |
| Japan | 64.1 | 28.9 |
| Korea | 88.9 | 9.5 |
| Philippines | 87.8 | 8.1 |
| Vietnam[d] | 98.8 | 1.1 |

SOURCES: 1969 *INS Annual Report*, tables 6, 6B, 7A, pp. 40–48; 1985 *INS Statistical Yearbook*, tables IMM 2.6, 3.1, pp. 33–37; 1989 *INS Advance Reports*, table 4.
[a] By 1985 no nonpreference visas were available, but some Asians were able to enter as nonimmigrant investors (see Table 5).
[b] Includes mainland China, Taiwan, and Hong Kong.
[c] Not including immigrants through legalization (amnesty).
[d] Not including refugee and Amerasian adjustments.

eased emigration of Chinese from mainland China. Taiwan and China had been counted as a single country for quota purposes, but Taiwan was given a separate quota of 20,000 in 1981.[10] Total immigration from Taiwan and mainland China increased from 25,000 in 1981 to 39,732 in 1985.[11] The increase of the colonial quota for Hong Kong from 600 to 5,000 in the 1986 Immigration Reform and Control Act has begun to add several thousand immigrants each year as well. Under 1990 amendments, the Hong Kong quota has been enlarged to 10,000 and will reach 20,000 in 1995.

*Gender ratio*

The 1965 relaxation of regulations also helped more Chinese women to immigrate. Since the 1943 Chinese Repealer overturned the draconian policy of excluding them, women have outnumbered men among Chinese immigrants.[12]

The greater numbers of Chinese women who have entered since the late 1940's do not fully account for the overall drop in the gender ratio to a 1980 level of 102.4 men for every 100 women.[13] Not until the deaths of earlier Chinese male immigrants, many of whom did not have female counterparts prior to 1965, did the ratio begin to balance out. As recently as 1960, most Chinese Americans over the age of 65 were men,[14] and in 1970 there were 15,244 men and 11,612 women.[15] By 1980, however, more women (28,663) than men (27,598) were over the age of 65.[16] At the current mortality and immigration rates, detailed 1990 census data will probably reveal that for the first time women outnumber men in the Chinese American community.

## Geographic Distribution and Residential Patterns

### Geographic distribution and urbanization

Early immigration policies and laws controlled Chinese settlement patterns by encouraging the recruitment of male Chinese laborers to the West Coast, particularly to rural areas. They were prevented from relocating outside the West in significant numbers, and those who traveled to the East Coast were mostly students and diplomats. The postwar relaxation of legal controls resulted in a larger proportion locating in New York, but before 1965 usually no more than fifteen hundred per year did so.

Chinese immigrants still prefer California because of the Chinese American communities there. Alien land laws and other legal schemes originally designed to limit them to certain areas thus influenced settlement patterns long after their revocation. Like California, the New York area has offered new immigrants a long-established Chinese American community and a multitude of economic opportunities. As a result, since 1965 New York has continued to be Chinese immigrants' second most popular choice after California. By 1990, 42.8 percent of Chinese Americans resided in California,[17] and 17.3 percent in New York.[18] In 1990, 4.2 percent lived in Hawaii.[19] The other most popular states for new Chinese immigrants are Illinois, Texas, Maryland, and Michigan.[20]

Cities in New York and California have many Chinese immigrants who followed the early arrivals into the security of Chinatowns, despite their predominantly rural, agricultural backgrounds. As a result of the 1965 changes in the immigration laws, however, the vast majority have been from Hong Kong, Taipei, Guangzhou, Beijing, and Shanghai and they have overwhelmingly preferred to live in urban centers. Those entering in family reunification categories (see Table 8) often resettle in metropolitan areas where their American relatives live.

In 1980, 96 percent of Chinese Americans were living in urban areas,[21] and today almost 90 percent of all Chinese immigrants intend to reside there.[22] In New York and Illinois almost 90 percent reside in New York City and Chicago.[23] The San Francisco and Oakland areas continue to be the home of the largest Chinese American population.[24] Yet since 1967 New York City has attracted more Chinese immigrants than San Francisco and Oakland.[25] This shift reflects in part the development there of the ethnic labor markets where Chinese is spoken and native skills are valued that historically have drawn them to the Bay Area.[26]

Trends toward urbanization may also be explained by generational differences in Chinese America. Many children of hardworking rural immigrants have had college educations. Better educated than their parents, this second generation's employment and social opportunities lie in urban areas. Eventually, many first-generation parents retire to the city where their children now work and reside. Few members of the second generation, who generally work fewer hours than did their parents but earn more in professional jobs, would seriously consider returning to their childhood rural homes to take the helm of family businesses.

### Ghettoization

Since 1965 immigrants have contributed to the rejuvenation of Chinatowns in San Francisco, New York, Los Angeles, and Chicago.[27] One need only walk along Grant Avenue or Stockton Street in San Francisco at noon, or on Mott, Canal, or East Broadway streets in Manhattan on Saturday evening to feel the vibrant intensity of these resilient enclaves. After World War II these Chinatowns began to shrink and even disappear as the older immigrants died. The first signs of their revival appeared in the early 1960's with the admission of refugees from mainland China. Family reunification categories of 1965 provided a steady flow of individuals and families attracted to the cultural familiarity, employment opportunities, and family ties available there.[28] Many working-class immigrants often have few housing options other than the lower rents in Chinatown.

Chinatowns endure because as the second and third generations leave they are replaced by immigrants and because they are sustained by the larger community.[29] Though most Chinese Americans do not reside in Chinatowns, they live nearby and regularly patronize their merchants.[30] Even those in rural settings retreat to Chinatown when visiting cities. Because of the permanent expansion of the Hong Kong quota even beyond 1997 and because the demands for visas from mainland China and Taiwan are at an all-time high, Chinatowns will continue to function for some time. Despite their overburdened infrastructures, they meet new immigrants' needs for housing, employment, resettlement support, and cultural activities.

## Careers and Socioeconomic Status

### Careers

Within five years of the 1965 reforms, it became evident that the numbers of professionals and technicians from all countries had increased largely because of the new professional and occupational categories.[31] Between 1953 and 1966 an annual average of about 22,000 immigrants worldwide (about 8 percent) indicated a prior professional or technical occupation. By 1969 the number was more than 40,000 (more than 11 percent of all immigrants).[32]

The shift was more dramatic among Chinese immigrants. Prior to 1965 about 12 percent from mainland China and Taiwan identified themselves as professionals or managers.[33] By 1977 the figure had increased to 25.1 percent, even though more were entering in family reunification categories.[34] It doubled because of the new categories and because of rapid modernization in Taiwan and Hong Kong.[35]

Some observers, who note fewer professionals among Chinese immigrants, contend that after the initial influx of professionals in the late 1960's and early 1970's, poorer, working-class Chinese began entering.[36] But this is only part of the story. The proportion who enter in professional and occupational categories decreased between 1969 and 1989 (see Table 9) in part because a 1976 law required all professionals to first secure a job offer from an employer.[37] The absolute number of professionals and executives, however, has increased. In 1969, for example, a total of 3,499 immigrated from mainland China, Taiwan, and Hong Kong.[38] In 1983 the total had jumped to 8,524.[39] Thus, the smaller percentage merely reflects the increase in other categories. The proportion of those who enter in professional and occupational categories from Taiwan is also much higher than for those from mainland China (28 percent to 5 percent in 1989). And though more than twice as many born in mainland China entered in 1989 (32,272 to 13,974), Taiwan had more occupational immigrants (3,842 to 1,599).[40]

Interest in emigration remains high among Chinese professionals. Taiwan's politically volatile environment has contributed to the desire of the educated class to look for residential options elsewhere, and the stability of the United States and its long-standing anti-Communist philosophy appeals to them. Similarly, the impending return of Hong Kong to mainland China's jurisdiction in 1997 has provided a strong impetus for its elite to look to the United States. And the Tiananmen Square massacre in June 1989 significantly accelerated emigration from Hong Kong.[41]

While the 1965 reforms have facilitated the entry of some professionals and executives, the family reunification provisions have also spurred the immigration of a large pool of service workers. After 1965 immigrants entering under family reunification provisions were required to prove that they were not likely to need public assistance.[42] Since this requirement could be fulfilled through a job offer or affidavit of support from a relative, it has not been difficult for service workers to gain admittance in the family reunification categories. Consequently, a large majority of Chinese immigrants have indicated that they are housewives or service workers or that they have had no occupation.[43]

The lack of English skills among new arrivals plays a part in the high proportions of service workers in Chinese American communities. In fact, because of racial discrimination and their own lack of skills, many immigrants are able to find work only in Chinatowns, but the jobs are low-paying, unstable, and seldom provide promotional opportunities.[44]

Opening categories for professionals and investors after 1965 greatly increased the percentage of professionals among Chinese Americans, as did the educational achievements of some American-born Chinese.[45] A higher percentage of Chinese immigrants (31 percent) than of white Americans (24 percent) are professionals or executives. At the same time, however, the percentage of foreign-born Chinese Americans who work in service occupations (22 percent) is twice that of white workers and is the highest for any group of foreign-born Asian Americans.[46] The simultaneous growth of the professional and the service-worker classes has created a divided community that bears little resemblance to the one before 1965.[47] By the early 1980's, 32.5 percent of all Chinese in the United States were professionals, managers, or executives, while 18.5 percent were in service work.[48]

Still, the proportion of Chinese classified as professionals and managers is misleading because it includes the scientific and technical fields into which they are often channeled.[49] Management statistics are also misleading because they include small-business owners. Chinese Americans have a slightly higher than average rate of small-business ownership (65.1 per thousand compared to 64 for the general population), especially in metropolitan areas where general economic expansion has occurred.[50] For example in 1987, Chinese-owned businesses in Los Angeles and San Francisco exceeded all other Asian American groups.[51] Management statistics also obscure the often unpublicized discrimination against Chinese Americans in promotions to management level or partnership positions in the professions.[52]

*Income and poverty*

The popular media have underscored the fact that the median family income for Chinese Americans is higher than that of the general population.[53] But this reporting has been misleading. Certainly, the postwar easing of controls has been reflected in Chinese American income, especially since 1965. However, they have more workers per family (1.9) than the general population (1.6).[54] And recent immigrants, who make up a large part of the community, earn less than American-born Chinese or those immigrants who came before them.[55]

The attention paid to successful Chinese Americans has often conveyed the false impression of a uniformly upper-income community.[56] The media and even some scholars tend to ignore the fact that more Chinese American families (10.5 percent) fall below the poverty level than white American families (7 percent).[57] Of those immigrants who entered between 1975 and 1980, 22.8 percent were below the poverty line in 1980.[58] Only 2.8 percent of those who immigrated before 1970 fell below it.[59]

Compounding the new immigrants' problems is their ineligibility for most government benefits. Under current rules for Supplemental Security Income, the income of the citizen or lawful permanent resident petitioning for an alien is included in the immigrant's income for three years in determining financial need.[60] This formula is followed even if the sponsor fails to provide financial support.*

## Filipino Americans

### Population and Gender Ratio

*Population*

The expansion of the Filipino American community, which was impeded by the 1934 Philippine Independence Act's yearly quota of 50, slowly increased after World War II. The 1965 reforms allowed the community to flourish. By 1990 the modest 1965 community of about 200,000 had grown to over 1,400,000.[61] Almost 982,000 Filipinos immigrated during that 25-year period, and today over two-thirds of the community is foreign-born, compared to about 40 percent in 1965.[62] Because of almost 60,000 immigrants each year, Filipino Americans are now the nation's second largest Asian community after the Chinese. Immigration from the Philippines, which is greater than that from China, Taiwan, and Hong Kong combined, is second only to Mexico.[63]

As with the Chinese, Koreans, and Indians, the surge in Filipino immigration after 1965 was not anticipated, even though strong evidence of what might happen was provided by patterns of entry before 1965 and by events in the Philippines. For example, the increase in the number of their professionals who entered after 1952 should have provided notice that Filipino immigrants would take advantage of the 1965 law's professional categories.

Filipinos entered in the family categories, but since their population was relatively small in the early 1960's, just after the 1965 amendments it was generally professionals who took advantage of the new occupational preference categories (e.g., accountants, doctors, nurses). As more arrived and became naturalized, they began to use the immigration categories for close relatives. Family reunification categories offered many more visas (80 percent of all preference and 100 percent of immediate-

---

* The 1965 reforms affected the Japanese American community so little that the account of that community has been moved to the end of the chapter to serve as a contrast to those communities that were deeply affected.

relative, nonquota, visas were designated for family reunification until the 1990 amendments) and less stringent visa requirements. A relationship as spouse, parent, child, or sibling is all that was necessary. In the occupational categories, on the other hand, a certification from the Department of Labor was needed to show that no qualified American worker could fill the position an immigrant was offered.[64]

The family-oriented culture of Filipinos helps to explain the surge in family reunification that could not have happened earlier because of the 1934 Independence Act. In 1969 and 1970 about 45 percent entered in the professional and 55 percent in the family unity categories (see Tables 9 and 10). Within a few years, however, family networks developed that enabled naturalized citizens to take advantage of reunification categories. By 1976 Filipino immigration in the occupational categories dropped to about 21 percent.[65] By 1989, just over 8 percent came from the occupational categories compared to 88 percent in the family categories[66] (see Table 9).

Political instability and economic problems in the Philippines convinced many people in the educated and the working classes that they would have better economic opportunities in the United States. After independence in 1946 the Philippine Islands experienced a succession of one-term presidents until 1965. Elections, which were called a "showcase of democracy in Asia," were commonly accompanied by violence and corruption.[67] The pattern of single-term presidencies ended when Ferdinand Marcos was elected in 1965 and re-elected in 1969, but violence and corruption did not cease.[68]

After someone tried to assassinate the secretary of national defense in 1972, Marcos declared martial law and began an era of repression.[69] The military immediately arrested dozens of oppositionists, including senators, congressmen, provincial governors, and prominent reporters, and detained several thousand others.[70] Many newspapers and radio and television stations were shut down, schools were temporarily closed, public rallies and demonstrations were forbidden, and a curfew was established and enforced.[71] Increasingly, the military emerged as a principal source of power.[72] Threats of Muslim and Communist insurgencies contributed to the political and social instability.[73]

The overall economy, which became heavily dependent on foreign capital, suffered during the Marcos era, even though segments of the private sector flourished.[74] Real wages fell 5 percent a year, reflecting the abundance of labor, while inflation rose 20 percent a year.[75] Industrial

## TABLE 10
### Proportions of Entries in Immediate Relative and Preference Categories, 1970, 1979, and 1988

| Country and Year | Total | Immediate Relatives | Preference (%) | | | | | | | Nonpreference (Including Investors) |
|---|---|---|---|---|---|---|---|---|---|---|
| | | | 1st | 2nd | 3rd | 4th | 5th | 6th | 7th | |
| M. China/Taiwan | | | | | | | | | | |
| 1970 | 14,093 | 17.1 | 0.86 | 18.3 | 13.4 | 6.0 | 22.3 | 11.7 | 1.3 | 2.6 |
| 1979 | 28,600 | 28.5 | 2.5 | 46.0 | 7.6 | 14.9 | 36.3 | 10.4 | 5.9 | 0.03 |
| 1988 | 28,717 | 26.9 | 0.5 | 29.2 | 10.3 | 11.7 | 44.4 | 2.7 | | |
| India | | | | | | | | | | |
| 1970 | 10,114 | 4.5 | 0.06 | 13.4 | 19.7 | 0.2 | 4.0 | 7.9 | | 54.7 |
| 1979 | 22,400 | 12.4 | 0.1 | 38.6 | 12.0 | 0.45 | 60.7 | 9.2 | | 0.45 |
| 1988 | 26,268 | 29.2 | 0.16 | 31.0 | 12.0 | 3.2 | 50.4 | 3.1 | | |
| Korea | | | | | | | | | | |
| 1970 | 9,314 | 44.3 | 0.3 | 16.1 | 9.3 | 0.65 | 26.2 | 13.5 | | 33.9 |
| 1979 | 31,800 | 37.8 | 0.17 | 35.6 | 4.2 | 1.3 | 62.8 | 5.0 | | 0.76 |
| 1988 | 34,703 | 40.4 | 0.3 | 34.5 | 5.1 | 3.7 | 46.4 | 9.9 | | |
| Philippines | | | | | | | | | | |
| 1970 | 31,203 | 23.9 | 1.3 | 24.6 | 47.8 | 7.1 | 19.2 | 0.05 | | 0.07 |
| 1979 | 47,000 | 53.0 | 4.9 | 49.2 | 12.8 | 13.5 | 32.4 | 4.6 | | 0.44 |
| 1988 | 50,697 | 56.7 | 19.7 | 24.8 | 9.6 | 10.9 | 24.1 | 10.6 | | |

SOURCES: 1970 INS Annual Report, 1979 and 1980 INS Statistical Yearbooks.
NOTE: Appendix B describes the immediate relative and preference categories.

development stressed capital and not labor, so there were relatively few opportunities for employment available to the rapidly growing labor force. Unemployment and underemployment created great inefficiency within the economy. Official reports of unemployment fluctuated between 5 and 10 percent between 1950 and 1970. Underemployment, which accounts for the number of workers employed in marginal jobs, might have affected over a quarter of the population.[76]

What impact the ouster of Ferdinand Marcos and the shift to democracy has had on emigration remains unresolved. Filipino immigration remains high, as backlogs in preference categories continue to grow. If political and economic instability persist, the demand for visas is likely to continue.[77]

*Gender ratio*

The post–World War II trend of more women than men entering from the Philippines continued after 1965 as the Filipino wives of citizens or lawful permanent residents came over. Family reunification was augmented by the entry of large numbers of female nurses throughout the 1970's under the 1965 law's occupational categories. Hospitals had a shortage of nurses, and many Filipino women had the language and medical skills necessary to meet the demand.[78]

Although there were about 125 men to 100 women in 1965,[79] the huge increase in women immigrants after 1965 significantly affected gender distribution. In 1969, 56.6 percent of the 20,744 Filipino immigrants admitted were women; in 1977, 59.6 percent of 39,111 were women.[80] By 1980 there were 93.2 men for every 100 women, and this trend seems to be continuing.[81] Most new immigrants in the immediate relative category in 1985 were wives of citizens[82] (including a small number of mail-order brides[83]), and 58.2 percent of the 66,000 Filipino immigrants in 1989 were women.[84]

Women will continue to predominate in the Filipino American community, even though the Philippines has slightly more men than women.[85] Marriages between many U.S. servicemen stationed at two large bases in the Philippines and Filipino women contributed to the influx,[86] although the closure of bases in 1992 will reduce the flow. The fact that more and better job opportunities are available to Filipino women in the United States also appears to figure significantly in their decision to immigrate.[87] Filipino women want to pursue economic opportunities out of a generally liberated consciousness. They appear willing to leave traditional extended families and eager to escape what they perceive to be an inegalitarian culture.[88]

## Geographic Distribution and Residential Patterns

### Geographic distribution and urbanization

California is home to most Filipino Americans. In 1990, 52 percent lived in California and 12 percent in Hawaii.[89] The population is spreading to Illinois (4.6 percent), New York (4.4 percent), Washington (3.1 percent), New Jersey (3.8 percent), and other parts of the country.[90] Remarkably, Filipinos are the largest Asian American community in California, Washington, and Illinois (tied with Asian Indians).[91] Only a larger proportion of Japanese Americans (75.9 percent) live in the West than Filipinos (70.5 percent). By contrast only a little more than half of Chinese Americans (52.4 percent) live in the West.[92]

Doubtless the existence of well-established Filipino American communities there helps explain the attraction California and Hawaii hold for new immigrants. But California and Hawaii also offer economically dynamic large cities and suburbs, which are especially alluring since most Filipino immigrants come from Manila and other urban centers.[93]

Over 90 percent reside in metropolitan areas,[94] and only about 20 percent of all new immigrants are headed for other areas.[95] They have not completely limited themselves to Western states, but have spread out to major Midwestern and Eastern cities as well.[96] In 1989, for example, 11,820 Filipino immigrants went to the Los Angeles–Long Beach–Anaheim area, 8,198 to San Francisco–Oakland–San Jose, 3,455 to San Diego, and 2,724 to Honolulu. Yet at the same time, 3,299 went to the New York–Newark metropolitan area and a like number to Chicago.[97]

### Ghettoization

Prior to World War II, Manilatowns served as temporary stopover points for migrant farm workers. But as the restrictions on status and immigration by the 1934 Philippine Independence Act took effect, they began to become more permanent. They became for Filipinos what Chinatowns had long been for Chinese Americans. The 1965 policies and the great upsurge in Filipino immigration have infused new life into some of these poorer, working-class urban communities. But they are not as visible as Chinatowns or Japantowns, and in San Francisco, Los Angeles, Stockton, Fresno, and Salinas, California, only a couple of city blocks survive.[98]

A different type of residential clustering has emerged as many middle-income Filipino immigrants have been drawn to suburban neighborhoods. In the San Francisco suburb of Daly City (the city with the largest concentration of Filipinos in North America), for instance, Filipino Americans are 30 percent of the population of 90,000 and are the majority in many neighborhoods.[99] These middle-class enclaves now make their presence felt in housing patterns, in increasing numbers of Philippine restaurants and food markets, and in the growing Filipino use of public parks, recreational facilities, and shopping malls.[100]

## Careers and Income

### Careers

The 1965 amendments contributed to a distinct shift toward large numbers of immigrants who were professionals. With the exception of Asian Indians, Filipinos have made the most of the new opportunities. Fully 42.3 percent entered in professional categories in 1969, almost double the proportion of any other Asian group except Asian Indians (see Table 9). As a result, the relatively large number of farm laborers that first distinguished Filipino American communities recently has fallen more precipitously, in contrast with the gradual decline between 1946 and 1965.[101]

After the early 1970's, family reunification began to dominate Filipino immigration, but the absolute number of professionals entering remained high. In 1969, 36.3 percent had been employed at professional or managerial levels.[102] In 1978, however, the figure declined to 22.8 percent.[103] By 1985, even though only 7.6 percent entered in the occupational categories, a significant proportion (16.2 percent) designated their occupations as professionals, executives, or managers[104] (see Table 9). While not as many immigrants in the 1980's were entering in categories reserved for professionals as in the late 1960's, thousands were in the professional ranks each year.[105]

The employment profile of the Filipino American community is therefore quite diverse. Not surprisingly, the 1980 census reported that the proportion employed in the professions or as managers and executives (24.8 percent) was about the same as that of white Americans.[106] This high percentage reflects in part large numbers of nurses.[107] And in some areas such as San Francisco, Filipino-owned businesses have steadily increased.[108] The proportion of blue-collar workers in 1980 was about the same as it was in the general population, but the percentage of service workers (16.5 percent) was higher than in the white population (11.6 percent).[109] Though not insubstantial, the gap between upper-income professionals and lower-income service workers is not as great as that in the Chinese American community.

The impact of the foreign-born on these demographics merits emphasis. A sizable 27 percent of foreign-born Filipino Americans in contrast to only 15 percent of those born in America were employed in 1980 as managers, professionals, and executives.[110] At the same time, 20 percent of immigrants between 1975 and 1980 held service-oriented jobs, helping to account for the high proportion of Filipinos in that sector.[111] Indeed, an increase in the proportion of service workers seems likely given the steady immigration of large percentages of Filipinos who indicate either employment as service workers or no occupation. The income disparity between foreign-born Filipino professionals and service workers is greater than between those born in America, auguring perhaps for a social and economic bifurcation like that of the Chinese American community.

*Income*

The median family income for Filipino Americans, particularly those who are foreign-born, is higher than that of the general population, but there are more workers per family among Filipinos. In fact, the median income for individual white American workers in 1980 was almost 14 percent higher than for Filipino Americans. Because so many professionals arrived after 1965, Filipino immigrants earn more than American-born Filipinos, particularly women, whose unemployment rate is the lowest among all Asian immigrant women.[112] A relatively large portion of Filipino women are in the professions, especially nursing, and fewer Filipino American families (6.2 percent) fall below the poverty level than white American families (7 percent), implying that the vast majority of Filipino immigrants are not poor.[113] Like the Chinese, however, a Filipino's income is lower if he is a recent immigrant.[114]

# Korean Americans

## Population and Gender Ratio

### Population

The expansion of the Korean American community has been remark-able. Families had begun reuniting and growing before 1965; still growth came slowly, and in 1965 the population totaled only about 45,000. By 1990, however, it was almost 800,000—nearly a staggering eighteenfold increase in 25 years.[115] The 1965 reforms and deteriorating economic and social conditions in Korea set the stage for emigration.

After 1965, there was virtually no emigration from the closed Communist dictatorship in North Korea. In the 1960's and 1970's, South Koreans' right to dissent or to criticize the government was sharply restricted, and the government maintained complete control over the media. The Korean Central Intelligence Agency became infamous for its unlimited authority to investigate or detain political dissidents.[116] The Korean War had crippled the economy, and a dubious reconstruction plan made the country depend on foreign exports, raw materials, and capital investment. The economy was left vulnerable to recessions in the Japanese and American markets, even though it has performed well compared with other industrialized nations.[117]

Between 1969 and 1971 Korean immigration more than doubled from 6,045 to 14,297,[118] and in 1987 it topped 35,000.[119] More than 620,000 entered between 1966 and 1990.[120] In fact, Koreans have since 1973 been the third largest Asian immigrant group behind Filipinos and Chinese.[121] By 1980 an incredible 81.9 percent of the community was foreign-born,[122] second only to that of the newly developing refugee Vietnamese American community. Since 35,000 Koreans immigrate each year, the proportion of foreign-born will remain high for some time.

After the 1965 reforms a noteworthy share of Koreans (though not as many as Filipinos and Indians) came as occupational migrants, but eventually the use of family categories dominated (see Tables 9 and 10). In 1969, for example, 23.2 percent of Koreans entered in the occupational categories, and an additional 11.6 percent took advantage of the newly created investor category. Immigrants who entered through these occu-pational categories were able, in time, to petition for their relatives under the family categories, so more began to come as family members. In 1969, for example, 64 percent of Korean immigration came through family categories, and that figure rose to 91 percent by 1988, when those entering through occupational categories declined to less than 9 percent.

### Gender Ratio

An unusually unbalanced gender ratio in the Korean American community—72.3 men to 100 women in 1980[123]—is accounted for by the predominance of women among Korean immigrants between the 1952 Act and the 1965 reforms and after the new 1965 immigration categories. The perpetuation of this ratio appears likely. In 1989, for example, 18,942 Korean women immigrated compared to 15,275 men.[124] This contrast is striking since men slightly outnumber women in Korea.[125]

There are several reasonable explanations why women dominated Korean immigration, beyond the fact that men were petitioning for families.[126] Over the last 25 years Korean female nurses were trained for work in U.S. hospitals by specially established companies in Korea.[127] Between 1965 and 1977, for example, over seven thousand of these nurses entered the United States.[128] Many other Korean women who immigrate prefer the employment opportunities in the United States to those in South Korea. Korean women perceive relatively progressive views on gender equality in the United States.[129] Marriages between U.S. servicemen stationed in South Korea and Korean women also contributed.[130]

## Geographic Distribution and Residential Patterns

Since the Korean American population was very small compared to Chinese, Japanese, and Filipinos in 1965, its current geographic distribution may represent how Asian Americans might have distributed themselves in the absence of stringent controls. In any event Korean American settlement choices seem to be relatively free of the lure of pre-existing ethnic enclaves, and that would seem to explain how they were dispersed.

Although early Korean laborers went to Hawaii, the Japanese ban on Korean emigration in 1905 precluded them from establishing communities there before 1965. They were prohibited from responding to the plantation recruitments that drew so many Japanese and Filipinos to the islands. Lacking well-established Korean American communities,

Hawaii still has not attracted many Koreans. In 1990, for example, only 3.1 percent resided in Hawaii—a small share when compared to the large proportion of Japanese (29.2 percent) and Filipinos (12 percent).[131]

Thus the 1965 amendments' easing of controls over Asian immigration dispersed Korean Americans throughout the United States. Unlike Chinese, Filipinos, Japanese, and Vietnamese, less than half (44.4 percent) live in the West. Almost 23 percent live in the Northeast, 19.2 percent in the South, and 13.7 percent in the Midwest.[132] Just under 32.5 percent of the entire population is in California.[133] But Koreans can also be found in New York (12 percent), Illinois (5.2 percent), New Jersey (4.8 percent), Texas (4 percent), Virginia (3.8 percent), and Washington (3.7 percent).[134]

*Urbanization*

By the 1960's South Korea's economic gains had extended primarily to its commercial and industrial sectors. As the country moved to industrialize, the gap between urban and rural living standards widened. From the mid-1960's to late 1970's, South Korea's urban population rose from about 28 percent to 55 percent because of rural migration to the cities.[135]

In 1989, 7,808 Korean immigrants settled in the Los Angeles–Long Beach–Anaheim area, 3,336 went to New York City, 1,854 to Washington, D.C.–Maryland–Virginia, 1,384 to Chicago, and 1,075 to Philadelphia.[136] Thus in New York and Illinois about 85 percent reside in New York City and Chicago,[137] and 92.5 percent in an urban-suburban environment.[138]

A significant 20 percent of Korean immigrants choose to live in southern cities, especially in Virginia and Texas.[139] This unusual attraction for the South appears to be attributable in part to a judgment that these areas present good economic opportunities. Relatives and other immigrant friends might follow for social as well as economic reasons.[140]

*Ghettoization*

Compared to other Asian groups, the emerging Korean American community has made very different choices regarding the resettlement options presented by the 1965 reforms. For example, unlike Filipino Americans, Korean Americans have not clustered in large residential enclaves, though some small pockets have developed. In 1980 more than 37,000 resided in the New York City–Newark–Jersey City area,[141] but the tendency of Korean immigrants has been to scatter throughout the sub-urbs after attaining some economic success in the cities.[142] They have tended to cluster in urban neighborhoods related to business interests. Koreans in New York, Los Angeles, and Chicago have established pock-ets of businesses.[143] Most of these businesses are small, with some cater-ing to Korean ethnic tastes. Others serve African Americans or Latinos who reside in the area. Unfortunately, some Koreans in places such as Los Angeles and New York have been involved in well-publicized conflicts with African American residents and customers.

The economic class of most Korean immigrants accounts for the relative absence of inner-city Korean ghettos. While some working-class immigrants have begun to reside in Koreatowns, such as in Los Angeles, most Korean immigrants are young and educated, and from the urban elite or middle classes of South Korean society.[144] They can afford to live in suburban neighborhoods. Instead of staying in touch by establishing suburban enclaves, they use churches for regular meeting places and often establish a center for social and cultural gatherings.[145] This rela-tively educated class does not have the same desire or need to live together as have working-class professional Filipinos.

### Careers

The professional and nonpreference investor categories established by the 1965 amendments facilitated the entry of a substantial number of wealthy and professional Koreans. As noted above, in 1969, 23.2 percent of Korean immigrants entered in occupational categories (which include professionals), and 11.6 percent entered on nonpreference visas, which were primarily used by investors (see Table 9). Between these two categories, then, over a third in 1969 had professional job skills or sufficient funds to start a business.

Like Asian Indians and Filipinos, many potential immigrants began tailoring their training to meet the technical requirements of occupa-tional categories.[146] The demand for specialized training was so strong that schools and companies in Korea were established solely to teach skills that would qualify.[147] Doctors, nurses, and pharmacists entered these training programs in large numbers. By 1977 thirteen thousand Korean medical professionals were working in the United States.[148]

Once Koreans had developed family ties in the United States, they were able to immigrate more easily through the family unity categories.

Since those immigrants are not required to demonstrate that no qualified workers are available for particular jobs, they are able to obtain visas much more quickly.[149] By the 1970's, moreover, many Korean war brides became naturalized.[150] Naturalization created new ways of requesting the admission of relatives, since citizens under the 1965 amendments could petition for parents, married sons and daughters, and siblings.[151] At the same time, the practice of bringing in wives for native citizens that had started before 1965 continued through the next decade.[152]

Some commentators attribute the late 1970's decline in the Korean use of occupational categories to the decade-long recession that plagued the United States.[153] The greater demand for family reunification visas, however, probably was more significant. Immigration law changes in the 1970's also contributed. In response to intense lobbying from the American Medical Association, which feared competition by specially trained Koreans, the laws were amended in 1976 to limit the number of foreign-trained physicians and surgeons entering the United States.[154] Most of these doctors could not enter to practice medicine unless they passed an American national examination and were competent in English. As a result, the number of Korean-trained doctors who could enter was substantially reduced. A 1977 change in the procedures for professionals that imposed more requirements on employers also made the professional entry route more onerous.[155]

Although 90 percent of all Korean immigrants enter through family categories today, many are of the same class as the professionals and investors who first immigrated through the occupational and nonpreference categories. So while the proportion of Koreans who have entered in the occupational categories has decreased in the last fifteen years, the absolute number of professionals has not. In 1969, 1,164 immigrants indicated that they were professionals or managers prior to entry. This figure rose to 3,955 in 1972, 2,782 in 1985, and 3,109 in 1989.[156]

Since the community is over 80 percent foreign-born and 35,000 immigrants are added annually, its career and economic profile reflects the characteristics of Korean immigrants. Again, the numbers alone tell much of the story. For example, 25 percent of foreign-born Korean Americans are employed as professionals or managers, and 24.8 percent overall. A high percentage of Koreans are employed in service jobs (16.5 percent) because 19 percent of recent Korean immigrants report holding that sort of job.[157] The share of Koreans employed in blue-collar service, farming, factory, and laborer occupations (47.7 percent) is comparable to that of the general population (45 percent).[158]

The proportion categorized as professionals, managers, and executives is also comparable to the proportion for the general population.[159] This figure, though, includes a high percentage of small-business owners. In 1980, there were 90 Korean-owned businesses for every thousand Korean Americans. In the general population those figures were 64 per thousand.[160] Between 1982 and 1987, the number of Korean-owned businesses in the United States more than doubled from 30,919 to 69,304.[161] In Los Angeles alone, Korean Americans operated 5,701 small businesses in 1987,[162] and 40 percent of Korean household heads and 34 percent of their spouses described themselves as proprietors.[163] In New York, where Korean Americans dominate the greengrocer business, 34 percent of the men run small retail businesses.[164] In the metropolitan areas with the most business-intensive Asian American communities (Dallas–Fort Worth, Houston, and Atlanta), Koreans have business rates of 130 or more per thousand.[165] These high rates of small-business ownership are more noteworthy when one considers that few of these immigrants had pursued merchant vocations before coming to the United States.[166]

From 1969 though the mid-1970's, the high percentage of Koreans operating small businesses stemmed partly from use of the nonpreference investor category available to those buying or starting American businesses.[167] Confronting strong barriers in the job market, lacking English fluency and knowledge of American customs, facing persistent discrimination, and refused a foothold in white-collar occupations, other Koreans turned to small business almost by default.[168]

Newly arriving immigrants, in turn, perceived their predecessors as successful in small businesses and were encouraged to try their hand. And, as more and more Koreans opened small businesses—such as the greengrocers in New York City—they established business and supply networks that made it easier for later arrivals to set up their own shops. The Korean small-business community has in fact become its own ethnic labor market.

Income figures reveal that family income is comparable to that of the general population, though there are more workers in Korean families.[169] The median income for Korean American full-time workers ($14,230) is lower than that of white Americans ($15,570). Recent arrivals are earning less still.[170] Not surprisingly, a wide discrepancy exists between men and women ($17,360 for men versus $10,260 for women).[171]

And foreign-born women earn less than if they were born in America ($10,070 versus $12,760).[172] A higher proportion of Korean American families (13.1 percent) than white American families (7 percent) fall below the poverty level.[173] Most of the poor are American-born who hold service jobs. Of recent immigrants, 11 percent fall below the poverty level,[174] compared to only 6 percent of those who immigrated between 1970 and 1974.[175]

## Asian Indian

### Population and Gender Ratio

*Population*

The Asian Indian American community increased from perhaps 50,000 before the 1965 reforms to 815,500 by 1990. During this period over 446,000 immigrated to the United States.[176] Not surprisingly, the population was over 80 percent foreign-born in 1980.[177] Since 1983 an average of more than 25,000 have entered annually.[178]

Immigration reform occurred when India had the highest rate of enrollment in postsecondary education of any low-income industrializing nation.[179] The Indian economy is divided between a small, relatively high-salaried modern sector and a large, impoverished traditional agricultural sector.[180] Demand for better wages created a great demand for higher levels of education.

Political and economic uncertainty engendered by the failure to meet economic expectations since Indian independence contributed to a willingness by many to leave. The economy has not been able to keep pace with the demand for modern-sector jobs, leaving many highly educated persons who cannot be absorbed.[181] Unemployment, frustration, and resentment have created conditions favoring emigration.

Throughout this period relations between the United States and India modulated. Immediately after the 1965 reforms India suffered a food shortage and sought U.S. aid. The United States delayed its response to survey the extent of the shortage and was severely criticized for its inaction. Then in 1971 it intervened on the side of Pakistan in the Indo-Pakistani War, and India's victory forced better relations.[182]

But even initially strained relations during this period could not stifle the interest in the United States among Indians who could take advantage of new immigration possibilities. More than any other group of Asian immigrants, Indians used the occupational and investor categories of the 1965 reforms to develop family networks in the United States. Few lived in the United States in 1965 and the occupational categories were the only ones available. In 1969, for example, 45 percent entered in the occupational categories, 26.8 percent as investors, and only 27 percent under family reunification (see Table 9). As family networks developed, the family reunification categories were used to petition for other relatives. This happened in the Chinese, Filipino, and Korean American communities as well, but the pattern was most evident in Indian immigration. By 1988 approximately 89 percent entered in the family categories, and less than 11 percent under occupational groupings.

### Gender ratio

Indians have the most balanced gender ratio of any Asian American community (99.8:100).[183] The balance is not uniform in each age group, however, and among those able to work, men constitute the majority (unlike Filipinos and Koreans); among older Indians, there are more women.[184]

The gender balance is counterintuitive since men have historically dominated immigration from India. The great majority of early Indian male immigrants have died, and there are more American-born women than men now in the older segment of the population.[185] More than 77 percent over age 65 are women, and 78 percent of these are American-born.[186]

Thus, the Asian Indian community is balanced between older American-born women and younger foreign-born men. Since 1965 more young or working men than women have immigrated. As of 1980, 60 percent between the ages of 35 and 54 have been men. Almost 96 percent of them were foreign-born,[187] most having immigrated between 1970 and 1980.[188] Unlike women from other Asian countries, few women have immigrated as nurses or through marriage to military men. So when only foreign-born members of the community are considered, men predominate, 119.9 to 100.[189]

Yet after the post-1965 increase in male immigrants,[190] the ratio remained fairly even[191] because the initial wave of post-1965 immigration was mainly in the male-dominated occupational and professional categories. Immigration today, however, which principally involves the gender-neutral family reunification categories, has resulted in greater gender balance. In 1989, for example, 15,993 men and 15,182 women immigrated.[192]

## Geographic Distribution and Residential Patterns

### Geographic distribution

The pre-1965 allure of California and New York has not weakened. Indians are the only Asian group not concentrated in the West. In 1990, only 23.1 percent lived there, while 35 percent lived in the Northeast—17.3 percent in New York alone—and 23.9 percent in the South.[193] Those in the West favor California, where 19.6 percent resided. New Jersey, Illinois, and Texas follow New York and California in popularity.[194] As a result, 9.7 percent live in New Jersey, 7.9 percent in Illinois, and 6.8 percent in Texas.[195] In fact, Indian Americans and Filipinos are the largest Asian American communities in New Jersey and Illinois.[196] This settlement pattern is due largely to perceived economic opportunities for this unusually professionalized group of immigrants, rather than to the presence of any existing community.

### Urbanization

Today, Indian immigrants overwhelmingly prefer living in urban centers. The more egalitarian policies of 1965 attracted immigrants from India's modernized urban areas, and they naturally sought out larger cities. Thus, over 90 percent live in major cities.[197] Metropolitan areas also attracted the professionals who began arriving after 1965. By the time they were using family-based immigration, a pattern for settlement had been established. In 1989, for example, 4,020 settled in the New York City–Newark–Jersey City area, 2,951 went to Chicago, and 2,216 to the Los Angeles–Long Beach–Anaheim area.[198]

### Ghettoization

Most professionals who arrived after 1965 did not cluster in residential enclaves. After the mid-1970's, as relatively fewer professionals entered and immigration shifted toward predominantly family-based categories, housing patterns began to shift. Less-skilled Indians now entering are as attracted to urban settings as their more affluent predecessors, but they find ethnic enclaves attractive because of better housing prices and working-class employment opportunities.[199] Their residential and economic enclaves can be found in various parts of New York and California and in Chicago, Newark, Washington, D.C., and Cincinnati.[200] And even in areas without such enclaves, social gatherings and religious centers bring many Indian Americans together on a regular basis.

## Careers

In 1969, over 70 percent of Indian immigrants entered through the occupational and investor categories, and almost 50 percent were professionals and managers[201] (see Table 9). As family immigration increased and investor visas became unavailable in the late 1970's, only one-fourth were professionals and managers.[202] By 1985 the share was under 20 percent.[203]

Yet while the proportion of professionals has decreased, their absolute number remains quite high. The number who designated their prior occupation as professionals or managers was 2,949 in 1969, 6,630 in 1977, 5,081 in 1983, and 6,681 in 1989.[204] The community includes an incredible 48.5 percent professionals, managers, or executives.[205] Indian Americans are the only Asian American group with a smaller proportion of service workers than the general population.

The post-1965 surge in professionals has created a relatively wealthy class with substantial capital.[206] The increase in family-based immigration, however, and the corresponding decrease in professionals will eventually affect the community's overall profile. Changes in the profile were already evident in 1989 as about 64 percent of new immigrants listed no occupation, and almost 12 percent listed blue-collar and service work occupations.[207] In 1970, by contrast, 42 percent listed no occupation and only 5 percent were blue-collar or service workers.[208]

Many who have been classified as managers, executives, and professionals own small businesses. In 1980 there were 70 Indian-owned businesses for every thousand Indian Americans, and even more in metropolitan areas that grew in the early 1980's.[209] The propensity to own small businesses is particularly evident in the motel and hotel industry where as many as fifteen thousand are owned by Asian Indians or about 20 percent of the U.S. total.[210] Indian Americans also own one-fourth of the trucking business in California.[211]

Small businesses are common among Indian Americans largely because after the 1965 amendments many immigrated under the non-preference investors category.[212] Purchasing a motel or restaurant qualified prospective immigrants for this classification. In 1969, 1,456 (over 26 percent) entered in this manner.[213] In 1972, the number was 8,753 (a staggering 53.7 percent of all Indian immigrants).[214] From 1978 to October 1991, however, no immigrant visas were available in the nonpreference investors category.[215] Even though a nonimmigrant investor category was available to nationals of many countries under current law, the necessary treaty has not existed between the United States and India.[216] A new investor's category implemented in October 1991 may, however, renew that option.

At $24,990 per year the 1980 median family income for Indian Americans was 25.5 percent higher than that of the general population.[217] This figure owes largely to the high salaries of foreign-born Indians, whose median income is significantly higher than those born in America.[218] Japanese Americans and Indian Americans are the only groups to have median incomes per worker higher than the general population's. As among other Asian American groups, more recent immigrants earn less than earlier arrivals, probably because of the ascendance of family immigration.[219]

To no one's great surprise, the median wage of the men is greater than that of the women.[220] Yet this disparity is not simply the result of low earnings among the women. In fact, immigrant women earn a bit more than their American-born counterparts. And Indian immigrant men earn 22.6 percent more than those born in America.

Unemployment and poverty are not insignificant among Asian Indians. The unemployment rate among immigrant Indian women (9.8 percent) is the highest among all immigrant Asian women and is higher than that among American-born Indian women.[221] Slightly more of their families (7.4 percent) fall below the poverty level than white American families (7 percent), reflecting the profile of recent immigrants. Of those who immigrated between 1975 and 1980, 10.7 percent were below the poverty line in 1980, compared to only 3.2 percent of those who immigrated between 1970 and 1974.[222]

# The Limited Effect on Japanese

## Population and Gender Ratio

*Population*

A variety of factors have combined to limit the impact of the 1965 amendments on Japanese America. Until 1924 Japan was able to prevent the imposition of harsh immigration policies, and Japanese newcomers were better able than other Asian immigrant groups to form families. Internment during World War II, however, destroyed many of the economic and social inroads they had made. Only against all odds did a strong family structure survive. The community grew because of a small, steady flow of immigrants after 1952. The 1965 amendments did not produce radical changes for Japanese Americans for three reasons. Tremendous economic growth in Japan by and large kept the Japanese at home. And because Japan had been so unusually successful in fighting off efforts to circumscribe family formation, fewer Japanese needed to emigrate to reunite with spouses and family members. Finally, internment led to bitterness and fear that discouraged a sentimental idea of what life in the United States might offer.

From 1965 to 1990 the Japanese American population increased by only 59 percent, from about 500,000 to a little over 847,500.[223] During this period only 116,000 Japanese immigrated.[224] Japanese Americans were in an excellent position to petition for relatives under the 1965 amendments' kinship provisions, yet they did not take advantage of this opportunity as other Asian American groups did.

The pattern of Japanese immigration is also noticeably different. Of the approximately five thousand who entered in 1969, about 75 percent were in family reunification categories, and 17.6 in the occupational category (see Table 9). Their limited use of the occupational categories is surprising because Japan was by 1969 well into its postwar economic recovery and was producing many professionals.[225] The source of new arrivals shifted by 1988, when 35 percent entered in the occupational categories, with 64 percent under family reunification provisions. Other Asian countries rely less on occupational categories today and more on family categories (see Table 9).

What had been the largest Asian American group in 1965 and 1970 slipped to third in 1980, where it has remained through the 1990 census—below Chinese and Filipinos and just above Asian Indians and Koreans (see Table 2). At current growth and immigration rates, by the end of the millennium Japanese Americans will be outnumbered by Vietnamese, Asian Indians, and Koreans. During the 1980's Japanese Americans grew by 21 percent, compared to 135 percent for Vietnamese Americans, 126 percent for Asian Indians, 125 percent for Koreans, 104 percent for Chinese, and 82 percent for Filipinos (see Table 2). And in the past few years the annual number of immigrants from Japan has averaged between 4,500 and 5,000, while the Philippines averages almost 60,000, Korea and China about 35,000, and India about 25,000.[226] The Japanese American community is the only one that is predominantly American-born today (71.6 percent in 1980). Since the same immigration categories were available to them as to Chinese, Koreans, Filipinos, and Asian Indians after the 1965 reforms, they evidently have a different attitude about or face different obstacles in leaving their homeland.

That Japanese Americans were the largest Asian community at the time of the 1965 reforms would suggest to some a unique potential to take advantage of the new family reunification categories. But Japanese American families were more stable and less in need of unification than were Chinese and Filipino families, so fewer immigration visas were necessary. But other factors must account for today's relatively low Japanese immigration. Filipino, Chinese, Korean, and Indian families have also been able to reunify, yet their demand for immigration is not subsiding.

Japan's relative economic and political stability appears to be the main reason for recent ebbs in immigration. By 1948 its economy was on solid footing. By 1954 national income had risen to 137 percent of prewar figures.[227] By 1969 its growth rate, as measured by gross national product, exceeded that of the United States and West Germany.[228] And in 1987 per capita income in Japan was higher for the first time than it was in the United States.[229] For many in Japan, therefore, economic opportunity is not a particularly powerful reason for emigrating. While a large proportion who do enter are professionals or skilled workers, many have reservations about moving to this country, partly because of the strengths of Japan's economy.[230] And Japan's negative birth rate (which contrasts with that of its Asian neighbors) will continue to provide job security for well-trained, young adults.[231]

Trauma suffered during World War II has also affected Japanese immigration since then. Of the 120,000 interned, 77,000 were citizens and the rest were mostly lawful permanent residents.[232] Anecdotal evidence strongly suggests that internment and the bitter fighting in World War II had a chilling effect on immigration.[233] Not only did internment destroy the economic structure of the community,[234] it served as an unequivocal reminder of the racism immigrants faced.[235]

In spite of the relatively slow growth of Japanese America, Japanese immigrants increased from 3,896 in 1981 to 5,734 in 1990.[236] This trend is worth watching in relation to changing economic and social conditions in Japan.

### Gender Ratio

Since the community is mostly American-born, current immigration demographics have little impact on its gender ratio. Prior to 1965 the story was different. Because of early agreements between Japan and the United States, most families were able to enter intact. From the McCarran-Walter Act of 1952 until the 1965 amendments, only the Japanese American community had more women than men, with approximately 85 men for every 100 women.[237] And this ratio has changed little. Even in 1980 there were 84.8 men to 100 women.[238]

Japanese immigrant women have continued to outnumber immigrant men. In 1985, for example, only 1,565 men immigrated compared to 2,521 women.[239] The women, moreover, have been disproportionately young, with over 70 percent between the ages of 20 and 39.[240] While few have studied these women, some speculate that many among them may be drawn to the United States by what they perceive as women's social standing here.[241]

## Geographic Distribution and Residential Patterns

### Geographic distribution

Their concentration in the West continued after the 1965 reforms. By 1990, 36.9 percent lived in California and 29.2 percent in Hawaii,[242] where they continue to be the largest community.[243] Slightly more than 4 percent resided in Washington. Since 1965 more are settling elsewhere. In 1980, 3.5 percent resided in New York, but by 1990 there were 4.2 percent.[244] But because these numbers are small compared to the overall Japanese American population, the pre-1965 geographic distribution will remain relatively constant for some time.

*Urbanization*

The community is mostly urbanized (88.9 percent), though it was initially drawn from rural agricultural areas.[245] In 1980 more than 190,000 Japanese lived in and around Honolulu and almost 150,000 in the Los Angeles–Long Beach–Anaheim area.[246] Of those in Illinois and New York, about 90 percent live in the Chicago and New York City areas.[247]

Current immigration policies seem, however, to have little to do with urbanization. Many early settlers started out as agricultural tenant farmers and small-business owners in western rural areas, but the alien land laws curtailed their development. Having lost their agricultural holdings as a result of internment, others moved to urban areas after the war, particularly because of continued racial animosity. Still others have simply followed the general population's movement toward urban-suburban living. Thus 11.2 percent of those who immigrated before 1960 compared with 6 percent after reside in rural areas.[248]

*Ghettoization*

The noticeable absence of large residential pockets of Japanese Americans has not changed since the 1965 reforms. Without an influx of working-class immigrants or refugees, Japantowns, even those in San Francisco and Los Angeles, have been deprived of the socioeconomic groups that generally sustain and need them. The predominantly American-born Japanese prefer suburban living, and a significant percentage can afford to settle in more expensive suburbs.[249]

San Francisco is a good example. Since World War II its Japantown has shrunk from 30 blocks to six. Although internment accounts for some of the community's population loss, and redevelopment in the 1970's—which supplanted housing with businesses—triggered further decline, most of the city's Japanese Americans live outside Japantown of their own accord.[250] San Francisco Japantown is today more a commercial than a residential center, where about 60 percent of the businesses are owned by Japanese Americans or Japanese companies.[251]

## Careers and Socioeconomic Status

Japanese America today is occupationally highly diverse. Statistically, it has a higher percentage (28.5 percent) of professionals, managers, and executives than the white population (24 percent), fewer blue-collar workers (37.3 percent to 45 percent) and a little higher percentage of service workers (12.8 percent to 11.6 percent).[252] In spite of the differences between them, however, the Japanese American employment profile corresponds closest to that of white Americans.[253]

It largely reflects the employment patterns of those in the second and third generation, though immigration appears to have added to the percentage of service workers. Of those who arrived prior to 1975, 21.8 percent were employed as professionals, managers, and executives; 24 percent were service workers.[254] This pattern changed markedly among more recent immigrants. Forty-six percent who immigrated between 1975 and 1980 were professionals, managers, and executives, but still 14 percent were service workers.[255] The proportion of Japanese Americans who are classified as professionals and managers is, however, skewed as in other Asian American communities by higher than average rates of small-business ownership.[256]

The median family income for Japanese Americans is unusually high. In 1980, for instance, it was more than 37 percent higher than the comparable figures for the general population but unemployment among Japanese Americans was only 3 percent, the lowest of any Asian American group.[257] Though there are more workers per household than in U.S. households generally, the median income for Japanese Americans ($16,830) is higher than that for white American workers ($15,570).[258]

Despite these glowing statistics, income differences within the community do exist. Indeed, differences between Japanese Americans and the general population are due largely to the achievements of those born in the United States. The median income for Japanese immigrants ($15,750) is about the same as for white workers, but significantly lower than for American-born Japanese Americans ($17,138).[259] Immigrant families earn almost 22 percent less than the average Japanese family.[260] Consistent with this, the proportion of immigrants who are poor is far greater than is that of the American-born. While only 4 percent of all Japanese American families fall below the poverty line (7 percent for white Americans), 10 percent of those who recently immigrated are classified as poor.[261]

## Nonimmigrant Factor

More Japanese nationals in nonimmigrant (temporary) categories enter than from any other country. Laws relating particularly to business rep-

TABLE 11

*Comparison of Entrants for Selected Nonimmigrant Categories, 1988*

| Country and total | Temporary workers | Business visitors | Intracompany transferees | Treaty investors[a] | Students |
|---|---|---|---|---|---|
| Japan 2,703,225 | 5,948 | 291,187 | 8,776 | 11,571 | 44,557 |
| India 146,945 | 2,648 | 28,096 | 862 | 39 | 13,000 |
| China/Taiwan 258,008 | 2,090 | 71,473 | 17,474 | 3,605 | 24,176 |
| Hong Kong 90,570 | 535 | 20,800 | 471 | 60 | 12,253 |
| Korea 151,034 | 1,811 | 38,942 | 843 | 4,884 | 14,473 |
| Philippines 152,157 | 5,868 | 22,312 | 1,078 | 1,804 | 2,613 |

SOURCE: 1988 *INS Statistical Yearbook*, table 43, pp. 72–74.
NOTE: Figures for business visitors, intracompany transferees, temporary workers, and students include accompanying spouses and minor children.
 [a]Includes treaty traders as well as treaty investors.

resentatives and temporary workers have been especially important for the Japanese. In 1989, for example, 2,985,573 nonimmigrant Japanese entered the United States. The vast majority of these were tourists (2,476,636).[262] But many nonimmigrants enter for temporary business purposes, and are then able to remain lawfully for several years (see Table 11). Intra-company transferees, traders/investors, and temporary workers best illustrate this practice.[263] In addition, many Japanese students matriculate and often remain for a long time.[264]

The presence of many nonimmigrant Japanese business people in cities has been noticeable.[265] In New York City, for example, the number of Japanese restaurants doubled in five years, and two cable television stations began airing Japanese soap operas and news reports.[266] At elementary schools in Scarsdale, one of four students is Japanese. And by 1987, twelve private Japanese schools had opened on weekends to supplement public education for 4,300 Japanese students.[267]

## Today's Undocumented Asian Population and Recent Policy Enforcement Issues

Although Asians have taken full advantage of the immigration routes opened by the 1965 amendments and through other policy changes in the past 25 years, an undocumented population does exist. It is difficult to know whether it consists more of overstayed students or overstayed visitors and travel industry crew members. Some hold professional jobs, while others are service workers.[268] Members of undocumented groups generally live in fear of detection. They are not inclined to cooperate with surveys, and they usually live where they can blend in with lawful resident aliens.

With those limitations in mind, estimates of the undocumented portion of the Asian American population range from 3 to 10 percent.[269] Of 7.3 million Asians (the 1990 count), from 219,000 to 730,000 could be undocumented. The limited availability of legalization (or amnesty) under the Immigration Reform and Control Act of 1986 did little to diminish even the lower estimate. Fewer than 49,000 applied under a program for those who had entered and become undocumented prior to January 1, 1982, and only a handful were expected to apply under an agricultural worker amnesty.[270]

Before 1965 the undocumented population was predominantly Chinese. It could very well be mostly Filipino today. Of the 49,000 who applied for legalization, 15,995 were Filipinos, compared to a total of 11,737 from China, Taiwan, and Hong Kong.[271] The number of deportable Asians arrested each year is decreasing, while the proportion and number of deportable Filipinos is increasing. For example, in 1970, of the 14,613 Asians apprehended, 5,397 were Chinese and 3,472 were Filipino.[272] By 1982, 13,965 Asians were arrested; 2,226 were Chinese, and 3,699 were Filipino.[273] Of course these figures provided by the Immigration and Naturalization Service cannot be viewed as statistically valid for all of Asian America, because INS enforcement tactics are likely to cause distortions. For example, over 90 percent of the deportable aliens arrested by the INS are Mexican,[274] yet according to most reliable estimates, which the INS does not dispute, Mexicans are at most only half of the undocumented population.[275]

Though some probably enter through smuggling or border jumping, most become undocumented after overstaying an initially valid nonimmigrant visa or by working without permission. In 1982, 62 percent arrested by the INS had violated their student or visitor visa; 22 percent left a vessel on which they were crew members.[276] These figures reflect a change in the profile of undocumented Asians—at least those apprehended by the INS. In 1970 only 46 percent had violated their nonimmigrant visas, while over 42 percent were crew members.[277]

Additional violations no doubt involve visa fraud. For example, some Asians purchase fraudulent immigrant visas or forged passports stamped with nonimmigrant visas. Others might be parties to sham marriages to U.S. citizens.[278] Alleged visa fraud among Filipinos is of special concern.[279]

Clearly the undocumented community is not insignificant, but policies regarding legal immigration categories and their implementation are more vital. The days when false documents and fictitious family trees pervaded the Chinese American community have, like gender imbalances, faded.

From time to time, INS procedures and the enforcement of post-1965 immigration laws affect each Asian American community. A few examples demonstrate their peculiarity.

### INS Attitude Toward Filipinos

As immigration rates from the Philippines began to increase significantly in the 1970's, a noticeably distrustful attitude emerged at the INS toward Filipinos as it had toward Chinese. Fueled by claims of rampant visa fraud in Manila,[280] local INS investigators, examiners, and clerical staff developed an especially demeaning and insensitive attitude toward them. As a group, natives of the Philippines are distrusted and interrogated more intensively by immigration inspectors at international airports. In visa cases involving marriage, when one party is from the Philippines, both are subjected to exhaustive questioning far beyond the already humiliating examinations conducted in most marriage cases. Often, as a matter of discretion in visa and citizenship cases, further investigation is requested by the U.S. Consul in Manila, forcing a delay of from six to twelve months.[281] As a general rule the validity of documents is questioned, and many deportation hearings demand corroborative evidence beyond that required of non-Filipinos.[282] This attitude is most succinctly captured by a federal immigration judge who stated on the record: "By now, everyone dealing with such matters is well aware that aliens from the Philippines will engage in any fraud to get here and will do anything to stay."[283]

### Exclusion of Elderly Asian SSI Recipients

In August of 1978 immigration inspectors in Honolulu began a systematic interrogation of returning elderly Asian Americans who were lawful permanent resident aliens of the United States.[284] The airport interrogation went far beyond the customary questioning as to purpose and length of stay abroad. It focused on whether they were then, or had ever been, recipients of Supplemental Security Income (SSI).[285] SSI is a public assistance program for the elderly and disabled made available to citizens and lawful permanent resident aliens.[286] If SSI had ever been received by the returning alien, immigration inspectors took possession of the person's alien card and passport and instructed the person to report for further inspection and interrogation in the INS district office in Los Angeles, San Francisco, Seattle, San Diego, or Boston.[287] At the inspection these elderly Filipinos, Chinese, Koreans, and Japanese were informed that they were excludable from the United States as "public charges"[288] and were generally given three options: return to their native country, request an exclusion hearing, or terminate SSI benefits and post a public-charge bond of $5,000.[289]

Note that the INS was dealing with lawful permanent resident aliens—not with first-time immigrants or undocumented aliens.[290] The authority for INS to reimpose the public-charge grounds of exclusion each time a lawful alien reenters the United States stems from the "reentry doctrine." It had traditionally been used against returning criminals, subversives, and other undesirables, and not under modern immigration laws against returning resident aliens who had sought public assistance.[291] Applying it to Asian recipients of SSI simply appears to have been arbitrarily instituted beginning in the summer of 1978.[292]

In more than five hundred reported cases, there was no question that the person had a right to apply for and to receive SSI under Social Security Administration regulations.[293] Fraudulent receipt of SSI benefits was never alleged by the government.[294] It was equally clear that if these persons had not proceeded abroad, they could not have been deported for receiving public assistance.[295] In fact, SSI recipients were permitted to leave the country for up to 30 days without affecting their eligibility, and in many instances they had been informed by Social Security representatives prior to their departure that there was nothing to worry about.[296]

Although former INS Commissioner Leonel Castillo issued guidelines in May 1979 to deal with these cases on a more humane level,[297] and one alien successfully appealed his case to the Board of Immigration Appeals,[298] the guidelines and board decision were largely ignored by immigration officials in Honolulu, where most of the cases originated, for some time.[299] This kind of harassment of elderly Asian SSI recipients continues from time to time.

Because most lawful permanent resident Asian travelers return through Honolulu, the impact of the policy fell squarely on elderly Asians. Immigrants at other ports were not questioned.[300] The action caused great alarm in Asian communities throughout the United States, in part because of its similarity to selective racial enforcement that haunted them in the past.[301]

## Visa Backlogs

Although the 1965 reforms facilitated huge increases in Asian population, country and territorial quotas have resulted in significant backlogs and delays. Although spouses, unmarried minor children, and parents of adult citizens can immigrate regardless of quota restrictions, adult sons and daughters of citizens, relatives of permanent residents, and siblings of citizens have been subject to numerical restrictions. Countries with high visa demand have gradually developed severe backlogs in these preference categories. Immigrants entering today under second preference (spouses and unmarried sons and daughters of permanent residents) from the Philippines have had to wait more than seven years.[302] Siblings of U.S. citizens (formerly fifth preference, but made fourth preference in 1991), a very popular category, have an even longer wait.[303] For most countries (including mainland China and India), it is more than eight years. For the Philippines, the wait is over thirteen years.[304] Appendix B provides examples of how these categories have been used.

Additional visa numbers made available under 1990 legislation will not reduce the waiting period for family preference categories. The larger allocation for second preference would seem to help ease the backlog, but given the three million additional permanent residents—mostly Latino—who obtained status through legalization (amnesty) under the 1986 Immigration Reform and Control Act, the number of new second-preference petitions will increase dramatically, and increase the backlog even more. Since no extra visas were provided for siblings, the waiting period will get longer and longer for that category as well.

Some 1990 changes will facilitate greater immigration from Hong Kong. Under the amendments the annual quota increases to ten thousand in 1992, then to twenty thousand in 1995. Under 1986 legislation the quota for Hong Kong (and all dependent areas) was increased from six hundred to five thousand. In 1986 the backlog for Hong Kong in second preference was over seven years, and in the sibling preference more than twelve years. By October 1989 the backlog in second preference was no greater than for other countries (two years), and the same was true for the sibling category by April 1991 (nine years).[305]

## Chinese Visa Petitions

Immigrants originally from mainland China who enter in large numbers each year face a procedural difficulty. The frequent nonuse of birth and marital records in China make reunion with family members in the United States today difficult. For most non-Chinese, the process is simple. If the relative abroad is in an immediate relative or preference category, evidence of the relationship is filed with the INS, such as birth certificates, marriage certificates, and family registries.[306]

But when a Chinese person files such a petition, a long list of secondary evidence of the relationship must be submitted to INS in support or else the petition will be returned. If secondary evidence is not available, the Chinese petitioner is usually effectively barred from reunification with the relative. Until the mid-1980's, interviews were also required in Chinese petition cases, causing an added delay of from six to eighteen months. While processing times varied from district to district on all visa petitions, an interview was not required in the vast majority of non-Chinese cases.[307] Today, interviews are not required in any visa petition cases except for marriages. The petitions are adjudicated at regional service centers, which often return them with requests for secondary evidence of the relationship. This continues to significantly delay the cases.

The secondary evidence required usually takes the form of photographs, old correspondence, school records, money receipts, affidavits, blood tests, and old Hong Kong documents, if either the petitioner or beneficiary had ever resided in Hong Kong. The burden to produce this evidence has always fallen on the shoulders of the petitioner who, by the nature of the requirements, is expected to be something of a pack rat. More often than not, the petitioner is advised to correspond with the relative abroad and to request the relative to obtain documents in China, even though most of those relatives remain in small villages and are not particularly mobile or familiar with formal documents.

Normalization of relations with mainland China did not, for the most part, alleviate the problems. Immigrants from China in the late 1970's and early 1980's generally had received approved petitions ten to fifteen years earlier. Many thousands were permitted out of China immediately after normalization but were not able to leave right away because of the backlogs in various preference categories. Ironically, after normalization certain documents of the local commune authorities that had been unquestioned by U.S. authorities were suddenly distrusted, and U.S. officials in China were required to verify the documents even though their offices were not fully operative.[308] Local commune officials reportedly would not provide the documents requested unless approval had already been granted by U.S. immigration officials, but the INS often conditioned its approval on the receipt of the requested Chinese document.

These inconsistencies have slowly been resolved with the advent of regional processing, though many petitioners, especially those without counsel, are confused over the requirements. One thing does remain certain. Because of secondary-evidence requirements, a Chinese petition will take more time to process than most others.[309]

## Conclusion

The 1965 amendments greatly expanded the possibilities for Asian American communities to develop and for Asian Americans to pursue their aspirations. Increases in population, shifts in demographics, and changes in gender balance and geographic preferences have been dramatic since 1965. Yet, because earlier efforts to control the social forces within each community differed, each group had developed differently. The social, economic, and political conditions in each Asian country have also strongly influenced patterns of immigration. Accordingly, population size, gender ratios, occupational profiles, ghettoization, residential preferences, and the like vary sharply.

Consider population. Roughly speaking, Chinese and Japanese communities had at least one thing in common when the 1965 reforms were instituted—each had a population in the hundreds of thousands. But while growth of the Japanese American community has been moderate since, the Chinese American community grew substantially, much more like the Filipinos, Koreans, and Asian Indians, which were not large in 1965. Political and economic stability in Japan in the past 25 years has reduced the desire of its nationals to emigrate, but the treatment of immigrants under U.S. laws is also important. Japanese were better able to form and maintain families in the United States before 1965 and did not take advantage of the family reunification provisions as other groups did.

Since Chinese and Filipino Americans substantially outnumbered Koreans and Asian Indians in 1965, they had a greater base from which to take advantage of the family-oriented admissions system of the reforms. Thus, as early as 1970, fairly large numbers of immigrants from mainland China, Taiwan, and the Philippines entered in the categories for immediate relatives, and for second (relatives of permanent residents) and fifth preference (siblings) (see Table 10). Filipinos also often used the category for professionals (third preference) in 1970, helping to build a base for family immigration in subsequent years. Asian Indians used the investor and professional categories to establish a family base. Koreans also immigrated as investors soon after the 1965 reforms, and as immediate relatives and as preference siblings in 1970 (see Table 10). For a group with a seeming small family base, this statistical oddity is attributable to the many Korean war brides and adopted orphans that continued to enter after the 1965 amendments.

To the surprise of U.S. policymakers, Asian American communities (except Japanese) grew dramatically between 1965 and the present. The small but substantial Filipino American population grew seven times by 1990 to become the second largest. The smaller Korean American and Asian Indian communities increased eighteen and sixteen times respectively in 25 years, approaching the size of the Japanese American community, which had been the largest group through the early 1970's. Chinese America, already relatively substantial in 1965, increased by four and a half times by 1990 to remain the largest group since 1980, just ahead of Filipinos. Overall, Asian America has increased from under 1.2 million in 1965 to almost 7.3 million in 1990. In the 1980's alone the Asian and Pacific Islander population grew 107.8 percent compared to only 9.8 percent for the entire nation.[310]

Filipinos, South Koreans, and Chinese are leaving behind political instability for a better economic environment. Many Indian nationals have pursued training abroad in specialties that cannot be absorbed by the Indian economy. Many Koreans and Filipinos have pursued careers, such as those in the medical field, that can be used both at home and in the United States. They have contributed to the higher proportion of female immigration from Korea and the Philippines since 1965. For many, economic independence, occupational opportunities, and progressive social attitudes (in short, greater gender equality) in the United States were influential. As a result, Korean and Filipino women outnumber men, as Japanese American women outnumber Japanese American men. Chinese Americans are evenly divided because of 25 years of female-dominated immigration and the passing of the older male-dominated community. The sexes in the Asian Indian community appear fairly balanced, but most of its working-age immigrants are men, while more of its elderly are women.

Except for Asian Indians and Koreans, Asian Americans prefer living in the West. Since 1965 a huge number of Asian Indians have settled in the Northeast, as have many Chinese. Filipinos and Japanese continue to have an affinity for Hawaii and California. Many Korean immigrants are attracted to California, but their settlement pattern has been more widespread, even stretching into the South.

Asian Americans generally prefer living in urban areas; the extent and types of enclaves each group establishes vary. Chinatowns, established historically as the result of harsh laws, racism, and family separation, have provided places to live and work to new immigrants, many working-class relatives, and refugees who arrived after 1965. Some urban Chinatowns have flourished. Filipino American enclaves have blossomed as well after 1965, but they are more in suburban areas. Because of fewer Japanese immigrants, Japantowns, while still visible, are much smaller, but do provide a social and political network.

The immigrant-driven profiles of the newer Asian Indian and Korean American communities have resulted in different enclaves. Before and just after 1965, when most Asian Indian immigrants were professionals or owned small businesses, enclaves were not prevalent. Recent arrivals from family categories and working-class backgrounds require social and economic networks, so residential enclaves are now quickly developing. Until recently, most Korean immigrants have had the means to reside in suburban areas and entered through occupational and investor categories. Their propensity for small business resulted in business blocks, rather than in residential enclaves. But some recent immigrants also live in Koreatowns.

The income in Asian American families has generally been higher than in the general population, mostly because more members work. Preliminary reports from the 1990 census agree but show that in California Asian American household income now lags behind white households.[311] Individual Chinese, Filipino, and Korean Americans make less than their white counterparts, but Asian Indian and Japanese American workers generally earn more.[312] Although a significant proportion of Asian Americans hold professional jobs, particularly Asian Indians, many immigrants—especially Chinese and Filipinos—are service workers or live below the poverty line. Professional and management proportions also reflect the prevalence of small businesses in Asian America. The number of businesses owned by Asian Americans increased six times faster than the national rate between 1982 and 1987.[313]

Demographic profiles of the Chinese, Japanese, Asian Indian, and Filipino American communities strongly reflect the 1965 reforms and will continue to even after recent changes. Size, gender ratios, residential patterns, and employment profiles manifest the presence of expanded opportunities after 1965. Immigration reforms enacted in 1990 will continue to facilitate Asian immigration in the family preferences, though perhaps not in the same proportions. Increases in the Hong Kong quota will allow thousands more Chinese each year. More visas for professionals and a new investor category are also accessible to Asians.[314]

The influence of immigration policies on demographics suggests an effect on social life as well. But before moving on to that issue, we will trace the special character of refugee policies and their peculiar impact on the Vietnamese American community.

## CHAPTER FOUR

# Shaping the Vietnamese American Community: Refugee Law and Policy

In 1975 when the United States withdrew its troops from Vietnam, the number of Vietnamese Americans was negligible. By 1990 their population surged to 614,547. The community's 134.8 percent rate of growth since 1980 is the fastest of the six largest Asian American groups, including Koreans and Asian Indians, whose own populations have undergone phenomenal growth since 1965.[1] What in 1975 was a totally obscure group has become a community not easily ignored.

Vietnamese Americans have made themselves noticeable by contributing to the revitalization of various urban centers, and their food enriches the cuisine of many cities. They have also been made conspicuous by the media—sometimes for the educational accomplishments of their children, sometimes for the economic threat they are perceived as posing to white fishermen, and sometimes for their experiences as victims of renewed anti-Asian violence.

For all this newfound prominence, the presence and growth of

Vietnamese America does not obviously translate into much that is revealing about immigration law and policy. After all, Vietnamese came here as part of our involvement in the war, mostly through refugee rather than immigration categories. Refugee law and policy has historically been understood by scholars and policymakers as importantly distinct from immigration law and policy. It expresses, we are told, the national community's need to make ad hoc judgments in response to its humanitarian sensibilities. Conventional immigration law and policy, by contrast, reflect judgments about growth in light of political, social, and economic concerns. In effect we are asked to believe that whatever might appear noteworthy about Vietnamese Americans and how they got here is largely separable from the experiences of other Asian immigrants.

But the themes that have already emerged in this study invite a closer look at largely unexamined facets of refugee policy. Attention should be focused on the likelihood of multiple national agendas, the hidden continuities between refugee and admissions laws and policies, the reassertion of familiar instruments of control, and the superficiality of our understanding of the Vietnamese.

Make no mistake. Vietnamese immigration does confirm that humanitarian concerns operate through refugee law and policy. At the same time, though, it reveals how the United States repeated many mistakes made earlier with other Asian immigrants. In trying to be sensitive to the Vietnamese, refugee law and policy revealed patterns of knowledge and inattention that found their origins in this country's historical experience with other Asians. Sadly missing was a careful analysis of the effects immigration policy had on earlier Asian American communities. The similarity between refugee and admissions law and policy seems at times pretextual.

The history of Vietnamese immigration does reveal conflicting and even contradictory aspirations, particularly by policymakers. The same drive to control the work, the location, and even the families of Asian Americans that over a century informed admissions law and policy emerges again. Perhaps a realist, layperson, or scholar would find all this unsurprising: no law could conceivably be entirely humanitarian. Yet policymakers and Congress continue to act and legislate in a manner that denies the political and social link between refugee and conventional immigration policies.

## Background on Refugee Policies

The United States takes considerable pride in its long history of providing refuge to foreign nationals displaced by the ravages of war or persecuted by totalitarian governments. As early as 1783, President George Washington proclaimed, "The bosom of America is open to receive not only the opulent and respectable stranger, but the oppressed and persecuted of all nations and religions."[2] For two centuries kindred statements by leaders and citizenry alike have helped project, even if they did not always accurately reflect, a certain national generosity of spirit.

Refugees from Asian nations were among those who took such statements at their word. By the turn of the century, for example, Chinese revolutionary Sun Yat Sen entered the United States and began raising funds for rebellion.[3] In 1905 three Korean political exiles fled here to avoid persecution after an abortive coup.[4] Between 1910 and 1918, 541 Korean "refugee students" fled Japanese persecution.[5] And Indian political refugees began arriving in 1908, using the United States as the base from which to lead anti-British activities.[6]

Thousands of other refugees, sometimes hundreds of thousands, were escorted here by an array of congressional acts that, on an ad hoc basis, superseded the national quota systems. Prominent among these was the 1948 Displaced Persons Act, which enabled 400,000 refugees and displaced persons to enter, most of whom were from Europe.[7] The 1953 Refugee Relief Act admitted 200,000 refugees, including 38,000 Hungarians and about 2,800 refugees of the Chinese Revolution.[8]

Refugee migration to the United States finds its origin in the noble pursuit of humanitarian-oriented foreign policy objectives. Refugee sympathizers invariably invoke the need to respond compassionately to those in other countries confronted with life-threatening crises. In passing the Displaced Persons Act, Congress explicitly adopted the definition of the terms "displaced person" and "refugee" set forth in the 1946 Constitution of the International Refugee Organization.[9]

> It is the historic policy of the United States to respond to the urgent needs of persons subject to persecution in their homelands, including, where appropriate, humanitarian assistance for their care and maintenance in asylum areas . . . admission to this country of refugees of special humanitarian concern to the United States, and transitional assistance to refugees in the United States.[10]

This rhetoric notwithstanding, refugee law and policy has reflected the tensions between humanitarian aims and practical domestic and international concerns. These tensions—evident over the years in even the least obvious situations—make plain the link between refugee and immigration policy. In the 1930's, for example, the United States turned away thousands of Jews fleeing Nazi persecution, in large part because of the powerful restrictionist views then dominating immigration laws.[11] Congress and U.S. consular officers consistently resisted Jewish efforts to emigrate and impeded any significant emergency relaxation of limitations on quotas.[12] A 1939 refugee bill would have rescued twenty thousand German children had it not been defeated on the grounds that the children would exceed the German quota.[13] And in 1972 the U.S. Coast Guard and Naval intelligence, confused over proper asylum procedures and indecisive in the face of conflicting objectives, returned an asylum-seeking Lithuanian seaman to his Soviet ship.[14]

As if collectively to deny these tensions, policymakers showed every sign through the early 1970's of being pleased by their system of policies, laws, and ad hoc decisions. As they saw it, whenever large numbers of deserving refugees appeared, new legislation could be enacted or existing laws and regulations manipulated. That sort of flexibility in a legal regime was, to their minds, to be unashamedly admired. It also permitted policy-making consistent with their political preference for refugees from communism.

A closer look at the basic structure of the system and the policies that informed it bears witness to this ideological bias. Consider the 1952 McCarran-Walter Act, which granted the attorney general discretionary authority to "parole" into the United States any alien for "emergent reasons or for reasons deemed strictly in the public interest."[15] Although the original intent was to apply this parole authority on an individual basis,[16] the 1956 Hungarian refugee crisis led to its expanded use to accommodate those fleeing Communist oppression.[17] The parole authority was also used to admit more than fifteen thousand Chinese who fled mainland China after the 1949 Communist takeover[18] and more than 145,000 Cubans who sought refuge after Fidel Castro's 1959 coup.[19]

Using that authority the attorney general did permit over 400,000 refugees from Southeast Asia to enter between 1975 and 1980.[20] By 1980, 99.7 percent of the more than one million refugees admitted under the parole system were from countries under Communist rule.[21] These figures betray any claim that refugee policy was based solely on humanitarian considerations.

The preference afforded refugees from Communist countries is also reflected in the 1965 reforms, when Congress created the first permanent statutory basis for the admission of refugees. Incorporating prior refugee language into a seventh preference category, conditional entry was provided for refugees fleeing Communist-dominated areas or the Middle East. Immigration controls were manifest as well in this category, since it included a worldwide annual quota of 17,400 and a geographic restriction that limited its use through 1977 to countries outside the Western Hemisphere.[22] Until its repeal in 1980 the seventh preference was used by tens of thousands of refugees fleeing China, the Soviet Union, and other Communist societies.[23]

Shortly after the creation of the seventh preference, the United States agreed in 1968 to the United Nations Protocol Relating to the Status of Refugees.[24] The protocol obligated compliance with the guidelines established by the United Nations Convention Relating to the Status of Refugees.[25] The ideological and geographic restrictions of the seventh preference, however, were inconsistent with the ideologically neutral protocol, so the United States attempted to juryrig compliance by using the attorney general's discretionary parole authority.[26] But that authority did not conform to the protocol's principles of neutrality either.

Few complaints about refugee policies and laws were registered on the floors of Congress during most of the 1970's. Some liberal observers did challenge the bias favoring refugees from Communist countries, but mostly as it affected applications for political asylum filed by individuals who had already gained entry. As for the greater numbers seeking refugee status from abroad, policymakers seemed satisfied with the status quo. Rather than being disingenuous, this attitude was entirely consistent with their sense of humanitarianism.

After 1975 policymakers became less complacent as Asians began entering in increasing numbers under existing guidelines. Only about 2,800 Chinese benefited before then from the 1953 Refugee Relief Act. Through 1966 about 15,000 were admitted under the parole provision. These low numbers were not perceived as threatening, since the seventh preference category restricted Chinese refugees through its annual worldwide limitation of 17,400. Indeed, until it was repealed in 1980, only 14,000 who fled mainland China were able to take advantage of the seventh preference.

Following the military withdrawal from Vietnam in April 1975, however, the flow of Asian refugees increased markedly almost overnight. Invoking numerical restrictions in the midst of a controversial and devastating war would have been unacceptable; too many understood such inflexibility as morally treacherous and politically high-priced. Consequently, the attorney general on several occasions used the parole authority to permit Asians to enter—the first time it was so employed since the 1965 amendments.

Initially, the United States merely wanted to evacuate from Vietnam the approximately 17,600 American dependents and government employees.[27] Immediately before the fall of Saigon in April 1975, however, former employees and others whose lives were threatened were included. These evacuees included approximately 4,000 orphans, 75,000 relatives of American citizens or lawful permanent residents, and 50,000 Vietnamese government employees and officials. Mass confusion permitted many who did not fit into these categories to also be evacuated.[28] Between April and December 1975, the United States thus admitted 130,400 Southeast Asian refugees, 125,000 of whom were Vietnamese.[29]

The exodus did not stop there. By 1978 thousands more were admitted under a series of Indochinese Parole Programs, authorized by the attorney general. The number of Southeast Asian refugees swelled to 14,000 a month by the summer of 1979.[30] Following the tightening of Vietnam's grip on Cambodia, several hundred thousand "boat people" and many Cambodian and Laotian refugees entered between 1978 and 1980.[31] In fact, annual arrivals of Southeast Asian refugees had increased almost exponentially: 20,400 in 1978, 80,700 in 1979, and 166,700 in 1980.[32]

In general the flow of Southeast Asians was poorly coordinated. The executive branch repeatedly waited until the number of refugees in countries of "first asylum" (those first reached by refugees) reached crisis proportions before declaring an emergency. Only then would a new parole program be instituted.[33] Attacks on the inconsistent treatment of refugees and calls for a consistent policy became commonplace. Many were uncomfortable with the attorney general's considerable unstructured power to hastily admit tens of thousands of refugees under the parole mechanism. Others were genuinely concerned with the government's erratic response to the plight of Southeast Asian refugees.[34] Dissatisfaction with ad hoc admissions provided the impetus for reform and, ultimately, the passage of the 1980 Refugee Act.[35]

The new refugee law was an attempt by Congress to treat refugee and immigration policies as separate and distinct. The Refugee Act was introduced, debated, and passed when the federal Select Commission on Immigration and Refugee Policy was preoccupied with other issues.

Members of the commission, perhaps the most important body assembled to consider such policies since 1900, were presented the act as a fait accompli and told that refugee and immigration polices were separable. Their work on immigration policies was to focus on selection and admission regulations in terms of their effects on the nation's economic, social, and political well-being.[36] A major catalyst for the new refugee law was a disturbing anxiety felt by some members of Congress that thousands of Southeast Asians would destabilize many communities.[37] Concerns about controlling immigration have dominated Refugee Act applications ever since.

Those who passed the 1980 Refugee Act and those who enacted earlier legislation claimed that they desired a less biased system. The ideologically and geographically restrictive seventh preference category was replaced with a general provision that allowed any person with a "well-founded fear of persecution" to enter as a refugee.[38] The act requires the president, after "appropriate consultation" with Congress, to determine who will be offered refuge and to establish corresponding limits on how many will be admitted. The reforms restrict the attorney general's authority to parole refugees, thereby foreclosing large, ex parte admissions.[39]

In practice, however, the new law has been administered in a manner reminiscent of the heavyhanded use of the seventh preference and parole provisions. Without much congressional opposition,[40] presidents have continued to favor refugees from Communist countries while consistently ignoring pleas of those from U.S. allies.[41] The number of Asian refugees has declined accordingly.

The executive branch and Congress established a limit of 234,000 refugees for fiscal 1980. The Carter administration then reserved 169,000 places for Southeast Asia, 33,000 for the former Soviet Union, 19,500 for Cuba, and 1,000 for the remainder of Latin America. By 1985 the total number of refugee admittees dropped to 70,000, with 50,000 reserved for East Asia. For 1992 the total was increased to 142,000, primarily to accommodate an increase to 61,000 for the Soviet Union. The number for East Asia remains at 52,000, despite dire circumstances in Asian refugee camps.[42]

Humanitarianism has occasionally taken precedence over the drive to control. Consider the 1982 and 1987 legislation concerning "Amerasian children."[43] Designed to enable Southeast Asian children whose natural fathers were U.S. servicemen to enter more easily, the legislation allows them the exceptional option of either filing on their own behalf or having an immigration visa petition filed for them.[44] Other prospective family-based immigrants cannot petition on their own behalf. The consequences of this technical accommodation are not insignificant. A large number of children were fathered by servicemen in Korea, Vietnam, Laos, Cambodia, and Thailand over the past forty years where they have suffered racial discrimination and ostracism in their native lands, which led to inadequate housing, substandard medical care, and nutritional deficiencies.[45] By October 1991, 18,280 Amerasians (mostly from Vietnam) had taken advantage of this law and migrated to the United States.[46] And unfortunately many of them have endured similar discrimination and ostracism here.[47]

Yet the decency evident in such legislation cannot conceal the ideological bias that has permeated refugee practices. One example of U.S. beneficence cannot negate the tensions between humanitarianism and practical concerns that regularly condition and constrain refugee law and policy-making. More often than not, the impulse to conceal and deny actual motivations has been followed. Expressly blurring the boundaries between immigration and refugee policies helps to avert the need for self-deprecation. This approach demands careful assessment of the idea of refugee so strongly implicated both in the U.S. self-image and in the making of Vietnamese America.

## Refugee Resettlement Policies

Southeast Asians posed a distinctive resettlement problem even for a country with experience in designing refugee plans that dates as far back as 1945.[48] They became the largest refugee group ever to so rapidly enter the country, and the challenge they presented began early when they came in entirely unanticipated numbers. Policymakers had planned for about 18,000 refugees, but instead about 130,000 entered within an eight-month period in 1975. When this first wave triggered widespread opposition and resentful propaganda, it became obvious to bureaucrats and politicians alike that something needed to be done to help minimize the economic and cultural disruptions.[49] On April 18, 1975, President Gerald Ford created a temporary Interagency Task Force (IATF) to coordinate the activities of twelve federal agencies, including the Department of Health, Education and Welfare, that were responsible for resettlement.[50]

From the outset IATF's temporary character proved problematic. As if to convince itself (and perhaps the president) that a temporary task force could manage the assignment, IATF perceived and treated the refugee problem as though it were temporary. As a result, its policies did not carefully consider the long-term effects on the refugee community.[51] IATF's rush to supervise led to sloppy sponsorship arrangements, some of which broke down almost immediately, leaving many refugees alone and unaided.[52] Others served employers looking for cheap labor or subservient workers and exploited refugees.[53]

More to the point, the short-sightedness of IATF led to the misguided decision to disperse Vietnamese refugees as widely as possible, rather than to concentrate them in assigned areas.[54] For those who wished to maintain control over the Vietnamese, assigning them to a few central locations seemingly promised to keep them where they could be more easily monitored and manipulated.[55] At the same time, however, it increased opportunities for refugees to communicate with and reinforce each other, perhaps enabling them to form alliances and mobilize.

Dispersal had its own appeal. It might help avoid acute economic stress in host communities, force a more rapid assimilation, and diffuse the potential for solidarity and organization. The logistical problems, however, were considerable. If refugees became restless, for example, it would be more difficult to contain them. Still, by compelling them to disperse and rely upon outsiders, IATF hoped to domesticate the refugees, easing their transition into and their burden on mainstream culture.

Policymakers soon discovered that dispersal was ill-advised and unpopular. Initially, the program produced a settlement pattern approximating that of the rest of the population. Refugees were "neatly" dispersed around the country, with 21 percent being placed in California. At least one hundred were relocated in every state except Alaska.[56] Relative isolation, however, quickly proved unacceptable to refugees who began moving from their assigned locations in substantial numbers, a practice commonly referred to as secondary migration.

While many factors contributed to refugees' decision to resettle, secondary migration principally resulted from poor policy decisions based upon superficial analysis. In a new and often hostile land, forced dispersal deprived Southeast Asians of desperately needed familial, cultural, and ethnic support. Their desire to develop these support systems seemed possible only by forming the kinds of ethnic enclaves that dispersal discouraged. So Vietnamese leaders, particularly the clergy, frequently coordinated ambitious secondary migrations to places like New Orleans, where living together as a community seemed feasible.[57]

Secondary migration resulted, too, from the poorly designed sponsorship program that was part of the dispersal policy. New arrivals were required to have a sponsor before they could leave the refugee processing camps.[58] Voluntary agencies ("volags") that had experience dealing with European and Cuban refugees were made responsible.[59] They found sponsors who agreed to assist families in adjusting to their new surroundings.[60] But unlike previous refugee groups, Southeast Asians had no indigenous community to rely upon for sponsorship. Instead, their sponsors were mostly U.S. volunteers motivated by humanitarian concerns and located throughout the country.[61] Because sponsorship entailed a major financial obligation, only a few could be found.[62] And since only some sponsors could accommodate the large extended families of Southeast Asians, the families often ended up separated and divided. Perhaps not surprisingly, many reunified soon after passing through the processing centers.[63]

By 1980, 45 percent of the first wave of Southeast Asian refugees had moved from their assigned locations to a different state, thereby frustrating the dispersal policy's goals of minimizing the impact of refugees on local economies.[64] They became concentrated most heavily in California, Texas, and Louisiana.[65] Urban areas having warm climates and an Asian population were preferred.[66] Thus, by the time the second wave began arriving in 1978, Southeast Asian refugees, particularly the Vietnamese, were no longer as widely dispersed as they had been under the original plan. And the secondary migration of the first wave affected the initial dispersion of the second because newcomers were placed near those with whom they had close ties.[67] Housing shortages, perceived job competition, and high welfare dependency became associated with many of these resettlement areas, only fueling hostility and resentment.

By the late 1970's the profile of Southeast Asian refugees changed as more Chinese ethnics began entering Malaysia to avoid mistreatment in Vietnam. And in the wake of Vietnam's invasion of Cambodia, thousands of Cambodians fled across the Thai border into refugee camps.[68] Both eventually found their way to the United States, where they arrived in much worse physical and mental condition than their predecessors.[69] Joined there by more Laotians, these newer arrivals were considerably poorer and less formally educated than those in earlier waves.[70] Experienced observers maintained that they constituted the "largest nonwhite, non-Western, non-English-speaking group of people ever to enter the country at one time."[71] Their influx emphasized the need to overhaul refugee resettlement policy.

In response the 1980 Refugee Act created the Office of the Coordinator for Refugee Affairs. Charged with organizing a resettlement program and establishing permanent relocation guidelines, it determined that exclusive reliance on volunteer associations and the private sector was inadequate.[72] It attempted to standardize resettlement programs through thoughtful planning directed at controlling the social forces driving mass resettlement.

The new administrators revised earlier policies. Though widespread dispersal remained the goal, more care was used in selecting sites.[73] Job opportunities, housing availability, viable voluntary organizations, service providers, and the existence of refugee populations at various sites all were considered. Consultation with local officials became standard practice.[74] Although it emphasized social assimilation and avoiding additional economic pressures, the office's relatively more studied approach gave greater weight to the refugee communities themselves.[75]

The official policy on ghettoization changed too. Administrators now acknowledged that "ethnic coalescence is not only a fact of life, but that it can [provide] a beneficial [support system] as long as clusters are not so large that they overburden local services."[76] This change in orientation was reflected in the 1981 Khmer Cluster Project. When the project began, Cambodian refugees were entering in substantial numbers for the first time. Unlike second-wave Vietnamese and some Laotians, they had no relatives drawing them to particular areas.[77] The project placed about 8,500 of these so-called free cases in clusters of from 300 to 1,300 in twelve sites located in ten states chosen for their capacity to absorb refugees.[78]

Despite the project's efforts, secondary migrations continued, especially among Hmong refugees. Sometimes entire communities relocated in response to suggestions by their leaders.[79] Between 1980 and 1986, for example, 30,000 Hmong migrated to Fresno in the Central Valley agricultural area of California.[80] In response the federal government experimented with financial incentives designed to attract refugees to appointed locations. Referred to as Planned Secondary Resettlement, the program was intended to encourage refugees to move from California to Phoenix where there are fewer refugees, more jobs, and perhaps a more hospitable environment.[81] So far the program has not generated much interest.[82]

Bureaucrats and politicians continue to hope that establishing community-based employment and social ties will eventually create patterns of internal migration for refugees that are more dispersed. Now, however, California remains the most popular destination for new arrivals and secondary migrants.[83] Although less than 25 percent of the refugee population is placed in California at first, an estimated 40 percent of the Southeast Asian population now resides there.[84] Perhaps because of government influence, secondary migration to California has decreased since 1983, and more Southeast Asians have begun moving to Texas, Washington, Massachusetts, and Minnesota.[85]

# The Effect of Refugee Policies on the Vietnamese Community's Demographics

## Geographic Distribution and Residential Patterns

The government's initial resettlement plans have failed largely because the Vietnamese were dissatisfied with them. The community has become widely dispersed.[86] By 1990, 54.3 percent resided in the West, but 27.4 percent were in the South, 9.8 percent in the Northeast, and 8.5 percent in the Midwest. More of them lived in the South and Midwest than Filipinos and Japanese.[87] About 45.6 percent of the entire community is found in California and 11.3 percent in Texas. It has also spread to Virginia (3.4 percent), Washington (3 percent), Louisiana (2.9 percent), and Pennsylvania (2.6 percent).[88]

Sponsorship requirements and the location of holding centers have contributed markedly to the geographic dispersion of Vietnamese Americans. Each refugee had to have a sponsor, and the sponsors were located near holding centers.[89] California, for example, is the home of Travis Air Force Base, where Vietnamese were first flown,[90] and Camp Pendleton, the nation's first and largest holding center.[91] Pennsylvania is the site of Fort Indiantown Gap, a holding center near Harrisburg that opened in 1975.[92] Refugees passing through these points were likely to remain in these states where they could most easily find sponsorships.[93]

### Urbanization

Despite the government's efforts to relocate significant numbers of Vietnamese in rural areas, 1980 figures reveal that approximately 92 percent resided in metropolitan areas.[94] Job opportunities and the availability of sponsors contributed to this trend, but there were sponsors and jobs in rural areas as well. At least as important was the compelling need to form enclaves that might provide security and emotional support.

There were large concentrations of Vietnamese by 1980 in Los Angeles–Long Beach–Anaheim and San Francisco–Oakland–San Jose.[95] Four years later, half of California's Southeast Asian refugees lived in Los Angeles and Orange counties.[96]

### Ghettoization

The goal of preventing ethnic enclaves ignored the dynamics of Vietnamese culture and perhaps even basic psychology. The need for ethnically based social, cultural, and economic support among refugees was either seriously misjudged or coldly ignored. Enclaves established earlier by Chinese, Filipino, and Japanese immigrants played key roles in easing their adjustment to American society. The need for a stable support system may be even more crucial for Southeast Asians, whose experience has been profoundly unsettling. Politically persecuted, unexpectedly driven from their homes, their hopes dashed, these refugees not surprisingly turned to the past for sustenance.[97]

In doing so, they turned to each other, and despite numerous obstacles have been remarkably successful in developing their own communities. They have, for example, transformed San Francisco's red-light district near Union Square into a bustling hub of Vietnamese hotels, residences, and small businesses.[98] Vietnamese Americans have likewise helped to develop a "booming" wholesale district out of Skid Row in Los Angeles and altered the downtown areas of San Jose and Santa Ana, California, as well as a section of the Washington, D.C., suburb of Arlington, Virginia.[99]

## Population, Age, and Gender

The rapid growth of the Vietnamese population has made it an important part of Asian America. The 614,547 Vietnamese in the United States in 1990 were 8.4 percent of the Asian and Pacific Islander population and sixth among Asian groups. This is remarkable since they did not begin entering the country in significant numbers until 1975. The Chinese, with almost a hundred-year head start, were 22.6 percent of the Asian American population.[100]

The current size of the Vietnamese American community is due almost exclusively to refugee admissions, though some Vietnamese immigration occurred after the 1965 amendments. Of the 18,000 who immigrated by 1974, many were the spouses of American businessmen and military personnel who had been stationed in Vietnam. But a dramatic upsurge in new arrivals began after 1975, with 125,000 admitted immediately after the troops pulled out. By 1980 more than 400,000 additional refugees were welcomed from Vietnam, Laos, and Cambodia,[101] approximately 90 percent of whom were from Vietnam.[102]

Although the 1980 Refugee Act established new controls, the flow of refugees continued due to persistent humanitarian pressure on the United States. After a second, sizable wave entered in 1980, the flow of new entries declined steadily. In 1984, 40,604 Vietnamese refugees entered, then the average dropped to about 22,000 until 1988 when 17,626 were admitted.[103] So by 1988, 540,700 Vietnamese refugees had arrived. By October 1991, 18,280 Amerasians (mostly from Vietnam) arrived along with another 44,071 relatives. Eventually as many 80,000 to 100,000 Amerasians and their relatives may enter.[104]

As a result, over 90 percent of the Vietnamese population is foreign-born, the highest percentage of all Asian American groups.[105] The overwhelming majority fled Vietnam after, and indeed because of, the war and have been admitted as refugees.

Following the pattern set by other Asian Americans, small but increasing numbers of Vietnamese are entering in family reunification categories. In order to take full advantage of these categories, U.S. citizenship is required,[106] and most Vietnamese have been residents long enough to qualify.[107] Some do so to demonstrate allegiance; others recognize that, as citizens, they may petition for more relatives. Though about 38 percent of the first wave of Vietnamese was naturalized between 1975 and 1984,[108] the rate for the second wave is significantly lower.[109] In 1983 roughly 3,300 entered in the family categories, but by 1988 more than 4,000 had.[110] Approximately 90,000 have been admitted in nonrefugee categories since the early 1950's.[111] These figures do not approach those of the other large Asian American communities for family category admissions (with the exception of the Japanese).

Nonrefugee admission is likely to remain low because in the absence of normal diplomatic ties between the United States and Vietnam, Vietnamese nationals attempting to obtain exit permits face tremendous difficulties.[112] After an immigration petition is filed by a resident on behalf of a relative in Vietnam, the Vietnamese government must approve it. In 1984 only 3,700 immigrants were allowed under the so-called Orderly Departure Program. More than half a million cases are currently backlogged.[113] As a result, sizable growth of the Vietnamese American community exclusively through existing nonrefugee categories is unlikely.[114]

Refugee policies also affect age and gender in Vietnamese America. In 1980 the median age was 21.5, significantly lower than that of both the general population and of other Asian American groups.[115] Refugees tend to be young because older people have been less likely to flee in times of crisis.[116] The median age for Vietnamese refugees who entered in 1984 and 1986 was about 20,[117] but recent births in the United States distort this figure. By 1980 about 10 percent of the Vietnamese American community was under age 5, of whom more than 61 percent were American-born.[118]

In 1980 there were 108.5 Vietnamese men per 100 Vietnamese women, compared to 94.5 per 100 in the general population.[119] This ratio is not as skewed as similar ones for initial waves of Filipinos and Chinese, who were much more male-dominated. The refugee policy that enabled Vietnamese to enter after 1975 under unique circumstances contributed to greater balance. Rather than fleeing individually, those departing Vietnam have done their best to keep their families intact.[120] Roughly 45 percent of recent arrivals are women.[121]

## Careers and Socioeconomic Status

The different profiles of early and later entrants influenced the quality of refugee life in the United States. The first wave was relatively well educated, proficient in English, and experienced in urban living. Though they accepted initial resettlement assistance, these refugees worked aggressively to minimize their subsequent reliance on government benefits.[122] What federal funds they did accept, they used to achieve professional status and create thriving businesses.[123]

The second wave, however, was much poorer and less educated and typically did not possess the skills needed for employment in a technologically complex society. Nor did they have the advantage of government programs designed to assist them with these problems.[124] Many have benefited from the solidarity generated within ethnic enclaves. Some, for example, despite having no established credit and no ability to procure loans from major financial institutions, have managed to start small businesses with money borrowed from friends.[125] Along with first-wave entrants, they help account for the fact that Vietnamese-owned businesses had the highest growth rate from 1982 to 1987—415 percent.[126] In general, though, the second wave has remained trapped in low-status, service sector jobs.

The 1980 census revealed that 13.3 percent of all Vietnamese Americans held professional, managerial, or executive positions; more than 55 percent had blue-collar jobs; and more than 15 percent were service workers.[127] Comparable figures for white Americans were 24 percent, 44 percent, and 12 percent, respectively.[128] These statistics probably do not accurately capture the occupational profile of contemporary Vietnamese America. The community grew by almost 135 percent between 1980 and 1990 alone.[129] Many of the newcomers were poorer, less well-educated refugees unqualified for high-status jobs.

Precise, up-to-date occupational data on Vietnamese Americans are not available. The Office of Refugee Resettlement, however, provides an annual report on the entire Southeast Asian refugee community that supplies some specific information. The proportion of Southeast Asians who hold professional or managerial jobs, for example, fell, so that by 1987 only 2.6 percent were so employed. At the same time the proportion of service workers rose to 22.3 percent and blue-collar workers had increased to about 58 percent. Unemployment rates fell from 24 percent in 1982 to 16 percent in 1986. Reported rates, however, are based only on those who are working or actively seeking work. In 1986 only 41 percent of the refugee population were in these categories, compared with 65 percent in the general population.[130]

Those who have withdrawn from (or were never in) the labor market give three reasons: family demands, health problems, and enrollment in training and education programs. For those under age 25, education seems to be the principal explanation. For those between 25 and 44, family concerns were cited most often. And for those over 44, health problems appear to be preeminent.[131] The lack of English proficiency is relevant, but less so than in the early 1980's, in part because of more job opportunities in ethnic enclaves where a command of English is not required.

The exact proportion of Vietnamese Americans who currently receive public assistance is unavailable. In 1980, 28.1 percent of their households did so, compared to 10 percent of Filipinos, the next highest

Asian group, and 6 percent of white households.[132] Nationwide, 64 percent of all Southeast Asian households headed by refugees arriving after 1980 are on public assistance, three times the rate of African Americans and four times that of Latinos.[133]

Not surprisingly, the Vietnamese have been accused of having developed a welfare mentality, and the government has responded in knee-jerk fashion. Their relatively low rate of labor-force participation has in fact led many Vietnamese refugees to depend on government assistance.[134] Many attribute this dependency to a welfare system that purportedly creates disincentives to work.[135] Policymakers have urged state and local resettlement agencies to expeditiously assist refugees with job placement.[136] Under the 1980 Refugee Act, refugees were given 36-month stipends of special refugee cash, medical assistance programs, and other support services.[137] But in 1982 amendments to the act reduced the stipends to 18 months to pressure refugees to become economically independent more quickly.[138] These changes came during the entry of the poorer, less-educated, and more devastated second wave. After 1982 most programs stressed employment-enhancing services such as vocational, English-language, and job-development training.[139] Most refugees are unable to acquire the skills that would qualify them for anything other than minimum wage jobs in 18 months. They were nonetheless constrained to take these positions in the absence of continued public assistance.[140]

Restrictions on federal assistance thus help to account for increased Vietnamese American concentration in entry-level, minimum wage jobs requiring little formal education or mastery of English.[141] For many refugees, in fact, these types of jobs and the poverty that results are unavoidable.[142] Indeed, figures show that in 1979, a striking 35.1 percent of Vietnamese families were living below the poverty level.[143] And by 1985 an astonishing 50 percent of all Southeast Asian refugees were.[144]

While the average Chinese, Filipino, and Korean American worker earns less than a white American, Vietnamese workers earn even less. In 1979 a full-time Vietnamese worker earned $11,640, compared with $15,570 for a white American worker.[145] Vietnamese women ($9,260) earned far less than men ($13,080).[146] Recent figures do, however, suggest that refugee families at the lowest socioeconomic levels are slowly advancing as more family members enter the labor market. Partly as a result of a decline in unemployment, income figures have increased for those who entered between 1975 and 1979.[147] More Southeast Asian households are becoming self-sufficient, with the number of wage earners per household increasing steadily. Because there are no recent income statistics, these trends may not reflect what those who entered after 1980 earn. What is known is that income among Vietnamese refugees remains below the national average.[148]

## Conclusion

The Vietnamese American community has been shaped by complicated, sometimes contradictory, self-serving and humanitarian foreign policy objectives, which create and reflect a close and controversial relationship between refugee and immigration laws and policies. Each scheme has been used strategically to control the size, location, and livelihood of the Vietnamese community, sometimes creating discernible tensions.

Because of the political schemes applied to Vietnamese refugee admissions since 1975, Vietnamese Americans have suddenly grown faster than any other Asian American group. By 2000 their population will surpass that of the Japanese American community, which had been the largest group for the first 70 years of this century. And the vast majority of the community will continue to be refugees.

Refugee policies have shaped other aspects of the Vietnamese American community. In spite of massive self-relocation the government's resettlement plans influenced its geographic distribution. Many Vietnamese and other Southeast Asian refugees have continued to reside where they first settled. Those who rejected the government's plans through secondary migration reconfirmed that residential enclaves were necessary for certain entrants who need emotional, economic, and cultural support. Over 90 percent live in urban areas. Much of the community is poor or relies on public assistance, and over 80 percent of those who do work are service or blue-collar workers because of limitations on job training and other programs.

The community remains strictly controlled by governmental policies. Refugee quotas have been reduced in recent years, and regulations continue to be applied once refugees have been admitted. In short, attempts at monitoring and regulating where Vietnamese live, what jobs are available to them, and other aspects of their lives continue to be oppressive.

# Immigration Policy and Asian American Life: Educational Performance, Political Participation, and Identity

We have seen how immigration policy and law, both before and after key 1965 reforms, helped make Asian America a mosaic of diverse communities. But these demographics, which have been ignored even by those policymakers, print and broadcast journalists, organizers, and activists who are most influential in how we all regard Asian Americans, raise other questions. Couldn't demographics reflect and condition Asian American life by helping to define the possibilities and limits of social action, though not always in obvious, direct, or simple fashion?

Two aspects of Asian American life—education and political participation—have been a principal focus of academics and others whose commentaries and analyses have helped to develop and sustain popular images. A third aspect—identity—attracts Asian Americans themselves, particularly activists. Yet observers and activists have not demonstrated a command of even basic demographics, much less a sense of how demographics have been influenced by immigration policies and might influence educational, political, and personal behavior and attitudes.

The typical images that invite our attention and scrutiny are that Asian American students are hardworking, intelligent students who value education and do well in school; that Asian Americans are not involved in politics; and that they are forming or are capable of forming a new identity. But given what we now know about the development of Asian America, aren't some of the premises behind these images suspect?

Consider diversity. Can it really be said that all Asian American students are smart or get good grades? Could the patchwork society of Asian America have something to do with a perceived lack of political involvement? Is it not difficult to imagine a unified identity given the assortment of backgrounds and cultures of Asian immigrants?

It seems plausible, for example, that the history of discrimination against Asian Americans could influence political participation and possibly even academic performance. Demographic changes brought about by the 1965 amendments would seem to have a tangible impact on identity and political life. Economic and immigrant status affect political participation as well.

My purpose here is to begin unraveling how immigration policies may ultimately influence attitudes and behaviors relating to education, political participation, and identity. We can begin by examining the assumptions underlying what many have come to believe about Asian American life.

## Educational Achievement

### The Popular Image of Asian American Educational Achievement

Particularly over the last decade or so, Asian American students have been portrayed as whiz kids, especially in math, science, and other technical fields. Magazines and newspapers routinely inform us of Asian American academic superstars who win national science contests and make up a large percentage of freshman classes at prestigious schools.[1] To some the notion that this image dominates seems implausible because they intuitively distinguish between Chinese, Japanese, Koreans, and the rest of Asian America. At the very least, they seem to believe that such stereotypes are more facilely perpetuated by the media than unquestioningly embraced by the public at large. Yet there is ample proof that this image is shared, informed, and reinforced by intellectuals, policymakers, and university admissions officers, who are quoted by the popular media and whose op-ed pieces appear in the *New York Times.*[2]

The history of these views reveals interesting dichotomies. Early Chinese, Japanese, Korean, Asian Indian, and Filipino settlers were uniformly regarded as diligent and industrious workers. Yet they came to be regarded as unassimilable. Chinese were thought to cling tenaciously to old customs and recalcitrantly oppose progress and moral improvement.[3] After all, in the words of a U.S. senator (speaking in support of efforts to exclude "Hindoos and all persons of the Mongolian or yellow race, the Malay or brown race, the African or black race"), "God Almighty Himself hates the hybrid."[4] They were either incapable of understanding our democratic principles,[5] or they "retained the habits and customs of their own country . . . without any interest in our country or its institutions."[6] The belief that Asian immigrants could not assimilate is ironic given today's image of exceptional academic performance, since seeking an education is consistent with conventional notions of assimilation. During World War II Americans regarded both Japanese and Chinese as "hardworking and intelligent." But Chinese were also characterized as "honest, brave, and religious," while Japanese were "treacherous, sly, cruel, and warlike."[7]

The popularity and persuasiveness of the current academic stereotype are hardly surprising given the types of reports and statistics readily disseminated by educational commissions, testing services, and some school districts. For example, the Department of Education reports that Asian American high school students get A's more often and fail less than whites or any other racial groups in subjects ranging from English to art.[8] The American Council on Education notes that "levels of educational attainment and income for Asian Americans are comparable to those for whites, and sometimes exceed them . . . offer[ing] valuable lessons as the nation seeks ways to promote minority advancement."[9] The Achievement Council cites that only 5.8 percent of Asian high school graduates had cumulative grade point averages (GPAs) below 2.0 compared to 14.1 percent of white graduates.[10]

Statistics reveal, moreover, that while Asian Americans are less than 3 percent of the population, they are 9 to 25 percent of the entering classes at Harvard, Stanford, MIT, the University of California at Berkeley, Princeton, and Cal Tech.[11] In fact, a larger percentage of Asian Americans graduate from high school and college than in the general population,[12] they earn the highest Scholastic Aptitude Test scores in math,[13] dominate the annual Westinghouse Science Talent Search,[14] and boast an inordinate number of engineers and medical professionals.[15] With regard to every aspect of education typically treated as a measure of success—years of schooling, grades, performance on standardized tests, and fields of study—Asian Americans must be seen as doing quite well.

Among those who promote the popular image, including some scholars, Asian American academic achievement is routinely attributed to a culturally grounded "achievement syndrome." Asian Americans are regarded as a racial group with a "particular orientation to achievement, like Jews."[16] A high regard for education is presumably "a characteristic of the [Asian] culture."[17] Children are endowed with "an underlying devotion to scholarship,"[18] largely because they have the advantage of stable families and Asian mothers who rear them for success.[19]

Major consequences flow from this popular image. Those in the so-called mainstream, other people of color, and Asian Americans themselves have grown to accept this image without questioning. And those who make significant decisions act on these understandings without knowing more. Elementary and secondary teachers and administrators, too often expecting all Asian American students to do well, make placements, design homework, and provide feedback with this image in mind.[20] University and college administrators, presuming that Asian Americans are performing at an unusually high level, see little reason to include Asian Americans in affirmative action programs and feel the need to place limits on their admissions.[21] Academics and grantmakers, accepting uncritically evidence of and explanations for high academic achievement among Asian Americans, frame and respond to grant proposals that focus almost exclusively on successes and their cultural antecedents.[22] Fellow students, believing that Asian Americans are incomparably intelligent and hardworking, both resent and admire them for their perceived talent and diligence.[23]

Yet for all the seeming persuasiveness of these related views, what we now know about the making and remaking of Asian American communities casts doubt on the accuracy of the popular image. Should we simply presume that the educational experiences of Korean American students are identical to those of Filipinos or Taiwanese? Are economically advantaged Korean and Asian Indian children better able to perform academically than less-advantaged Vietnamese refugees? Do children from the economically bifurcated Chinese American community perform differently? What differences, if any, are there between Asians who live in residential enclaves and those who do not? Did those who entered before and after the 1965 immigration law reforms perform similarly? In fact, what we know about the growth and diversity of Asian America suggests the need to explore these possible variations in academic performance across ethnicities, classes, and cohorts.

## How Well Does the Popular Image Hold Up?

Several scholars have begun to carefully examine Asian American academic performance, believing that Asian Americans cannot be treated generically. Some explore differences between ethnic groups; others stress gender, class, or generational differences. Some assume that the 1965 immigration law reforms were an important turning point; others do not. Some consider the significance of residential patterns; others disregard them.

Researchers have also begun to abandon the exclusive reliance on cultural factors in explaining educational performance. Some examine more carefully the relationship between academic performance and family structure. They appreciate that these relationships may vary across groups, classes, and cohorts. Others remind us that family structure and dynamics may only be part of the story. They underscore the importance of economics and class as determinants of educational performance.

For all its strengths this newly critical research frequently lapses into imprecise thinking. Those who concentrate on family life, for example, rely on vaguely defined concepts. Those who stress class sometimes overstate Asian American economic advantage and discount the accomplishments of the economically disadvantaged. In fact, this research often fails to escape the premises underlying the popular image. Nor does it take advantage of what we now know about the effects of immigration law and policy nor provide a useful synthesis of relevant findings. Perhaps most important, this work has failed to penetrate the public consciousness, possibly through no fault of the authors. Most studies remain unpublished and are typically available only through specialized research services as dissertations and conference papers.[24]

*The myth of exclusive Asian American concentration in math, science, and technical fields and uniformly high academic achievement*

Limited available evidence contradicts the popular notion that most Asian American students specialize in math, science, and technical fields. In a 1984–85 survey of college and university students, Asian Americans, like all other groups, made business and management their first choice as a major.[25] Of those who did not, a majority were more likely to choose engineering, physical sciences, mathematics, and computer science than the humanities and social sciences.[26] In this regard they did differ from their non-Asian counterparts. But the same survey revealed that the choice of majors for Asian Americans was as varied as for other ethnic groups.[27]

The evidence fails to sustain an even more central tenet of the popular image—the idea that Asian Americans generally outperform non-Asians. It is true that Asian Americans score the highest of all groups on the math section of the Scholastic Aptitude Test. Their verbal scores, however, are lower than those of whites.[28] Likewise, Asian American high school students score above the norm in math on the California Assessment Program achievement test. Yet they score at or below the norm in reading and writing.[29] This pattern perhaps explains why 54 percent of Asian American freshmen in 1986 compared to 37 percent of all freshmen at UC Berkeley were required to take "bonehead English,"[30] further undermining the image of the all-around whiz kid.

Even the image of the math and science superstar may be apocryphal. Asian American math abilities as high school students may carry over to college and university, where their mean grades in math, science, and related fields may be higher than those of non-Asians. Still, this tells us little about how Asian American math and science majors do compared with their non-Asian counterparts. There are, to be sure, increasing numbers of Asian Americans—some of whom are highly visible—whose accomplishments in these fields are noteworthy.[31] But these successes may owe more to the absolute number of Asian Americans in these fields than to any peculiar Asian American genius for math and science.

If those operating in the popular image pay too little attention to what we know and don't know about standard measures of Asian American performance, they ignore altogether other aspects of educational experience that bear on academic achievement. A growing number of Asian American students, for example, drop out or become discipline problems. Their dropout rates are currently lower than for whites, but they are increasing.[32] Reported increases in truancy and suspension rates contrast with declining rates among whites.[33]

Those advancing the popular image compound their difficulties by failing to contemplate possible differences in academic performances between ethnic groups. The popular image makes much of enrollment figures for Asian Americans. Data from the 1980 census, for instance, do support the popular claim that Asian Americans see education as a way of realizing their aspirations. Compared with whites, African Americans, and Latinos, each of the six largest groups included discernibly higher percentages of enrolled students among those aged 20–24. But closer attention reveals that Filipinos (27.1 percent) were enrolled at significantly lower rates than Koreans (40.1 percent), Vietnamese (41.8 percent), Asian Indians (44.5 percent), and Japanese (48 percent). And a striking 59.8 percent of college-aged Chinese Americans were attending school when surveyed.[34]

As a group Asian Americans do have proportionately more high school graduates than the general population, but the proportion without a high school degree is about the same as Latinos and the numbers also vary widely from group to group.[35] Compared to whites, for example, a significantly higher percentage of Japanese Americans and a slightly higher percentage of Asian Indians are high school graduates. For Korean Americans, the percentage is about the same. But the percentages for Chinese, Filipino, and Vietnamese Americans are lower than for whites.[36]

Paying attention to particular ethnic groups also casts doubt on popular ideas about high grade point averages. Those few studies that have broken down GPA information by group reveal important differences. A 1988 review of Hawaiian high school students, for example, reported that Koreans (3.56), Japanese (3.26), and Chinese (3.21) had higher GPAs than whites (3.18), while the GPAs for Filipinos (3.10), Native Hawaiians (2.88), and Samoans (2.59) were lower.[37] In San Diego in 1987, 34.6 percent of all white high school students had GPAs above 3.0.[38] The figures were, however, substantially higher for a combined grouping of Japanese, Chinese, and Koreans (52.1 percent), and for Vietnamese (53.7 percent). The percentages for Filipinos (38.3) and Hmong (40.4) were also higher than, but closer to, those for whites.[39] On the other hand, the totals for Laotians (32.8 percent), Samoans and Guamanians (24.2 percent), and Cambodians (20 percent) were all lower.[40]

Variance is also apparent in the reading and writing scores on the

California Assessment Program achievement test. Though all Asian-fluent, English-proficient students whose primary language is not English scored near or below the norm of 50, noticeable differences between groups were uncovered: Chinese—reading 38.3, writing 50; Filipinos—reading 37.9, writing 45.2; Japanese—reading 45.4, writing 54.2; Korean—reading, 41.1, writing 53.0; Southeast Asians—reading 28.5, writing 34.2. And although all groups scored above the norm in math, marked differences were detected here as well: Chinese (71.2), Japanese (72.1), Koreans (74.9), Filipinos (53.3); and Southeast Asians (56.9).[41]

Just as the popular image downplays differences between groups, it pays little attention to variations in academic performance within each community. A Chicago cohort analysis revealed that third-generation Asian American students have lower grades than immigrant children.[42] But researchers reported in a similar San Francisco Bay Area study that only grades for Filipinos decreased from the first to the second generation, while those for Koreans and Chinese remained the same. And grades for Japanese American students actually increased across generations.[43] Other researchers, focusing on residential patterns, found that Japanese who moved away from ethnic enclaves attained higher educational levels than those who remained.[44] Others have discovered that within particular groups educational performance may vary by gender and class.[45]

Differences in preferred fields of study within groups have also surfaced, though the data are limited. Chinese Americans born in the United States, for instance, were, according to one study, more likely to major in social sciences than those born elsewhere.[46] A 1985 survey of Chinese American students at the City University of New York revealed that most were enrolled in science and technical fields. At the same time, an unusually high number of students from Chinatown were majoring in accounting and business.[47] Other studies document differences along gender lines. For example, Chinese American men were more likely than women to major in engineering and were less likely to select the humanities.[48]

In failing to apprehend differences within groups, the popular image perhaps most notably overlooks the effects of the 1965 amendments. Much is made of the current median number of years of schooling for all Asian Americans. This figure is implicitly contrasted with the corresponding figure for whites, leading all to believe that this contrast says a great deal about what Asian Americans have achieved.[49] This view fails to appreciate, however, that the current median number of years of schooling for all Asian Americans largely reflects the profile of a foreign-born population educated abroad. It ignores that this profile changed dramatically after 1965.[50]

Consider some of the available data. In 1960 foreign-born Chinese adult men (25 years and older) had a mean of 8.1 years of schooling; by 1980 the figure was 14.3.[51] The 1960 figure for foreign-born Filipino men was 7.0, and it was 13.5 by 1980.[52] In 1960 the figure for foreign-born Japanese men was 10.3, and it was 14.8 in 1980.[53] For foreign-born Asian Indians, the figures were 3.4 in 1940 and 16 in 1980.[54] Though the median level of education for each of these groups and for all Asian Americans went from below to above the median level for white Americans over these years, this says more about what immigrants brought with them than what they have done here.[55]

### The failure of cultural and economic explanations

Popular explanations for Asian American academic success are straight-forward. Asian Americans place a high value on education and adopt parenting styles that are conducive to high achievement. Their children are presumably instilled with a great desire to succeed and a work ethic that serves them well academically. They are frequently described as being "similar to the Jewish immigrants of the 1930's with their empha-sis on learning and the family and the sheer energy they get from their opportunity in America."[56]

The family is featured prominently in these explanations. Asian Americans, the argument goes, have supportive, selfless, stable, and enduring families that emphasize the development of children.[57] This family-centered life-style is thought to strengthen academic perfor-mance because youngsters are kept at home when not in school, and older siblings take the place of playmates, role models, and tutors.[58] And cultural values inspire students to "bring honor" to the family by suc-ceeding in school.[59] Such family-centeredness is presumed to exist not only among early generations of Asian American immigrants, but also among more recent Southeast Asian refugees because of the value they "attach to self-discipline and respect for elders."[60] In weaving together these themes, one observer notes that the "major factor in [Asian American] educational" achievement centers on family structure and value systems.[61]

There are obvious reasons to doubt these accounts. Is it really possible that a common cultural heritage could explain academic performance? Given the diversity of Asian American origins and experiences, could their socialization uniformly instill an ability and inclination to persevere and do well? Can achievement actually be attributed to a distinctively stable and focused family structure? Cultural explanations at the very least require the sort of uniformity in performance that the evidence belies. In the absence of such uniformity, must we assume that those who perform less ably are somehow less Asian?[62]

However obvious the difficulties with these and related explanations, many researchers (and not just those who readily accept and reinforce the popular image) apparently remain convinced of the potential of the cultural paradigm. They fail to question the categories that define the analytical scheme. They believe that the critical inheritance is not genes or economic circumstance, but cultural resources. They treat the idea of culture as a knowable bundle of traits that can confidently be identified and passed from one generation to another. And they believe that these transferable cultural resources can to some significant degree be parlayed easily into academic advantages.[63]

Indeed, much of this work especially emphasizes its reliance on the cultural paradigm. One careful survey of what Asian Americans study in colleges and postgraduate work was based on the idea that they had attained "high academic achievement" both because of "their high expectation of education [and] great emphasis on learning," and because "Asian Americans value greatly . . . educational opportunity."[64] Another researcher, in criticizing and attempting to discourage the backlash against Asian Americans on college campuses, calls for a recognition that their achievement is not the product of ability but the result of "cultural factors" such as diligence and family sacrifices.[65] Others searching for clues from Indochinese students to help all U.S. students sense that "it is possible to identify culturally compatible values, behaviors and strategies for success that might enhance scholastic achievement."[66]

None of this is to say that, taken together, the best scholars operating within the cultural paradigm have not helped to focus attention on certain realities of Asian American family life. For the first time they have begun examining family structure and interaction in detail. They seem to appreciate that the families do not conform to any generic vision of domestic life in the United States, much less to some fanciful

Bill Cosby television family world. They seem in search of something beyond the hackneyed explanations. The problem we can see after a review of the immigration history and a brief look at demographic factors is that because there are so many distinctive Asian American experiences, a single theory cannot address them all without oversimplifying their answers and negating the uniqueness of each community.

These researchers have discovered that in most Asian American families both parents work, often to support themselves and their children. Many have limited opportunity to learn English. Parents are by and large unable to track progress in school, in part because they do not understand a report card or have time to participate in organizations like the PTA.[67] Children frequently must act for them as interpreters and conduits to the outside world and often become caught up in traditional family responsibilities. They hassle with landlords, arrange for medical care, deal with the legal system, and otherwise assume adult obligations.[68] Some, like those young Southeast Asians who live without their parents,[69] really must be adults before their time. This added tension and responsibility can detract from concentration and study time and increase the possibility of dropping out.[70]

For all their sensitivity to these special qualities and details, researchers using a cultural paradigm either continue to stress vaguely defined notions of family stability or never square what we know about educational performance with their otherwise carefully constructed typologies of socialization. They rarely clarify to whom, if anyone, they are comparing the so-called prototypical Asian American family. Even when they sensibly begin to disentangle the complicated relationship between parenting and educational achievement, their efforts remain muddled if not utterly contradictory, often failing to examine their own assumptions. For example they imply that certain parenting styles must be strongly related to high academic achievement.[71] Yet they never explain, much less address, how the penchant for "authoritarian" parenting among first-generation Asian Americans is with every other group typically linked to poor academic performance.[72] Nor do they tell us how to think about those families where parental pressure has contributed to the student's decision to drop out[73] or even to contemplate suicide.[74]

Perhaps most tellingly, these researchers never force themselves to examine what it might mean to insist that Asian Americans value education. One can value education and still reject the relevance of school. Many Vietnamese in San Diego and Orange County high schools graduate at the top of their classes, whereas Vietnamese in the same schools have the highest truancy and dropout rates among Asians.[75] Must we assume that Vietnamese dropouts, truants, and those in Seattle who were measured as showing the lowest effort among Asian Americans do not value education?[76] Hmong and Cambodian parents have had very little formal schooling. Yet Hmong refugee students are getting good grades while Cambodians and other second-wave refugees score below the average.[77] Does this mean that Hmong parents value education, but Cambodian parents do not? Do any of these results vary under a first-wave versus second-wave cohort analysis?

Some scholars have noticed that the popular conception of Asian Americans in education is oversimplified. Without knowing much in detail about the demographic data, they sense that the communities are simply too diverse to be understood as a monolithic culture. These scholars claim not to discount the impact of culture, but their position suggests otherwise. They insist that "cultural factors have little independent effect on educational outcomes, [and] are influential only as they interact with class factors."[78] But, in the final analysis, they offer their own "simple truth: that what is inherited is not genes, and not culture, but class advantage and disadvantage."[79] Asian Americans should be expected to perform well, say these scholars, since large segments of their communities are educated and prosperous, reflecting in part that the 1965 immigration amendments allowed "only highly selected Asians . . . who very often had [superior] educational qualifications."[80]

While the impulse to look beyond family structure, attitudes, and values makes sense, merely substituting economic for cultural explanations is too simple. Class-based explanations are premised on exaggerated claims about the degree to which the post-1965 influx of Asians overwhelmingly, if not exclusively, involved economically privileged immigrants. They are based upon the mistaken notions that academic successes were rare before 1965, and that the vast majority since then owes exclusively to economic advantage. In fact, we now know based on demographic data that pre- and post-1965 immigrant communities have been highly stratified. There is, moreover, certainly evidence of academic successes before 1965[81] and after among those who can hardly be characterized as privileged.[82]

*The need for new ways of understanding Asian Americans
and education*

The precise meaning of Asian American educational achievement remains elusive. Though scholars, commentators, and educators presume its importance, the concept is almost never analyzed. Some think achievement is unambiguously correlated with personal fulfillment and economic, social, and political power.[83] Those who are more skeptical think it potentially reflects some illiberal narrowness.[84] For others achievement seems to represent nothing but escapist, careerist ambitions.[85] Its vague and shifting meanings seem uniformly linked to visions of the good life in the United States.

The myth of uniformly successful students who concentrate in math and science and whose accomplishments owe entirely to traditional values passed on through unusually stable families obviously needs revision, as do those hypotheses based on economic advantage. Some scholars have started paying closer attention to performance differences between and within various groups.[86] Others have begun to observe and speculate about the interaction of cultural and class factors to explain variations in achievement.[87]

One set of scholars argues that Asian Americans have a history of adapting to high-demand economic "niches."[88] In their view earlier Asian Americans did "poorly" because they were "fitted into niches reserved for low-paying undemanding jobs." Today they are meeting the need for the "mathematically inclined" and are doing much better. Though theirs might be an interesting hypothesis, these scholars retreat to a rather conventional explanation for performance linked to culture and family, thereby reiterating the popular image.[89]

Whatever their strengths and weaknesses, these newer studies stop short of rethinking educational achievement. They continue to abide by familiar, if undissected, definitions of achievement in documenting and explaining what can be observed. Yet their findings suggest the need to explore new ways of understanding the meaning and place of educational achievement in the lives of Asian Americans. Necessarily related to identity and community, educational achievement is ethnically specific and conditioned by age, class, and gender, and sophisticated accounts of educational achievement would seem best framed in these terms.

We must begin to appreciate the multifaceted, perhaps even contradictory, significance of achievement in Asian America. Is it really true, as most researchers suggest, that conventional success is the only way Asian Americans can assert themselves in a society where they might otherwise be consigned to low-status positions that presumably provide little social, political, or cultural capital? Are there not important costs associated with success, particularly when it sometimes requires suppressing certain qualities and characteristics that are central to one's identity? Can we imagine students who refuse to, or who are unable to, change in this way? What are we to make of them?

Once we begin to ask such questions, what we now know about Asian American academic achievement—who achieves at what levels and how this can be explained—might be viewed in a different light. Take, for example, the matter of language. Rather than merely being technically more difficult to master or less well suited to capabilities that are supposedly uniquely and uniformly Asian American, English implicates ethnic identity and pride in complicated ways. That some students may not master the language as quickly as they do math and that their grasp of it varies across ethnicities likely has as much to do with a sense of self as with intellectual ability.[90] Clinging to one's native language may affirm self and culture more than call for remedial treatment.

Truancies, dropouts, and fisticuffs likewise are not just indications that some Asian Americans are performing poorly in school, having difficulty adjusting, or are simply malcontents. That kind of behavior may be an attempt to cope with an adverse environment in which the dominant white culture exposes Asians to a broad range of individual and systemic racist insults. Students frequently are faced with the same overtly racist hostility and harassment earlier generations endured.[91] In a more subtle way their fellow students, faculty, and staff often compel them to deny important aspects of themselves and their cultural heritages in order to adapt and succeed. Fighting is not always a sign of mischievousness and maladjustment.

Rethinking achievement encourages us to examine students' successes as an affirmation of identity and culture. Whereas some Asian American students withdraw or lash out when faced with overt or subtle racism, others doubtless redouble their efforts to excel. Though they appear to be narrowly self-serving and accommodationist, this response may ultimately be every bit as political as other methods of individually and collectively acquiring ethnically based power and prestige. Striving is as much about racial and ethnic pride as about capitulation and narcissistic selfishness.

None of this is meant to romanticize what might genuinely be seen as discipline problems or empty academic achievements. Truancies, dropouts, and rebellious behavior present difficulties for all involved even if viewed as cultural resistance to hostile environments. And educational success does provide opportunities to escape ethnically charged conflict even if grounded in political pride and aspirations. In short, responses by Asian Americans to educational circumstances are paradoxical. What can be understood as self-affirming often can turn out to be self-defeating. Even Asian Americans, like those who attempt to study and respond to them, may well find themselves unable to get a firm grip on the nature and wisdom of any particular response. Rethinking the meaning and place of their educational achievement must proceed with this in mind.

## Political Participation

### The Popular Image of Asian American Political Participation

Until quite recently, not much attention has been paid to Asian American political participation. Yet a popular image has emerged that underscores the presumed lack of involvement by Asian Americans in political life. In 1960 Chinese Americans were considered "not politically astute or active in American politics."[92] Asian Americans outside of Hawaii in the late 1980's were described as not being "very important politically,"[93] a people whose "presence in U.S. politics remains poorly defined."[94] Nor have they been consistently associated with either liberalism or conservatism.[95]

The popular perception of political inactivity and ineffectiveness is grounded in a presumed set of cultural attributes. Asian Americans are understood to be passive, accommodating, unemotional people who keep their noses to the grindstone, are satisfied with their academic and economic achievements, and are averse to political participation.[96] These assumptions, shared and popularized by many Asian American commentators, draw on time-worn and well-rehearsed beliefs. The Chinese, for example, have long been regarded as unsuited for political participation because they were not equipped for the "highly competitive, masculine-oriented [United States] culture."[97] Like other Asian Americans, they have been both roundly praised and criticized for their lack of aggressiveness. President Nixon praised the Japanese for their civic-mindedness and law-abiding behavior, and S. I. Hayakawa lauded their "cultural value" of not being a nuisance.[98] At the same time, they have been castigated by Asian American activists for "quietly" conforming to stereotype in becoming socially and politically apathetic.[99]

The popular image drew support from widely read histories that describe the Chinese, for instance, as a "quiet, docile, nonaggressive" people who regard government as both "oppressive" and unresponsive to "concerted democratic procedure."[100] All "Oriental immigrants" were depicted as being "not politically inclined . . . from semi-feudal countries without the democratic tradition of citizen participation in public affairs."[101] Borrowing from these histories and apparently failing to recognize formal disenfranchisement as more than coincidental, media accounts regularly interpreted election results as products of these traditional customs and attitudes. If, for example, Asian Americans did not run for office or win elections in areas with significant Asian American populations, it was because they did not traditionally register or vote in significant numbers. Infrequent successes in electoral politics, often profiled in biographies of notable people, were merely the exception that proved this rule. Anecdotes captured what hard data had not yet confirmed: Asian Americans just were not much involved in electoral politics for reasons everyone pretty much understood.

The same familiar sources of confirmation for the popular image did not make much of, nor pay particular attention to, political persuasions. Asian Americans were uninterested, uninformed, and uninvolved—what we typically think of as apolitical. Taking too seriously an apolitical people's political persuasion seemed pointless. Their successful candidates included Democrats and Republicans whose platforms revealed no obvious programmatic consistency.[102] If Asian Americans were seen as having any particular ideological commitment, it was to a vague and evolving political agenda that would permit them to continue to achieve academically, do well economically, and keep to themselves.

This image is significant. Those who research voting patterns have for a long time seen little reason to gather and analyze data about phenomena they believed they already understood. Political parties typically made little effort to direct time, energy, or resources to Asian American communities whose residents they presumed were not only uninvolved but uninvolvable. They did, of course, solicit donations from major Asian American contributors, but did so with the unusual expectation that the money came with few strings attached.[103] This perhaps in part explains why they seemed routinely unafraid of repercussions from failing to provide whatever they may have promised.[104] Regularly "written out" of party agendas in this way, Asian Americans grew increasingly disenchanted and frustrated.[105] They may well have withdrawn from electoral politics in ways that can be described at once as self-affirming and self-defeating responses to the marginalization they experienced.

What we have learned about how immigration law has helped make and remake Asian American communities casts uncertainty on the validity of this popular image, just as it does on the accuracy of popular views regarding educational performance. Can Asian Americans from such different homelands all be viewed as passive and accommodationist? If so, is it plausible that these traits are easily transmitted across generations? Once in the United States, do Asian Americans all draw on some shared cultural identity that shapes their electoral involvements? Do we even know just how active each Asian American group has been? Are we satisfied, having learned that so much of the Asian American experience has been informal and unreported, that electoral affairs adequately explain their political lives? In short, there is more than good reason to press hard on the popular image.

## How Well Does the Popular Image Hold Up?

The work of some scholars who have begun to take stock of how Asian Americans act in and regard electoral politics parallels what we have learned about the force of immigration laws. For the first time some researchers have attempted to aggregate and carefully analyze data on electoral involvement. They seem to be reacting against the inattention to detail shown by earlier scholars. To their credit they appreciate both the need to explore the distinctions between groups and the importance of activities besides registering, voting, and running for office.

Other scholars have begun to question cultural explanations of putative Asian apathy. They have focused upon the pervasive discrimination Asians have encountered and their marginalization in electoral politics. Others have begun to explore the relationship between economic status and the propensity to participate. They examine the question of whether economic success leads to greater or lesser participation, and they also address the belief that Asian Americans uniformly hold high economic status. Together, these researchers have captured a degree of media attention.[106] This nascent challenge to the popular image may well be on its way to informing a newly critical view of Asian American electoral activity.

Yet these researchers cannot escape the logic of the same popular image they aim to question. For example, investigators who attempt to identify differences between Asian American groups unwittingly share with those who continue to promote the popular image the tendency to treat Asian Americans generically in certain important respects, a tendency no doubt reinforced by positivist social science.

### The myth of the apolitical character of Asian Americans

In recognizing the problems inherent in relying exclusively on anecdotal accounts and popular histories for conclusions about political participation, a handful of researchers have begun to measure data regarding Asian Americans and electoral politics. Their effort is particularly noteworthy because scholars had developed a substantial literature on the differences between African American and white participation and now pay increased attention to Latino electoral activity, but they had until recently entirely ignored Asian Americans.[107] This newly focused attention has so far produced a 1984 study in San Francisco,[108] a 1986 study in Los Angeles County,[109] and a 1984 survey of California.[110]

The San Francisco and Los Angeles County studies reported findings that seem startling. While the voter registration rate for the general population in California was about 73 percent in 1986,[111] at about the same time in San Francisco the rate for Japanese Americans was only 36.8 percent and for Chinese Americans it was 30.9 percent.[112] Similarly, in Los Angeles County Japanese had a registration rate of 43 percent, while Chinese registered at 35.5 percent. Other groups had even lower rates: 27 percent for Filipinos, 16.7 percent for Indians, 13 percent rate for Koreans, and 4.1 percent rate for Vietnamese.[113] These findings caught the attention of the popular media, no doubt because they seemed to support the popular notion that many Asian Americans able to register did not.[114]

But anyone familiar with the makeup of Asian American communities would have been skeptical about what these numbers might mean. Should it not have been suspicious that the groups reported to have the lowest voter registration rates just happen to have the highest proportion of foreign-born members? As it happens, such a suspicion would have been reasonable because neither survey distinguished between those who qualified by law to register and those who did not—they failed, in other words, to "adjust for noncitizens." This failure may not explain the low rate for the predominantly American-born Japanese Americans, but it certainly helps to account for the low registration rates for the other groups, which include high proportions of foreign-born noncitizens. And it is yet another example of studies that perpetuate traditional misconceptions by failing to factor in immigration patterns determined by law and policy.

One study that does adjust for noncitizens makes plain how important such sensitivity is to understanding Asian American participation in electoral politics. Drawing on 1984 interviews of California Latinos, African Americans, Asian Americans, and whites, it revealed registration rates that contradict both the popular image and the media's loose interpretation of the San Francisco and Los Angeles County studies. In this study, registration statistics for Asian Americans were much higher: 77 percent of California Asian American citizens were registered compared to 87 percent of the whites.[115]

This same statewide study revealed voting patterns suggesting that registered Asian Americans are as likely to vote as some registered whites. Only 69 percent of the Asians who registered voted compared to 80 percent of whites and 81 percent of African Americans.[116] When groups were viewed separately, however, Chinese were more similar to whites in their voting pattern, while Vietnamese and Koreans had the lowest voter turnouts among Asians.[117] This lends some credence to, or at least renders less implausible, unpublished surveys in San Francisco that report that on certain issues, Chinese Americans actually vote at a rate 5 to 10 percentage points above the general electorate.[118]

What we know about Asian American communities strongly suggests that economic status and income likely figure prominently in registration and voting. The San Francisco and Los Angeles County studies suggest that those areas commonly believed to have higher concentrations of middle- as opposed to lower-income residents have higher registration rates. In San Francisco, for example, the Chinese registration rate in Chinatown was 23.1 percent compared to 39.9 percent in the more middle-income Richmond district. Yet because these studies fail to distinguish between citizens and noncitizens, they leave us to wonder whether lower rates in presumably less affluent areas are the result of the proportion of foreign-born residents, economic status, or something else.

Even more careful attention to noncitizenship and economic status may not provide the explanations one would expect, however. Among whites, African Americans, and Latinos, higher socioeconomic status characteristically implies higher voter participation. But those who simply presume that the same is true of Asian Americans might be puzzled to learn, as were the scholars of the statewide survey investigating this relationship for the first time, that at least in California the generally expected correlation between economic status and electoral participation is not there.[119] Asian American political participation, unlike that of whites, African Americans, and Latinos, is not predictably influenced by levels of employment, educational attainment, and home ownership. These findings do seem to resist facile explanations, but perhaps they should not be regarded as altogether puzzling. They appear simply to reflect a possibility that is too often either never entertained or stubbornly resisted: economic circumstance may have different consequences within different ethnic communities.

If ethnic diversity makes a sensible appreciation of Asian American politics difficult, so does the fact that electoral affairs involve more than registering and voting. Understanding this, those who conducted the statewide survey considered other forms of political activity. In particular, they also inquired about contributing money, exhibiting a campaign poster or sticker, working for a party or candidate, and attending a political meeting or rally. And they asked about nonelectoral activities like contacting the media or officials and working with groups. What these scholars learned supports the notion that there is no simple or easily intuited pattern to the political behavior of African Americans, whites, Latinos, or Asian Americans.

Contrary to the popular image of Asian Americans as uniformly inactive, this research reveals that involvement varies according to the type of political activity. While it is true that Asians and Latinos seemed to be less inclined than whites to work on campaigns, attend political rallies, and exhibit political signs and bumper stickers, Asian Americans are more likely than other groups to contribute money to candidates.[120] Latinos are less likely than African Americans or whites to work in groups, but they contact news media at about the same rates. Asian Americans are as likely as whites to work in groups and more likely than anyone to convey opinions to news media. Filipinos and Koreans were more likely to convey their opinions to the news media than Vietnamese, Japanese, and Chinese, but Japanese were more likely to work in groups than Filipinos, Vietnamese, Chinese, and Koreans.[121]

Asian Americans are not only more active along certain electoral and nonelectoral dimensions than is typically believed; their affiliations and attitudes belie the popular image. Rather than having no (or "only" weak) allegiances or viewpoints, they show about the same rates of party loyalty and commitment as the general population. For example, the statewide study indicated that of those Asian Americans surveyed in 1984, 42 percent were registered Democrats, 41 percent were registered Republicans, and 16 percent declined to choose either party.[122] The Los Angeles study indicated that of the 1983 list of registered voters for certain tracts, 52.4 percent of Asian Americans registered as Democrats, 31 percent as Republicans, and 15 percent were independent.[123] And the 1984 survey in sample districts of San Francisco revealed that 51.5 percent were registered Democrats, 21.3 percent were registered Republicans, and more than a quarter declined to state a party.

For many Asian Americans party loyalties are strong. In the statewide survey 19 percent said they were "strong Republicans" and another 10 percent said they were "strong Democrats." To be sure, strength of party affiliation is a complicated matter. A strong Republican may not think much about either candidates or issues. A "weak" or "leaning Republican" may both know and care deeply about every candidate and issue. In any case, the figures for Asian Americans are similar to those obtained for whites (38 percent either strong Democrat or Republican) and for Latinos (34 percent either strong Democrat or Republican). Only the findings for African Americans (56 percent strong Democrats, 2 percent strong Republicans) differed significantly, no doubt reflecting their well-documented and historically grounded ties to the Democratic party. These statistics seem at least to rebut the popular image of Asian Americans who have allegiances that are weaker than most.

Careful examination would ultimately reveal the differences in the loyalties and commitments within Asian American groups that the limited information gathered to date points to. Of those included in the Los Angeles study, for instance, Filipinos had the highest percentage affiliated with the Democratic party at 63.3 percent compared with 22.8 percent Republican. Asian Indians were 59.1 percent Democrat and 23.6 percent Republican. Japanese followed at 54.9 percent Democrat and

32.3 percent Republican. Koreans were 48.5 percent Democrat and 29.4 percent Republican. Chinese (41.9 percent) and Vietnamese (40 percent) had the lowest proportions of Democrats, and the highest proportions of Republicans (36.4 percent and 35.9 percent, respectively).[124]

Likewise, in the San Francisco study of Chinese and Japanese, 48.6 percent of the Chinese were Democrats and 21.4 percent were Republicans; 66.7 percent of the Japanese were Democrats and 20.2 percent Republicans.[125] It would be unwise to draw any definitive conclusions from the patterns found in either the Los Angeles or San Francisco studies about the allegiances of particular groups, their intensity, or their relationship to other aspects of political life. The patterns do, however, begin to unmask a people far more interestingly affiliated than the popular image has ever contemplated. And they would seem obviously to suggest the need for more scholars who are inclined to inquire rather than presume.

The limitations of the popular image and the need for more careful scholarly attention are more striking when one takes into account what we now know about how Asian Americans think about particular issues. The California survey indicates that attitudes are not easily categorized. Like whites, Asian Americans are less likely than African Americans and Latinos to favor increased spending on welfare and more likely to favor the death penalty. Like whites and African Americans and unlike Latinos, a majority of Asian Americans do not favor amnesty for undocumented aliens. Like Latinos and African Americans and unlike whites, most favor bilingual education programs. And unlike whites, African Americans, and Latinos, most favor a ban on handguns but not prayer in public schools.[126]

As with party affiliation, the little data we have suggest that attitudinal differences between groups may be at least as great as those between Asians and other ethnic groups. In the California study Koreans were more likely than Japanese to favor bilingual ballots, bilingual education, and amnesty for undocumented aliens. Filipinos were the strongest supporters of prayer in public schools and increased military spending. Japanese political attitudes resembled those of whites more than of other Asian groups. And in the view of the authors, "There was no distinguishing pattern to Chinese American attitudes other than being generally conservative."[127]

Voting patterns, which seem to defy party affiliation, may provide further evidence about Asian American attitudes toward particular issues. In the 1984 presidential election, for example, California Asian

Americans, though predominantly registered Democrats, favored Ronald Reagan over Walter Mondale by 67 to 32 percent. Then in 1992 they voted 39 percent for Bill Clinton, 33 percent for George Bush, and 25 percent for Ross Perot[128] (although differences were measured between Chinese, Japanese, and Filipinos). Nationwide Asians favored Bush (52 percent to 32 percent for Clinton and 17 percent for Perot). In 1986 California Asian Americans favored Republican Governor George Deukmejian over Tom Bradley by 53 to 47 percent, and Deukmejian won, 62 to 38 percent. In the same election controversial Proposition 63, the "English only" initiative, passed by 77 to 23 percent but received only 52 percent of the Asian vote. And while the state rejected Supreme Court Justice Cruz Reynoso, a self-proclaimed liberal opponent of the death penalty and the court's only Latino judge, 60 to 40 percent, Asians favored him 54 to 46 percent.[129]

Perhaps this contrast confirms, as some believe, that Asian Americans are more inclined than others to cross party lines.[130] After all, African Americans and Latinos preferred Clinton and Mondale by margins that roughly paralleled formal party affiliations.[131] Yet party labels may simply be a poorer proxy for what Asian Americans care about and how strongly they care. And formal party affiliation may not reveal at all how responsive particular candidates are to their concerns or at least how responsive Asian Americans perceive them to be. In any case voting patterns raise far more questions than they answer. Like the other forms of electoral and nonelectoral activity we are finally beginning to learn more about, they expose the myth of the Asian apolitical character.

The distinctions between Asian American groups are undoubtedly reflected in other subcategories affected by immigration policies. More research is needed into patterns of electoral participation between generations, between urban and rural groups, between residents of enclaves and dispersed communities, and between pre- and post-1965 immigrants, to name just a few.

### Failure of familiar cultural explanations

The presumed political disengagement of Asian Americans is traced by the popular image to a character type supposedly ill-suited to political activism. Asians are seen as historically docile, acquiescent, and deferential, and as having come from homelands where the absence of democracy has taught them to be apathetic and uninvolved. They are portrayed as both the reason for and the product of authoritarian institutions and traditions that deny the social possibilities and individual growth democracies nurture and demand. They supposedly reproduce in the United States a civic self that readily accommodates their past. All this, in the popular image, is understood in a powerfully general and vague way to be cultural.

Some who have balked over the years at these reflexive explanations stress how historically anomalous they appear. They note, for example, that early Chinese, Japanese, and Indian immigrants did not come from serene, harmonious homelands. To the contrary, early Japanese immigrants lived through the Meiji Restoration.[132] Asian Indian immigrants were aggressively involved in liberation movements as early as 1908.[133] And most of those who immigrated from China in the nineteenth century were from a province where peasant rebellions, local wars, and actively antiestablishment secret societies were a tradition.[134]

Others who have questioned the familiar cultural explanations focus on what happened to Asians once they arrived. These critics insist that every interpretation of Asian American political life must be filtered through a central fact: for decades Asians as noncitizens could not vote.[135] Activities, events, successes, and failures in electoral politics should all be reported and interpreted in light of this disenfranchisement. "Banned from the political system and relegated to what was supposed to be a permanently inferior sociocultural status," they were, according to this dissenting view, "forced inward upon themselves as individuals, families, and communities."[136]

Those who emphasize disenfranchisement sensibly point to ostracism and degradation as plausible explanations for perceived disengagement. Asian Americans, they argue, are not silent and passive simply because of their cultural backgrounds but because "they are scared."[137] This fear is understandable given a "legacy of discrimination worse than that endured by any other group that came to this country voluntarily."[138] And when Asian Americans encountered "white racism, they cut as many ties with the white world as possible and withdrew into family and community."[139] From this perspective the effects of mistreatment continue today, and the absence of any apparent "linkage" with the broader society is largely explained by the pervasive "feeling of outgroup rejection and exclusion."[140] Asian Americans, in this account, remain "perpetual foreigners in their own home country."[141]

This dissenting view has spawned, even more recently, a range of other hypotheses about why they remain politically disengaged. Some critics contend that Asian immigrants, to the degree they focus on politics at all, remain concerned principally with the affairs of the home-land.[142] This, the dissenters claim, has been true of Chinese migrants who were preoccupied with China's wars, Japanese threats, and the 1949 revolution;[143] of Koreans who were concerned with Japanese imperialism and the 1948 partitioning of Korea; of Asian Indians who were involved in the Indian freedom movement;[144] of Filipinos who worried about and sometimes fought over the legitimacy of the Marcos regime; and of Southeast Asians who remain intimately connected to and concerned about relatives and friends in the midst of one war or another.

Other critics emphasize that many Asian Americans are recent immigrants who need time to adjust to their new environment.[145] The great majority, they note, do not speak English. These critics presume that those who do not use English as their primary language are less likely to understand domestic issues. Besides, they point out, immigrants may see little reason to care. American political parties can seem relatively indistinguishable, particularly to those who come from countries where politics covers a broader ideological spectrum. Even when agendas can be distinguished, electoral politics may seem inconsequential to people whose hopes have been betrayed time and again by candidates who fail to include Asian American priorities on their agendas and by officeholders who fail to distinguish themselves from previous regimes.

Among those who stress the experiences of Asians in the United States, some turn to economics to explain political inaction. They assert that recently arrived and perhaps all poorer Asians are by necessity too preoccupied with economic survival to worry about political affairs. Others contend that highly educated and successful Asians ignore politics because they have become preoccupied with their own success. Affluent Asian professionals have become "yappies" (young Asian professionals) who are consumed with "doing their own thing"—making careers for themselves, buying homes, and the like.[146] A few critics go so far as to argue that the socially and politically isolating nature of their scientific and technological jobs accounts for political indifference and passivity.[147]

One needn't find any of these hypotheses appealing, much less convincing, to agree with the impulse that gave life to them. In fact, there is currently little ethnographic, survey, or other empirical data available to support (or, for that matter, to refute) many of the more recent interpretations. Some of them may seem to be unduly hyperbolic. Need one believe, for example, that Asian Americans were the victims of a "legacy of discrimination worse than that endured by any other group" in order to feel justified in challenging familiar cultural explanations? Yet, together these hypotheses offer potentially provocative alternatives to hasty presumptions that Asian Americans are uniformly successful, passive, and careerist. They passionately urge that any explanation that focuses exclusively on the presumed character traits of Asians ignores the systemic disenfranchisement, ostracism, and degradation that have influenced their political life. Read both generously and skeptically, these hypotheses foreshadow a more basic challenge to the popular image.

*New ways of understanding Asian American political life:*
*electoral politics and beyond*

Drawing inspiration from recent critiques of the cultural paradigm, we can begin to develop a more systematic, empirically based framework for understanding Asian American political life. This framework borrows from a range of theoretical and empirical studies that provide important insights. More important, it builds on what we have learned about the making and remaking of Asian American communities. An appreciation of this history, together with new ways of analyzing and interpreting political involvements and commitments, enables us to identify and better comprehend the sometimes contradictory ways in which Asian Americans have been politically active from the moment of their arrival.

Underlying the popular image of Asian American participation is a conception of politics left largely tacit in this debate that values only conventional electoral affairs. Narrowly defined, they include only registration and voting. More broadly understood, they encompass a range of less high-profile activities like lobbying officials and their representatives.[148] Electoral politics are presumed to be the only way people voice their views, register the intensity of their feelings, and advance their interests. They are taken to be the unambiguous measure of each and every ethnic group's political life.

This powerful conception of politics has unwittingly influenced many, if not most, critics of the popular image of Asian Americans. Those who underscore the failure of familiar cultural explanations do so by emphasizing ignored aspects of Asian history, the degradation and ostracism of life in the United States, and other formal and informal obstacles to political participation. All the while, however, their focus, like the traditional view, remains principally on voting patterns and registration.

Those who try to expose the myth of the apolitical character of Asian Americans and the misconception that their electoral participation is uniformly low often preface their studies with allusions to the limits of electoral politics. They try to measure other forms of activism (including, for example, the California study's treatment of access to the media).[149] Nonetheless, even their analyses end up concentrating almost entirely on the electoral dimension.[150] Perhaps this simply reflects the impulse to study whatever is popular, or maybe foundations and government agencies circumscribe intellectual agendas through research grants. In any event the conception of politics underlying the popular image remains the focus of these otherwise discriminating scholars.

Had these critics followed their instincts and made better use of their own surveys, their analyses might well have benefited from a critique of the politics that underlies the popular image.[151] This critique proceeds from a more expansive vision of meaningful political life. It recognizes the importance of both electoral and nonelectoral activities, refusing to privilege either. It aims to study each in its own right and insists that neither can be understood without the other. In so doing it makes obvious that a people's political culture involves more than voting and registration rates.

Unfortunately, this more elaborated critique introduces its own failings. In seeking to expand the definition of the political, it turns more or less regularly to mass protest as the only, or certainly the most important, form of nonelectoral activity. Featured prominently in this analysis are the 1930's and 1960's protest movements.[152] Each was national in scope and demonstrated that mobilized mass defiance can sometimes be an effective exercise of power. Each revealed a complicated, interdependent relationship between mobilized mass defiance and electoral politics.

As helpful as this analysis is, it suffers from its disregard of an almost boundless range of nonelectoral activities that may qualify as meaningfully political. In focusing so exclusively on national movements, it neglects regional, state, and local mobilizations, overlooks smaller popular uprisings, and passes over mobilizations that may not cut across class, race, or ethnic lines. In centering so much attention on mobilizations that are openly defiant, it slights the more subtle ways in which people cope with and sometimes subvert conventional power. And in light of what we have learned about the making and remaking of Asian America, this analysis fails to appreciate the way life in and around particular ethnic communities helps shape both what people ultimately treat as political and, therefore, what should be defined as meaningful electoral and nonelectoral activities.

Relying uncritically on this more elaborate critique may be as misleading as unquestioned reliance on the popular image or on those who in their criticism do not move beyond its underlying conception of politics. Critics of the popular image have effectively drawn attention to time-worn notions that Asian Americans are by their nature uniformly politically passive, and those who critique conventional conceptions of politics have helped underscore the limits of these efforts. What we now know about the sociology and history of Asian America insists upon the need to explore more thoroughly and critically how various communities come to identify what is worth fighting about, how to wage such battles, and in what institutional arenas. It would seem to make sense, for example, to include the many smaller-scale, more-localized mobilizations and uprisings that have marked Asian American history.

As early as 1870 Chinese Americans protested a San Francisco "queue ordinance" requiring Chinese male prisoners, jailed for defying a "cubic air ordinance" aimed at reducing the population of Chinatown, to cut off their braided hair, their badge of Chinese identity.[153] In 1934 a farm worker strike against lettuce growers in Salinas over poor working conditions and low wages was organized and promoted by the Filipino Labor Union.[154] In the 1970's elderly Filipino and Chinese tenants joined with lawyers, community activists, and local politicians to forestall evictions from the International Hotel, a low-income residential hotel in San Francisco.[155] More recently, a coalition of Asian Americans lobbied intensely in 1988 to block Governor George Deukmejian's nominee for state treasurer from taking office.[156]

It would also seem necessary to include the many Asian American organizations and associations where experiences and aspirations are shared, identities and cultures formed and reformed, and a range of activities involving everyday survival, collective oppositions, and electoral agendas are galvanized and supported.

By the 1850's the San Francisco–based Chinese Consolidated Benevolent Association (popularly known as the Chinese Six Companies) had begun to be a vehicle for self-governance and mutual aid against discriminatory laws.[157] Similar organizations thrived in the 1930's in Japanese American communities throughout the West Coast.[158] They enhanced the legal status of Japanese citizens and noncitizens alike and were eventually combined in a single national body known as the Japanese American Citizens League. The formation of such associations is remarkable because in Asia family life formed the basis for most aspects of social life.[159]

Churches have also served as centers of social and political activities. In the 1980's, for instance, Korean Presbyterians in San Francisco and Los Angeles and Vietnamese Catholics in San Jose often made their churches the hub of life in their communities.[160]

What Asian Americans identify as mattering and worth fighting about casts a different light on a whole range of notions that have dominated both the popular image and more recent critical accounts of it. Certainly, the long-standing history of Asian American activism raises questions about their passivity. Perhaps it is true that, compared with other groups, some or even most Asian Americans have at one time or another been disinclined to register and vote and to participate in national protest movements. They may, moreover, be demonstrably more achievement-oriented than most. Yet can a people be called apolitical who form enduring organizations and associations, and risk real harm to assert their interests, confirm their own identities, and cope with economic discrimination, social ostracism, and political marginalization?

More careful study of Asian Americans might, in fact, lead to a rethinking of what even the most enlightened critics of the popular image have said about electoral disenfranchisement. For them it is the principal impediment to electoral participation and the moral and legal focal point of contemporary politics. Yet, however much one agrees with the impulse to excavate basic facts of Asian American history, too great an emphasis on disenfranchisement can obscure and mislead.

Rather than being the only obstacle to participating electorally, it might well be one piece of a more complicated puzzle. Had Asian Americans not been formally and informally blocked from registering and voting, they might still have refrained from treating conventional electoral activity as the principal means of political action and expression. They may well have chosen—and to some degree may continue to choose—alternative forms of political action for a variety of ethnically specific reasons. This would hardly be surprising of people who conceivably have different senses of what is powerful, effective, comfortable, and possible.

Operating in a liberal political/legal culture where aggrieved groups are encouraged (perhaps even forced) to demand restitution, Asian Americans sometimes feel obliged to exaggerate the discernible discriminatory effects of having been denied the right to register and vote.[161] Predictably, they end up mired in debates about historical accounts of disputed relationships and classes of identifiable victims. As a result, attention is drawn away from those political and social practices that continue to marginalize and degrade. Disenfranchisement may well be important to understanding and grappling with these more recent practices, but it cannot be the sole preoccupation of insightful analysis, much less the basis of an effective political movement.

## Asian American Identity

### Popular Images

An activist call for unity among Asian Americans has been sustained since the 1960's. The plea is for a movement that, given the growth of Asian America since 1965, is perceived as the means to political strength. It comes in response to the popular conception of Asian Americans as politically passive, unsuited for the political system, and not important. Activists believe that a unified effort of small individual populations would at the very least increase the size of the constituency several fold. Mobilizing separately as Chinese, Japanese, Filipinos, Asian Indians, Koreans, or Vietnamese results in fragmented politics and a dilution in impact. To attain political, social, and economic influence (or power), the diverse communities must "rally their numbers and money around common issues."[162] Put more bluntly, "We'll never be white people no matter how long we've lived here. . . . We cannot afford to live in America scattered and isolated. Only through unity can our people protect our rights and pass on a great legacy to our children."[163]

This view is not limited to political activists; it pervades much of Asian America. Educators, community leaders, social agency workers, and middle-class suburban residents alike believe that mobilizing a united Asian America is possible and necessary. Community organizers and others are likely to ask the same question: "Can you imagine the influence that Asian Americans will have in places such as San Francisco where they make up almost 30 percent of the population?"[164]

The notion of an Asian American identity seemed to be emerging when I was a freshman at Berkeley in 1967. Until then people of Chinese ancestry generally thought of themselves as Chinese Americans, those of Japanese heritage as Japanese Americans, and so forth. They may also have thought of themselves as Oriental, and there might have even been a socially unifying aspect to that term, but it was more a label of convenience for the mainstream than a term of mobilization.[165] Influenced by ethnic studies programs and the civil rights movement, Asian Americans on campus came together and began working toward common goals. Their vision of ethnic unity was fostered by ethnic studies programs that freed them to express themselves socially and politically. Historical animosity between groups was suppressed among these "radicalized" students.[166]

Even the origins of the term *Asian American* can be traced to efforts to form a unified ethnic identity for mobilization purposes. Unlike Indian (for Native Americans) or Hispanic, which were labels of convenience for the mainstream,[167] Asian American was a political label chosen by the people themselves in the 1960's.[168]

That choice was an act of collective mobilization—of empowerment—and intended as a symbolic expression of the similarity in treatment all Asian Americans experienced[169] and others shared after immigration.[170] In that era of nascent civil rights and ethnic studies, ethnic identification was promoted and popular. Rallying around a common identity was natural.[171]

To some the new image is not limited to political identity or mobilization. A new cultural identity is evolving from a common American experience and is viewed as a new "culture coming of age. It's a bold culture, unashamed and true to itself. It's a culture with a common destiny, a *community of the mind and soul*. And it's taking many forms—in plays and films, in literature and journalism, in history and the social sciences, in professional groups and political caucuses."[172]

Asian American represents a new ethnicity, the permanent adoption of an identity that radically changes nationalistic identity. It entails broadening a sense of oneself.

The viability of these images is hardly surprising given impressive accounts of Asian American organizational efforts, political victories, and cultural developments. In calling for legislation to combat anti-Asian violence (and for the federal indictment of the racially motivated assailants of Vincent Chin),[173] an Asian American community effort involving Japanese, Chinese, Southeast Asians, Filipinos, and Koreans surfaced.[174] When California Governor George Deukmejian sought to appoint conservative Republican Congressman Dan Lungren (who opposed reparations to Japanese Americans interned during World War II) as state treasurer in 1988, he was blocked by a broad coalition of Asian Americans.[175] When *Rolling Stone* magazine published an article offensive to Koreans, a coalition of the Asian American Journalists Association, the Japanese American Citizens League, the Korean American Bar Association, and the Asian Pacific American Legal Center protested, and the magazine acceded to demands for an editorial apology, the publication of critical letters, and the hiring of Asian American (not limited to Korean American) interns.[176]

Beginning in the 1980's lobbying efforts to maintain family reunification goals in immigration reforms and to challenge admissions policies in major universities that discriminate against Asian American applicants have involved a cross section of groups working together. Headlines such as "History in the Making: Nikkei, Koreans Join Hands," have become more common.[177] The National Democratic Council of Asian Pacific Americans is working closely with the Democratic National Committee to garner support for a variety of Asian American candidates and issues. Japanese American Congressmen Norman Mineta and Robert Matsui and Senator Daniel Inouye have come to be regarded as national leaders for their work on behalf of many Asian American groups.[178]

The number and types of professional, community-based organizations and social groups, such as the Asian Business League, Asian American Bar Association, and professional organizations for educators, journalists, writers, doctors, and pharmacists have proliferated as have community agencies, such as the Asian American Drug Abuse Program, Asian American Legal Defense and Education Fund, and Asian Pacific Advocacy and Resource Council (human services advocacy). There are Asian American tennis tournaments, jazz festivals, college fraternities and sororities, women's organizations, and newspapers. Since 1979 Asian and Pacific American Heritage Week (or month) has been celebrated each May. A genre of literature rooted in an interest in identity and the American experience has evolved, and Asian American theater groups performing plays by Asian American playwrights have flourished on both coasts.

As encouraging as these signs might be to those who operate in the image of a unified Asian American identity, what we now know about the making and remaking of Asian America calls into question the formation of a unified identity. Given the diversity of Asian America, is such an identity likely? Does political mobilization or the development of a political agenda require a new ethnicity? Is there even the genesis of that ethnicity? Is it even wise for diverse communities to be unified given the impact such an image has on affirmative action in education and employment, the census, the Small Business Administration, and even on the scope of Asian American studies programs? Can anyone claim to speak for Asian America?

## How Well Do the Popular Images Hold Up?

Much of the unity building by Asian American activists and social commentators has been supported by community workers and educators since the 1960's. But even before so many Asian Americans immigrated in the 1970's and 1980's, certain community members and scholars were cognizant of the diversity of Asian America and how that would challenge efforts to establish a new culture or unified movement. Yet, as the community grew, more attention was paid—by activists and commentators alike—to the cognizance of commonalities and the urgency of united action, as more and more Asians searched for political solutions to social injustice.

For all the attention to calls for unified action, until the 1980's little attention was given to the growing diversity. The rising chorus of independent Vietnamese, Filipino, Asian Indian, and Korean American voices has changed all that. By no means has this newfound attention resolved the serious questions of political mobilization or ethnicity. But it has made clear the need to focus on the issues that challenge the notions of Asian American identity.

*The challenge that diversity presents to images of
Asian American identity*

The most obvious challenge to the formation of a single Asian American ethnicity or identity is its diversity. In the early 1970's, some commentators noticed the middle-class roots of the campus-generated Asian-American movement and its "cultural, economic and political differences" with the communities as well as with the "street movement."[179] Asian America has been further made and remade since then through immigration policies. Today it is predominantly foreign-born and made up of many communities, and immigration trends suggest that these conditions will continue for some time.

The diversity is multi-leveled. The substantial foreign-born and American-born populations in each community give rise to cultural, social, and political differences within them.[180] The foreign-born are from a variety of countries, many of which harbor historical animosities toward one another. Language differences exist in each community between English and non-English speakers, among immigrants from different countries, and even within a community of non-English speakers (e.g., Mandarin versus Cantonese Chinese).[181] Community differences in class and urban/rural backgrounds are difficult to ignore as are gender differences.[182] Income disparities and differences in residential patterns exist as well. Asian America is many different people, including third- and fourth-generation Japanese and Chinese Americans, business entrepreneurs from Korea and Taiwan, Hmong hill farmers, Indian scientists, Filipino nurses, and Amerasian beach peddlers.

The diversity is apparent in political affiliations and attitudes on social issues. A wealthy Taiwanese immigrant who owns a business may be uninterested in low-income housing for elderly residents of Chinatown or even oppose it.[183] Country of origin also influences attitudes. Immigrants who fled communism or who lived next door to it may have supported military aid to the Nicaraguan Contras in the 1980's, but the American-born influenced by the anti–Vietnam War movement may have been staunchly opposed. Vietnamese Americans (90 percent of whom are foreign-born) lean toward the Republican party, possibly because they perceive the GOP as more anti-Communist.[184] The same might be expected of Chinese who fled mainland China after 1949, certain South Koreans, and Chinese from Taiwan. Yet not all Vietnamese Americans (53 percent in Santa Clara County and 36 percent Los Angeles) are registered Republicans.[185] The highest percentage of Asian Americans affiliated with the Democratic party in Los Angeles were Filipinos (63.3 percent), perhaps in part because most fled during the Marcos era and the Republican party was viewed unfavorably as the greater Marcos supporter. Plenty of other Filipinos (22.8 percent), however, are aligned with the Republican party. Thus, the group most sympathetic with the Democrats has a greater proportion of Republicans than other communities of color.[186]

Diversity is also evident in the variety of personality types who struggle to reconcile the tension between ethnic identification and assimilation. Traditionalists may have a strong desire to maintain their ethnic culture and heritage, even to the point of minimizing contact with the Western political environment.[187] Others may be willing to strip themselves of their old culture and become immersed in the new.[188] They might even discontinue speaking the language of the homeland within the family in the belief that this will help them and their children become accepted. Between those extremes falls a variety of personalities, who in varying degrees want to balance the old culture and the new and at the same time deal with the racism inherent in American culture.[189] The mélange of psychological attitudes about ethnicity and assimilation that exist among Asian Americans presents special challenges to the notion of a uniform ethnicity.[190]

Agreement is difficult to reach because of the hostility or conflicts inherent in different personalities, cultures, languages, socioeconomic status, and the like.[191] Racism can invert the normal relation among members of a racial group, replacing trust with mistrust and charitable feelings with hatred.[192] The more militant may regard the less militant as sellouts or as part of the bourgeoisie.[193] They may become impatient with those who do not seek to combat discrimination faster. The militants are viewed as extremists by moderates who are willing to mobilize but through different tactics. These conflicts are particularly problematic to those who envision a unified ethnicity as essential to political mobilization. The traditionalist's withdrawal and isolation from society is inconsistent with conventional notions of political mobilization requiring group action within mainstream institutions.[194] For those who reject their Asian identity, ethnic politics is incompatible with the goal of complete assimilation.

Though it is clear that the continued influx of Asians as refugees, professionals, family members, and business owners will perpetuate all forms of diversity, who can say what personality categories each immigrant or refugee falls into? Do Southeast Asian refugees or family immigrants necessarily cling to traditional cultural values, or do they respond to sympathetic mainstream efforts to help them assimilate? Because of their education and financial self-sufficiency, are professional-class entrants viewed more favorably by the mainstream, making them more likely to seek assimilation? Or are they more threatening? And if hostility or racism from the mainstream surfaces, how does one necessarily respond? By withdrawing from society? By seeking economic or educational prominence? Through violence? By stripping oneself of ethnic culture?

Diversity challenges popular images of political mobilization and the development of a new culture. For all the so-called Asian American political mobilization efforts, community-based organizations, professional groups, newspapers, and social events, separate Korean, Japanese, Filipino, Vietnamese, Chinese, Asian Indian political mobilization efforts, community-based organizations, professional groups, newspapers, and social events continue to be sustained and expanded as well.[195] Not all Asian American leaders think in terms of unity among the groups. Many activists concerned with political mobilization write about the need to mobilize their specific communities without mention of coalescing with other Asian American communities.[196] In the streets one finds Vietnamese gangs, Chinese gangs, Filipino gangs, not Asian American gangs. And for all the broad support for Japanese American political leaders such as Mineta and Matsui, Chinese Americans, Filipino Americans, Korean Americans, Asian Indians, and Vietnamese Americans are seeking to get "their own" community leaders elected.[197]

*The limitations of conventional descriptions of ethnicity to account for Asian American identity*

As troubling as the notion of a new political and/or cultural identity might be, given the challenges presented by diversity, it is difficult to ignore the level of mobilizing that has taken place. Political, community, and social groups, events, and activities are real and ever-growing. In fact, the concept of a new ethnicity is not so farfetched in light of the emergence of political-ethnic groups in other parts of the world, often from "unorganized ethno-cultural categories."[198] The Brahmauris and Gaddis in north India are exotic examples.[199] Their ethnic identity developed from complex psychological, historical, economic, political, and other situational phenomena. Closer to home there are the Native Americans.[200] Since the 1960's ethnic politics involving other people of color has become a major fixture of the American political culture, even though their American-born generations are assimilated to various degrees.[201]

Commentators offer an array of explanations and descriptions for the new ethnic political movement. For example, as boundaries between groups dissolve, two principal phenomena are said to occur. The first is *amalgamation* when the new, larger group is different from any of the component parts; the other is *incorporation*, when a group loses its identity by merging into another that retains its identity.[202] With ethnic political mobilization, there are supposedly four overlapping categories, the *common background, utilitarian, shaped-by-the-mainstream*, and *situational.*

The common background model applies to persons with a common origin or a common culture who are more likely to work together collectively to achieve political goals.[203] The utilitarian view is that ethnic politics is motivated by pragmatism—the strategic utility of concerted ethnic action. A common interest in political and socioeconomic power keeps the group together.[204] Under the shaped-by-the-mainstream category, recognition of certain ethnic groups by a government, administrative unit, or by mainstream society enhances identification and group formation.[205] Finally, in the situational model ethnicity is fluid and volitional and is activated by the competition and oppression the group is experiencing.[206]

Whether these categories actually describe the development of Asian American identity is questionable given what we know. Take the amalgamation-incorporation dichotomy. It is doubtful that the threatened loss of identity of one group through incorporation is desirable. And it seems that through amalgamation every group stands to lose its original identity. Both categories are also antithetical to the retention of the culture that many Asian Americans desire.

The categories of ethnic political mobilization provide a basis for understanding issues affecting the development of identity. At first glance, the common background premise does not apply to Asian Americans given their diversity. Yet among many of my friends of various Asian ancestries who socialize with one another, a definite sense of a shared background and culture has developed. For some it flows from having been immigrants. For many others (myself included), it largely derives from our American experience—our racial features in a predominantly white society, our two-culture (or multiculture) lives, our treatment by the mainstream. In the early stages of the Asian American movement, there was a sense of a united "struggle for liberation" for Asian people around the globe.[207] From this perspective a common background is unmistakable. Those who have not had the same experiences (or the same reactions), however, would not share that background.[208]

The utilitarian perspective has some appeal because mobilization owes something to the recognition that collective activism has tactical utility in seeking particular goals. The push to prosecute the murderers of Vincent Chin served to increase awareness of increasing incidents of anti-Asian violence, and lobbying efforts to maintain family reunification goals in immigration reforms benefited every Asian group. The utilitarian explanation, however, fails to account for the sense of commonality among some Asian Americans that extends beyond the moment.

The shaped-by-the-mainstream model raises complicated issues. Consider, for example, efforts to have Asian Americans recognized for special admissions or affirmative action plans. Mobilizing out of utilitarian motives may allow certain institutions to validate and perpetuate the group identity. Other institutions pick up on the Asian American label, further perpetuating the group identity. The more these institutions and the mainstream (including the media) refer to Asian Americans instead of to Chinese Americans, Korean Americans, Vietnamese Americans, and so forth, the greater the prospects that some will act collectively.

Others might react negatively to these generalizations. Responding as a unit may be inconsistent with their desire to demand recognition of group individuality and independent needs. Asian Americans opposed the Census Bureau's plan, for example, to lump them and Pacific Islanders into one category for the 1990 census.[209] Thus, the shaped-by-the-mainstream theorists might at first say, "Listen, stop treating us as one group. We have different advantages and disadvantages, with varying needs," only to add, "but regard us as one group in terms of the complaints that we have about your treatment of us."

The situational model does a better job of describing mobilization experiences of Asian Americans. Here mobilization is triggered by a policy, event, or condition. This model assumes that ethnicity (identity) is fluid because class, religion, language, nationality, race, age, or gender may become prominent depending on the context, pulling together people with the same trait.[210] Because ethnic identity is fluid, a certain amount of identity switching can also occur. It can be assumed for a short period, a long period, or perhaps permanently, depending on changing experiences and problems.[211]

At times, nationality, language, and residential factors produce independent mobilization. Chinese and Filipinos, for example, relied on families, friends, and community to build the Chinatowns and Manilatowns that gave them some collective control over their existence.[212] Japanese Americans obtained reparations or redress for those interned during World War II.[213] Vietnamese Americans showed antipathy toward politicians who appeared sympathetic to North Vietnam during the Vietnam War along community lines.[214] Korean Americans rallied in response to the targeting of Koreatown stores during the 1992 uprising in south central Los Angeles.[215] But in combating most anti-Asian violence, lobbying for immigration reforms, or seeking state funds for health-care services, coalitions of many groups have been formed.[216]

The situational model recognizes that at times Asian American communities should work together, but that doing so is sometimes neither necessary nor beneficial. It accommodates identity switching and recognizes that for some the achievement of identity is an ordered and structured psychic process that continues throughout the life of the individual.[217]

As well as this situational model seems to account for much of the mobilization in Asian America, it too is incomplete. Like the utilitarian model it fails to account for the sense of commonality that has emerged among some Asian Americans. Both models fail to address the issue of representation, a derivative of diversity.

Diversity challenges the ability to forge a unified political agenda, much less a new cultural identity, and raises problematic questions about the propriety and wisdom of claiming such an identity. The leadership (or at least the organizers) of Asian American political mobilization efforts, community-based organizations, professional groups, and social events are generally Chinese and/or Japanese Americans (often American-born). The idea that Japanese and Chinese Americans view themselves, or are viewed by others, as spokespersons for Vietnamese or Asian Indians is troubling. All too often, the agenda in these settings has been given a Japanese and/or Chinese American emphasis, amounting to virtually a de facto incorporation or loss of identity for other Asian Americans. Japanese and/or Chinese American experiences cannot duplicate the Vietnamese refugee, Asian Indian, Korean, or Pacific Islander immigrant experience. The same is true of the writers of the new Asian American literature or plays,[218] as well as the more senior faculty of Asian American studies programs.[219] As sensitive as they may be about other Asian Americans, they cannot represent the majority, which we now know is non-Japanese and non-Chinese American.

Even the more thoughtful academic descriptions of ethnic mobilization and identity formation fail to include the voices of group members at the center of political, social, and cultural struggles. Though they are aware of different personality types, these scholarly examinations would benefit from the reflections and voices of those affected, as we struggle to get a real feel for what is happening and what is likely to happen.

### *Developing new ways of understanding Asian American identity*

Throughout this book I have used the term Asian Americans to describe all Asian immigrants to the United States as well as American-born citizens of Asian ancestry. But no one should infer that a singular ethnicity has evolved. In fact, the immigration-generated mosaic of diverse communities calls into question the very use of the term Asian American. Yet the assumption of a single ethnicity might very well be resented even if the broader Asian Pacific American term were used to include those from the Pacific Islands. Clashing personality types and extreme political and socioeconomic polarities suggest that the more plausible picture is one of relative unity only among certain segments of Asian America. We need to ask what that new limited ethnicity means to the rest of Asian America and to the mainstream.

Whether there is, will be, or even should be a single ethnicity is a complicated question. While the various communities share elements of a common history, their individual histories, demographics, and experiences are unique. The current diversity within and between groups—demographically, culturally, socially, politically, and economically—would appear to create too many obstacles to such a single identity. Today as I walk around a predominantly foreign-born neighborhood like Chinatown, it is hard to imagine (although they should be asked) that the people on the street would not first think of themselves as Chinese American, or even Chinese. They are Chinese immigrants who look Chinese, speak Chinese, and spend most of their time in Chinatown. Yet similarities in terms of race, experience, treatment by the mainstream, and political values have drawn some Asian Americans (not only the American-born) together, and not always simply for utilitarian political purposes or because the situation calls for it.

A look through the eyes of Asian Americans would no doubt enlighten our understanding of identity and ethnic formation. My views and experiences might be relevant here.

I generally think of myself as Asian American rather than Chinese American, but that may in part be because I was born in the United States, I have many Japanese, Chinese, Korean, and Filipino friends who are also American-born or have lived here most of their lives, I communicate with them in English, and despite our different opinions I share with them many experiences. I work in a university where Asian American is a common label, and the vast majority of my Asian American co-workers and students are American-born Japanese and Chinese Americans. I also have been a member of many political and social groups (formal and informal) that are labeled or regarded as Asian American and have members of varied Asian backgrounds. I do regard myself as Chinese American when specific cultural signals are invoked, such as when I am with relatives (most of whom are Chinese American), in Chinatown, or a Chinese restaurant. I do not recall ever being able to regard myself simply as an American. My racial features inevitably evoke certain reactions, looks, body language, and treatment from the people with whom I interact, so that I am constantly reminded that I am Asian American or Chinese American.[220]

But I cannot serve as the standard. Asian America today is predominantly foreign-born and not of Chinese ancestry. Informal surveys, which I and others have conducted of Asian Americans on how they identify themselves, reveal a range of responses. Many, even some born in the United States, see themselves as Chinese Americans, Japanese Americans, or Vietnamese Americans. Others insist that they are simply Americans, resent any prefix, and claim that because they act and think of themselves as Americans, they are treated as such. Still others respond that their identity depends on the time of day. In a work environment lacking other Asian Americans, some regard themselves as simply Americans, while others are reminded that they are Asian American, and all might regard themselves as Filipino or Chinese American if they volunteer after work at a community center.

Here is a sampling of the varied comments about identity I have heard from a predominantly middle-class cross section of Asian Americans:[221]

> I think of myself primarily as Taiwanese. I think of myself as Asian American when I'm in a political situation, like in voting and supporting candidates, because the Taiwanese community is pretty small. So I think of what candidates would represent the Asian community or if there happens to be a Taiwan-related issue at hand, I'll look at that first. (Taiwan-born woman, age 41, immigrated at age 22)

I think of myself as Vietnamese. Sometimes I think of myself as Vietnamese American. I never think of myself as Asian American. I don't feel more affinity with other Asian groups such as the Japanese or Chinese. Historically, Vietnam has not had a friendly relationship with these countries because these countries dominated us. I check the box Asian American in all my forms (employment, etc.), but that's because they don't have a Vietnamese American box. (Vietnam-born man, age 50, entered as refugee at age 38)

I think of myself as Asian American. I think of myself as Vietnamese when I'm with other Vietnamese, and I think of myself as American when I'm in Europe. (Vietnam-born woman, age 20, immigrated at age 4)

I regard myself as an American. I grew up in a setting with few other Asians, and I was treated as a regular person by my white friends. So I think of myself as simply an American. (American-born woman, Chinese ancestry, age 42)

I think of myself as an American. My parents are Chinese, but I grew up in the United States. A few years ago I went to China where I couldn't relate and I realized I wasn't Chinese. In the United States, we have to think of ourselves as American in order to get respect. (American-born man, Chinese ancestry, age 45)

I think of myself as Japanese American. The racism that I and my friends have experienced over the years is a constant reminder that I am different and will never be accepted simply as an American. (American-born man, Japanese ancestry, age 66)

I think of myself as Taiwanese American. I rarely identify myself as anything else, but sometimes if I'm at an Asian dance, I will consider myself as Asian. It depends on the environment. . . . It's hard for me to relate to the Vietnamese. I identify more with Chinese and Taiwanese. (Taiwan-born man, age 25, immigrated at age 3)

I think of myself as Chinese American. I grew up in Chinatown and went to Chinese school after regular school every day. Both my parents were immigrants. I've never been out of the Bay Area, and I continue to work, eat, and shop a lot in Chinatown even though I live in the Richmond district [with many Chinese American neighbors] of San Francisco. (American-born man, age 45)

I'm Filipino. I fought in World War II for the United States in the Philippines and not until recently are they going to give me the citizenship I earned. I want to be an American citizen, but I will always be a Filipino. (Philippine-born man, age 75, immigrated at age 63)

Through high school I told people I was Chinese, and if I wanted to refer to all Asians I used the word Orientals. . . . At college I was told that the proper label for me was Asian American, that Oriental was a word to describe furniture, not people. But what is the difference? . . . Minority groups want new labels to give themselves a more positive image. But unless the stereotypes disappear as well, is it really going to help very much? (Chinese American sophomore at Yale)[222]

The complexity of Asian American identity underscores the need for a more sophisticated understanding of it and its continuing evolution. This understanding must account for those many Asian Americans who switch identities from situation to situation and who tell us that Asian American is not an identity for all times and all purposes. And it must respect the unique cultural backgrounds that the foreign-born majority represent.

When we speak of an Asian American identity, are we referring to a new ethnicity with common traits, customs, and cultural characteristics, a political identity for mobilization purposes, or both? Is it proper to use these terms interchangeably as some do? Assuming that a new ethnicity would entail a cultural identity, would that be different from political identity? A new cultural identity or ethnicity could very well be established for collective mobilization for political purposes, but diverse groups can be mobilized without forming a new cultural identity. It's a substantial leap to a new ethnic identity from collective mobilization. Otherwise, the so-called new Asian American ethnic identity must be limited to those like myself—those middle-class, American-born Chinese or Japanese Americans with exposure to an array of community issues and similar educational experience.

To many, then, the concept of Asian American identity may not involve a new cultural identity. Rather, it might properly be viewed as a means of achieving political integration. For some, this may simply be situational political mobilization. But for others it could involve a more permanent process of developing a political identity or platform while maintaining separate ethnic identities for non-political purposes. In that sense, it is a civic identity that transcends single situations and is more lasting in nature. On the other hand, it falls short of a new ethnic or cultural identity since it can be established simply for political reasons. This type of ethnic mobilization is essentially a form of social interaction between culture groups.

Situational mobilization acknowledges a more pliant character than identity formation. Though independent community mobilization may damage prospects for pan–Asian American efforts,[223] given the diversity of Asian immigrants it is too much to expect that intra-community organizing and a turning inward will not occur. The persistence of Chinatowns, Filipino American suburbs, and Vietnamese business pockets promotes intra-community mobilization. The flexibility of the situational model permits more than one mobilization response without foreclosing the possibility of others in different contexts, in light of different issues.

A less flexible view of Asian American identity is dangerous. Rudimentary calls for unity or uninformed claims of an emerging uniform culture involve several interrelated risks. First among them is exclusivity. Those who do not find themselves in the description of Asian America are likely to be turned off or alienated, and that would be counterproductive to unity. Second is the notion of the incorporation, or loss of identity, by smaller groups. Finally, the dominance of middle-class, American-born Chinese and Japanese Americans risks distorting information about Asian America.

The dangers of inflexibility should also give great pause to those who believe in cultural pluralism. At what expense are we willing to assume or call for a new Asian American ethnicity? Are there not elements of cultural sacrifice in that notion that affront us for the same reasons we abhor strict demands of Americanization or assimilation? A single ethnicity smacks of the same cauldron-like approach we have resisted in the Anglo-conformity or melting-pot models of Americanization.[224] The formation of Asian American political, social, and cultural identity must be accompanied by the same respect of cultural heritages and democratic development that we have so long sought from the mainstream. Just as most Asian Americans have come to realize that developing and identifying an alternative, pluralistic structure may be a natural (and possibly necessary) response to the barriers erected to exclude them from mainstream institutions, so the retention of ethnic culture, heritage, and values, or a multitiered mobilization is also natural and possibly necessary.[225]

Is it misguided to regard Asian American identity as one might view a coalition of people of color, gays and lesbians, and feminists? The racial identification shared by Asian Americans does distinguish the two.[226] Yet, just as in people of color–gay–feminist coalition work where varied interests are respected and understood, and time to caucus independent from the larger coalition is honored, immigration-generated diversity demands respect and space. We must also remember that identity may be linked less to race than to gender, class, and perhaps even geography. These are worthwhile lessons for those who challenge the feasibility of Asian American mobilization or ethnic formation on diversity grounds. Diversity exists within any mobilized coalition or, for that matter, any ethnicity.

No one can claim to know what Asian American ethnicity is or what it will become. No one can claim that a uniform identity exists. And certainly no one can claim to speak for Asian America.

## Conclusion

While the relationship between immigration policies, demographics, and social life may as yet not be fully understood or validated, it does exist.

Diversity strains the development of an Asian American identity, distorts academic performance, and creates nonmonolithic social and political groups. The history of private, local, and codified animosity against Asian Americans and their responses to it contribute to their level of political participation. The enclaves that led to social organizations help to explain the reliance on alternative modes of political participation today. The demographic changes forced by the 1965 amendments influenced economic rank and citizenship status, which affect conventional measures of political participation such as voter registration. And academic performance—poor as well as exemplary—is a collection of possibly complicated responses to modern discrimination.

In short, important aspects of Asian American life—academic performance, political participation, and identity—are deeply influenced by the demographics that have been shaped and reshaped by immigration policy. These demographics reveal a diversity that questions the popular images of Asian Americans and the methodology if not thoroughness of even more sophisticated scholars and researchers. More recent, but limited, attempts to reinterpret some aspects of demographics—diversity, family differences, residential patterns, economic differences, pre- and post-1965 distinctions—are noteworthy. But the evolution of Asian America entails a rethinking and understanding of what academic performance, political participation, and Asian American identity really mean.

# Epilogue

At the outset of this project, I noted its major themes: the effect of immigration policies and the attitudes and events they reflect on Asian demographic/socioeconomic profiles; the great diversity within and between Asian groups; the effort to control them, their sense of family, their recruitment for agricultural labor, and the inattention to their development.

We have seen that the communities are a patchwork of distinctive groups and that their diversity developed from the early effect of law on their demographics. Early policymakers controlled the Chinese largely by excluding Chinese women and through antimiscegenation laws. Entry of Japanese nationals was negotiated with Japan, a world power at the turn of the century, allowing Japanese wives and picture brides to enter. As a result, the Japanese American population grew even after Japanese immigration was cut off in 1924. Restrictions were timed to stop one group while another was recruited.

After the Chinese exclusion act, for example, Japanese immigration was open for twenty years. The Asiatic barred zone established in 1917 covered neither Japanese nor Filipinos, who entered by the hundreds of thousands in the 1920's and early 1930's. Postwar policy changes, especially the egalitarian 1965 amendments that abandoned the racial national-origins quota system, reflected and maintained the diversity of each Asian American community. The driving force behind the evolution of the Vietnamese American community, which today is growing faster than any Asian group, is refugee law and policy.

Control emerged as a theme as I proceeded in this project.

Principally, it concerns exclusion and numbers. But the more carefully I looked at it, the more it became reasonably evident that it was more manipulative than that. The evidence might be regarded as anecdotal, but some information cannot be ignored.

Take Chinatowns, for example. Keeping early Chinese contained in them might not have been an accident. In Tucson in 1885 a petition was drafted urging that the Chinese should be forced to a Chinatown where they could be watched and monitored, and in San Francisco landlords refused to rent to Chinese outside the ghetto. Keeping Chinese women out of the country can be viewed as a way of assuring that the men would stay either rootless and migrant or confined to their Chinatown families. Control of this nature is complicated, of course, especially when ghettoization is compared with the dispersal of Vietnamese 90 years later. Yet the latter did make Asians less powerful, while the former was a way of keeping an eye on them.

The type of work Asians would do here was also controlled. Those allowed to immigrate were recruited as laborers, and they were expected to remain in the laborer class. Refusal to extend citizenship rights, alien land laws, and other restrictions (Yick Wo–type) on business were designed to perpetuate this class restriction. The migrant nature of railroad and agricultural work compounded the rootlessness of early immigrants who could not bring their families over nor start new ones. The inability to settle down kept many immigrants from starting their own farms and businesses.

As to a sense of family, I do not mean to overstate or urge the recognition of some unique Asian value. I do not really know if Asians were any more committed to the family than other immigrant groups. But when it came to reunification, they certainly had to be more resourceful. Chinese women were kept out, so to have a conventional family Chinese and other Asian men had to reunite with relatives from abroad because of antimiscegenation and expatriation laws. They were forced to imagine their past family as their future family. When the 1965 amendments favored reunification, Asians gradually expanded their communities. Koreans and Asian Indians expanded first through investor and employment categories, then by taking full advantage of the family categories. Asians' drive to reunify was important to their growth and their progress toward gender balance.

Immigration policy allowed Chinese to be recruited to work in the plantations of Hawaii and the farmlands of California after placer mining gave out and the transcontinental railroad was completed. Growers there actually protested much of the move to exclude Chinese. After exclusion Japanese and Koreans (until their emigration was cut off by Japan) were recruited to Hawaii and to the West, and after their entries were limited, Asian Indian and particularly Filipino labor was sought.

Throughout all this, however contradictory it may seem, policymakers were also guilty of inattention to Asia and Asian Americans, especially after the 1965 amendments. No one predicted how social forces would be unleashed. The amendments were supposed to permit a few thousand immigrants initially; then the numbers would trail off. Policymakers failed to anticipate that Asians would come to dominate legal immigration.

In Chapter 5, the most provisional section of the book, I examine three aspects of Asian American social life. It is now evident to me that, given their diversity and what I now know about the communities, some popular conceptions of the experiences of Asian Americans miss the mark. Their lack of involvement in political life is generally attributed to cultural traits or historical disenfranchisement, but Asian Americans actually participate on many levels. Their opinions on social and political issues are not monolithic. The generalized whiz-kid image varies within and between groups, casting doubt on simple cultural or class explanations of performance. A more sophisticated analysis is needed of the possibilities for Asian American political mobilization and the formation of a new ethnicity.

I began this project with the sense that much less is known about Asian American communities than is commonly believed. The more I learned, the more I realized we had to learn. Questions abound regarding each community's unique history, demographics, and experiences and their relationship to immigration policies and laws and the forces behind them. These questions, which remain largely unanswered, underscore how limited the available information is. They expose unexamined assumptions. And, ultimately, they generate skepticism about the opinions and assertions of those of us who claim expertise. If a certain disquiet prompted me to undertake this study, what I have come to understand proved more humbling than I would have expected.

Like so many others who try to get a handle on complex legal and social phenomena, I find myself acknowledging how much more light remains to be shed on the making and remaking of Asian America. There are, for instance, no detailed ethnographies of the communities these people come from or of how they change and are changed by those they enter. Qualitative studies would help us better understand what made immigration attractive or necessary and how changes in the law affected sending and receiving communities. For example, my preliminary findings on the economic situation in India compared with that in Korea and the Philippines suggest that the so-called brain drain needs more than a mere head count. By the same token, only a few surveys provide the kind of data necessary to more precisely gauge demographics and to relate attitudes and behaviors to shifts in immigration policies and laws.

For all that seems to me in need of study, I appreciate that even now a wide range of people are acting and are compelled to act on the basis of one or another understanding of Asian America. Policymakers, print and broadcast journalists, organizers, and activists—no doubt often under intense pressure to produce—look for immediate payoffs in scholarly efforts like mine. They insist upon easy answers that no one can provide but which they hope to parlay into striking legislative proposals, clever story lines, or inventive mobilizations. They rarely appreciate the need for more thoroughly reorienting themselves, for understanding Asian American life and its relationship to immigration policies and laws more deeply.

My research provides no solace for those seeking ready-made answers. Indeed, it may well prove a source of frustration. Even those with whom I've worked most closely over the years may find maddening the gaps, complications, and contradictions I have uncovered. Yet preconceptions and misguided policies must be challenged and research that will enable real expertise must be stimulated if we are to move beyond the popular images that currently inform policy, reporting, organizing, and even scholarly inquiries.

My work, whatever else it offers, moves us in this direction. More than most people apparently realize, immigration policies and laws and the social and political forces that gave rise to them helped determine the size, residential patterns, gender ratios, and socioeconomic profiles of Asian American communities. And these basic demographics shape Asian American life even to the present day. They will continue to play an important role in the evolution of Asian America.

Perhaps as important, Asian Americans have been implicated in the making and remaking of U.S. immigration policy, as well as state and local laws affecting immigrants. From the beginning Asians themselves induced a radical rethinking of the role immigration law might play in the construction of our national community. Employers, policymakers, commentators, and others began to recognize how immigration laws might foster economic and social welfare. They began to realize, too, that those laws communicated what they thought about their community and about the others who might want to enter. Asians thus made obvious the self-defining capacity of a nation's immigration laws, thereby laying the foundation for their use in controlling the migration of other groups.

Certain implications of my findings are inescapably relevant to immigration policies and the social character of the United States. The unanticipated impact of the 1965 amendments on Asian America makes one wonder about the reliability of our underlying vision, especially since some policymakers intended to limit Asian American growth through a family-oriented system. For example, today some policymakers are concerned about the impact of immigrants on the nation's economy. But even though Asians are almost half the legal immigrants to the United States annually, they are less than 3 percent of the population. Broader national economic and education policies would seem better places on which policymakers should focus attention. This anxiety over immigration smacks of scapegoating and is reminiscent of the support for anti-Filipino legislation as a partial quick fix during the Great Depression. Likewise, proposals to shift from a family- to a skills-based admission system seem suspiciously racial given the current backlogs in family reunification categories for Asian (as well as Latin) countries, and especially since the number of Asian professionals entering has remained high. Policymaking demands careful attention to the demographics of communities and immigrant groups. No matter how well informed, it can never produce the exact results intended. Immigrants themselves always will help define immigration policy.

My findings, particularly those related to diversity and social life in Chapter 5, also concern the social character of the United States. The vast majority of immigrants today are from Asia and Latin America. More than 300,000 Asian immigrants, 56,000 Mexican immigrants, along with 30,000 from Central America and 46,000 from South America, entered in 1990.[1] The growth of communities of color makes it evident that identity and Americanization are important issues in many areas of the country. The multiethnic fabric of many regions raises questions of diversity associated with language, culture, and sociology that demand a sophisticated understanding of communities—of the need for separate space yet to coexist, if we are to live in a workable, culturally pluralistic society.

My look at Vietnamese refugee policies has serious implications for those concerned with this issue. What becomes clear in my examination of how policies emerged in response to the Indochina war is that our foreign policies were prominent in creating refugee pressures. This raises special issues related to our involvement in the affairs of other regions of the world.

Perhaps the most striking ramifications of my findings involve the extent to which policies have touched virtually every aspect of Asian American life. Immigration and refugee policies have influenced gender ratios, where people live, how people live, the jobs they have, their income, as well as personal identity. Policymakers should realize the potential far-reaching effects of their decisions.

We can learn much from Asian America and from the attempts to control its making and remaking. Yet we have never understood the limits of legally imposed control or the frequently unpredictable and sometimes paradoxical consequences of immigration policies and laws. Policymakers typically saw Asia and Asian Americans as a monolith, seldom acknowledging their social and cultural diversity. They characteristically viewed Asians and Asian Americans as merely objects, rarely respecting their ingenuity in responding to regulation. They regarded what little they knew as sufficient, hardly ever bothering to study the dynamics they aimed to control. If they were sometimes successful at controlling the flow of Asian immigration, it was usually because they were able and willing to bully.

Times have changed, however. The social forces turned loose in Asian America (or, for that matter, in Asia) will not allow containment, no matter how forceful or even cruel. We all confront a different world both within and beyond our borders. Though law and policymakers played a prominent role in its making, that new world now seems to resist their shrewdest designs. Rather than trying to push people around, they would be better served attempting to understand and adapt. The United States need not be submissive in order to sometimes compromise and accommodate. In struggling to come to terms with Asians and Asian Americans, we in this country may find entirely new ways to identify and assert our interests—ways that incorporate Asian American history, demographics, and experiences as our own. Whether we are up to the task will tell us much about ourselves.

# Appendixes

# Chronology of Selected Events and Policies Affecting Asian Immigration

| | |
|---|---|
| 1600's–1700's | Open policies from U.S. perspective; emigration bars in Japan, China, Korea |
| 1565 | Small settlement of Filipinos established in Louisiana |
| 1800–75 | Open policies from U.S. perspective |
| 1840's | Chinese begin to enter in appreciable numbers |
| 1850 | California enacts foreign miners' tax, resulting in depopulation of Latino mining force, leaving mostly Chinese |
| 1850's | Chinese actively recruited; but anti-Chinese sentiment also arises |
| 1854 | Peace treaty with Japan, ending Japan's policy of seclusion |
| 1868 | Burlingame Treaty with China, officially ending China's strict emigration policy; but anti-Chinese sentiment grows |
| 1870 | Citizenship rights extended to African Americans, but not to Chinese |
| 1875 | Page Law barring entry of Chinese prostitutes |
| 1882 | Chinese Exclusion Act barring entry of laborers for 10 years |

| 1882 | Treaty with Korea ending Korea's self-imposed isolation |
| 1884 | Supreme Court holds that wives of Chinese laborers cannot enter |
| 1884–85 | Japan permits laborers to work in Hawaii and passes first modern emigration law, as recruitment of Japanese workers increases |
| 1894 | Additional treaty with Japan, reaffirming its commitment to open travel; but anti-Japanese sentiment grows |
| 1895 | Japan defeats China in war |
| 1898 | U.S. takes jurisdiction over Philippines |
| 1902–5 | 7,500 Koreans arrive in Hawaii |
| 1904 | Chinese exclusion made indefinite |
| 1905 | Japan defeats Russia in war; Korea becomes a Japanese protectorate |
| 1906 | San Francisco public schools segregate Japanese students |
| 1907–8 | Under Gentlemen's Agreement, Japan agrees to restrict travel documents to laborers |
| 1911 | Japan agrees to further restrictions on the emigration of laborers |
| 1913 | California enacts Alien Land Law |
| 1911–17 | 2,000 Asian Indians enter; anti-Asian sentiment grows |
| 1917 | Asiatic barred zone is created |
| 1920's | Recruitment of Filipino workers is stepped up |
| 1922–23 | Supreme Court rules that Japanese and Asian Indians are not eligible for citizenship |
| 1924 | National Origins Quota Act, barring any "alien ineligible to citizenship" |
| 1932–34 | Influx of Filipinos hits its peak, as does anti-Filipino sentiment |
| 1934 | Tydings-McDuffie Act grants Philippine independence in 12 years and establishes interim immigration quota at 50 |
| 1942 | Internment of 120,000 West Coast Japanese Americans begins |
| 1943 | Chinese exclusion repealed |
| 1946 | Asian Indians and Filipinos granted citizenship rights; quotas increased to 100 |
| 1952 | McCarran-Walter Act abolishes Asiatic barred zone, but limits immigration to 2,000 within Asia-Pacific triangle |

| | |
|---|---|
| 1962 | Attorney general paroles in 15,111 refugees from mainland China |
| 1965 | Asia-Pacific triangle repealed; country quotas of 20,000 established under family reunification premised system |
| 1975 | U.S. withdraws from Indochina and opens doors to refugees |
| 1980 | Refugee Act establishes refugee procedures |
| 1981 | Separate quota established for Republic of China (Taiwan) |
| 1990 | Expansion of Hong Kong quota (to 10,000; then to 20,000 in 1995); naturalization extended to Filipino veterans of World War II |

# How the Immigration System Worked After 1965

Under the 1965 reforms immigrants essentially were categorized as immediate relatives of U.S. citizens or under the preference system. As immediate relatives they were not subject to quotas or numerical limitations. The category included the spouses and minor, unmarried children of citizens, as well as the parents of adult citizens.

The preference system included seven categories:

*First preference*: adult, unmarried sons and daughters of citizens.

*Second preference*: spouses and unmarried sons and daughters of lawful permanent resident aliens. Permanent residents (green card holders) can petition for relatives only through this category.

*Third preference*: members of the professions or those with exceptional ability in the sciences or the arts. Proof from the Department of Labor that the immigrant would not be displacing an available worker was required for third and sixth preference.

*Fourth preference*: married sons and daughters of citizens.

*Fifth preference*: siblings of adult citizens.

*Sixth preference*: skilled or unskilled workers, of which there was a shortage of employable and willing workers in the United States.

*Seventh preference*: persons fleeing from a Communist-dominated country, a country of the Middle East, or who were uprooted by a natural catastrophe.

Seventh preference was eliminated in 1980. Third and sixth preferences became a part of a larger employment-based immigration scheme in 1990, and an additional pool of visas was set aside for spouses and minor children of lawful permanent residents—most of second preference. The married sons and daughters category was made the third preference, and the sibling category is now fourth preference.

Some examples of how the immigration system worked between 1965 and 1990:

A. A Korean woman who had married a U.S. serviceman (presumably a citizen) could immigrate in the immediate relative category, thereby becoming a lawful permanent resident of the United States. After three years of marriage, she could apply for naturalization and become a citizen. She could then petition for her parents under the immediate relative category, and also for siblings under the fifth preference. Once her parents immigrated, they, as lawful permanent residents, could petition for other unmarried sons and daughters under the second preference. Married siblings entering under the fifth preference could be accompanied by spouses and minor, unmarried children.

B. A doctor or engineer from India could immigrate under the third preference as a professional. He/she could be accompanied by a spouse and unmarried, minor children. After five years of permanent residence, the doctor/engineer could apply for naturalization, and upon obtaining citizenship could petition for parents under the immediate relative category, siblings under the fifth preference, and married sons and daughters under the fourth preference (who could also bring their spouses and minor, unmarried children). The same scenario is possible even if the first Indian immigrant in this family had entered as a non-preference investor when such visas were available.

C. A nurse from the Philippines might be able to immigrate under the third preference. After qualifying for citizenship five years later, she could petition for her parents. Her parents could petition for other unmarried sons and daughters under the second preference or the nurse could petition for these siblings under the fifth preference. If the son or daughter married on a visit to the Philippines, that spouse could then be petitioned for under the second preference.

D. A Chinese American citizen might marry a foreign student from Taiwan. The student would then be able to become an immigrant under the immediate relative category. After three years of marriage to a citizen, naturalization opens immigration possibilities for parents under the immediate relative category and siblings under the fifth preference.

As illustrated in Table 8, nationals from Asian countries generally used the occupational categories more in 1969 than in 1985. Table 9 compares immigrants from China/Taiwan, India, Korea, and the Philippines for 1970, 1979, and 1988. The table reveals that by the late 1970's, second preference and fifth preference were used heavily by immigrants from all of these countries. Substantial numbers of immigrants from all of these countries enter in the immediate relative category today, but Chinese and particularly Indians relied less on it at first. About half of the immigrants from India in 1970 came under the nonpreference category, which was mostly for investors. A large proportion also entered as third preference professionals. But Indians shifted to family-based immigration by the late 1970's. A substantial proportion of Koreans also immigrated as nonpreference investors and in labor categories in 1970, but in the same year, most of them entered in family categories as immediate relatives (e.g., spouses and adopted children of citizens).

# Excerpts from Selected Laws and Cases Affecting Asian Immigration

## Statutes

### 1850 California Foreign Miners Tax
### Passed April 13, 1850

§1. No person who is not a native or natural born citizen of the United States, or who may not have become a citizen under the treaty of Guadalupe Hidalgo (all native California Indians excepted), shall be permitted to mine in any part of this State, without having first obtained a license so to do according to the provisions of this Act. . . .

§6. Every person required by the first section of this Act to obtain a license to mine, shall apply to the Collector of Licenses to foreign miners, and take out a license to mine, for which he shall pay the sum of twenty dollars per month. . . .

### The Burlingame Treaty
### 16 Stat. 739 (July 28, 1868)

Article V. The United States of America and the Emperor of China cordially recognize the inherent and inalienable right of man to change his home and allegiance, and also the mutual advantage of the free migration and emigration of their citizens and subjects, respectively, from the one country to the other, for purposes of curiosity, of trade, or as permanent residents. . . .

Article VI. Citizens of the United States visiting or residing in China shall enjoy the same privileges, immunities, or exemptions in respect to travel or residence as may there be enjoyed by the citizens or subjects of the most favored nation. And, reciprocally, Chinese subjects visiting or residing in the United States, shall enjoy the same privileges, immunities, and exemptions in respect to travel or residence, as may there be enjoyed by the citizens or subjects of the most favored nation. But nothing herein contained shall be held to confer naturalization upon citizens of the United States in China, nor upon the subjects of China in the United States.

Article VII. Citizens of the United States shall enjoy all the privileges of the public education institutions under the control of the government of China, and, reciprocally, Chinese subjects shall enjoy all the privileges of the public education institutions under the control of the government of the United States, which are enjoyed in the respective countries by the citizen or subjects of the most favored nation. . . .

*Statutes of California*
*Eighteenth Session of the Legislature, 1869–70*
*[Chinese and Japanese Prostitutes]*

Chap. CCXXX. Whereas, the business of importing into this State Chinese women for criminal and demoralizing purposes has been carried on extensively during the past year, to the scandal and injury of the people of this State, and in defiance of public decency; and whereas, many of the class referred to are kidnapped in China, and deported at a tender age, without their consent and against their will. . . .

Sec. 1. It shall not be lawful, from and after the time when this Act takes effect, to bring, or land from any ship, boat or vessel, into this State, any Mongolian, Chinese or Japanese females, born either in the Empire of China or Japan, or in any of the islands adjacent to the Empire of China, without first presenting to the Commissioner of Immigration evidence satisfactory to him that such female desires voluntarily to come into this State, and is a good person of correct habits and good character, and thereupon obtaining from such Commissioner of Immigration a license or permit particularly describing such female and authorizing her importation or immigration.

*Page Law*
*18 Stat. 477 (Mar. 3, 1875)*

Chap. 141. That in determining whether the immigration of any subject of China, Japan, or any Oriental country, in the United States, is free and voluntary, . . . it shall be the duty of the consul-general or consul of the United States . . . to ascertain whether such immigrant has entered into a contract or agreement for a term of service within the United States, for lewd and immoral purposes. . . .

Sec. 3. That the importation into the United States of women for the purposes of prostitution is hereby forbidden. . . .

Sec. 5. That it shall be unlawful for aliens of the following classes to immigrate into the United States, namely, persons who are undergoing a sentence for conviction in their own country of felonious crimes other than political or growing out of or the result of such political offenses, or whose sentence has been remitted on condition of their emigration, and women "imported for the purposes of prostitution." . . .

*Chinese Exclusion Act*
*22 Stat. 58 (May 6, 1882)*

Chap. 126. In the opinion of the Government of the United States the coming of Chinese laborers to this country endangers the good order of certain localities within the territory thereof. . . .

That from and after the expiration of ninety days next after the passage of this act, and until the expiration of ten years next after the passage of this act, the coming of Chinese laborers to the United States be, and the same is hereby, suspended; and during such suspension it shall not be lawful for any Chinese laborer to come, or, having so come after the expiration of said ninety days, to remain within the United States. . . .

Sec. 3. That the two foregoing sections shall not apply to Chinese laborers who were in the United States on the seventeenth day of November, eighteen hundred and eighty, or who shall have come into the same before the expiration of ninety days next after the passage of this act, and who shall produce to such master before going on board such vessel, and shall produce to the collector of the port in the United

States at which such vessel shall arrive, the evidence hereinafter in this act required of his being one of the laborers in this section mentioned. . . .

Sec. 6. Every Chinese person other than a laborer who may be entitled by said treaty and this act to come within the United States, and who shall be about to come to the United States, shall be identified as so entitled by the Chinese Government in each case, such identity to be evidenced by a certificate issued under the authority of said government . . . stating such right to come, and which certificate shall state the name, title, or official rank, if any, the age, height, and all physical peculiarities, former and present occupation or profession, and place of residence in China of the person to whom the certificate is issued and that such person is entitled conformably to the treaty in this act mentioned to come within the United States. . . .

Sec. 7. That any person who shall knowingly and falsely alter or substitute any name for the name written in such certificate or forge any such certificate, or knowingly utter any forged or fraudulent certificate, or falsely personate any person named in any such certificate, shall be deemed guilty of a misdemeanor; and upon conviction thereof shall be fined a sum not exceeding one thousand dollars, and imprisoned in a penitentiary for a term of not more than five years. . . .

Sec. 15. That the words "Chinese laborers", wherever used in this act, shall be construed to mean both skilled and unskilled laborers and Chinese employed in mining.

*Scott Act*
*25 Stat. 504 (Oct. 1, 1888)*

Chap. 1064. An act a supplement to an act entitled "An act to execute certain treaty stipulations relating to Chinese," approved the sixth day of May eighteen hundred and eighty-two. . . .

That from and after the passage of this act, it shall be unlawful for any chinese laborer who shall at any time heretofore have been, or who may now or hereafter be, a resident within the United States, and who shall have departed, or shall depart, therefrom, and shall not have returned before the passage of this act, to return to, or remain in, the United States.

Sec. 2. That no certificates of identity provided for in the fourth and fifth sections of the act to which this is a supplement shall hereafter be issued; and every certificate heretofore issued in pursuance thereof, is hereby declared void and of no effect, and the chinese laborer claiming admission by virtue thereof shall not be permitted to enter the United States. . . .

*Geary Act*
*27 Stat. 25 (May 5, 1892)*

Chap. 60. That all laws now in force prohibiting and regulating the coming into this country of Chinese persons and persons of Chinese descent are hereby continued in force for a period of ten years from the passage of this act. . . .

Sec. 5. That after the passage of this act on an application to any judge or court of the United States in the first instance for a writ of habeas corpus, by a Chinese person seeking to land in the United States, to whom that privilege has been denied, no bail shall be allowed, and such application shall be heard and determined promptly without unnecessary delay.

Sec. 6. And it shall be the duty of all Chinese laborers within the limits of the United States, at the time of the passage of this act, and who are entitled to remain in the United States, to apply to the collector of internal revenue of their respective districts, within one year after the passage of this act, for a certificate of residence, and any Chinese laborer, within the limits of the United States, who shall neglect, fail, or refuse to comply with the provisions of this act, or who, after one year from the passage hereof, shall be found within the jurisdiction of the United States without such certificate of residence, shall be deemed and adjudged to be unlawfully within the United States, and may be arrested, by any United States customs official, collector of internal revenue or his deputies, United States marshall or his deputies, and taken before a United States judge, whose duty it shall be to order that he be deported from the United States as hereinbefore provided, unless he shall establish clearly to the satisfaction of said judge, that by reason of accident, sickness or other unavoidable cause, he has been unable to procure his certificate, and to the satisfaction of the court, and by at least one credible white witness, that he was a resident of the United States at the time of the passage of this act; and if upon the hearing, it shall appear that he is so entitled to a certificate, it shall be granted upon his paying the cost. Should it appear that said Chinaman had procured a certificate which has been lost or destroyed, he shall be detained and judgment suspended a reasonable time to enable him to procure a duplicate from the officer granting it, and in such cases, the cost of said arrest and trial shall be in the discretion of the court. And any Chinese person other than a Chinese laborer, having a right to be and remain in the United States, desiring such certificate as evidence of such right may apply for and receive the same without charge. . . .

Sec. 8. That any person who shall knowingly and falsely alter or substitute any name for the name written in such certificate or forge such certificate, or knowingly utter any forged or fraudulent certificate, or falsely personate any person named in such certificate, shall be guilty of a misdemeanor, and upon conviction thereof shall be fined in a sum not exceeding one thousand dollars or imprisoned in the penitentiary for a term of not more than five years. . . .

*Chinese Exclusion Laws*
*33 Stat. 428 (1904)*

Sec. 5. That section one of the Act of Congress approved April twenty-ninth, nineteen hundred and two, entitled "An Act to prohibit the coming into and to regulate the residence within the United States, its Territories, and all territory under its jurisdiction, and the District of Columbia, of Chinese and persons of Chinese descent" is hereby amended so as to read as follows:

"All laws in force on the twenty-ninth day of April, nineteen hundred and two, regulating, suspending, or prohibiting the coming of Chinese persons or persons of Chinese descent into the United States . . . are hereby, reenacted, extended, and continued, without modification, limitation, or condition: and said laws shall also apply to the island territory under the jurisdiction of the United States, and prohibit the immigration of Chinese laborers, not citizens of the United States, from such island territory to the mainland territory of the United States. . . .

*Act of March 2, 1907*
*34 Stat. 1228*

Sec. 3. That any American woman who marries a foreigner shall take the nationality of her husband. At the termination of the marital relation, she may resume her American citizenship, if abroad, by registering as an American citizen within one year with a consul of the United States, or by returning to reside in the United States. . . .

*Telegram of January 1, 1908*
*[Part of the Gentlemen's Agreement]*

(Enclosure No. 3 with Mr. O'Brien Dispatch No. 120 of Jan. 2.)
(Reading of telegram sent January 1, 1908.)
(Secstate, Washington. January 1, 1908. 12 P.M.)

Have received from Minister for Foreign Affairs an extended memorandum in reference to our several conversations and my note to him of November sixteen(period) Am sending herewith important portions by cable and full text by mail January third (paragraph)

(quote) It affords Count Hayashi sincere pleasure to express at the outset his appreciation of the genuinely friendly and conciliatory spirit which is so conspicuously present in the Ambassador's official and personal utterances regarding this subject(period) Fully realizing as they do the weighty character of the considerations which influence the opinions of the American Government(comma) the Imperial Government are gratified to perceive in the views expressed by the Ambassador on behalf of his Government reciprocal recognition of the delicate and difficult nature of the problem which confronts Japan(period) Count Hayashi is confident that he does not err in believing that this mutual acknowledgement of the difficulties to be overcome on both sides will aid materially in reaching a satisfactory settlement of the matters at issue(end quote) (paragraph)

(quote) The Imperial Government recognize as a matter of course the right of the American Government to regulate such matters in the manner best calculated to promote American interests(period) They are confident however that the Government at Washington(comma) while acting upon this principle(comma) will deal with the situation to which the Ambassador refers in the same liberal and enlightened spirit which has been such a marked characteristic of American intercourse with Japan(end quote) (paragraph)

(quote) It is sufficient for the purpose which both Governments have in view to assure the Ambassador that the Imperial Government (comma) appreciating the manifest intention of his communications and of the views of his Government as explained therein(comma) are desirous by frank and cordial cooperation to reach an understanding which will eliminate all the difficulties of the present situation(end quote) (paragraph)

He refers to belief of American authorities (quote)That existing administrative regulations have proved inadequate for the regulation of the influx of Japanese laborers to the American mainland(period) The Imperial Government are not prepared to admit without qualification that this view is entirely correct(period) They believe that the partial failure of the measures in question to accomplish the results hoped and expected has been due partly to causes of a temporary nature(comma) the recurrence of which will be rendered extremely improbable in the future(colon) and partly to causes which the measures which they are willing to adopt will wholly remove(end quote) (paragraph)

He draws attention (quote)to what appeared to him to be some inaccuracy in the figures reported by the American immigration authorities(period) To illustrate(comma) it is stated that the number of Japanese coming to the United States instead of decreasing has largely increased(comma) twelve thousand four hundred seven having arrived during the last twelve months as against six thousand four hundred fifty-four during the preceding year(comma) and that the number of laborers coming in has increased(comma) one thousand eight hundred fifty-eight Japanese laborers having passports for the continental territory of the United States having been admitted during the six months ending September thirty(period) (paragraph)

As regards the first of these statements it may be noted that the official Japanese statistics show that the total number of passports issued to persons of all classes proceeding to American territory in nineteen six was nineteen thousand eight hundred eighty-eight of whom fourteen thousand seven hundred twenty-six went to the Hawaiian Islands and five thousand one hundred sixty-two to the mainland the latter number including all persons in transit to other countries(period) In nineteen seven from January to October inclusive the total number was fifteen thousand one hundred sixty-eight of whom ten thousand seven hundred thirty-two went to the Hawaiian Islands and four thousand four hundred thirty-six to the main land(period) Of the latter three thousand six hundred eighty-four belonged to the non laboring classes and seven hundred fifty-two were laborers(comma) either persons returning to the United States(comma) the members of the families of laborers already resident there(comma) or agricultural settlers(period) Count Hayashi is at a loss to account for the discrepancies thus disclosed but believes it may confidentially be stated that the number of passports alleged to have been granted to laborers emigrating to the main land in nineteen seven cannot possibly be correct(period) It is true that it has come to the knowledge of the Japanese Government that some laborers in the guise of merchants or students have obtained passports to the American main land(comma) but making reasonable allowance for cases of that description the total number must fall far short of that reported to the Ambassador(end quote) (paragraph)

(quote) By way of recapitulation and of additional explanation Count Hayashi now begs to present(comma) for the information of the American Government(comma) the following summary of the views of the Imperial Government and of the measures they are prepared to take (paragraph)

One. The Imperial Government are determined to continue their announced policy of issuing no passports good for the American main land to either skilled or unskilled Japanese laborers(comma) except to those who have previously resided in the United States or the parents wives or children of Japanese residents (paragraph)

Two. They intend however to continue to grant passports to settled agriculturists(period) As was made known to the predecessor of His Excellency the Ambassador on the twenty-sixth of May last the Japanese Government have exercised with reference to those persons very careful and rigorous supervision and restriction(period) The privilege has only been granted to bona fide agriculturists intending to settle in certain specified localities(period) In order to avoid all possible subterfuge the central administration will continue rigidly to apply the precautionary measures set forth in the explanatory memorandum of May twenty-sixth (paragraph)

Three. The Imperial Government have formulated instructions to local Governors that in every case of application for a passport to the United States by a student(comma) merchant(comma) tourist or the like(comma) thorough investigation must be made to determine whether the applicant is not likely to become a laborer after reaching the United States(period) A material and indispensable part of this investigation relates to the financial status of the applicant(period) If he is not rich enough in his own right to assure the permanence of his status as a student(comma) merchant or tourist(comma) surety will be required of his family or special patron in the case of a student(comma) or of his firm or company in the case of a merchant or mercantile employee (comma) guaranteeing the payment of expenses and a monthly allowance of say forty yen(colon) and(comma) in the case of tourists (comma) the payment of sufficient traveling expenses(period) The passport applied for will only be issued after this surety has been given (period) As a further precaution in the case of students no such pass-ports will be issued except to students who have passed through the middle schools (paragraph)

Four. So far as concerns the Hawaiian Islands(comma) which it is proposed to set aside from the scope of the questions under considera-tion(comma) it is the present intention of the Imperial Government experimentally to stop all emigration to those Islands for some time to come except in isolated cases of returning emigrants and of the parents wives and children of those already resident in the islands (paragraph)

Five. The Imperial Government intend to take measures regarding the emigration of Japanese laborers to foreign territory adjacent to the United States(comma) which(comma) in their opinion(comma) will effectually remove all cause for complaint on that account (paragraph)

Count Hayashi sincerely trusts that His Excellency the Ambassador and his Government will find in the foregoing recapitulation ample evi-dence of the desire and the intention of the Imperial Government to adopt administrative measures of regulation and control which will effectually meet the requirements of the situation(end quote)

In a conversation thirtieth I received memorandum in which Japanese Minister for Foreign Affairs discusses your suggestions(period) As to clause four he says passports entitle holder to protection (quote) It is a right upon which all Governments are want to insist as regards their subjects or citizens abroad even where the latter are accused of viola-tions of the law(period) The domestic control and restriction of emigra-tion are purely administrative functions(comma) and confer no power upon the Japanese Government to agree in advance that the evasion of such control and restriction at home(comma) or the violation of similar laws or regulations abroad(comma) shall deprive the offender in toto of the protection guaranteed to him by treaty(end quote) As to clauses five and six (quote) the Japanese Consulate General in New York has seven-teen states and one district within its consular district(colon) the Consulate of Chicago has twenty States and one district(colon) the Consulate General at San Francisco has four States and two dis-tricts(comma) while the Consulate at Seattle has six states in its dis-trict(period) Most of these states and districts extend over several hundred miles(comma) and Japanese residents in the United States (comma) more than one hundred thousand in number(comma) are scattered over these great areas(period) The Japanese Consulate can have no exact knowledge as to the whereabouts of these Japanese residents or means of communicating with them all(period) The result will be that with the suggested system of registry most(comma) if not all(comma) of these residents will find themselves after one year from January one nineteen eight(comma) unqualified to remain legally in the United States and may be dealt with accordingly(comma) without the least fault on their part(period) In order to compel a steamship company to carry back(comma) without expense to the Japanese Government(comma) any Japanese or Korean subjects who may have acted in contravention of any regulations(comma) possibly it may be months or years after the alleged offense is said to have occurred (comma) legislation will be necessary(period) Japanese Government can entertain no hope that such legislation(comma) if submitted to the Diet(comma) will receive its approval(period) The suggestions made by the American Government under sections five and six would appear therefore wholly impracticable if not entirely impossible (comma) to say nothing of the indignity and humiliation to which Japanese residents in the United States would be liable at any moment(period) The Japanese Government are afraid moreover that if these Japanese who have entered the United States and are peacefully earning their livelihood were to be subjected to the same rigorous measures of personal examination and vexations identification as on the occasion of entry an almost intolerable amount of injustice and humiliation would be inflicted upon Japanese residents other than laborers(end quote) I believe that they strongly resent as a blow to their national pride the similarity between our proposals in this respect and the terms of the Chinese exclusion act and they have plainly intimated that the provisions of clauses five and six would be less acceptable to Japan than an exclusion law(period) As to section five of the recapitulation I am informed that the Japanese Government believe that their proposed measures in reference to Canada and Mexico (comma) together with the suspension of emigration to Hawaii(comma) will effectively stop all illicit immigration(period) I have some reason to believe that the following may be agreed to(colon) first that there be plainly printed on passports the conditions upon which they are granted and possibly some penalty for violation of these limitations Second that number to Hawaii be restricted to one thousand With potential for greater number whenever President believes additional laborers needed. Third provision for more strict rules as to agriculturalists Fourth to arrange for registration of those going to the US hereafter (paragraph)

Minister for Foreign Affairs admits that methods in the past have been too lax but I believe in his sincere intention to remedy this difficulty

O'Brien

SOURCES: O'Brien to Root, telegram, January 1, 1908, S.D. File 2542/331–334; Records of Department of States, National Archives, Numerical Series, 1906–1910: 2542 Japanese Immigration, cited in Esthus, fn. 68, p. 164.

*Alien Land Law*
*1913 California Statutes*
*Approved May 15, 1913*

Chap. 113. Section 1. All aliens eligible to citizenship under the laws of the United States may acquire, possess, enjoy, transmit and inherit real property, or any interest therein, in this state, in the same manner and to the same extent as citizens of the United States, except as otherwise provided by the laws of this state.

Sec. 2. All aliens other than those mentioned in section one of this act may acquire, possess, enjoy and transfer real property, or any interest therein, in this state, in the manner and to the extent and for the purposes prescribed by any treaty now existing between the government of the United States and the nation or country of which such alien is a citizen or subject, and not otherwise, and may in addition thereto lease lands in this state for agricultural purposes for a term not exceeding three years. . . .

*Immigration Act*
*39 Stat. 874 (Feb. 5, 1917)*

Sec. 3. That the following classes of aliens shall be excluded from admission into the United States . . . persons who are natives of islands not possessed by the United States adjacent to the Continent of Asia, situate south of the twentieth parallel latitude north, west of the one hundred and sixtieth meridian of longitude east from Greenwich, and north of the tenth parallel of latitude south, or who are natives of any country, province, or dependency situate on the Continent of Asia west of the one hundred and tenth meridian of longitude east from Greenwich and east of the fiftieth meridian of longitude east from Greenwich and south of the fiftieth parallel of latitude north, except that portion of said territory situate between the fiftieth and the sixty-fourth meridians of longitude east from Greenwich and the twenty-fourth and thirty-eighth parallels of latitude north, and no alien now in any way excluded from, or prevented from entering, the United States shall be admitted to the United States. . . .

All aliens over sixteen years of age, physically capable of reading, who can not read the English language, or some other language or dialect, including Hebrew or Yiddish. . . .

Sec. 38. That this Act shall not be construed to repeal, alter, or amend existing laws relating to the immigration or exclusion of Chinese persons or persons of Chinese descent. . . .

*The Cable Act*
*42 Stat. 1021 (Sept. 22, 1922)*

Sec. 3. That a woman citizen of the United States shall not cease to be a citizen of the United States by reason of her marriage after the passage of this Act, unless she makes a formal renunciation of her citizenship before a court having jurisdiction over naturalization of aliens: *Provided,* That any woman citizen who marries an alien ineligible to citizenship shall cease to be a citizen of the United States. . . .

*Immigration Act*
*43 Stat. 153 (May 26, 1924)*

Sec. 11.(a) The annual quota of any nationality shall be 2 per centum of the number of foreign-born individuals of such nationality resident in continental United States as determined by the United States census of 1890, but the minimum quota of any nationality shall be 100. . . .

Sec. 13. (c) No alien ineligible to citizenship shall be admitted to the United States unless such alien (1)is admissible as a non-quota immigrant under the provisions of subdivision (b), (d), or (e) of section 4, or (2) is the wife, or the unmarried child under 18 years of age, of an immigrant admissible under such subdivision (d), and is accompanying or following to join him, or (3) is not an immigrant as defined in section 3. . . .

### Tydings-McDuffie Act
### 48 Stat. 456 (March 22, 24, 1934)

Sec. 1. The Philippine Legislature is hereby authorized to provide for the election of delegates to a constitutional convention . . . to formulate and draft a constitution for the government of the Commonwealth of the Philippine Islands, subject to the conditions and qualifications prescribed in this Act, which shall exercise jurisdiction over all the territory ceded to the United States by the treaty of peace concluded between the United States and Spain on the 10th day of December, 1898. . . .

Sec. 8. (1) For the purposes of the Immigration Act of 1917, the Immigration Act of 1924 . . . this section, and all other laws of the United States relating to the immigration, exclusion, or expulsion of aliens, citizens of the Philippine Islands who are not citizens of the United States shall be considered as if they were aliens. For such purposes the Philippine Islands shall be considered as a separate country and shall have for each fiscal year a quota of fifty. . . .

(2) Citizens of the Philippine Islands who are not citizens of the United States shall not be admitted to the continental United States from the Territory of Hawaii. . . .

(4) For the purposes of sections 18 and 20 of the Immigration Act of 1917, as amended, the Philippine Islands shall be considered to be a foreign country. . . .

Sec. 10. (a) On the 4th day of July immediately following the expiration of a period of ten years from the date of the inauguration of the new government under the constitution provided for in this Act the President of the United States shall by proclamation withdraw and surrender all right of possession, supervision, jurisdiction, control, or sovereignty then existing and exercised by the United States in and over the territory and people of the Philippine Islands. . . .

Sec. 14. Upon the final and complete withdrawal of American sovereignty over the Philippine Islands the immigration laws of the United States (including all the provisions thereof relating to persons ineligible to citizenship) shall apply to persons who were born in the Philippine Islands to the same extent as in the case of other foreign countries. . . .

*The Chinese Repealer*
*57 Stat. 600 (Dec. 17, 1943)*

An Act
To repeal the Chinese Exclusion Acts, to establish quotas, and for other purposes.

*Be it enacted by the Senate and House of Representatives of the United States of America in Congress assembled,* That the following Acts or parts of Acts relating to the exclusion or deportation of persons of the Chinese race are hereby repealed: May 6, 1882 (22 Stat. L. 58); July 5, 1884 (23 Stat. L. 115); September 13, 1888 (25 Stat. L. 476); October 1, 1888 (25 Stat. L. 504); May 5, 1892 (27 Stat. L. 25); November 3, 1893 (28 Stat. L. 7). . . .

Sec. 2. With the exception of those coming under subsections (b), (d), (e), and (f) of section 4, Immigration Act of 1924 . . . all Chinese persons entering the United States annually as immigrants shall be allocated to the quota for the Chinese computed under the provision of section 11 of the said Act. A preference up to 75 per centum of the quota shall be given to Chinese born and resident in China.

Sec. 3. Section 303 of the Nationality Act of 1940, as amended (54 Stat. 1140; 8 U.S.C. 703), is hereby amended by striking out the word "and" before the word "descendants", changing the colon after the word "Hemisphere" to a comma, and adding the following: "and Chinese persons or persons of Chinese descent" [making them eligible for naturalization].

*Filipino and Indian Naturalization Act*
*60 Stat. 416 (July 2, 1946)*

An Act
To authorize the admission into the United States of persons of races indigenous to India, and persons of races indigenous to the Philippine Islands, to make them racially eligible for naturalization, and for other purposes.

That section 303 of the Nationality Act of 1940 . . . be amended to read as follows:

"Sec. 303 (a) The right to become a naturalized citizen under the provisions of this Act shall extend only to—

"(1) white persons, persons of African nativity or descent, and persons who are descendants of races indigenous to the continents of North or South America or adjacent islands and Filipino persons or persons of Filipino descent. . . .

"(3) Chinese persons and persons of Chinese descent, and persons of races indigenous to India. . . . "

*McCarran-Walter (Immigration and Nationality Act of 1952)*
*Public Law 414, 66 Stat. 163*

To revise the laws relating to immigration, naturalization, and nationality; and for other purposes.

Sec. 201. (a) The annual quota of any quota area shall be one-sixth of 1 per centum of the number of inhabitants in the continental United States in 1920, which number, except for the purpose of computing quotas for quota areas within the Asia-Pacific triangle, shall be the same number heretofore determined under the provisions of . . . the Immigration Act of 1924. . . .

Sec. 202. (a) Each independent country, self-governing dominion, mandated territory, and territory under the international trusteeship system of the United Nations, other than the United States and its outlying possessions and the countries specified in section 101(a)(27)(C), shall be treated as a separate quota area when approved by the Secretary of State. . . .

(5) notwithstanding the provisions of paragraphs (2), (3), and (4) of this subsection, any alien who is attributable by as much as one-half of his ancestry to a people or peoples indigenous to the Asia-Pacific triangle defined in subsection (b) of this section, unless such alien is entitled to a nonquota immigrant status . . . shall be chargeable to a quota as specified in subsection (b). . . .

(b) With reference to determination of the quota to which shall be chargeable an immigrant who is attributable by as much as one-half of his ancestry to a people or peoples indigenous to the Asia-Pacific triangle comprising all quota areas and all colonies and other dependent areas situate wholly east of the meridian sixty degrees east of Greenwich, wholly west of the meridian one hundred and sixty-five degrees west, and wholly north of the parallel twenty-five degrees south latitude—

(1) there is hereby established, in addition to quotas for separate quota areas comprising independent countries, self-governing dominions, and territories under the international trusteeship system of the United Nations situate wholly within said Asia-Pacific

triangle, an Asia-Pacific quota of one hundred annually, which quota shall be subject to the provisions of subsection (e). . . .

(6) such immigrant born outside the Asia-Pacific triangle who is attributable by as much as one-half of his ancestry to peoples indigenous to two or more separate quota areas situate wholly within the Asia-Pacific triangle, or to a quota area or areas and one or more colonies and other dependent areas situate wholly therein, shall be chargeable to the Asia-Pacific quota. . . .

(e) After the determination of quotas has been made as provided in section 201, revision of the quotas shall be made by the Secretary of State, Secretary of Commerce, and the Attorney General, jointly, whenever necessary, to provide for any change of boundaries resulting in transfer of territory from one sovereignty to another, a change of administrative arrangements of a colony or other dependent areas, or any other political change, requiring a change in the list of quota areas or of the territorial limits thereof, but any increase in the number of minimum quota areas above twenty within the Asia-Pacific triangle shall result in a proportionate decrease in each minimum quota of such area in order that the sum total of all minimum quotas within the Asia-Pacific triangle shall not exceed two thousand. . . .

## Cases

*Chew Heong v. United States*
*112 U.S. 536 (1884)*

MR. JUSTICE HARLAN delivered the opinion of the court.

This case comes before us upon a certificate of division in opinion upon questions that require a construction of the act of Congress approved May 6, 1882, ch. 126, 22 Stat. 58, entitled "An Act to execute certain treaty stipulations relating to Chinese,"—commonly known as the Chinese restriction act—and of the act amendatory thereof, approved July 5, 1884, ch. 220, 23 Stat. 115.

The facts deemed important in the consideration of these questions, and as to which there is no dispute, are these: The plaintiff in error, Chew Heong, is a subject of the Emperor of China, and a Chinese laborer. He resided in this country on the 17th of November, 1880, on which day commissioners plenipotentiary, upon the part of the United States and China, concluded, at Peking, a treaty containing articles in modification of former treaties between the same countries. 22 Stat. 826. He departed from the United States for Honolulu, in the Hawaiian Kingdom, on the 18th of June, 1881, and remained there until September 15, 1884, when he took passage on an American vessel bound for the port of San Francisco. Arriving at that port on September 22, 1884, his request to be permitted to leave the vessel was denied, and he was detained on board, under the claim that the act of Congress of May 6, 1882, as amended, forbade him to land within the United States. He was thereupon brought before the Circuit Court of the United States for the District of California upon a writ of habeas corpus. The United States Attorney for that District, who was permitted to intervene in behalf of the government, objected to his discharge, and asked that such orders be made as would effect his removal from the country. It was held that he was not entitled to re-enter or to remain in the United States, and must be deported to the place whence he came, to wit, Honolulu.

The questions certified involve the inquiry, whether §4 of the act approved May 6, 1882, as amended by that of July 5, 1884, prescribing the certificate which shall be produced by a Chinese laborer as the "only evidence permissible to establish his right of re-entry" into the United States, is applicable to Chinese laborers who, residing in this country on November 17, 1880, departed by sea prior to May 6, 1882, and remained out of the United States till after July 5, 1884.

What injustice could be more marked than, by legislative enactment, to recognize the existence of a right, by treaty, to come within the limits of the United States and, at the same time, to prescribe, as the only evidence permissible to establish it, the possession of a collector's certificate, that could not possibly have been obtained by the person to whom the right belongs? Or to prevent the re-entry of a person into the United States upon the ground that he did not, upon his arrival from a foreign port, produce a certain certificate, under the hand and seal of a collector, and upon forms prescribed by the Secretary of the Treasury, which neither that nor any other officer was authorized or permitted to give prior to the departure of such person from this country? Or what incongruity is more evident than to impose upon a collector the duty of going on board of a vessel, about to sail from his district for a foreign port, and making and recording a list of its passengers, of a particular race, showing their individual, family, and tribal names in full, their age, occupation, last place of residence, physical marks and peculiarities, when such vessel had sailed long before the law passed which imposed that duty on the collector? These questions suggest the consequences that must result, if it is held that Congress intended to abrogate the treaty with China, by imposing conditions upon the enjoyment of rights secured by it, which are impossible of performance.

But there is another view which tends to show the unsoundness of the construction upon which the government insists. It is this: If Chinese laborers who were here at the date of the treaty, or who came within ninety days next after the passage of the act of 1882, being out of the country when the act of 1884 was passed, can re-enter only upon producing the certificate required by the latter act, then Congress must have intended to exclude even those who were in this country at the time the act of 1882 was passed, and who, upon going away, received the certificate mentioned in it; for the certificate prescribed by the act of 1882 is not the certificate prescribed by that of 1884; they differ in several particulars; and yet, if the act of 1884 is to be taken literally, all Chinese laborers are excluded who do not produce the very certificate mentioned in it. The original act expressly provides that the certificate prescribed therein "shall entitle the Chinese laborer to whom the same is issued to return to and re-enter the United States, upon producing and delivering the same" to the collector of the district at which he seeks to re-enter. Congress did not intend, by indirection, to withdraw from those who received and relied upon the certificate mentioned in that act the privilege of returning, simply because they did not (and could not) produce the certificate required by the amendatory act, passed during their rightful absence. Those who left the country with certificates under the original act were entitled to return upon the production of those certificates. If, then, the act of 1884 did not defeat the rights given by that of 1882, it follows that there are Chinese laborers who, having been in the United States prior to July 5, 1884, may re-enter without producing the certificate required by the act of the latter date; . . . The Chinese laborer who, under the act of 1882, was entitled to return and re-enter the United States upon producing the certificate therein prescribed, and the Chinese laborer who, after the act of 1884 was passed, could re-enter the country only upon producing the certificate required by the latter act, is described as one "to whom the same is issued." It would be a perversion of the language used to hold that such regulations apply to Chinese laborers who had left the country with the privilege, secured by treaty, of returning, but who, by reason of their absence when those legislative enactments took effect, could not obtain the required certificates.

Yick Wo v. Hopkins
118 U.S. 356 (1886)

MR. JUSTICE MATTHEWS delivered the opinion of the Court.

[A San Francisco ordinance made it unlawful to operate a laundry without the consent of the board of supervisors except in a brick or stone building. Yick Wo, a Chinese alien who had operated a laundry for 22 years, had certificates from the health and fire authorities, but was refused consent by the board. For violating the ordinance, he was fined $10 and jailed for nonpayment. It was admitted that "there were about 320 laundries in the city [and] about 240 were owned [by] subjects of China, and of the whole number, viz., 320, about 310 were constructed of wood"; that "petitioner, and more than 150 of his countrymen, have been arrested" for violating the ordinance "while those who are not subjects of China, and who are conducting 80 odd laundries under similar conditions, are left unmolested."]

[T]he facts shown establish an administration directed so exclusively against a particular class of persons as to warrant and require the conclusion that, whatever may have been the intent of the ordinances as adopted, they are applied [with] a mind so unequal and oppressive as to amount to a practical denial by the State of [equal protection]. Though the law itself be fair on its face and impartial in appearance, yet, if it is applied and administered by public authority with an evil eye and an unequal hand, so as practically to make unjust and illegal discriminations between persons in similar circumstances, material to their rights, the denial of equal justice is still within the prohibition of the Constitution. . . .

The present cases [are] within this class. It appears [that] petitioners have complied with every requisite deemed by the law, or by the public officers charged with its administration, necessary for the protection of neighboring property from fire, or as a precaution against injury to the public health. No reason whatever, except the will of the supervisors, is assigned why they should not be permitted to carry [on] their harmless and useful occupation, on which they depend for a livelihood; and while this consent of the supervisors is withheld from them, and from 200 others who have also petitioned, all of whom happen to be Chinese subjects, 80 others, not Chinese subjects, are permitted to carry on the same business under similar conditions. The fact of this discrimination is admitted. No reason for it is shown, and the conclusion cannot be resisted that no reason for it exists except hostility to the face and nationality to which the petitioners [belong]. The discrimination is therefore [a] denial of [equal protection].

*The Chinese Exclusion Case*
*Chae Chan Ping v. United States*
*130 U.S. 581 (1889)*

MR. JUSTICE FIELD delivered the opinion of the court.

The appeal involves a consideration of the validity of the act of Congress of October 1, 1888, prohibiting Chinese laborers from entering the United States who had departed before its passage, having a certificate issued under the act of 1882 as amended by the act of 1884, granting them permission to return. The validity of the act is assailed as being in effect an expulsion from the country of Chinese laborers, in violation of existing treaties between the United States and the government of China, and of rights vested in them under the laws of Congress.

The discovery of gold in California in 1848, as is well known, was followed by a large immigration thither from all parts of the world, attracted not only by the hope of gain from the mines, but from the great prices paid for all kinds of labor. The news of the discovery penetrated China, and laborers came from there in great numbers, a few with their own means, but by far the greater number under contract with employers, for whose benefit they worked. These laborers readily secured employment, and, as domestic servants, and in various kinds of out-door work, proved to be exceedingly useful. For some years little opposition was made to them except when they sought to work in the mines, but, as their numbers increased, they began to engage in various mechanical pursuits and trades, and thus came in competition with our artisans and mechanics, as well as our laborers in the field.

The competition steadily increased as the laborers came in crowds on each steamer that arrived from China, or Hong Kong, an adjacent English port. They were generally industrious and frugal. Not being accompanied by families, except in rare instances, their expenses were small; and they were content with the simplest fare, such as would not suffice for our laborers and artisans. The competition between them and our people was for this reason altogether in their favor, and the consequent irritation, proportionately deep and bitter, was followed, in many cases, by open conflicts, to the great disturbance of the public peace.

The differences of race added greatly to the difficulties of the situation. Notwithstanding the favorable provisions of the new articles of the treaty of 1868, by which all the privileges, immunities, and exemptions were extended to subjects of China in the United States which were accorded to citizens or subjects of the most favored nation, they remained strangers in the land, residing apart by themselves, and adhering to the customs and usages of their own country. It seemed impossible for them to assimilate with our people or to make any change in their habits or modes of living. As they grew in numbers each year the people of the coast saw, or believed they saw, in the facility of immigration, and in the crowded millions of China, where population presses upon the means of subsistence, great danger that at no distant day that portion of our country would be overrun by them unless prompt action was taken to restrict their immigration. The people there accordingly petitioned earnestly for protective legislation.

In December, 1878, the convention which framed the present constitution of California, being in session, took this subject up, and memorialized Congress upon it, setting forth, in substance, that the presence of Chinese laborers had a baneful effect upon the material interests of the State, and upon public morals; that their immigration was in numbers approaching the character of an Oriental invasion, and was a menace to our civilization; that the discontent from this cause was not confined to any political party, or to any class or nationality, but was well-nigh universal; that they retained the habits and customs of their own country, and in fact constituted a Chinese settlement within the State, without any interest in our country or its institutions; and praying Congress to take measures to prevent their further immigration. This memorial was presented to Congress in February, 1879.

So urgent and constant were the prayers for relief against existing and anticipated evils, both from the public authorities of the Pacific Coast and from private individuals, that Congress was impelled to act on the subject. Many persons, however, both in and out of Congress, were of opinion that so long as the treaty remained unmodified, legislation restricting immigration would be a breach of faith with China. A statute was accordingly passed appropriating money to send commissioners to China to act with our minister there in negotiating and concluding by treaty a settlement of such matters of interest between the two governments as might be confided to them.

This court is not a sensor of the morals of other departments of the government; it is not invested with any authority to pass judgment upon the motives of their conduct. When once it is established that Congress possesses the power to pass an act, our province ends with its construction, and its application to cases as they are presented for determination. Congress has the power under the Constitution to declare war, and in two instances where the power has been exercised—in the war of 1812 against Great Britain, and in 1846 against Mexico—the propriety and wisdom and justice of its action were vehemently assailed by some of the ablest and best men in the country, but no one doubted the legality of the proceeding, and any imputation by this or any other court of the United States upon the motives of the members of Congress who in either case voted for the declaration, would have been justly the cause of animadversion. We do not mean to intimate that the moral aspects of legislative acts may not be proper subjects of consideration. Undoubtedly they may be, at proper times and places, before the public, in the halls of Congress, and in all the modes by which the public mind can be influenced. Public opinion thus enlightened, brought to bear upon legislation, will do more than all other causes to prevent abuses; but the province of the courts is to pass upon the validity of laws, not to make them, and when their validity is established, to declare their meaning and apply their provisions. All else lies beyond their domain.

There being nothing in the treaties between China and the United States to impair the validity of the act of Congress of October 1, 1888, was it on any other ground beyond the competency of Congress to pass it? If so, it must be because it was not within the power of Congress to prohibit Chinese laborers who had at the time departed from the United States, or should subsequently depart, from returning to the United States. Those laborers are not citizens of the United States; they are aliens. That the government of the United States, through the action of the legislative department, can exclude aliens from its territory is a proposition which we do not think open to controversy. Jurisdiction over its own territory to that extent is an incident of every independent nation. It is a part of its independence. If it could not exclude aliens it would be to that extent subject to the control of another power.

For local interests the several States of the Union exist, but for national purposes, embracing our relations with foreign nations, we are but one people, one nation, one power.

To preserve its independence, and give security against foreign aggression and encroachment, is the highest duty of every nation, and to attain these ends nearly all other considerations are to be subordinated. It matters not in what form such aggression and encroachment come, whether from the foreign nation acting in its national character or from vast hordes of its people crowding in upon us. The government, possessing the powers which are to be exercised for protection and security, is clothed with authority to determine the occasion on which the powers shall be called forth; and its determination, so far as the subjects affected are concerned, are necessarily conclusive upon all its departments and officers. If, therefore, the government of the United States, through its legislative department, considers the presence of foreigners of a different race in this country, who will not assimilate with us, to be dangerous to its peace and security, their exclusion is not to be stayed because at the time there are no actual hostilities with the nation of which the foreigners are subjects.

*Fong Yue Ting v. United States*
*149 U.S. 698 (1893)*

These were three writs of *habeas corpus,* granted by the Circuit Court of the United States for the Southern District of New York, upon petitions of Chinese laborers, arrested and held by the marshal of the district for not having certificates of residence, under section 6 of the act of May 5, 1892, c. 60, which is copied in the margin [footnote omitted].

The power to exclude or to expel aliens, being a power affecting international relations, is vested in the political departments of the government, and is to be regulated by treaty or by act of Congress, and to be executed by the executive authority according to the regulations so established, except so far as the judicial department has been authorized by treaty or by statute, or is required by the paramount law of the Constitution, to intervene.

The treaty made between the United States and China on July 28, 1868, contained the following stipulations:

"ARTICLE V. The United States of America and the Emperor of China cordially recognize the inherent and inalienable right of man to change his home and allegiance, and also the mutual advantage of the free migration and emigration of their citizens and subjects, respectively, from one country to the other, for purposes of curiosity, of trade, and as permanent residents."

"ARTICLE VI. Citizens of the United States visiting or residing in

China," "and reciprocally, Chinese subjects visiting or residing in the United States, shall enjoy the same privileges, immunities and exemptions, in respect to travel or residence, as may there be enjoyed by the citizens or subjects of the most favored nation. But nothing herein contained shall be held to confer naturalization upon citizens of the United States in China, nor upon the subjects of China in the United States."

After some years' experience under that treaty, the government of the United States was brought to the opinion that the presence within our territory of large numbers of Chinese laborers, of a distinct race and religion, remaining strangers in the land, residing apart by themselves, tenaciously adhering to the customs and usages of their own country, unfamiliar with our institutions, and apparently incapable of assimilating with our people, might endanger good order, and be injurious to the public interests; and therefore requested and obtained from China a modification of the treaty.

In view of that decision, which, as before observed, was a unanimous judgment of the court, and which had the concurrence of all the justices who had delivered opinions in the cases arising under the acts of 1882 and 1884, it appears to be impossible to hold that a Chinese laborer acquired, under any of the treaties or acts of Congress, any right, as a denizen or otherwise, to be and remain in this country, except by the license, permission and sufferance of Congress, to be withdrawn whenever, in its opinion, the public welfare might require it.

Chinese laborers, therefore, like all other aliens residing in the United States for a shorter or longer time, are entitled, so long as they are permitted by the government of the United States to remain in the country, to the safeguards of the Constitution, and to the protection of the laws, in regard to their rights of person and of property, and to their civil and criminal responsibility. But they continue to be aliens, having taken no steps towards becoming citizens, and incapable of becoming such under the naturalization laws; and therefore remain subject to the power of Congress to expel them, or to order them to be removed and deported from the country, whenever in its judgment their removal is necessary or expedient for the public interest.

The act of May 5, 1892, c. 60, is entitled "An act to prohibit the coming of Chinese persons into the United States"; and provides, in section 1, that "all laws now in force, prohibiting and regulating the coming into this country of Chinese persons and persons of Chinese descent, are hereby continued in force for a period of ten years from the passage of this act."

The manifest objects of these sections are to provide a system of registration and identification of such Chinese laborers, to require them to obtain certificates of residence, and, if they do not do so within a year, to have them deported from the United States.

The effect of the provisions of section 6 of the act of 1892 is that, if a Chinese laborer, after the opportunity afforded him to obtain a certificate of residence within a year, at a convenient place, and without cost, is found without such a certificate, he shall be so far presumed to be not entitled to remain within the United States, that an officer of the customs, or a collector of internal revenue, or a marshal, or a deputy of either, may arrest him, not with a view to imprisonment or punishment, or to his immediate deportation without further inquiry, but in order to take him before a judge, for the purpose of a judicial hearing and determination of the only facts which, under the act of Congress, can have a material bearing upon the question whether he shall be sent out of the country, or be permitted to remain.

If no evidence is offered by the Chinaman, the judge makes the order of deportation, as upon a default. If he produces competent evidence to explain the fact of his not having a certificate, it must be considered by the judge; and if he thereupon appears to be entitled to a certificate, it is to be granted to him. If he proves that the collector of internal revenue has unlawfully refused to give him a certificate, he proves an "unavoidable cause," within the meaning of the act, for not procuring one. If he proves that he had procured a certificate which has been lost or destroyed, he is to be allowed a reasonable time to procure a duplicate thereof.

*Takao Ozawa v. United States*
*260 U.S. 178 (1922)*

MR. JUSTICE SUTHERLAND delivered the opinion of the Court.

The appellant is a person of the Japanese race born in Japan. He applied, on October 16, 1914, to the United States District Court for the Territory of Hawaii to be admitted as a citizen of the United States. His petition was opposed by the United States District Attorney for the District of Hawaii. Including the period of his residence in Hawaii, appellant had continuously resided in the United States for twenty years. He was a graduate of the Berkeley, California, High School, had been nearly three years a student in the University of California, had educated his children in American schools, his family had attended American churches and he had maintained the use of the English language in his home. That he was well qualified by character and education for citizenship is conceded.

The District Court of Hawaii, however, held that, having been born in Japan and being of the Japanese race, he was not eligible to naturalization under §2169 of the Revised Statutes, and denied the petition. Thereupon the appellant brought the cause to the Circuit Court of Appeals for the Ninth Circuit and that court has certified the following questions, upon which it desires to be instructed:

"2. Is one who is of the Japanese race and born in Japan eligible to citizenship under the Naturalization laws?

"3. If said Act of June 29, 1906, is limited by said Section 2169 and naturalization is limited to aliens being free white persons and to aliens of African nativity and to persons of African descent, is one of the Japanese race, born in Japan, under any circumstances eligible to naturalization?"

In 1790 the first Naturalization Act provided that, "Any alien, *being a free white person*...may be admitted to become a citizen. . . . " C. 3, 1 Stat. 103. This was subsequently enlarged to include aliens of African nativity and persons of African descent. These provisions were restated in the Revised Statutes, so that §2165 included only the procedural portion, while the substantive parts were carried into a separate section (2169) and the words "An alien" substituted for the words "Any alien."

In all of the Naturalization Acts from 1790 to 1906 the privilege of naturalization was confined to white persons (with the addition in 1870 of those of African nativity and descent), although the exact wording of the various statutes was not always the same. If Congress in 1906 desired to alter a rule so well and so long established, it may be assumed that its purpose would have been definitely disclosed and its legislation to that end put in unmistakable terms.

. . . Is appellant, therefore, a "free white person," within the meaning of that phrase as found in the statute?

On behalf of the appellant it is urged that we should give to this phrase the meaning which it had in the minds of its original framers in 1790 and that it was employed by them for the sole purpose of excluding the black or African race and the Indians then inhabiting this country. It may be true that these two races were alone thought of as being excluded, but to say that they were the only ones within the intent of the statute would be to ignore the affirmative form of the legislation. The provision is not that Negroes and Indians shall be *excluded* but it is, in effect, that only free white persons shall be *included*. The intention was to confer the privilege of citizenship upon that class of persons whom the fathers knew as white, and to deny it to all who could not be so classified.

We have been furnished with elaborate briefs in which the meaning of the words "white person" is discussed with ability and at length, both from the standpoint of judicial decision and from that of the science of ethnology. It does not seem to us necessary, however, to follow counsel in their extensive researches in these fields. It is sufficient to note the fact that these decisions are, in substance, to the effect that the words import a racial and not an individual test, and with this conclusion, fortified as it is by reason and authority, we entirely agree. Manifestly, the test afforded by the mere color of the skin of each individual is impracticable as that differs greatly among persons of the same race, even among Anglo-Saxons, ranging by imperceptible gradations from the fair blond to the swarthy brunette, the latter being darker than many of the lighter hued persons of the brown or yellow races. Hence to adopt the color test alone would result in a confused overlapping of races and a gradual merging of one into the other, without any practical line of separation. Beginning with the decision of Circuit Judge Sawyer, in *In re Ah Yup*, 5 Sawy. 155 (1878), the federal and state courts, in an almost unbroken line, have held that the words "white person" were meant to indicate only a person of what is popularly known as the Caucasian race. Among these decisions, see for example: *In re Camille*, 6 Fed. 256; *In re Saito*, 62 Fed. 126; *In re Nian*, 6 Utah 259; *In re Kumagai*, 163 Fed. 922; *In re Yamashita*, 30 Wash. 234, 237; *In re Ellis*, 179 Fed. 1002; *In re Mozumdar*, 207 Fed. 155, 117; *In re Singh*, 257 Fed. 209, 211–212; and *Petition of Charr*, 273 Fed. 207. With the conclusion reached in these several decisions we see no reason to differ. Moreover, that conclusion has become so well established by judicial and executive concurrence and legislative acquiescence that we should not at this late day feel at liberty to disturb it, in the absence of reasons far more cogent than any that have been suggested. *United States v. Midwest Oil Co.*, 236 U.S. 459, 472.

The determination that the words "white person" are synonymous with the words "a person of the Caucasian race" simplifies the problem, although it does not entirely dispose of it. Controversies have arisen and will no doubt arise again in respect of the proper classification of individuals in border line cases. The effect of the conclusion that the words "white person" mean a Caucasian is not to establish a sharp line of demarcation between those who are entitled and those who are not entitled to naturalization, but rather a zone of more or less debatable ground outside of which, upon the one hand, are those clearly eligible, and outside of which, upon the other hand, are those clearly ineligible for citizenship. Individual cases falling within this zone must be determined as they arise from time to time by what this Court has called, in another connection (*Davidson v. New Orleans*, 96 U.S. 97, 104) "the gradual process of judicial inclusion and exclusion."

We have no function in the matter other than to ascertain the will of Congress and declare it. Of course there is not implied—either in the legislation or in our interpretation of it—any suggestion of individual unworthiness or racial inferiority. These considerations are in no manner involved.

*United States v. Bhagat Singh Thind*
*261 U.S. 204 (1923)*

MR. JUSTICE SUTHERLAND delivered the opinion of the Court.

This cause is here upon a certificate from the Circuit Court of Appeals, requesting the instruction of this Court in respect of the following questions:

"1. Is a high caste Hindu of full Indian blood, born at Amrit Sar, Punjab, India, a white person within the meaning of section 2169, Revised Statutes?

"2. Does the act of February 5, 1917 (39 Stat. L. 875, section 3) disqualify from naturalization as citizens those Hindus, now barred by that act, who had lawfully entered the United States prior to the passage of said act?"

Section 2169, Revised Statutes, provides that the provisions of the Naturalization Act "shall apply to aliens, being free white persons, and to aliens of African nativity and to persons of African descent."

If the applicant is a white person within the meaning of this section he is entitled to naturalization; otherwise not.

The conclusion that the phrase "white persons" and the word "Caucasian" are synonymous does not end the matter.

Mere ability on the part of an applicant for naturalization to establish a line of descent from a Caucasian ancestor will not *ipso facto* and necessarily conclude the inquiry. "Caucasian" is a conventional word of much flexibility, as a study of the literature dealing with racial questions will disclose, and while it and the words "white persons" are treated as synonymous for the purposes of that case, they are not of identical meaning—*idem per idem.*

In the endeavor to ascertain the meaning of the statute we must not fail to keep in mind that it does not employ the word "Caucasian" but the words "white persons," and these are words of common speech and not of scientific origin. The word "Caucasian" not only was not employed in the law but was probably wholly unfamiliar to the original framers of the statute in 1790.

But in this country, during the last half century especially, the word by common usage has acquired a popular meaning, not clearly defined to be sure, but sufficiently so to enable us to say that its popular as distinguished from its scientific application is of appreciably narrower scope. It is in the popular sense of the word, therefore, that we employ it as an aid to the construction of the statute. . . .

They imply, as we have said, a racial test; but the term "race" is one which, for the practical purposes of the statute, must be applied to a group of living persons *now* possessing in common the requisite characteristics, not to groups of persons who are supposed to be or really are descended from some remote, common ancestor, but who, whether they both resemble him to a greater or less extent, have, at any rate, ceased altogether to resemble one another. It may be true that the blond Scandinavian and the brown Hindu have a common ancestor in the dim reaches of antiquity, but the average man knows perfectly well that there are unmistakable and profound differences between them today; . . .

The term "Aryan" has to do with linguistic and not at all with physical characteristics, and it would seem reasonably clear that mere resemblance in language, indicating a common linguistic root buried in remotely ancient soil, is altogether inadequate to prove common racial origin. There is, and can be, no assurance that the so-called Aryan language was not spoken by a variety of races living in proximity to one another. Our own history has witnessed the adoption of the English tongue by millions of Negroes, whose descendants can never be classified racially with the descendants of white persons notwithstanding both may speak a common root language.

What we now hold is that the words "free white persons" are words of common speech, to be interpreted in accordance with the understanding of the common man, synonymous with the word "Caucasian" only as that word is popularly understood. As so understood and used, whatever may be the speculations of the ethnologist, it does not include the body of people to whom the appellee belongs. It is a matter of familiar observation and knowledge that the physical group characteristics of the Hindus render them readily distinguishable from the various groups of persons in this country commonly recognized as white. The children of English, French, German, Italian, Scandinavian, and other European parentage, quickly merge into the mass of our population and lose the distinctive hallmarks of their European origin. On the other hand, it cannot be doubted that the children born in this country of Hindu parents would retain indefinitely the clear evidence of their ancestry. It is very far from our thought to suggest the slightest question of racial superiority or inferiority. What we suggest is merely racial difference, and it is of such character and extent that the great body of our people instinctively recognize it and reject the thought of assimilation.

It is not without significance in this connection that Congress, by the Act of February 5, 1917, c. 29, §3, 39 Stat. 874, has now excluded from admission into this country all natives of Asia within designated limits of latitude and longitude, including the whole of India. This not only constitutes conclusive evidence of the congressional attitude of opposition to Asiatic immigration generally, but is persuasive of a similar attitude toward Asiatic naturalization as well, since it is not likely that Congress would be willing to accept as citizens a class of persons whom it rejects as immigrants.

# Reference Matter

# Notes

*For complete author names, titles, and publication data for the works cited here in short form, see the Bibliography, pp. 309–27. Complete publication data for references to the Departments of Commerce, State, and Health and Human Services are found under "U.S." in the Bibliography.*

## INTRODUCTION

1. Statements of Senator Edward Kennedy and Congressman Howard Berman, in support of NP-5/Berman Programs under §314 of the *Immigration Reform and Control Act of 1986*, and §2 of the *Immigration Amendments of 1988*, Public Law no. 100-658.

2. The only Asians who benefited from these adjustments were Japanese, and only slightly.

3. Senate Bill 358, 101st Cong., 1st sess.

4. J. Getlin, "Senate Backs Cap on Immigration," *Los Angeles Times*, July 14, 1989, part I, p. 1. "Kennedy and other sponsors said that the Senate legislation would redress an imbalance in the current immigration system, under which about 85% of all U.S. visas are granted each year to persons from Latin America or Asian nations" (ibid.).

5. Statement of Senator Alan K. Simpson in *Final Report of the Select Commission on Immigration and Refugee Policy* (March 1981), pp. 412–13 [emphasis added].

6. Testimony of Colorado Governor Richard Lamm in *Hearings Before the Subcommittee on Economic Resources, Competitiveness, and Security Economics*, Joint Economic Committee of Congress, May 29, 1986.

7. A. Arocha, "1980's Expected to Set Mark as Top Immigration Decade," *Washington Post*, July 23, 1988, p. A1.

8. See, e.g., Kellogg 1988: 199–204.

9. Bouvier and Gardner 1986: 34–35.

10. Ibid., p. 30.

11. Testimony of Otis Graham, *Hearings Before the Subcommittee on Economic Resources, Competitiveness, and Security Economics*, Joint Economic Committee of Congress, May 29, 1986, pp. 399–400, quoting from R. Rodriguez,

"Hispanics, in Changing, Change America," *Los Angeles Times*, May 23, 1986.

12. Testimony of Barry Chiswick, *Hearings Before the Subcommittee on Economic Resources, Competitiveness, and Security Economics*, Joint Economic Committee of Congress, May 29, 1986, p. 235; see also Chiswick 1982: 123–30, 141–45.

13. Uhlaner et al. 1989: 207.

14. Ibid., 213–14.

15. See, e.g., F. Viviano, "Poll Shows Ethnic Groups Torn by Bias, Cultural Ties—Chinese, Filipinos in Bay Area Slow to be Assimilated," *San Francisco Chronicle*, Mar. 27, 1990, p. A1: "The results [of a Bay Area poll] showed Asian Americans, especially, to be far more concerned about developments in their ancestral countries than about current events in California. Such findings 'tend to mean less interest in assimilating into American culture,' said [pollster Mark] Baldassare."

16. See, e.g., F. Butterfield, "Why They Excel," *Parade Magazine*, Jan. 21, 1990, pp. 4–6; F. Viviano, "When Success Is a Family Prize," *San Francisco Examiner, This World* section, Oct. 8, 1989, pp. 7–8; M. Kasindorf, "Asian-Americans: A 'Model Minority,' " *Newsweek*, Dec. 6, 1982, pp. 39, 41.

17. See T. Abate, "Survey Probes Asian Families' Median Incomes," *San Francisco Examiner*, Sept. 18, 1992. In fact, the household income for Asian Americans ($47,974) in California is lower than white households ($49,103); per capita income for Asian Americans ($13,733) is much lower than that of white Americans ($19,028). S. Johnson, "Minorities' Income Higher in South Bay," *San Jose Mercury News*, May 13, 1992, p. 1A.

18. Episodes of the television show "Grand" featured such a Japanese businessman in April and May 1990. See also U.S. Commission on Civil Rights 1992: 180–82.

19. W. Chan 1986: 26.

20. Ibid.

21. Unfortunately I fear a similar disregard for the plight of pro-democracy demonstrators in Thailand who have been pursued by the military in late Spring of 1992.

22. W. Wong, "Asian Americans and Political Power," *East West News*, Sept. 3, 1987, p. 4. I discuss this more fully in Chapter 5.

23. Two popular histories of Asian America are Professor Ronald Takaki's *Strangers From A Different Shore* and Professor Sucheng Chan's *Asian Americans: An Interpretive History*.


CHAPTER ONE

1. Chy Lung v. Freeman, 92 U.S. 275 (1875); Lyman 1974: 71; Tsai 1986: 43–44; Coolidge 1909: 69–82. Appendix C contains an excerpt of action taken by the

California legislature in 1870 to prevent "the kidnapping and importation of Mongolian, Chinese and Japanese females, for criminal or demoralizing purposes." In 1873 it enacted Section 2952 of the 1872 California Political Code requiring bonds of five hundred dollars for two additional categories: "a convicted criminal, or a lewd or debauched woman." Jayne Lee, a Spaeth Fellow at Stanford Law School from 1991 to 1993, is looking closely at the historical treatment of Asian immigrant women and its impact on their lives.

2. The state and local laws aimed at restricting or discouraging Asian immigration were precursors to modern statutes that discriminate on the basis of alienage. For example, states have enacted laws making it unlawful to hire undocumented workers (employer sanctions), making public schools unavailable to undocumented children, requiring residency requirements for welfare, and requiring citizenship for certain "public function" jobs. See DeCanas v. Bica, 424 U.S. 351 (1976); Plyler v. Doe, 457 U.S. 202 (1982); Graham v. Richardson, 403 U.S. 365 (1971); Foley v. Connelie, 435 U.S. 291 (1978); Ambach v. Norwick, 441 U.S. 68 (1979). Certainly, the intent behind some of these statutes reflects a general xenophobic sentiment or a discriminatory attitude against groups such as Mexican immigrants.

3. During the nineteenth century emigration from Japan was limited to traders and explorers. Between 1542 and 1638 there were some Japanese settlements in Siam and the Philippines. But the fear of foreign encroachment curtailed contact with Western countries and led to Japan's strict policy of exclusion and seclusion, which prohibited emigration until 1868. (Ichihashi 1915: 1–3.) After the destructive invasion by the Manchus in 1627 and 1636, Korea began two and a half centuries of self-imposed isolation, during which it was known as the Hermit Kingdom. (Choy 1979: 19; Kim 1971: 3; Kitano and Daniels 1988: 107.) The Qing dynasty (1644–1911) refused to sanction emigration or exile until 1868 when China entered into the Burlingame Treaty. (Tsai 1986: 8–11; Hsu 1975: 4.)

4. A small, educated class of scholars, diplomats, and political dissidents from China, India, Japan, and Korea entered in the early 1800's. (Ichioka 1988: 7–8; Hata 1977: 14; Lee 1960: 86; Jensen 1988: 1, 20–21; Choy 1979: 239.) Filipino seamen attached to Spanish galleons between 1565 and 1815 jumped ship, initially in Mexico, and made their way to Louisiana (Espina 1988: 38–39).

5. "During this period there was little legislation. An early attempt at restriction was the Alien Act of 1798 [Act of June 25, 1798, 1 Stat. 570], a part of the Alien and Sedition Laws, which authorized the President to expel from the United States any alien he deemed dangerous. This legislation was very unpopular and was allowed to expire at the end of its two-year term. Subsequent statutes, commencing in 1819, sought to improve conditions on ships bringing immigrants to the United States. As late as 1864 Congress passed legislation designed to encourage immigration [Act of July 4, 1864, 13 Stat. 385. Repealed by

sec. 4, Act of March 30, 1868, 15 Stat. 58]. And some of the states had active programs to promote immigration" (Gordon and Mailman 1991: §1.2a. See also Vialet 1980: 10).

6. Tsai 1986: 10.

7. Coolidge 1909: 16–17; Miller 1969: 111–12; Kwong 1987: 16–18.

8. Coolidge 1909: 22.

9. Sandmeyer 1939: 44. Other immigrants were welcomed in the West as well. "The migration west of [white] immigrants was also encouraged by western States by brochures and agents sent to New York and abroad, and by reducing the residence period required to vote. The Homestead Act of 1862 made western lands available to immigrants as well as the native-born" (Vialet 1980: 10).

10. Konvitz 1946: 11–12.

11. Coolidge 1909: 21; see also Mooney 1984: 571; Cheng and Bonacich 1984: chaps. 4 and 5.

12. Saxton 1971: 60–65; Coolidge 1909: 52.

13. Coolidge 1909: 15–18; Tsai 1986: 12–15.

14. Coolidge 1909: 28–29.

15. See generally Higham 1963.

16. Coolidge 1909: 29–30; Sandmeyer 1939: 41–43.

17. Coolidge 1909: 25. Exclusion during this period is usually attributed to a general nativism. I sort nativism or restrictionist sentiment into three categories. Concerns over employment and entrepreneurial competition, wages, and protectionist notions I consider economic nativism. Racial nativism (or racism) embraces a belief in racial superiority and antagonism based on skin color. Social nativism incorporates concerns over cultural, political, language, and religious differences, perceived inability to assimilate, health, and criminality. These overlap to some extent.

18. Sandmeyer 1939: 41–43; Kitano and Daniels 1988: 21; Takaki 1989: 81–82.

19. Saxton 1971: 73–75.

20. *Oregon Laws* pp. 48–49 (1857–58), cited in Mooney 1984: 569. California was responsible for several laws and rulings directed at Chinese, such as an 1854 state Supreme Court ruling in People v. Hall, 4 Cal. 399 (1854), which prevented Chinese from testifying in court against white men, and an 1855 law that required owners of vessels to pay a fee for each passenger who was ineligible for citizenship (Lyman 1974: 71; Tsai 1986: 43–44; Coolidge 1909: 69–82). Perhaps the most infamous anti-Chinese local law was the San Francisco ordinance that eliminated the use of wooden buildings for hand laundries. The Supreme Court declared the law unconstitutional because all Chinese persons owning such laundries were forced to give up their businesses while white owners were exempt [Yick Wo v. Hopkins, 118 U.S. 356 (1886); excerpts in Appendix C].

21. If asked about their program, its members were instructed to answer, "I know nothing about it" (Kennedy 1964: 70).

22. Coolidge 1909: 58; Wynne 1978: 1.

23. Higham 1963: 12–13.

24. Sandmeyer 1934: 45–46; Mooney 1984, 63: 573–75.

25. Coolidge 1909: 392. One commentator of the time described the Chinese in this manner: "The Chinaman, it is claimed, and apparently with truth, will learn any given mechanical operation in one-third of the time required by a white workman. He has no family; he lives in the most frugal manner; he lodges upon a wooden bench; he has been used at home to wages that would hardly more than sustain life. His sole ambition is to accumulate two hundred to four hundred dollars. . . . By means of all this he is enabled to life as no white man could live. . . . The result has been to prevent the immigration of a strong and healthy laboring class of kindred and easily affiliated races from the Eastern States and from Europe" (Whitney 1888: 113–14).

26. Daniels 1962: 19.

27. *Statutes at Large of the United States, 1789–1873* (Washington, D.C., 1850–73), 16: 739; 1 Malloy, Treaties 234, excerpted in Appendix C.

28. Miller 1969: 131, citing *New York Times,* Feb. 25, 1871, p. 2, quoting Secretary of State William Seward.

29. Miller 1969: 132; *Daily Evening Transcript,* Feb. 27, 1868.

30. For a more thorough review of the causes of Chinese exclusion, see Saxton 1971; Coolidge 1909; Sandmeyer 1939; Miller 1969; Tsai 1986; Barth 1964.

31. McClain 1984: 529–31, 564–67 (discussing sec. 16 of the Civil Rights Act of 1870).

32. Years later when Japanese immigrants unsuccessfully sought naturalization as "free white persons," the Supreme Court reaffirmed that the framers of the 1790 naturalization statute intended that African Americans and Native Americans were to be denied naturalization [Ozawa v. United States, 260 U.S. 178, 196 (1922); excerpt in Appendix C].

33. *Statutes at Large* 16: 254 (July 14, 1870).

34. The Senate defeated one amendment that would have read: "That the naturalization laws are hereby extended to aliens of African nativity, and to persons of African descent, and to persons born in the Chinese empire" (Hutchinson 1981: 5–6). In her comprehensive history Professor Sucheng Chan points out that the compiler of the 1873 U.S. Revised Statutes omitted the limiting reference to whites in the naturalization section, and the error was not corrected until 1875. Therefore, between December 1873 and February 1875, "no racial or color restriction existed with regard to citizenship, and a number of Chinese in New York were naturalized" (Chan 1991a: 92).

35. Act of March 3, 1875, *Statutes at Large* 18: 477. See Sandmeyer 1939: 34–35. To control Chinese prostitutes a San Francisco court in 1854 encouraged the Chinese madames to locate their houses outside certain limits (Chan 1991a: 56).

36. Coolidge 1909: 418.

37. Professor Ronald Takaki points out that the number of Chinese women entering between 1876 and 1882 declined from the previous seven-year period by 68 percent. In 1882, during the few months between the passage of the Chinese Exclusion Act and its enforcement, 39,579 Chinese slipped into America. But this massive migration included only 136 women, testifying to the effectiveness of the Page Law (Takaki 1989: 40). See also Peffer 1986: 28–46; Chan 1991a: 105–6.

38. Heizer and Almquist 1971: 166.

39. Hutchinson 1981: 80–81; Saxton 1971: 178.

40. Heizer and Almquist 1971: 158.

41. Act of May 6, 1882, *Statutes at Large* 22: 58. Excerpt in Appendix C.

42. A remarkable number of Chinese challenged the application of the exclusion law (over 9,200 between 1882 and 1905), primarily on the grounds that they were citizens (Salyer 1989: 91–117). But this number is small compared to the number that had been entering before 1882.

43. Excerpt in Appendix C.

44. 112 U.S. 536 (1884 [excerpt in Appendix C]); see also United States v. Jung Ah Lung, 124 U.S. 621 (1888).

45. Under the renegotiated Burlingame Treaty of 1880, China agreed to allow the United States to regulate or limit migration in exchange for its help in forcing Japan to withdraw from Okinawa. Tsai 1986: 50–60; Coolidge 1909: 158–80.

46. In United States v. Mrs. Gue Lim, 176 U.S. 459 (1900), the Court ruled that the wives and minor children of Chinese merchants in the United States were permitted to enter because the 1880 treaty protected them. See also Nee and Nee 1973: 55.

47. See also Chan 1991a: 105–14.

48. Gordon and Mailman 1991: §1.2b.

49. Higham 1963: 17–18.

50. Act of October 1, 1888, *Statutes at Large* 25: 504. Excerpt in Appendix C.

51. Chae Chan Ping v. United States, 130 U.S. 581 (1889). Excerpt in Appendix C.

52. Unfortunately the all-Asians-look-alike excuse is still with us. A UCLA engineering lecturer asked his Asian American students to submit a photo with their 1991 winter-quarter project because he had difficulty matching Asian names and faces (Garcia, "UCLA Lecturer Subject of Probe After Complaints by Students," *Los Angeles Times*, May 24, 1991, p. B3).

53. Saxton 1971: 230–31.

54. Act of May 5, 1892, *Statutes at Large* 27: 25. Excerpt in Appendix C. See Gordon 1943: 10; Coolidge 1909: 214. Likewise, in 1979 all Iranian students in the United States were required to report to the INS in response to the hostage crisis in Tehran. See Narenji v. Civiletti, 617 F.2d 745 (D.C. Cir. 1979).

55. Act of May 5, 1892, *Statutes at Large* 27: 25, §4.

56. Wong Wing v. United States, 163 U.S. 698 (1892).

57. 149 U.S. 698 (1892); see also Saxton 1971: 230–31.

58. Saxton 1971: 231–32; Higham 1963: 107.

59. The Qing (or Ch'ing) dynasty (1644–1911) was the last of the Chinese dynasties (Hsu 1970: 4).

60. *Statutes at Large* 28: 1210; 1 Malloy, Treaties, 241.

61. Act of April 27, 1904, *Statutes at Large* 33: 428. Excerpt in Appendix C.

62. Higham 1963: 46.

63. Act of Feb. 26, 1885, 23 Stat. 332; Act of Feb. 23, 1887, 24 Stat. 414; Act of Oct. 19, 1888, 25 Stat. 566; Gordon and Mailman 1991: §1.2b.

64. Higham 1963: 68–70, 106.

65. The Meiji Restoration of 1868 marked the emergence of Japan from centuries of feudalism and isolation into modern industrialism, international commerce, cultural exchange, and war (Jansen 1968: 163).

66. F. Chuman 1976: 4–5; Otsuka 1969: 35.

67. Chatters 1966: 15; Allen 1971: 8; Ichihashi 1915: 5.

68. Jansen 1968: 163.

69. *1982 INS Statistical Yearbook*, table IMM.2; Bennett 1963: 36.

70. "Labor agents" traveled to Japan to recruit laborers. The arrival of Japanese laborers in Hawaii did not go unnoticed by Chinese exclusionists. Almost immediately, they lobbied against the entry of this new source of "cheap" labor (F. Chuman 1976: 9–11). In the 1890's, agriculture expanded so swiftly in California that farmers short of workers unsuccessfully called for relaxation of the Chinese exclusion laws (Higham 1963: 107; see generally Cheng and Bonacich 1984).

71. Ichihashi 1932: 392. Emigration pressure had increased because farmers in Japan faced increased economic hardship as a result of financial policies of the Meiji government instituted to industrialize and militarize Japan (Takaki 1989: 43).

72. Ichihashi 1915: 5; Takaki 1989: 44–45.

73. Irons 1983: 9.

74. Akagi 1936: 435.

75. Kim 1971: 3.

76. A group of Korean diplomats had entered the United States on a brief goodwill mission following the 1882 treaty ratification. The first Koreans who intended to reside permanently were a trio of political exiles, fleeing prosecution in 1884 after an abortive coup designed to seize the government for liberal reform. Two subsequently went to Japan, but the third received a medical education and lived in the United States for the rest of his life (Houchins and Houchins 1974: 549; Kim 1971: 3). Korean emigrants also traveled to Japan, Manchuria, or the Russian Maritime Provinces; some of the first Korean immigrants to the United States in 1899 came from those regions. Boyd 1974: 507; Kim 1974: 24.

77. Kim 1974: 25; Kim 1971: 4.

78. A major reason for Japan's restrictions was the fear that students in the United States might stir up anti-Japanese sentiment (Houchins and Houchins 1974: 555–58).

79. Ichihashi 1932: 392; F. Chuman 1976: 10–11.

80. Ichihashi 1932: 87–89; Kitano 1969: 17–18.

81. Kitano 1969: 16–17; Takaki 1989: 43–46.

82. Takaki 1989: 46.

83. Ichihashi 1932: 87–89; Kitano 1969: 18.

84. Saxton 1971: 247–48, 251–52; F. Chuman 1976: 19; see also Higham 1963: 131, 165–66.

85. Daniels 1962: 27–29.

86. Thompson 1978: 82–83.

87. Penrose 1973: 1; Ichihashi 1932: 228–29. In 1892 and again immediately after the turn of the century, legislation analogous to Chinese exclusion laws was introduced to exclude Japanese and Filipinos for twenty years (Hutchinson 1981: 129).

88. Hall 1970: 286.

89. Thompson et al. 1981: 145; Steiner 1917: 65–66; Thompson 1978: 249–54.

90. Bailey 1934: 11; Hall 1970: 207; F. Chuman 1976: 22.

91. "[After the San Francisco earthquake of 1906], bands of young hoodlums were roaming the streets, assaulting Japanese businessmen and shopkeepers. Restaurants owned and operated by Japanese were being boycotted and their customers threatened and harassed. A Japanese professor of seismology, investigating the results of the earthquake and fire, was assaulted and insulted in the streets. An architect, also sent from Japan to study the structural damage caused by the earthquake, was severely beaten." Ironically, at the same time, the people of Japan were raising almost $250,000 in earthquake relief for San Franciscans that was later channeled through the Red Cross (F. Chuman 1976: 23).

92. When school officials ordered the transfer of all Japanese pupils in San Francisco public schools to the Oriental school in Chinatown, the segregation immediately sparked international controversy, and the Japanese ambassador protested to President Roosevelt. In an effort to defuse the tension, Roosevelt sent his secretary of commerce and labor to San Francisco, yet school authorities refused to vacate the order. Roosevelt's administration had difficulties negotiating the restriction of further entries of Japanese laborers with Japan because of the San Francisco segregation order, and it stalled the Gentlemen's Agreement (Esthus 1969: 146–66; Wollenberg 1976: 52–68; Ringer 1983: 690–95; Saxton 1971: 254–57; F. Chuman 1976: 19–21, 23–29).

93. In February 1907 Congress authorized President Roosevelt to block Japanese laborers from Hawaii, Mexico, and Canada (Immigration Act of Feb. 20, 1907, *Statutes at Large* 34: 898). The president's subsequent executive order

under this authority effectively stopped the flow of Japanese laborers from Hawaii to the mainland. These actions greatly offended the Japanese government (Hutchinson 1981: 142; Esthus 1966: 161–67; Chan 1991a: 37).

94. Excerpt in Appendix C. Esthus 1966: 146–64; Akagi 1936: 434; Hutchinson 1981: 157.

95. Akagi 1936: 434–35. The agreement was not a formal document but more of a "voluntary arrangement" between the two countries and consisted of a series of cables, telegrams, notes, and correspondence (Esthus 1966: 163–64). One such telegram is in Appendix C.

96. Esthus 1966: 163–66; Wollenberg 1976: 66–67; F. Chuman 1976: 35–36; Takaki 1989: 46–47. Many of the women who entered were picture brides who were married by proxy in Japan to men in the United States they had never met (F. Chuman 1976: 36). It was the Japanese custom during this period to arrange marriages (Reischauer 1986: 280).

97. Higham 1963: 110–11.

98. Gordon and Mailman 1991: §1.2b.

99. Steiner 1917: 57.

100. In 1911 the Japanese government was able to stave off total exclusion by its assurances that it would continue to restrict the emigration of Japanese laborers (F. Chuman 1976: 43–46; Ichihashi 1932: 255; Inui 1926: 191).

101. Steiner 1917: 57.

102. Irons 1983: 10.

103. Washington state passed a similar alien land law in 1921 (Yanagisako 1985: 4). See also McGovney 1947: 7.

104. Woolsey 1921: 58; Akagi 1936: 437.

105. Japanese Americans challenged the citizenship act, arguing that they were free white persons under the naturalization laws. But, in Ozawa v. United States, 260 U.S. 178, 185 (1922), the Supreme Court ruled that the words "white person" were synonymous with the words "a person of the Caucasian race." See also Yamashita v. Hinckle, 260 U.S. 199 (1922). Since the inability of Asians to own land severely discouraged Japanese immigration, *Ozawa* marked a victory for exclusionists. Excerpt in Appendix C.

106. Patterson 1983: 94.

107. The bloody and violent conflict between U.S. troops and the Philippine resistance is the subject of "The First Viet Nam—The Philippine-American War of 1899–1902," *Letters in Exile: An Introductory Reader on the History of Filipinos in America* (UCLA Asian American Studies Center, 1976), 1–19.

108. The current provision regarding noncitizen nationals [*United States Code* 8: §1101(a)(22) (1992 ed.)] is identical to the provision in force at that time (Hing 1985: 12, 386–87). Only persons born in American Samoa or Swains Island are considered noncitizen nationals [*U.S. Code* 8: §1101(a)(29) (1982 ed.)].

109. According to one group of researchers, 2,767 Filipinos were counted in

1910 (Gardner et al. 1985: 8, table 2, table F-1); another has reported about 2,300 Filipinos in 1910 (Smith 1976: 322).

110. The British colony in South Africa, for example, imported Indian workers as indentured laborers under three-year contracts. But by 1890 Indians in South Africa were treated as Chinese and Japanese had been treated on the West Coast—with the same exploitation, racial discrimination, and violence. Many were even pejoratively called "coolies." Their situation differed from that of the Chinese in the United States, however, in that the colonial government in India had some influence on its counterpart in South Africa. It successfully insisted, for instance, that Indian workers in Africa had to be accompanied by women (40 to every 100 men), which allowed some Indian immigrants to find wives and have children in South Africa (Hoyt 1974: chap. 5).

111. Chan 1991a: 22.

112. Hess 1976: 417; Kitano and Daniels 1988: 90; see generally Gonzales 1986: 40–54.

113. *1984 INS Statistical Yearbook*, pp. 2–3. Some who entered in the early 1900's were spillovers from Canada where the government, yielding to anti-Asian sentiment, instituted an exclusion policy of its own in 1909 (Hess 1976: 414; Chan 1991a: 23; Hoyt 1974: chap. 9; Cheng and Bonacich 1984: 332).

114. Hess 1976: 415.

115. The Asiatic Exclusion League claimed that "from every part of the Coast complaints are made of the undesirability of the Hindoos, their lack of cleanliness, disregard of sanitary laws, petty pilfering, especially of chickens, and insolence to women" (*Proceedings*, Feb. 16, 1908, pp. 8–10).

116. Hess 1976: 29–30.

117. On Sept. 5, 1907, in Bellingham, Washington, five hundred whites tried to drive the Indians, who were working at the lumber mills, out of town (Wynne 1966: 174). A month later white workers in eastern Washington met Indians migrating from Canada and forced them back across the border. The Asiatic Exclusion League reported that the "immodest and filthy habits of the Hindoos are continually involving them in trouble, beatings and otherwise. . . . In all cases, we may say that the Oriental is at fault" (*Proceedings*, Sept. 20, 1908, p. 12). On Mar. 21, 1910, white lumbermen, with the support of local police and fire departments, again attacked Indian immigrants, this time in St. Johns, Oregon, and succeeded in driving out all of them ("Race War in St. Johns Results in Bloodshed and Injuries," *Oregon Journal*, Mar. 22, 1910, pp. 1–2).

118. Hess 1976: 416. The public-charge ground of exclusion, which remains a part of today's immigration law, authorizes the visa-issuing official or the port of entry inspector to condition entry on the likelihood that the immigrant will not need public assistance or "welfare." *U.S. Code* 8: §1182(a)(15) (1982); Matter of Harutunian, Immigration and Nationality Decisions 14: 583 (Reg. Comm'r 1974); Hing 1985: 4.46–4.47.

119. California Board of Control. 1920. *California and the Oriental: Japanese, Chinese, and Hindus* (Sacramento: State Printing Office), 101–2.

120. Kitano and Daniels 1988: 93; Takaki 1989: 298–99.

121. United States v. Bhagat Singh Thind, 261 U.S. 204 (1923). Excerpt in Appendix C.

122. *Hearings Before the Committee on Immigration*, Senate, 69th Cong., 2d sess., on *S.J. Res. 128, Providing for the Ratification and Confirmation of the Naturalization of Certain Persons of the Hindu Race*, Dec. 9 and 15, 1926, p. 2.

123. Kitano and Daniels 1988: 93–94.

124. U.S. Immigration Commission 1911: 75–76; Cheng and Bonacich 1984: 216; Hess 1976: 413.

125. Act of Feb. 5, 1917, *Statutes at Large* 39: 874. Gordon and Mailman 1991: §1.2c; Higham 1963: 159. The literacy provision had failed to become law in 1913 and 1915 after presidential vetoes by Taft and Wilson. But in 1917 Congress overrode President Wilson's second veto, and the law was enacted. (Leibowitz 1983: 2-46 to 2-48.) Until 1990 the literacy requirement remained in the law. *U.S. Code* 8: §1182(a)(25) (1982). The impact of the literacy requirement was never fully measured.

126. *Statutes at Large* 39: 874, sec. 3. Excerpt in Appendix C.

127. *Statutes at Large* 43: 153. Excerpt in Appendix C.

128. Schwartz 1968: 107; Gordon and Mailman 1991: §1.2c; Higham 1988: 316–24.

129. Kennedy 1964: 74–76; Hutchinson 1981: 483–85.

130. Higham 1963: 318.

131. Immigration Act of 1924, §13 (c), *Statutes at Large* 43: 153.

132. F. Chuman 1976: 101–3; Bennett 1963: 39.

133. Smith 1976: 322.

134. Catapusan 1940: 13; DeWitt 1976: 13; Kitano and Daniels 1988: 79. Of course this is similar to how Japanese were substituted in large numbers for Chinese after Chinese exclusion, and later how Mexicans were used as a cheap source of labor (López 1981: 641–72).

135. Catapusan 1940: 13; Kitano and Daniels 1988: 79–80.

136. Lasker 1931: 25–27; Smith 1976: 307.

137. Lasker 1931: chap. 12; Clifford 1976: 74.

138. Catapusan 1940: chap. 4.

139. See Adeva 1932; De Witt 1976: 13.

140. Kitano and Daniels 1988: 81; Morales 1976: 31.

141. De Witt 1976: 17–24.

142. Catapusan 1940: chap. 4; De Witt 1976: 12–15; Bogardus 1929: 61.

143. Bogardus 1929: 64.

144. Ibid., 63–64.

145. Crow 1913: 516, 519–20.

146. De Witt 1976: 22–23; Kitano and Daniels 1988: 80. Much of the contact with white women came at taxi-dance halls. See, e.g., Catapusan 1934: 45–55.

147. De Witt 1976: 33–63.

148. Smith 1976: 322; De Witt 1976: chap. 3.

149. Catapusan 1934: 29–32; Melendy 1974: 526–27.

150. Catapusan 1934: 32.

151. Ibid.

152. Act of Mar. 24, 1934, *Statutes at Large* 48: 456. Excerpt in Appendix C. See also Catapusan 1934: 34–44.

153. One bill introduced between 1929 and 1931 that made no headway provided that citizens of American Samoa, Guam, and the Philippine Islands would be treated in the same way as the citizens of other countries (Hutchinson 1981: 220–21).

154. Catapusan 1934: 34–44.

155. Act of March 24, 1934, *Statutes at Large* 48: 456, §14. This divestiture of noncitizen national status was challenged unsuccessfully in Rabang v. Boyd, 353 U.S. 427 (1957).

156. Act of Mar. 24, 1934, *Statutes at Large* 48: 456, 462, §8; *U.S. Code* 48: §1238 (1934 ed.).

157. Act of May 26, 1924, *Statutes at Large* 43: 153, §11(a), (b).

158. Toyota v. United States, 268 U.S. 402, 410 (1925). A provision in a 1908 law did, however, make an exception for Filipinos and Puerto Ricans who enlisted.

159. See, e.g., Gordon 1943.

160. Hutchinson 1981: 264–65, 312.

161. Act of Dec. 17, 1943, *Statutes at Large* 57: 600. Excerpt in Appendix C. Hutchinson 1981: 264–65.

162. Act of Dec. 17, 1943, *Statutes at Large* 57: 600. By becoming eligible for citizenship, Chinese who were unregistered (undocumented), but who had entered prior to July 1, 1924, also became eligible for the amnesty or registry provision enacted in 1929 and modified in 1939 (Act of Mar. 2, 1929, *Statutes at Large* 45: 1512; and Act of Aug. 7, 1939, *Statutes at Large* 53: 1243).

163. Hutchinson 1981: 264.

164. Public Law 713, Act of Aug. 9, 1946, *Statutes at Large* 60: 975; *1946 INS Annual Report* 1; Hutchinson 1981: 272. The law covered only subsequent marriages, but eventually the racial barrier to admission was also waived for Chinese spouses of citizens, regardless of the date of marriage (Act of July 22, 1947, *Statutes at Large* 61: 401).

165. Act of July 2, 1946, *Statutes at Large* 60: 416. Excerpt in Appendix C. This was important to Filipinos since Philippine independence would have subjected them (as with other Asians except Chinese after 1943) to exclusion under the "ineligible to citizenship" provision of the 1924 Immigration Act. The Nationality Act of 1940 had perpetuated naturalization requirements that precluded Asians from such citizenship rights (Act of Oct. 14, 1940, *Statutes at Large* 54: 1137, §303a).

166. Tewari 1977: 7; Kitano and Daniels 1988: 96.

167. Hutchinson 1981: 272–73; Kitano and Daniels 1988: 83.

168. Discussed more fully in Chap. 2.

169. Certainly, mainstream attitudes toward Chinese in contrast to Japanese had improved during World War II. But the shift resulted from the political alliance between the United States and China.

170. War Brides Act of Dec. 28, 1945, *Statutes at Large* 59: 659.

171. Fiancees Act of June 29, 1946, *Statutes at Large* 60: 339.

172. Act of June 25, 1948, *Statutes at Large* 62: 1009.

173. S. Rept. 1515, 81st Cong., 2d sess.; H. Rept. 1365, 81st Cong., 2d sess., *U.S. Code Congressional and Administrative News*, 1653 (1952).

174. Act of June 27, 1952, Public Law 414, *Statutes at Large* 66: 163. See Appendix C.

175. Hutchinson 1981: 304–13; Gordon and Mailman 1991: 1.3a, 1.3b.

176. H. Rept. 1365, 81st Cong., 2d sess., *U.S. Code Cong. & Adm. News*, 1653, 1679 (1952). Some said that the exclusion policy was an important factor in the anti-American feeling in Japan prior to World War II.

177. Act of June 27, 1952, Public Law 414, *Statutes at Large* 66: 163, §202.

178. The Japanese quota was 185; the Korean, 100; the Chinese, 100; and the Indian, 100. The two thousand annual visas were allocated to the countries located in the Asia-Pacific Triangle [H. Rept. 1365, 81st Cong., 2d sess., *U.S. Code Cong. & Adm. News*, 1653, 1681 (1952); see Scully 1966: 234].

179. *U.S. Code* 8: §1152(a) (1956 ed.).

180. Scully 1966: n. 11; *U.S. Code* 8: §1152(a)(5) (1956 ed.); *U.S. Code Cong. & Adm. News*, 1653, 1679 (1952); see Hutchinson 1981: 480.

181. Scully 1966: n. 11.

182. Bernstein and Matusow 1966: 143. The inclusion of McCarthy-era grounds for political exclusion in the legislation was also repulsive to Truman (Cole 1990: 52).

183. Scully 1966: 228.

184. *H. Doc. 520*, 82d Cong., 2d sess.

185. Scully 1966: 229; see e.g., *Letter From the President to the Speaker of the House*, Aug. 25, 1965. 111 Cong. rec. 20996 (daily ed. Aug. 25, 1965).

186. *Executive Order 10392*, Sept. 4, 1952.

187. Whom We Shall Welcome, Report of the President's Commission on Immigration and Naturalization (1953).

188. See *H. Doc. 1*, 85th Cong., 1st sess., p. 7; *H. Doc. 329*, 84th Cong., 2d sess.; *H. Doc. 85*, 85th Cong., 1st sess.; *H. Doc. 360*, 86th Cong., 2d sess.; *H. Doc. 255*, 86th Cong., 2d sess.; *H. Doc. 385* (p.5); *S. Doc. 115*, 86th Cong., 2d sess., p. 4; *H. Doc. 1*, 87th Cong., 1st sess.

189. In 1961 a provision included in a series of amendments eliminated the ceiling of two thousand imposed on the total of quotas for the Asia-Pacific

Triangle (Act of Sept. 26, 1965, Public Law 87-301, *Statutes at Large* 75: 650, 654).

190. *White House Press Release,* July 23, 1963; Gordon and Mailman 1991: §1.4A.

191. See Kennedy 1964; see generally Schwartz 1968.

192. Hutchinson 1981: 105, 359–61.

193. Kennedy 1964: 62–63, 78. Another problem with the national origins system was that it was administratively unpredictable in the hands of those that were inclined to be influenced by compassionate pleas. After the 1952 law, nearly two-thirds of those who entered did so through the nonquota system, through huge volumes of special legislation, and through administrative grace (Kennedy 1964: 78–79; Schwartz 1968: 110–11).

194. Kennedy 1964: 103, 107.

195. In spite of the administration's support for it, the reform campaign met with opposition. The national origins quota system was not without its advocates, like Senators Ervin, Thurmond, and Eastland. They remained loyal to what they perceived as the idea underlying the national origins quota system. Along with other supporters they branded the new proposals discriminatory against prospective English-speaking immigrants, condemned the legislation as an assault on immigration laws by those who "appeal to organized minority blocs in the great urban areas," and charged that the purpose of the bill was to increase immigration and change its composition (Hutchinson 1981: 376). In Senator Ervin's words, the law "recognized the obvious and natural fact that those immigrants can best be assimilated into our society who have relatives, friends or others of similar backgrounds already here." Comments of Senator Sam J. Ervin, Jr. (D.-N.C.), *S. Rept. 748,* 89th Cong., 1st sess., pp. 52–55 (1965); see also Reimers 1982: 34–35.

196. After the assassination of President Kennedy, his proposals received unexpected support from President Johnson, who had no record of sympathy for immigration reform. Yet he followed through on the Kennedy plan, and in his 1964 State of the Union address attacked the national origins quota system and included a call to eliminate the Asia-Pacific Triangle [see *H. Doc. 251,* 88th Cong., 2d sess., p. 5; *White House Press Release* of Jan. 13 and Jan. 17, 1964, 110 Cong. Rec. (daily ed., Jan. 23, 1964) 989, 1006; *H. Doc. 52,* 89th Cong., 1st sess.]. Even an unsympathetic Secretary of State Rusk was an effective spokesperson at congressional hearings. While Johnson's unexpected support for immigration reform encouraged many advocates of Kennedy's plan, it later appeared that his interest was primarily based on keen political strategizing and did not reflect a deep commitment to the cause (Schwartz 1968: 117–21; Hutchinson 1981: 366–75).

197. House Subcommittee 1 of the Committee on the Judiciary, *Immigration: Hearings,* 88th Cong., 2d sess., 1964, p. 418.

198. Reimers 1982: 35.

199. Senator Edward Kennedy, opening statement at the Subcommittee on

Immigration and Naturalization of the Committee on the Judiciary, Feb. 10, 1965, p. 2; see also Kennedy 1966: 138.

200. Kitano and Daniels 1988: 16.

201. One prominent immigration lawyer from San Francisco Chinatown testified: "Let it not be said that Chinese immigration would be opened. Under the pending proposals, any increase in volume of immigration of the Chinese would still be limited, but nevertheless, the Chinese communities throughout the United States are in favor of this proposal as a final step in proving to the world that all men are equal when it comes to selecting immigrants" (Jack Wong Sing, testifying before the Subcommittee on Immigration and Naturalization of the Committee on the Judiciary, July 15, 1965, p. 727).

202. Hutchinson 1981: 276.

203. *U.S. Code* 8: §1152(a) (1969 ed.). The Western Hemisphere included Canada, Mexico, Central America, South America, and the "adjacent islands" of Saint Pierre, Miquelon, Cuba, the Dominican Republic, Haiti, Bermuda, the Bahamas, Barbados, Jamaica, the Windward and Leeward Islands, Trinidad, Martinique, and other British, French, and Netherlands territory or possessions in or bordering on the Caribbean Sea. *U.S. Code* 8: §1101(b)(5). Under the 1965 amendments the Western Hemisphere countries had one pool of 120,000 immigrant visas to share without a per-country limitation. *U.S. Code* 8: §1151(a) (1969 ed.). In 1977 the Western Hemisphere was included in the preference system and a single worldwide numerical limitation was set. *Immigration and Nationality Act Amendments of 1976*, Public Law 94-571, *Statutes at Large* 90: 2703–07; see also DeAvila v. Civiletti, 643 F.2d 471 (7th Cir. 1981).

204. The immediate relative category included spouses, unmarried children under age 21, and parents of adult citizens. *U.S. Code* 8: §1151(a), (b) (1969 ed.).

205. Reimers 1982: 38. For some who were more candid, the family reunification bias was a method of perpetuating the Western European preference of the national origins system. Because the nation was predominantly of Western European descent, a family-oriented system would increase the chance that Western Europeans would have relatives to petition for them (Briggs 1986: 49).

206. *U.S. Code* 8: §1153(a)(3), (6) (1982 ed.). Eligibility under the occupational categories was established if a "labor certification" was obtained from the Department of Labor, determining that qualified workers were not available and that employment of the alien would not adversely affect prevailing wages. §1182(a)(14) (1982 ed.).

207. The availability of nonpreference visas was determined by the numbers of unused visas in preferences one through six. *U.S. Code* 8: §1153(a)(8) (1969 ed.).

208. Wasserman 1979: 138–59.

209. Scully 1966: 243.

210. *U.S. Code* 8: §1153(a)(7) (1969 ed.); discussed more fully in Chap. 4.

211. *U.S. Code* 8: §1153(a)(7) (1969 ed.). The 1965 amendments also updated the registry/amnesty provisions of the law (§1259) to grant lawful permanent residence to aliens who had resided in the United States continuously since June 30, 1948. This provided a mechanism for additional Asians who entered or remained illegally to legalize their status.

212. *U.S. Code* 8: §1152(c) (1964 ed.). Under the 1952 Act, immigrants from colonies or dependent areas were charged to the quota of the governing country, up to a maximum of 100 [§1152(c) 1958 ed.]. While small increases to the dependent area quota were made over the years, a substantial increase to 5,000 was enacted as part of the Immigration Reform and Control Act of 1986, Public Law 99-603, *Statutes at Large* 100: 3359. Pursuant to legislation enacted in 1990, the quota for Hong Kong will be increased to 10,000 from 1992 to 1995; thereafter, persons born in Hong Kong will be allotted 20,000 visas under the preference system (Public Law 101-649). In 1976 amendments were enacted that primarily impacted immigration from the Western Hemisphere by extending the annual limitation of 20,000 for each country to that area (Act of Oct. 20, 1976, Public Law 94-571, *Statutes at Large* 90: 2703). Before the amendment Mexicans were using about 40,000 of the 120,000 annual visas allotted to the Western Hemisphere. By creating an across-the-board country limit of 20,000, the amendments essentially cut immigration from Mexico in half. Furthermore, due to Congress's failure to clarify the effective date and the government's fiscal year, the transition from a single Western Hemisphere quota to a per-country limitation resulted in only 5,797 visas for Mexico during the first three quarters of 1977. See DeAvila v. Civiletti, 643 F.2d 471 (7th Cir. 1981).

213. Hong Kong has been a colony of Great Britain since 1842 when the Treaty of Nanking ended the Opium War (Cheng 1984: 3). Great Britain's lease on the territory will expire in 1997, and Hong Kong will then revert to the People's Republic of China. The lease is actually only on the new territories outside of metropolitan Hong Kong, but Great Britain is by treaty ceding the entire area back to China. See Wesley-Smith 1980: 187–90. Macao was a colony of Portugal from 1887 to 1974 when Portugal divested itself of all colonies (Coates 1978: 102–3). On the date of its independence, it became a foreign state for purposes of numerical limitations and entitled it to its own 20,000 allotment. *U.S. Code* 8: §1152(a) (1969 ed.).

214. *U.S. Code* 8: §1152(b) (1969 ed.). Of the 3,803,000 residents of Hong Kong in 1968, about 58 percent were actually born there. About 1.5 million were estimated to be refugees from the People's Republic of China (Hong Kong Census and Statistics Department, *Hong Kong Social and Economic Trends 1968–1972,* table 5, p. 10; Hong Kong Census and Statistics Department, *Hong Kong Population and Housing Census,* 1972, table 6, p. 30). The refugees from China might emigrate to the United States if they qualified under the new preference system, or as conditional entrants under the seventh preference, refugee-type

category. Under either method the visa would be charged to China rather than Hong Kong if the refugee was born in China. The 20,000 visas for countries and 200 for colonies and dependent territories resulted in several anomalies. While a country as small as Singapore, with a population of 1.99 million in 1968, had a full 20,000 available, Hong Kong with its 2.2 million native-born had only 200. A country the size of the People's Republic of China, with a population of 733.37 million in 1968 would have only a total of 20,000, and, on top of that, the Republic of China on Taiwan with a population of 13.47 million shared that allotment (Statistical Office of the United Nations 1971: table 4, 128–31).

## CHAPTER TWO

1. Chinese immigrants commonly referred to the United States as Gold Mountain—a term derived from the dreams of early Chinese migrants lured by the gold rush. Lee 1960: 1; Takaki 1989: 7.

2. Chan 1991a: 104.

3. Cheng and Bonacich 1984: 391, 395.

4. Discussed more fully in Chap. 1.

5. Act of Mar. 2, 1907, *United States Statutes at Large* 34: 1228. Excerpt in Appendix C.

6. Act of Sept. 22, 1922 (The Cable Act), *Statutes at Large* 42: 1021. Excerpt in Appendix C.

7. The Oregon antimiscegenation law, which was initially aimed at African Americans, added Chinese, Hawaiians, and Native Americans in 1866. It prohibited marriage between a white person and a person more than half Chinese (Mooney 1984: 572). The California law, enacted in 1880, prohibited marriage between a white person and a "negro, mulatto, or Mongolian" [*California Codes*, Chap. 41 §1, 1880 (deleted by statute and amendments to the code Sept. 18, 1959)].

8. U.S. Treasury Dept. 1903: 4354.

9. Tong 1973–74: 186–87; Takaki 1989: 31, 65, 117.

10. Based on Sung 1967: 320, table A-3.

11. Tsai 1986: 18–19; Takaki 1989: 47–48.

12. Takaki 1989: 48–49; Lee 1960: 204–5.

13. Takaki 1989: 37–39.

14. Based on data from Kitano and Daniels 1988: 24.

15. Saxton 1971: 104–5, 148–50; Coolidge 1909: 255–60, 350–51.

16. Treasury Dept. 1903: 4354.

17. Ibid., 4338.

18. Based on *1975 INS Annual Report*, table 1, p. 31.

19. Discussed more fully below.

20. *1983 INS Statistical Yearbook*, table IMM 1.2.

21. Lyman 1977: 15–16. By definition, students were classified as nonimmigrants who were required to intend to remain only temporarily. See, e.g., Ex parte Tsiang Hsi Tseng, 24 F.2d 213 (N.D. Calif. 1928); Hing 1985: §3.3.

22. Gordon 1943: 10, n. 28.

23. Between 1913 and 1924, 5,806 Chinese women immigrated, compared to 27,768 men (*1913 to 1924 Annual Reports of the Commissioner General of Immigration*, Dept. of Labor, table 7).

24. Immigration was lowest during the 1930's for all countries (see the figure in Chap. 1). The 1924 law, the depression, and war in Europe and Asia discouraged emigration. Although the Act of June 13, 1930, waived the racial exclusion for Chinese wives of citizens married before the 1924 Act, its effect was insubstantial. Only a few were affected, and Chinese were unable to come up with Western-style marriage certificates and documents required by the immigration authorities. In China marriages and births were often not registered and were established through secondary forms of evidence such as affidavits, photographs, and correspondence (Hing 1979: 299–300; Hing 1983: 24–26).

25. The spouses of citizens were exempt from the quota restrictions, but the quotas for others were still minimal. From 1951 to 1955 fewer than four hundred Chinese entered each year (based on *1951 and 1956 INS Annual Reports*, table 13).

26. Based on *Annual Reports of the Immigration and Naturalization Service 1946–1952*, table 9.

27. Sung 1967: 116, 320, figure 8-B, table A-3; Lee 1960: 43.

28. Based on Sung 1967: 320, table A-3; Gardner et al. 1985: 8, table 2. The Displaced Persons Act of 1948 gave permanent resident alien status to 3,465 Chinese students, visitors, and seamen. The elimination of the Asiatic barred zone in the 1952 Act provided a slight increase in the Chinese quota; the Refugee Relief Act of 1953 permitted the entry of 2,777 refugees of the Chinese Revolution; the Act of August 8, 1958, advanced a registry/amnesty provision to those who had entered prior to June 28, 1940 (*Statutes at Large* 72: 546), and the attorney general's parole authority permitted 15,111 Chinese refugees who had fled to Hong Kong to enter in 1962 (Schwartz 1968: 139–40; Chinn et al. 1969: 19).

29. *1985 INS Statistical Yearbook*, pp. 3–5; Schwartz 1968: 139–40.

30. Estimated from Lee 1960: 42; and Sung 1978: table 2.

31. There the majority of Chinese men, many of whom were merchants and intellectuals, married other ethnic minorities and women of Irish descent ("Asian Immigrant Women—1850 to 1940," an address by Professor Ronald Takaki to the Chinese Historical Society, San Francisco, Sept. 18, 1987).

32. *1959 INS Annual Report*, table 12A, p. 37. The figures for all immigrants that year were 49,673 to California and 64,698 to New York.

33. Estimate based on Sung 1978: table 1.

34. Lee 1960: 58–59; Lyman: 1977: 134–44; Wunder 1989: 142. My own parents fit this description as do other Chinese Americans I have met whose parents or grandparents settled in rural areas of California, Wyoming, Utah, Mississippi, and Arizona.

35. Lee 1960: 53–58.

36. Lee 1960: 13.

37. Chan 1991a: 56.

38. Wunder 1989: 141.

39. Chan 1991a: 57.

40. Tsai 1986: 79–100.

41. Lee 1960: 142–52; Kitano and Daniels 1988: 25–26.

42. Li 1987: 102–3; Nee and Nee 1973: 20–24.

43. Tsai 1986: 72–73.

44. Lee 1960: 58–60.

45. Sung 1967: 144.

46. Schwartz 1968: 139–40; Nee and Nee 1973: 253–55.

47. Sung 1976: 1.

48. Working for $8 per month (compared to $30 for white workers), Chinese began helping to prepare the land for the first vineyards in 1858 (Schoenman 1979: 28).

49. Sung 1972: 5. For an excellent history of Chinese agricultural workers in California, see Sucheng Chan 1986.

50. Sung 1972: 14–15.

51. Ibid., 5. Some Chinese went to the Monterey peninsula of northern California where they found work in the canneries (Hemp 1986: 22–25).

52. Saxton 1971: 183.

53. Sung: 1972: 33–34; Takaki 1989: 93.

54. For a discussion of the conditions that induced Chinese to set up laundries and restaurants see Blalock 1967: 79–84; see also Landa 1978.

55. Many students did go back to China after they had completed their studies. After the Communist victory in the Chinese civil war in 1949, though, some returned to the United States or fled to Taiwan or Hong Kong as political refugees (Nee and Nee 1973: 257–58).

56. Ibid., 149.

57. In a Gallup poll taken in 1942, respondents characterized the Chinese as "hardworking, honest, brave, religious, intelligent, and practical." In contrast, during the World War II hysteria that led to internment Japanese were "treacherous, sly, cruel, and warlike" though also "hardworking and intelligent" (Chan 1991a: 121, citing Isaacs 1958).

58. "How to Tell Your Friends from the Japs," *Time*, Dec. 22, 1941, p. 33; "How to Tell the Japs from the Chinese," *Life*, Dec. 1941.

59. Sung 1976: 2–4.

60. Based on Ling–chi Wang, "The Politics of Assimilation and Repression" (unpublished manuscript), cited in Chan 1991a: 121.

61. Wong 1980: 521.

62. Treasury Dept. 1903: 4354.

63. *1985 INS Statistical Yearbook*, table IMM 1.2, pp. 2–4; F. Chuman 1976: 11.

64. *1983 INS Statistical Yearbook*, table 1.2.

65. *1924 Annual Report of the Commissioner General of Immigration*, Dept. of Labor, table 14.

66. *Japanese Immigration Legislation: Hearings on the Johns Bill S. 2576 Before the Senate Committee on Immigration*, 68th Cong., 1st sess., 130 (1924).

67. Professor Sucheng Chan downplays the significance of the provisions of the Gentlemen's Agreement permitting Japanese women to immigrate: "As for Japanese women, the Gentlemen's Agreement did not explicitly deal with them, concerned primarily as it was with laborers. Women were just mentioned in passing: only laborers 'previously domiciled' in the United States or the parents, wives, and minor children of such laborers could enter after the agreement went into effect" (Chan 1990: 90–91). The Gentlemen's Agreement consisted of an exchange of telegrams, cables, and other communications, rather than a statute as in the case of the various Chinese exclusion laws (see Appendix C). And this "passing" mention of wives and children of Japanese laborers had no counterpart for Chinese laborers at the time. Obviously, the issue of laborers was largely what exclusion efforts were all about. So provisions that allowed laborers to bring their spouses and children are noteworthy.

68. Takaki 1989: 46–47. Gender balancing among Japanese Americans was caused by a large increase in the immigration of Japanese women in the twelve years before the 1924 Act when more Japanese women (62,991) than men (46,191) were admitted. In contrast, 5,806 Chinese women and 27,768 men immigrated between 1913 and 1924. Based on *1912 Through 1924 Annual Reports of the Commissioner General of Immigration*, Dept. of Labor, table 7.

69. Sung 1976: 320, table A-3.

70. Kitano 1969: 39–40; Takaki 1989: 47, 72–73; F. Chuman 1976: 107; Glenn 1986: 42–66.

71. *Japanese Immigration Legislation: Hearings on the Johns Bill S. 2576, Before the Senate Committee on Immigration*, 68th Cong., 1st sess., p. 134 (1924).

72. Ibid., p. 26. Under today's immigration laws, a citizen can petition for a fiancé(e) under circumstances that are not unlike those surrounding the picture bride phenomenon. *United States Code* 8: §1101(a)(15)(f) (1992 ed.); see Hing 1985: §3.22.

73. *Japanese Immigration Legislation: Hearings on the Johns Bill S. 2576, Before the Senate Committee on Immigration*, 68th Cong., 1st sess., p. 134 (1924), p. 26. One senator from California alleged that this was all part of a conspiracy to take over land in California.

74. In Hawaii in 1930 the number stood at over 91,000 (Chan 1991a: 109).

75. Professor Chan argues that in spite of the Burlingame Treaty's recognition of the right, "Chinese statutes prohibiting emigration were not removed from the books until the turn of the century." Therefore, all Chinese emigration until then was technically illegal (Chan 1990: 91). Whether China actually regarded emigration as illegal, however, is doubtful. In international law, treaty provisions generally take precedence over statutory law.

76. Ibid., 86–87.

77. Compare Takaki:

> While women in China were restricted to the farm and the home, women in Japan in the nineteenth century were becoming wage-earning workers away from home.... By 1900, women composed 60 percent of Japan's industrial laborers.... The movement of Japanese women to Hawaii and the United States was an extension of a proletarianization process already well under way in Japan. (1989: 47–48)

with Chan:

> Despite its rapid industrialization, Japan remained an overwhelmingly agrarian country in the early decades of this century: its industrial labor force represented only a little over one percent of the country's total population.... I know of no studies that show a causal connection between factory experience and the tendency of Japanese women to emigrate. In the available oral histories of Japanese immigrant women, few, if any, mention that having been factory or industrial workers in Japan was what had encouraged them to come to the United States. (1990: 87)

78. As a result of China's far slower pace of modernization, very few Chinese women held similar status during the same period. Professor Ronald Takaki suggests that Japanese women were more receptive to the idea of traveling overseas than Chinese because they were more educated (1989: 47–49). But Professor Sucheng Chan argues that some Chinese girls were also going to public schools by the early twentieth century (1990: 88). But as I have shown, by the early twentieth century the enforcement of the exclusion laws effectively curtailed the entry of most Chinese women, while different rules applied to Japanese women.

79. In China all sons received a piece of their parents' land (Takaki 1989: 48–49; Chan 1990: 89–90). A final factor encouraging the immigration of Japanese women was the type of jobs their husbands had in the United States. Many of the first Chinese immigrants had worked in migratory jobs—on farms, in mines, and on the railroad. The Japanese who went into agricultural work in California, however, would try to become tenant farmers, which was a life-style more conducive to establishing a conventional family (Takaki 1989: 190–91).

80. Ichihashi 1932: 396–98; Steiner 1917: 65–66.

81. F. Chuman 1976: 311.

82. Based on *1952 to 1961 INS Annual Reports*, table 38.

83. *1959 INS Annual Report*, table 9.

84. *1961 INS Annual Report*, table 9.

85. Estimate based on 1970 census data. Dept. of Commerce 1975a: table 33, p. 30 (indicating that in 1970 there were 271,000 Japanese American men and 320,000 women for a ratio of 84.7:100).

86. From 1956 to 1959, an average of almost 6,500 Japanese immigrated annually while Chinese constituted the second largest group with only 1,500 each year (*1959 INS Annual Report*, table 13, p. 41). Though from 1961 to 1965 Japanese annual immigration averaged under 4,000, this was still over twice the average of 1,850 for the Chinese. *1966 INS Annual Report*, table 13, p. 57.

87. Gardner et al. 1985: 8, table 2.

88. Ichihashi 1932: 392.

89. Takaki 1989: 182–86; Kitano 1969: 17–23.

90. Ichihashi 1915: 21.

91. Kitano and Daniels 1986: 58–59; C. Kang, "Japantown: A Community Losing Its Identity," *San Francisco Examiner*, Sept. 14, 1987, B-4.

92. See Korematsu v. United States, 323 U.S. 214 (1944); Hirabayashi v. United States, 320 U.S. 81 (1943).

93. F. Chuman 1976: 143–63; Kitano 1969: 69–88; Takaki 1989: 379–405; Chan 1991a: 122–39. Congress went out of its way to accommodate interned Japanese Americans who wanted to renounce their citizenship as a form of protest. It enacted special legislation in 1944 to allow renunciation, presumably paving the way to deport these Japanese after the war. Although over six thousand applied for renunciation, subsequent lawsuits and political pressure enjoined the enforcement of the legislation, largely on the grounds that the applicants acted under duress and coercion (Chan 1991a: 139).

94. See Buss 1985: 85–105 (account of Mary Tsukamoto).

95. "The tendency of the nation is to keep the Japanese in a permanently separate group distinct from the main part of the population. Such a policy will probably result eventually in not only a distinct but an inferior position, in much the same manner in which the Negro problem has resulted. The difficulty lies in the refusal of the Japanese to accept inferiority. Their ambitions are in direct conflict with the racial consciousness of the whites" (Paul 1978: 102–3).

96. Korematsu v. United States, 584 F.Supp. 1406 (N.D. Cal. 1984).

97. Clark 1980: 8, 11–12.

98. Chan 1991a: 139. There is, however, some empirical evidence that points to a large-scale resettlement in the Chicago area after World War II (Kim 1978: 115).

99. Kim 1978: 115.

100. In 1959, for example, 285 Japanese immigrants settled in New York, 196 in

Pennsylvania, 235 in Texas, and 259 in Illinois. In 1961, 235 went to New York, 126 to Pennsylvania, 134 to Texas, and 195 to New York (*1959 and 1961 INS Annual Reports*, table 12A).

101. *1952 to 1965 INS Annual Reports*, table 12A.

102. Ibid.

103. *1952 to 1968 INS Annual Reports*, table 12A.

104. Steiner 1917: 58.

105. Nikki Bridges, wife of labor activist Harry Bridges, was told by War Relocation Authority officers prior to her release from camp that she should avoid being seen in groups with Japanese Americans, speak English at all times, and dress and act American.

106. C. Kang, "Japantown: A Community Losing Its Identity," *San Francisco Examiner*, Sept. 14, 1987, p. B-1; see also Kitano and Daniels 1986: 58–59.

107. Chan 1991a: 39.

108. Hosokawa 1969: 59; Petersen 1971: 28.

109. Thernstrom 1980; Hosokawa 1969: 71; see generally Kitano 1974: 500–519. In the 1890's, a small community of Japanese American abalone fishermen was established near Monterey Bay in northern California (Hemp 1986: 34–39).

110. Kitano 1969: 16–17.

111. Glenn 1986: 68–76.

112. Kawakami 1921: 191–92. The law permitted aliens ineligible for citizenship to hold leaseholds for three years, thereby technically satisfying the terms of the 1911 treaty (Kimura 1988: 301).

113. Daniels 1981: 16. It was clearly established by that time that the Fourteenth Amendment conferred citizenship on children born in the United States of lawful resident alien parents. See United States v. Wong Kim Ark, 169 U.S. 649 (1898).

114. Section Four of the statute effectively provided that no ineligible alien could become a guardian of a minor's estate in land. Section Nine provided a catchall provision in anticipation of new loopholes: "Every transfer of real property, or an interest therein, though colorable in form, shall be void as to the state and the interest thereby conveyed shall escheat to the state if the property interest involved is of such a character that an ineligible alien is inhibited from acquiring, possessing, enjoying or transferring it, and if the conveyance is made with intent to prevent, evade or avoid escheat as provided herein." Other West Coast states, including Washington, followed the California model for alien land laws (See McGovney 1947: 7).

115. Webb v. O'Brien, 263 U.S. 313 (1923). The law was held not to violate equal protection or the 1911 treaty. See also Frick v. Webb, 263 U.S. 326 (1923); Powell 1924: 259.

116. Masaoka v. California, 39 Cal. 2d 883 (1952); Fujii v. California, 38 Cal. 2d 718 (1952).

117. Kitano and Daniels 1986: 58.

118. Kitano 1969: 20–21.

119. Ibid.: 23–24.

120. Strong 1933: 214–15.

121. Yanagisako 1985: 4 (citing Miyamoto 1939: 71).

122. For example, prior to the evacuation order, Los Angeles County dismissed all its clerks of Japanese ancestry, and the California State Personnel Board barred all descendants of enemy aliens from civil service positions, but enforced the rule only against Japanese Americans (Chan 1991a: 125; see also Yanagisako 1985: 5).

123. Strong 1933: 90–97; Chan 1991a: 139.

124. Kitano and Daniels: 1988: 59–60.

125. Based on *1959 and 1961 INS Annual Reports*, table 8.

126. Gardner et al. 1985: table 2, p. 8. Others have reported about 2,300 Filipinos in 1910 (Smith 1976: 322).

127. Ibid.

128. *1983 INS Statistical Yearbook*, table IMM 1.2.

129. Smith 1976: 322. Gardner et al. 1985: 8, table 2; Lasker reports that in 1931 there were 75,000 Filipinos in Hawaii and 60,000 on the mainland (1931: pt. I, chap. 3).

130. Takaki 1989: 58–59.

131. Kitano and Daniels 1988: 95. Housing patterns in Los Angeles in the early 1930's revealed that Filipinos were better treated in Mexican neighborhoods than in white neighborhoods (Catapusan 1934: 5–6).

132. Catapusan 1934: 40–44. To encourage Filipinos to return to the Philippines, Congress enacted a Repatriation Act in 1935 that offered travel money to any Filipino (Thernstrom 1980: 361). Over two thousand accepted the offer (Takaki 1989: 332–33; Kitano and Daniels 1988: 82–83).

133. Act of March 27, 1942, *Statutes at Large* 56: 182; *1945 INS Annual Report*, p. 97. Besides the 1942 statute, Filipino veterans were also eligible to apply under a 1940 provision if they sought naturalization within six months of an honorable discharge. Act of Oct. 14, 1940, *Statutes at Large* 54: 1137, §§303(a), 324(a). It exempted alien servicemen from the usual requirements for naturalization, including residency, English literacy, and filing within the jurisdiction of a U.S. court. Although about four thousand took advantage of the 1942 law, thousands more were denied the opportunity for approximately nine months, and others were unaware of the law and/or its filing deadline of December 31, 1946. See Immigration and Naturalization Service v. Pangilinan, 486 U.S. 989 (1988); Immigration and Naturalization Service v. Hibi, 414 U.S. 5 (1973); Naturalization of 68 Filipino War Veterans, 406 F.Supp. 931 (N.D. Calif. 1975). Under legislation enacted in 1990 the opportunity for these World War II Filipino war veterans to apply for naturalization has been renewed.

134. Discussed more fully in Chap. 1.

135. *1951 INS Annual Report*, table 39. From 1951 to 1959, about two thousand were naturalized annually (*1959 INS Annual Report*, p. 79).

136. Based on *1959 and 1961 INS Annual Reports*, table 9; see also Barkan 1983: 33.

137. Chan 1991a: 140.

138. Based on Smith 1976: 325. Approximation for 1965 based on Smith 1976: 325, and Gardner et al. 1985: 16.

139. Of the 2,633 immigrants from the Philippines in 1960, 2,300 were spouses and children of citizens (*1959 INS Annual Report*, table 6, p. 17; *1970 INS Annual Report*, table 14).

140. The proportion living in Hawaii was 53.5 percent in 1930 and 49.7 percent in 1950 (Smith 1976: 322).

141. Kitano and Daniels 1988: 80.

142. Originally, these Little Manila districts were used as "stopover points" for agricultural workers in transit (De Witt 1976: 21).

143. Catapusan 1934: 1.

144. Melendy 1974: 524.

145. DeWitt 1976: chap. 3.

146. Melendy 1974: 530; Catapusan 1934: 30–31; Chan 1991a: 40.

147. Morales 1976: 31.

148. Barber shops, restaurants, embroideries, photo studios, rooming houses, and employment agencies were among the small Filipino-owned businesses in Los Angeles (Catapusan 1934: 2, 12–13). The existence of a merchant class in the Philippines was suppressed by U.S. and European business people and by Chinese middlemen. Thus, less than 1 percent of the early Filipino migrants had business backgrounds (Yu 1980: 84).

149. Kitano and Daniels 1988: 78.

150. Smith 1976: 322; De Witt 1976: chap. 3.

151. Morales 1976: 31.

152. Melendy 1974: 530–31.

153. Based on *1959, 1961, and 1963 INS Annual Reports*, table 8.

154. Melendy 1974: 530–31.

155. Vreeland 1976: 67; Bunge 1984: 41–42.

156. Bunge 1984: 42–46.

157. Koreans did not mind being strikebreakers because of animosity between them and Japanese over aggression and establishment of the Protectorate, and they received relatively good pay (Patterson 1988: 151).

158. Houchins and Houchins 1974: 549–50; Boyd 1974: 24–25; Kim 1971: 4, 11; Shin 1971: 200–201; Patterson 1988: 103. Koreans were labeled by plantation owners as mediocre workers. The planters had high expectations because reports from Korea had spoken of their stellar physical strength and fitness. But most who actually went to Hawaii were not typical peasants, and were from the cities and thus unaccustomed to agricultural labor (Patterson 1988: 121).

159. Kim 1971: 4, 23.

160. Ibid., 22–23.

161. Ibid., 23–24. Houchins and Houchins 1974: 558. Another group of 289 students arrived between 1921 and 1940 with passports issued by the Japanese government in Korea. Yet they were not eligible for permanent residence, primarily because of the 1924 Act. Though most returned to Korea, a few were able to remain in the United States during World War II to serve as interpreters or in the military (Kim 1971: 24).

162. Boyd 1974: 25.

163. Gardner et al. 1985: 8, table 2; Xenos et al. 1987: table 11.1, pp. 252–53.

164. Boyd 1974: 25–26.

165. Kihl 1984: 49.

166. Bunge 1982: 31.

167. Many Korean students opposed to South Korean leader Rhee were denied extensions on their passports and were forced to return to Korea before completing their schooling (Choy 1979: 183).

168. H. Rept. 1365, 81st Cong., 2d sess., *U.S. Code Cong. & Adm. News*, 1653, 1681 (1952).

169. *1961 INS Annual Report*, table 14. In 1960 only 11,000 foreign-born Korean Americans were in the United States (Knoll 1982: 139).

170. From *1961 and 1969 INS Annual Reports*, table 14.

171. This is an estimate based on the 1960 and 1970 data in table 7.

172. Boyd 1974: 25; Houchins and Houchins 1974: 559; Kim 1976: 40.

173. Takaki 1989: 273.

174. Kim 1976: 40–41; Chan 1991a: 140.

175. *1959–1960 INS Annual Reports*, table 9.

176. Boyd 1974: 26–28.

177. Ibid.; Kim 1981: 39–41 (Americans have adopted about thirteen thousand Korean children since 1955); Kitano and Daniels 1988: 110–11.

178. Shin 1971: 201; Takaki 1989: 275–77.

179. Shin 1971: 201–2; Houchins and Houchins 1974: 559–60.

180. Shin 1971: 203.

181. Ibid.

182. Some of the major Korean American political groups established between 1905 and 1920 included the Korean National Association, the League of Korean Independence, the Comrade Society, the Korean Women's Patriotic League, the Korean's People's Revolutionary Party in Los Angeles, and the Sino-Korean People's League in Hawaii (Choy 1979: 115–20).

183. Shin 1971: 203; Houchins and Houchins 1974: 561.

184. Houchins and Houchins 1974: 561–62.

185. Takaki 1989: 276.

186. *Los Angeles Times*, June 27, 1913, pp. 1, 5; June 28, 1913, p. 1.

187. Based on *1959, 1961, and 1963 INS Annual Reports*, table 8.

188. Political or cultural exchanges promoted a better understanding between the two countries, although it was more a matter of mutual curiosity than any economic or social interest. See Tewari 1977: chaps. 1 and 2.

189. Kitano and Daniels 1988: 90.

190. See Tewari 1977: chaps. 1 and 2.

191. Hoyt 1974: chap. 9; Minocha 1987: 3; Hess 1976: 413–14.

192. Hess 1976: 416.

193. Ibid., 419.

194. La Brack and Leonard 1984: 527–37.

195. Leonard 1986: 71.

196. Ibid., 71–72.

197. These marriages created tension in India, but the men would continue to send money to their families and some Mexican wives and Mexican-Asian Indian children eventually visited India (Leonard 1986: 73; see also Hess 1976: 32).

198. Tewari 1977: 9–10.

199. Discussed more fully in Chap. 1.

200. *1947 INS Annual Report*, table 6.

201. Anti-Indian feeling and discrimination in South Africa was assuming the same proportions as had the anti-Oriental fever on the Pacific coast. Finally, the movement for the exclusion of Asian Indians in the 1960's resulted in the mass exodus of Indian laboring classes to Britain and to British territories, such as Canada, New Zealand, and the British West Indies. Only a few entered the United States directly—most were spillovers from Canada (Hoyt 1974: 103, 108; Cheng and Bonacich 1984: 332).

202. From *1969 INS Annual Report*, table 13. From 1820 to 1965 less than seventeen thousand immigrants from India entered (*1965 INS Annual Report*, table 13).

203. Dept. of Commerce 1975b: 117. Population figures for the entire Asian Indian community were not collected for these periods.

204. See generally Dandekar 1968; United Nations 1983; Todaro 1985.

205. Hess 1976: 413; Kitano and Daniels 1988: 90. These Punjabis traveled abroad as free emigrants, unlike Indians from north central and southern India who were recruited as indentured laborers to the British West Indies, Uganda, Maritius, and British Guiana (Chan 1990: 95). Asian Indian immigrants after the 1965 amendments are still from the Punjab, but are not predominantly Sikhs (Hess 1976: 98).

206. Hess 1976: 414.

207. Kitano and Daniels 1988: 95. New York is where Asian Indians thought they would go when they came to America (conversations with Druv Khana and Raj Prasad, March 1989).

208. Hess 1976: 415.

209. Jensen 1969: 335–40.

210. Hess 1986: 32; Tambs-Lyche 1980: 12, 97.

211. Cheng and Bonacich 1984: 558–59; Hess 1976: 414–15.

212. Hess 1976: 413–14; Hess 1986: 29.

213. Hess 1976: 417; see also Chan 1986: map 19.

214. In 1933 a grand jury indicted more than 60 Asian Indians for evading the California alien land law (Leonard 1986: 70).

215. Sucheng Chan 1986: 40.

216. Hess 1976: 419.

217. See generally Dandekar 1968; United Nations 1983; Todaro 1985.

218. Based on 1959 INS Annual Report, table 8.

219. Based on 1963 INS Annual Report, table 8.

220. Melendy 1972: 112.

221. Ichioka 1988: 63–64.

222. Hess 1976: 419; Melendy 1977: 205–6.

223. Sung 1967; Lee 1960: 300–307; Conwell 1871: 212; Chinn et al. 1969: 15; Kitano and Daniels 1988: 28–30; Takaki 1989: 234–39.

224. Coolidge 1909: 316.

225. Lyman 1974: 69; Takaki 1989: 234.

226. Around the turn of the century one estimate placed the number of Chinese smuggled in at twenty thousand annually. In 1932 and 1933 about five thousand Chinese were allegedly caught illegally crossing the Mexican border into Arizona (Tsai 1986: 99; Lyman 1974: 105–9).

227. Mirandé 1987: 108.

228. In my experience as a legal services attorney in Chinatown in the 1970's, it was quite common for clients to have a relative who had made a false claim to citizenship.

229. Daniels 1988: 91. Though I am speaking here principally of the period from 1882 to 1965 (particularly around the turn of the century), many practitioners feel that distrust of Chinese, however subtle, persists among INS examiners. On a formal tour of the San Francisco INS office in 1975, I heard a suspicion of Chinese expressed bluntly. Then Senior Immigration Judge Chester Sipkin candidly stated that he never accepted at face value the testimony of any Chinese person appearing before him.

230. Tsai 1986: 99–101; Takaki 1989: 231–39. My mother, who was born in Scranton, Pennsylvania, in 1901, was detained at Angel Island for a week in 1925 (see B. Hing, "No Place for Angels," Asian Week, Dec. 22, 1979, p. 1). Before Angel Island an infamous wooden shack near the beach on San Francisco Bay was used to inspect Chinese (Coolidge 1909: 315).

231. A marvelous collection of Angel Island poetry is contained in Lai et al. 1980.

232. Daniels 1988: 92; Lyman 1974: 69.

233. Chen 1980: 215; Daniels 1988: 308.

234. Lyman 1974: 111; Chen 1980: 216; Daniels 1988: 309.

235. Lowenstein 1960: 6–10.

236. See, e.g., Ng v. Pilliod, 279 F.2d 207, 211 (7th Cir. 1960); Takaki 1989: 416. Vestiges of the complications that these fictional relationships created in the Chinese immigration process continue to haunt Chinese American families. See, e.g., Jen Hung Ng v. Immigration and Naturalization Service, 804 F.2d 534 (9th Cir. 1986). A misconception has developed among some otherwise careful scholars that special legislation was enacted to protect Chinese who confessed. In fact, relief for any alien who had resided in the United States for seven years and who would suffer extreme hardship if deported was available, but only as a matter of discretion. I represented many Chinese who had confessed and many who had not when I practiced in Chinatown.

237. Tsai 1986: 135–36; Chen 1980: 215; Takaki 1989: 416.

## CHAPTER THREE

1. See Table 3.

2. Gardner et al. 1985: 8, table 2.

3. A total of 42,478 immigrated in 1987, *Immigration Statistics: Fiscal Year 1987, Advance Report*, table 4, Immigration and Naturalization Service, June 1988.

4. From *1970 INS Annual Report*, table 13; *1988 and 1989 INS Statistical Yearbooks*, table 2. INS Statistical Branch, Detail Run 401—Total FY 1990.

5. *1972–78 INS Annual Reports*, table 7A; *1977 INS Annual Report*, table 6E. Although this provision did not apply to aliens who had firmly resettled in a third country—Rosenberg v. Woo, 402 U.S. 49 (1971)—many of the Chinese who were admitted under seventh preference had resided in Hong Kong for many years. See, e.g., Matter of Ng, 12 I.&N. Dec. 411 (Reg. Comm'r 1967); Matter of Chai, 12 I.&N. Dec. 81 (Reg. Comm'r 1967).

6. There is, however, a noticeable variation in these proportions between immigrants from Taiwan and those from mainland China. In 1987, 93 percent entered in the family categories and 4.2 percent in the occupational categories from mainland China. But for Taiwan, it was 64.3 percent family and 34.5 percent occupational (based on *Immigration Statistics Fiscal Year 1987, Advance Report*, table 4).

7. Based on Dept. of Commerce 1988a: table 1.

8. The Immigration and Naturalization Systems of the United States, *Rept. of the Committee on the Judiciary Pursuant to S. Res. 137*, Apr. 20, 1950, p. 141; Takaki 1989: 254; Lee 1960: 42, 117.

9. Tabulations from *1985 INS Statistical Yearbook*, table IMM 1.2; *1988 and 1989 INS Statistical Yearbooks*, table 2; 1990 data supplied by Blanche V. Shanks, Statistical Assistant, Immigration and Naturalization Service, Washington, D.C., June 13, 1991.

10. A separate quota for Taiwan was established as a rider to a defense bill to aid the Republic of China. *International Security and Development Cooperation Act of 1981*, Public Law 97-113, *United States Statutes at Large* 95: 1519.

11. Gardner et al. 1985: 37. L. Harrison, "Asians 40 Percent of 1985's Legal Immigrants," *Asian Week*, May 23, 1986, p. 24.

12. In typical years after the Chinese Repealer and other changes that facilitated the entry of Chinese wives, more Chinese women than men entered. In 1951, 957 women entered and only 126 men (*1951 INS Annual Report*, table 10). And in 1959, 3,185 Chinese women immigrated, compared to 2,846 men (*1959 INS Annual Report*, table 10, p. 33). After the 1965 amendments, this pattern continued. In 1969, 10,892 women immigrated compared to 10,001 men from China and Hong Kong; in 1976, 12,770 women arrived compared to 11,819 men; and in 1985, 23,644 Chinese women entered, compared to 21,209 men (*1969 INS Annual Report*, table 9, pp. 52–53; *1976 Annual Report*, table 9, pp. 68–69; *1985 INS Statistical Yearbook*, table IMM 4.3).

13. Based on Dept. of Commerce 1988a: table 1. In the general population there are more women than men, the ratio being 100 women for every 94.5 men (based on *The Europa World Year Book 1989*: K–Z; see Gardner et al. 1985: 16; Sung 1980: 39).

14. Sung 1967: 120.

15. Sung 1978: table 1.

16. Based on Dept. of Commerce 1988a: table 18.

17. Dept. of Commerce 1991: table 5b. The California proportion seems to be increasing. In 1980, 40.1 percent resided in California (Gardner et al. 1985: 11), and about 39.5 percent in 1970 (Sung 1978: table 1).

18. Dept. of Commerce 1991: table 5b. The proportion of Chinese in New York has been dropping (although the actual populations are increasing). In 1970 it was 19 percent (Sung 1978: table 1); in 1980 it was 18.1 percent (Gardner et al. 1985: 11). A preference for California among all immigrants was clear in the 1980's. In 1976 about the same number of immigrants settled in California (88,700) as in New York (85,928); but by 1985 many more immigrants preferred California (155,403 to 104,734) (*1985 Statistical Yearbook*, table IMM 5.2, p. 58).

19. Based on Dept. of Commerce 1991: table 5A.

20. Based on *1985 INS Statistical Yearbook*, table IMM 5.3, pp. 59–61. In 1990, 3 percent lived in Illinois, 3.8 percent in Texas, 1.9 percent in Maryland, and 1.2 percent in Michigan. Washington (2.1 percent), Massachusetts (3.3 percent), and New Jersey (3.6 percent) also show growing Chinese American populations (Dept. of Commerce 1991: table 5b).

21. Gardner et al. 1985: 12.

22. Based on *1985 INS Statistical Yearbook*, table IMM 5.3, pp. 59–61.

23. Dept. of Commerce 1983a: table 4, p. 12; 1983b: table 248.

24. Dept. of Commerce 1983b: table 248.

25. Sung 1979: 17, 21.

26. Mar 1985: 83–87, 106.

27. Kwong 1987: 3–9; Nee and Nee 1973: 253–55; Butterfield, "Chinatown's Year of Snake Marks Era of Change," *New York Times,* Jan. 7, 1989.

28. Sixty-one percent in 1969 and 81 percent in 1985 entered in family categories (see Table 9).

29. Nee and Nee 1973: 253–55; Sung 1967: 145; interview with Gordon Chin, executive director, Chinatown Resource Center, Feb. 24, 1989.

30. Sung 1967: 147–49; Tsai 1980: 329.

31. See generally Wong 1980: 511; Keely 1975: 179; Keely 1974: 89; Keely 1971: 157.

32. Based on table 8 of *1953–1966, 1969 INS Annual Reports.*

33. From *1961 and 1966 INS Annual Reports,* table 8.

34. Based on *1969 and 1977 INS Annual Reports,* table 8. This is consistent with general findings today that family reunification categories provide most of the new immigrant professionals (Bach and Meissner 1989: 11–12).

35. Since immigrants are charged to their country of birth, many immigrants from Hong Kong were born in China and are regarded as coming from China. *United States Code,* 8: §1152(b) (1990 ed.).

36. Consider, for example, the statements of Barry Chiswick, the dean of Economics and Business Administration at the University of Illinois in Chicago, cited in the Introduction.

37. Visas were set aside for "qualified immigrants who are members of the professions or who [have] exceptional ability in the sciences or the arts." To qualify the applicant had to obtain a labor certification, which required a job offer from an employer. See *U.S. Code* 8: §§1153(a)(3), 1182(a)(14) (1982 ed); Hing 1985: chap. 5.

38. From *1969 INS Annual Report,* table 8.

39. From *1983 INS Statistical Yearbook,* table IMM 6.1.

40. Based on *1989 INS Statistical Yearbook,* tables 5 and 6, pp. 12, 14.

41. Waller and Hoffman 1989: 313; "Beijing Death Toll at Least 200; Army Tightens Control of City But Angry Resistance Goes On," *New York Times,* June 5, 1989, p. 1; conversation with Eugene Chow, Aug. 15, 1989, private attorney in Hong Kong.

42. The statute requires every applicant for admission to demonstrate that he or she is "not likely to become a public charge" [*U.S. Code,* §1182(a)(4) (1992 ed); see also Hing 1985: §§4.46–4.47].

43. In 1961, 8.5 percent were service or household workers and 69.4 percent were housewives or had no prior occupation; in 1966, 14.7 percent were service or household workers and 54 percent were housewives or had no prior occupation (based on *1961 and 1966 INS Annual Reports,* table 8). This occupational breakdown held until 1969, when 11.5 percent were household or service workers, and 52 percent were housewives or had no prior occupation (based on *1969*

*INS Annual Report,* table 8). By 1977, the proportion who designated household or service work jobs dropped to 5.4 percent, but 53 percent were housewives or had no prior occupation (*1977 INS Annual Report,* table 8). As recently as 1985, 57.5 percent continued to indicate no prior occupation (with 4.6 percent indicating service work) (*1985 INS Statistical Yearbook,* table IMM 6.1).

44. Mar 1985: 10–11, 83–87, 106.

45. See generally Wong 1980: 518, 522; Ng 1977: 106; Sung 1976: 69.

46. Gardner et al. 1985: 31 (corrected data based on telephone conversation with authors).

47. The bifurcation of labor in the Chinese American community is not uncommon. Sociological and economic literature often accounts for the labor experience of immigrants through a "split market theory" (higher-paid labor deals with the undercutting potential of cheaper labor by excluding them from certain types of work) or the "human capital model" (the labor market contains at least two groups of workers whose price differs for the same work, or would differ if they did the same work). For a discussion of the split market theory, see Piore 1979; Bonacich 1972. For a discussion of the human capital theory, see Chiswick 1980; Ng 1977: 101; Chiswick 1978: 897.

48. Dept. of Commerce 1988a: table 21.

49. Discussed more fully in Chap. 5.

50. Even in Minneapolis, which is the second lowest ranking metropolitan area, the rate is 74.9 per 1,000 for Chinese (Manning and O'Hare 1988: 35–37).

51. In Los Angeles, Chinese owned 7,664 businesses, Japanese 5,853, and Koreans 5,701 (Pei 1987). In the San Francisco Bay Area, the figures were Chinese 13,784, Filipinos 4,261, Japanese 4,075, Koreans 2,286, Asian Indians 1,707, and Vietnamese 1,339 (D. Waugh, "Asian American Businesses See Explosive Growth in State," *San Francisco Examiner,* Aug. 2, 1991, p. A-16).

52. Yu, "Asian-Americans Charge Prejudice Slows Climb to Management Ranks," *Wall Street Journal,* Sept. 11, 1985, p. 35; Chinese for Affirmative Action 1989: 20–22, 26–27; McLeod 1986: 51.

53. See, e.g., A. Ramirez, "America's Super Minority," *Fortune,* Nov. 24, 1986, p. 149; M. Kasindorf, "Asian-Americans: A 'Model Minority,'" *Newsweek,* Dec. 6, 1982, p. 39.

54. From Dept. of Commerce 1988b: table 7, p. 13.

55. Gardner et al. 1985: 34, table 14. Some scholars who note the higher earnings of older immigrants argue that immigrants assimilate quite well and over time their earnings overtake even native workers. But more thoughtful observers warn that the use of cross section data is misleading, because many immigrants eventually return to their country of origin—quite possibly those who have failed economically—and the average quality of the immigrant pool (in terms of education and job preparedness) may have been declining recently (Borjas 1986: 13–14).

56. Ignoring the existence of low-income Chinese Americans, Philip Martin of the University of California at Davis, who served on the staff of the Select Commission on Immigration and Refugee Policy, told a congressional committee, "In California it's hard to tell exactly what the [impact of the new wave of immigration has] been, but it seems as if Anglos and Asians tend to dominate the top of the income or wealth pyramid, while blacks and Hispanics tend to be over-represented at the bottom" (testimony before the Subcommittee on Economic Resources, Competitiveness, and Security Economics, May 29, 1986, p. 607).

57. Gardner et al. 1985: 34.

58. Ibid., table 14.

59. Ibid.

60. *U.S. Code* 42: §§1381, 1382 (1990 ed.).

61. Based on Dept. of Commerce 1991: table 1.

62. Dept. of Commerce 1988b: 3; 1965 figure estimated from Smith 1976: 325; *1989 INS Statistical Yearbook*, table 2; INS Statistical Branch, Detail Run 401—Total FY 1990.

63. Based on Immigration and Naturalization Service, *Immigration Statistics: Fiscal Year 1987, Advance Report*, table 4. The total for Hong Kong, Taiwan, and mainland China was 42,478 in 1987. So even with the territorial quota increase for Hong Kong provided in 1986 (from 600 to 5,000), the annual total immigration for those three areas will still be less than the Philippines. By 1995 the Hong Kong quota will be increased to 20,000.

64. *U.S. Code* 8: §1182(a)(5) (1992); see generally Hing 1985: chaps. 4 and 5.

65. Based on *1976 INS Annual Report*, tables 6, 6B, 7A.

66. The availability of nonpreference visas for investors was never significant for Filipinos. As Table 8 shows, less than 1 percent entered as investors in 1969, compared to 26.8 percent of Asian Indians and 11.6 percent of Koreans. Although during the Marcos era, Filipino asylum applicants were approved at the relatively high rate of up to 25 percent in 1984, that only amounted to about 30 per year. Polish nationals were granted asylum at a rate of 30 percent, Nicaraguans at 17 percent, El Salvadorans at 1 percent, Guatemalans at 0.3 percent, Iranians at 63 percent (Hing 1985: 196–97).

67. Vreeland 1976: 67; Bunge 1984: 197.

68. Vreeland 1976: 67, 218; Bunge 1984: 49.

69. Bunge 1984: 49; Vreeland 1976: 191.

70. Vreeland 1976: 221; Bunge 1984: 49. Senator Benigno Aquino was among the arrested group, as he was considered by many to be Marcos's key rival. He was sentenced to eight years in solitary confinement (Steinberg 1982: 102). The assassination of Aquino on his return from exile in 1983 helped stir the public's outrage against Marcos, and resulted in the installation of Aquino's widow, Corazon, to the presidency ("Anatomy of a Revolution," *Time*, Mar. 10, 1986, 28–29).

71. Vreeland 1976: 221.

72. Bunge 1984: 52, 92.

73. Steinberg 1982: 104–6; Bunge: 1984: 50, 231.

74. Steinberg 1982: 122; Bunge: 1984: 120.

75. Steinberg 1982: 106; Bunge: 1984: 120.

76. Bunge 1984: 116; Vreeland 1976: 36; Steinberg 1982: 111.

77. See, e.g., T. Abate, "Money Woes Driving Many Filipinos to the U.S.," *San Francisco Examiner*, Dec. 24, 1991, p. A-3; Berlow, "U.S. Immigration Bill Seen as a Way Out of Philippines," *San Francisco Chronicle*, Nov. 23, 1990, p. B-18.

78. Mangiafico 1988: 42; J. Johnson, "Separation Anxieties: Immigration Quotas Keep Filipina Nurses from Their Families," *Los Angeles Times*, May 13, 1991, p. B-3.

79. In 1970 the Filipino sex ratio was 123.4 men to 100 women (Gardner et al. 1985: 16).

80. Based on the *1969 and 1977 INS Annual Reports*, table 9.

81. Gardner et al. 1985: p. 16; calculations based on unpublished data provided by Robert W. Gardner of the Population Institute, East-West Center, Honolulu, Hawaii.

82. Based on *1985 INS Statistical Yearbook*, tables IMM 2.6 and IMM 6.1. In 1985, 29,738 Filipino immigrants were listed in the INS occupation table under "no occupation." That includes those whom INS previously labeled "housewives" (see, e.g., *1977 INS Annual Report*, table 8, p. 47).

83. Reported on KTVU Channel 2, Oakland, Calif. Segment 2 news series, May 16–20, 1988; S. Mydans, "Philippines Trying to Regulate One of Its Most Profitable Exports: Women," *New York Times*, May 12, 1988, p. A6.

84. *1989 INS Statistical Yearbook*, tables 4 and 12, pp. 4, 27.

85. The 1980 census in the Philippines counted 24,128,755 men (50.1 percent) and 23,969,705 women (*Europa World Year Book 1989*: K–Z).

86. Mangiafico 1988: 45–46; Chan 1991a: 140, 149.

87. Conversations with Llorette Tamayo, paralegal, International Institute; Professor Amado Cabezas, UC Berkeley Asian American Studies dept.; Lillian Galledo, director, Filipinos for Affirmative Action, William Tamayo, immigration lawyer, Asian Law Caucus, Feb. 18–25, 1990.

88. Interview with Professor Anderson, anthropology dept., UC Berkeley, Mar. 15, 1990.

89. Dept. of Commerce 1991: table 5b. In contrast, in 1980, 45.8 percent lived in California and 16.9 percent in Hawaii. Gardner et al. 1985: 11.

90. Dept. of Commerce 1991: table 5b.

91. The 1990 census counted 731,685 Filipinos in California and 704,850 Chinese. There were 43,799 Filipinos in Washington (Chinese were second with 33,962), and 64,224 in Illinois (64,200 Asian Indians). Filipinos were the second

largest community in Hawaii (168,682) after the Japanese (247,486). Dept. of Commerce 1991: table 5A.

92. Dept. of Commerce 1991: table 3C.

93. Cariño 1987: 313–14; Mangiafico 1988: 42–44.

94. Dept. of Commerce 1988a: table 1.

95. *1985 INS Statistical Yearbook*, table IMM 5.3, p. 61.

96. Filipinos in New York and Illinois are concentrated in the New York City and Chicago metropolitan areas (Smith 1976: 335–41). Of the 35,630 in New York, in 1980, 31,902 (89.5 percent) resided in the New York City standard metropolitan statistical area. And of the 44,317 in Illinois, 41,511 (93.7 percent) resided in the Chicago metropolitan area. (Dept. of Commerce 1983a: table 4, p. 12 and 1983b: table 248.)

97. *1989 INS Statistical Yearbook*, table 18, p. 38.

98. Yu 1980: 81.

99. Data from Daly City Community Development Dept. supplied Feb. 4, 1988; D. Waugh, "Daly City: New Manila," *San Francisco Examiner*, Sept. 17, 1989, p. A-1.

100. See, e.g., D. Kelley and P. Pascual, "Filipinos Put Down Roots in Oxnard," *Los Angeles Times*, Mar. 10, 1991, p. B-1.

101. Filipino farm workers held the first modern agricultural strike in California, walking out of ranches on Sept. 8, 1965. A week later they were joined by Mexican farm workers in the grape strike that started the United Farm Workers (interview with Susan Bowyer, former UFW organizer, Mar. 18, 1991).

102. *1969 INS Annual Report*, table 8.

103. Based on *1975 and 1978 INS Annual Reports*, table 8.

104. Based on *1985 INS Statistical Yearbook*, table IMM 6.1, p. 63.

105. In 1969, 7,530 Filipino professionals or managers entered, 9,584 in 1970, 6,649 in 1983, and 8,127 in 1988 (*1969 and 1970 INS Annual Report, 1983 and 1988 INS Statistical Yearbook*).

106. Xenos et al. 1987: table 11.25.

107. "Emigration from Philippines Soars as Thousands Come to U.S.," *San Jose Mercury News*, June 24, 1985: "The Philippines graduates thousands of health workers every year, often more than the economy can absorb, and then routinely loses a large portion of these to the United States, Canada, and the Mideast."

108. In the San Francisco Bay Area in 1987, Filipinos owned more businesses (4,261) than Japanese (4,075) and Koreans (2,386), but not more than Chinese (13,784) (D. Waugh, "Asian American Businesses See Explosive Growth in State," *San Francisco Examiner*, Aug. 2, 1991, p. A-16).

109. Xenos et al. 1987: 31.

110. Gardner et al. 1985: 31, fig. 6 (corrected figures based on telephone conversation with authors).

111. Ibid.

112. Dept. of Commerce 1988a: table 29.

113. Gardner et al. 1985: 34.

114. While the proportion of families under the poverty line is only 4.6 percent for Filipino Americans who immigrated prior to 1970, a higher proportion (8.8 percent) of more recent (1975–80) immigrant families is below the line (Gardner et al. 1985: 34, table 14).

115. Based on Dept. of Commerce 1991: table 1.

116. Choy 1979: 196–98.

117. Ibid., 205–7.

118. *1971 INS Annual Report*, table 14. Over 25,000 Koreans immigrated from 1966 to 1970 (*1969 and 1971 INS Annual Reports*, table 14).

119. *1979 and 1987 INS Statistical Yearbook*, table 14.

120. *1989 INS Statistical Yearbook*, table 2; INS Statistical Branch, Detail Run 401—Total FY 1990.

121. INS Statistical Branch, Detail Run 401—Total FY 1990; *1973–1989 INS Annual Reports and INS Statistical Yearbooks*.

122. Dept. of Commerce 1983a: table B. In 1965 most Koreans in the United States were American-born. By 1970, 54 percent were foreign-born (Kim 1974: 24, 36).

123. Dept. of Commerce 1988a: table 1.

124. *1989 INS Statistical Yearbook*, table 12, p. 26. The difference between the numbers of Korean men and women is decreasing, however. The difference in 1985 (20,942 females, 14,818 males), for example, was greater than in 1989 (*1985 INS Statistical Yearbook*, table IMM 4.3).

125. In 1985 there were 20,243,765 men in Korea, compared to 20,204,721 women (*The Europa World Year Book 1989*: vol. 2).

126. Although there was a period when large numbers of female Korean orphans were adopted by U.S. citizens, and when Korean war brides married U.S. servicemen (Kim 1976: 40; Kim 1974: 36), those explanations do not account for the current gender ratio of Korean immigrants.

127. Kim 1981: 60–61.

128. Ibid., 148.

129. Conversations with two Korean American women, Sallie Kim and Joanne Chung, Mar. 1–2, 1991; interview with Jayne Lee, Feb. 4, 1992; see also Terry, "Korean Women Fight 2nd-Class Status," *San Francisco Examiner*, June 18, 1990, p. A-15.

130. Mangiafico 1988: 91; Chan 1991a: 140.

131. Dept. of Commerce 1991: table 5b.

132. Dept. of Commerce 1991: table 3C.

133. Gardner et al. 1985: 11.

134. Dept. of Commerce 1991: table 5b.

135. Bunge 1982: 41; Kim 1981: 38, 71.

136. From *1989 INS Statistical Yearbook*, table 18, p. 37.

137. Based on Dept. of Commerce 1983a: table 4, p. 12, and Dept. of Commerce 1983b: table 248.

138. Dept. of Commerce 1988a: table 1. The 100,000 Koreans who reside in the Los Angeles metropolitan area constitute the largest single Korean community in the United States (Kim 1981: 42).

139. From *1985 INS Statistical Yearbook*, p. 60, table IMM 5.3.

140. Conversations with Tom Kim, executive director, Korean Service Center, and Sallie Kim, Mar. 1–2, 1990.

141. Dept. of Commerce 1983b: table 248.

142. Kim 1981: 184, 281.

143. The Korean enclave in downtown Los Angeles is more economic than residential (Bonacich et al. 1988: 167; Portes and Bach 1985: 59). Korean-operated grocery stores, churches, gas stations, barber shops, restaurants, and travel agencies can be found there (Takaki 1989: 436–37). Many of these businesses were looted and destroyed in the uprising following the April 29, 1992, verdict in the trial of police officers who beat African American motorist Rodney King.

144. H. C. Sunoo, "Reinvent Koreatown from the Center to the Sidewalks," *Los Angeles Times*, May 15, 1992, p. T5; Kim 1981: 37–38, 71.

145. Kim 1978: 178; Adams, "Ethnic Battle over Purchase of S.F. Building," *San Francisco Examiner*, Feb. 1, 1988, p. B-1.

146. Kim 1981: 42–44. With some exceptions, occupational preference categories require a labor certification issued by the Dept. of Labor (see Hing 1985: chap. 5).

147. Kim 1981: 57.

148. Kim 1981: 42–44, 148.

149. See generally Hing 1985: chaps. 4 and 5. The immediate relative category for citizens is unlimited [*U.S. Code* 8: §1151(b) (1990 ed.)]. In 1990 amendments more visas were added for occupational and professional immigrants.

150. Kim 1981: 32–33, 35. A large number of adopted Korean children also became citizens (Kim 1974: 35).

151. Those holding only lawful permanent resident alien status cannot petition for those relatives [*U.S. Code* 8: §§1151(b), 1153(a) (1982 ed.)].

152. Kim 1981: 32–33.

153. See, e.g., Kim 1981: 32–33.

154. *U.S. Code* 8: §1182(a)(32) (1990 ed.), added by Act of Oct. 12, 1986, Public Law 94-484, *Statutes at Large* 90: 2301, and amended by sec. 302(q)(j), Act of Aug. 1, 1977, Public Law 95-83, *Statutes at Large* 91: 383; Kim 1981: 153–55. However, until Dec. 31, 1986, graduates of foreign medical schools who were going to be employed in areas Health and Human Services had designated as "manpower shortage" areas were actually given preferential treatment [*Code of*

*Federal Regulations* 8: §656.22(c) 1986], so long as they had passed the National Board of Medical Examiners examination [*U.S. Code* 8: §1182(a)(32) (1982 ed.)]. Although this preferential treatment was deleted, general labor certification under occupational preferences is still available (see Hing 1985: §5.17, chap. 5). Under certain conditions foreign medical students may enter for graduate medical education or for training in residency or fellowship programs [*U.S. Code* 8: §§1101(a)(15)(J), 1182(j) (1990 ed.); *Code of Federal Regulations* 22: §514.1 (1990)]. South Korea–trained doctors have also had a difficult time passing a visa-qualifying examination implemented in 1977 (Kim 1981: 172–73).

155. Chan 1991a: 147–49.

156. Based on *1969 and 1972 INS Annual Report*, table 8; *1985 INS Statistical Yearbook*, table 6.1, p. 62; *1989 INS Statistical Yearbook*, table 20, p. 40.

157. Dept. of Commerce 1988a: table 45. Gardner et al. 1985: 31, fig. 6 (corrected data based on telephone conversation with authors).

158. Dept. of Commerce 1988a: tables 21, 45. This significantly exceeds that of the Chinese American population (37.3 percent).

159. Dept. of Commerce 1988a: table 45.

160. Manning and O'Hare 1988: 35.

161. D. Waugh, "Asian American Businesses See Explosive Growth in State," *San Francisco Examiner*, Aug. 2, 1991, p. A-16.

162. Pei 1987: 2.

163. Cariño 1987: 419; see also Gardner et al. 1985: 10.

164. Kim 1981: 38.

165. Manning and O'Hare 1988: 36–37.

166. See generally Min 1984: 333–52; Kim 1981: 102.

167. Wasserman 1979: 138–50.

168. See generally Min 1984: 333–52.

169. Dept. of Commerce 1988b: 9.

170. Gardner et al. 1985: 34, table 14, p. 34.

171. Dept. of Commerce 1988a: table 47.

172. Xenos et al. 1987: table 11.25.

173. Similar figures apply to Chinese, but not to Filipinos and Asian Indians (Gardner et al. 1985: 34).

174. Ibid., table 14.

175. Ibid.

176. Based on *1970 INS Annual Report*, table 13 and *1976 INS Annual Report*, table 14, p. 89; *1989 INS Statistical Yearbook*, table 2; INS Statistical Branch, Detail Run 401—Total FY 1990.

177. Based on Dept. of Commerce 1988a: table 1.

178. Based on *1983 INS Statistical Yearbook*, table IMM 1.2, and *1988 INS Statistical Yearbook*, table 2.

179. *World Development Report*, 1984, annex table 25 (New York: Oxford University Press).

180. *India to 1990, How Far Will Reform Go?*, Economist Intelligence Unit Special Report no. 1954, prospect series, p. 24.

181. Dandekar 1968: 121.

182. Tewari 1977: 132–37.

183. Dept. of Commerce 1988a: table 1.

184. Gardner et al. 1985: 15.

185. Ibid., 14–15.

186. Dept. of Commerce 1988a: table 36.

187. Ibid.

188. Gardner et al. 1985: 15, fig. 3.

189. Dept. of Commerce 1988a: table 1.

190. For example, in 1969 and 1970, 6,457 women entered from India and 16,077 men (based on *1969 and 1970 INS Annual Reports*, table 9).

191. In 1983–85, 38,405 men from India immigrated and 36,909 women (based on *1983, 1984 and 1985 INS Statistical Yearbooks*, table IMM 4.3).

192. *1989 INS Statistical Yearbook*, table 12, p. 26.

193. Dept. of Commerce 1991: tables 3C and 5B. The 23.1 percent for the West is, however, an increase over the 19.2 percent in 1980 (Gardner et al. 1985: 11; Dutta 1982: 78).

194. Dutta 1982: 78.

195. Dept. of Commerce 1991: table 5B.

196. In 1990, 79,440 resided in New Jersey. In Illinois, 64,200 Asian Indians were counted and 64,224 Filipinos (Dept. of Commerce 1991: table 5A).

197. Dept. of Commerce 1988a: table 1.

198. From *1989 INS Statistical Yearbook*, table 18, p. 37.

199. Asian Indians started settling in Jersey City in increasingly large numbers about twenty years ago because of its proximity to New York City and its then-modest housing costs (Marriot, J. "In Jersey City, Indians Face Rise in Violence and Hatred," *New York Times*, Oct. 12, 1987, p. 14).

200. Residential enclaves can be found in New York's Jackson Heights (Queens) and Artesia, California (where a section of this Los Angeles suburb is known as Little India) (Kitano and Daniels 1988: 107; *India West*, July 1, 1988, p. 46 and July 22, p. 39). Economic enclaves of Indian immigrants (as with Koreans and Vietnamese) have also been established in Chicago, Washington, D.C., and Cincinnati (Kitano and Daniels 1988: 102.)

201. Based on *1969 INS Annual Report*, table 8, p. 49.

202. Based on *1978 and 1979 INS Annual Reports*, table 8.

203. Based on *1984 and 1985 INS Statistical Yearbooks*, table IMM 6.1.

204. From *1969 and 1977 INS Annual Reports*, table 8; *1983 INS Statistical Yearbook*, table IMM 6.1; *1989 INS Statistical Yearbook*, table 20, p. 40.

205. Based on Dept. of Commerce 1988a: table 39.

206. In Dec. 1986, the nation's first publicly held bank with shareholders exclusively of Asian Indian origin, First Indo, opened. The initial capitalization

of the bank was $7.5 million, which was above the average ($3 million) for most newly organized California banks. Although the trend is changing, most minority-owned banks, except for Chinese American institutions, historically have had poor performance records in California despite the state's ethnic diversity (P. Ragsdale, "Bank Hopes to Capitalize on Its Origin," *San Francisco Examiner*, Jan. 30, 1987, C-1).

207. Based on *1989 INS Statistical Yearbook*, table 20, p. 40. The "no occupation" category included spouses and children.

208. Based on *1970 INS Annual Report*, table 8, p. 49. Many from the poorer working class in India continue to migrate to Great Britain instead of the United States where a majority may obtain unskilled jobs (Kitano and Daniels 1988: 101–2).

209. Among Asian Americans, this rate was second only to Koreans, and ranked above Japanese (68.5 per 1,000) and Chinese (65.1 per 1,000). Comparable figures for the general population were 64 per 1,000 (Manning and O'Hare 1988: 35–36).

210. "Surge in Indian Immigration," *Asian Week*, May 22, 1987, p. 5. Forty percent of the motels on Interstate 75 (between Detroit and Atlanta) are operated by Indians (Kitano and Daniels 1988: 101).

211. *India West*, Apr. 1, 1988, p. 47.

212. In fact, many reported cases involving legal interpretations of the investor category involve Asian Indians. See, e.g., Patel v. INS, 638 F.2d 1199 (9th Cir. 1980) (motel); Mawji v. INS, 671 F.2d 342 (9th Cir. 1982) (fast-food restaurant, then grocery store); Matter of Kumar, 11 I.&N. Dec. 315 (BIA 1980) (clothing store, then motel).

213. Based on *1969 INS Annual Report*, table 7A, p. 48.

214. Based on *1972 INS Annual Report*, table 7A, p. 35.

215. See Hing 1985: §4.13.

216. A commerce treaty is required under the law [*U.S. Code* 8: §1101(a)(15)(E) (1992 ed.)].

217. Dept. of Commerce 1988b: 9; Dept. of Commerce 1988a: table 38.

218. Dept. of Commerce 1988a: table 38.

219. Gardner et al. 1985: 34, table 14.

220. Dept. of Commerce 1988a: table 38.

221. Ibid., table 41.

222. Gardner et al. 1985: 34.

223. Based on Dept. of Commerce 1991: table 1.

224. Based on *1970 INS Annual Report*, table 13; *1989 INS Statistical Yearbook*, table 2; 1990 data supplied by Blanche V. Shanks, Statistical Assistant, Immigration and Naturalization Service, Washington, D.C., June 13, 1991.

225. Dept. of Commerce 1975b (comparing growth rates of Japan, the United States, and West Germany, as measured by percent of GNP); see also Burks 1964: 43–49.

226. *1988 INS Statistical Yearbook,* table 2, p. 4.

227. See Burks 1964: 43–49.

228. Dept. of Commerce 1975b.

229. P. Wechsler, "The Signs of Decline; Middle-Class Standard of Living Harder to Achieve," *Newsday,* May 8, 1988, p. 5.

230. Forty percent in a Chicago survey expressed such reservations (Kim 1978: 124–25).

231. Japan's negative birth rate was the topic of "Primetime Live," ABC-TV, May 31, 1991.

232. "Bill Apologizing to War Interns Goes to Reagan," *New York Times,* Aug. 5, 1988, p. A7.

233. Conversations with Rose Matsui Ochi, former member of the Select Commission on Immigration and Refugee Policy, and Paul Igasaki, of the Washington, D.C., office of the Japanese American Citizens League, Feb. 3, 1990.

234. See Boyd 1971: 50; C. Kang, "War, Redevelopment Drove 'Niseis' Away," *San Francisco Examiner,* Sept. 14, 1987, p. B-4.

235. U.S. Commission on Civil Rights 1986: 11, 32; Kim 1988: 125; Kennedy 1964: 62–63. It is difficult to measure the deterrent effect of the internment policy on would-be immigrants in Japan. After the war Japanese were still within the Asian exclusion provisions, and after 1952 they had a quota of 180. But as noted above, from 1960 to 1964 Japan sent more immigrants than any other Asian nation.

236. *1982 INS Statistical Yearbook,* table IMM 1.3, p. 6; 1990 data supplied by Blanche V. Shanks, Statistical Assistant, Immigration and Naturalization Service, Washington, D.C., June 13, 1991.

237. Based on 1970 census data (271,000 men, 320,000 women) (Dept. of Commerce 1975: table 33, p. 30).

238. Based on tables in Dept. of Commerce 1988a. The ratio for the general population was 94.5:100.

239. *1985 INS Statistical Yearbook,* table IMM 4.3, p. 50.

240. Over 40 percent are 20–29 years of age, and another 30 percent are 30–39. Among all immigrants 50 percent are between the ages of 20 and 39; 30 percent are 20–29; and 18 percent 30–39 (from *1985 INS Statistical Yearbook,* table IMM 4.3).

241. Conversations with Rose Matsui Ochi, former member of the Select Commission on Immigration and Refugee Policy, and Sandy Ouye, director, Kimochi Japanese Senior Citizens Center, Feb. 3, 1990. These women are also able to move into the U.S. economy more easily as well because they are perceived as less threatening than men and are more flexible about taking work that is available (conversation with Professor Mari Matsuda, Feb. 8, 1990).

242. Dept. of Commerce, 1991: table 5B. Both figures are down from the 1980 proportions when 37.5 percent lived in California and 33.5 percent in Hawaii (Gardner et al. 1985: 11, table 4, p. 110).

243. The 1990 census counted 247,486 Japanese and 168,682 Filipinos (Dept. of Commerce 1991: table 5A).

244. Dept. of Commerce 1991: table 5B; Gardner et al. 1985: 11.

245. Gardner et al. 1985: 12.

246. Dept. of Commerce 1983b: table 248.

247. Of the 24,754 Japanese Americans in New York in 1980, 23,241 (93.9 percent) lived in the New York City area; of the 18,432 in Illinois, 16,042 (87 percent) resided in or near Chicago (based on Dept. of Commerce 1983a: table 4, p. 12; and Dept. of Commerce 1983b: table 248).

248. Based on unpublished data supplied by Robert W. Gardner, Population Institute, East-West Center, Honolulu, Hawaii.

249. See, e.g., Kim 1978: 116; D. Chuman 1976: 38.

250. C. Kang, "Japantown: A Community Losing Its Identity," *San Francisco Examiner*, Sept. 14, 1987, p. B-1. Redevelopment and Japan-based corporations also played a role in the "slow and painful death" of Little Tokyo in Los Angeles (D. Chuman 1976: 37–38; Little Tokyo Anti-Eviction Task Force 1976: 327–37).

251. C. Kang, "Japantown," *San Francisco Examiner*, Sept. 14, 1987, p. B-1.

252. Based on Dept. of Commerce 1988a: table 33; Xenos et al. 1987: table 11.25.

253. Gardner et al. 1985: 31.

254. Based on Gardner et al. 1985: fig. 6, p. 31, and on unpublished tabulations provided by Robert Gardner.

255. Gardner et al. 1985: fig. 6, p. 31 (corrected figures provided by Gardner in telephone conversation).

256. In 1980, 68.5 Japanese-owned businesses were counted for every 1,000 Japanese Americans (compared to 64 per 1,000 in the general population), and the rate was even higher in metropolitan areas that experienced economic expansion in the early 1980's. Japanese Americans are also involved in more medium and large corporations than are Chinese and Koreans (Manning and O'Hare 1988: 35–36).

257. Based on Dept. of Commerce 1988a: table 35.

258. Based on Dept. of Commerce 1988a: table 35; Gardner et al. 1985: 34, table 14.

259. Based on Dept. of Commerce 1988a: table 35.

260. Ibid. In all Asian groups foreign-born men earn more than foreign-born women; for Japanese, foreign-born men make double the earnings of foreign-born women ($20,670 to $10,150). As with most Asian groups, foreign-born Japanese women earn less than their American-born counterparts ($10,150 to $12,510). On the other hand, only foreign-born Japanese and Indian men earn more than their American-born counterparts. Foreign-born Japanese men earn $20,668 compared to $20,160 for American-born.

261. Gardner et al. 1985: 34, table 34; Xenos et al. 1987: table 11.13, pp. 276–77.

262. The United Kingdom was second with a total of 2,361,698 nonimmigrants (1,869,238 tourists) (*1989 INS Statistical Yearbook*, table 44, p. 74).

263. L-1 visa holders are aliens being transferred to a U.S. corporate subsidiary or affiliate. They must have worked for the company one year before entry in a managerial or executive position or in one requiring specialized knowledge. Treaty traders and investors (E-1 or E-2 visa holders) are those entering to carry on substantial trade with another country or to develop and direct an enterprise in which they have made a substantial investment. H-1 visa holders are members of the professions, entertainers, artists, and sports figures. And the business visitor category (B-1) is for those entering to do business for employers abroad or for themselves if they are representing their company. Business visa holders generally visit for shorter periods. Reforms in 1990 added two categories (O and P) for athletes and entertainers. *U.S. Code* 8: §1101(a)(15)(B), (H), (E), (L), (O), (P); see generally Hing 1985: §§3.25–3.42.

264. Most nonimmigrant students enter with F-1 visas, although in 1981 the M category was added for vocational and nonacademic students [*U.S. Code* 8: §1101(a)(15)(F), (M)]. The F-1 category is generally used by students entering to attend a college or university.

265. D. Kleinman, "The New York Commuter May Be Japanese," *San Francisco Examiner, This World* section, July 12, 1987, p. 16. The Korean American dominance of the greengrocer business in New York City visibly contributes to the Asian presence in the area (Kim 1981: 85).

266. D. Kleinman, "The New York Commuter May Be Japanese," *San Francisco Examiner, This World* section, July 12, 1987, p. 16. New York has about 60,000 Japanese residents.

267. Ibid.

268. For a discussion of undocumented Korean workers employed in the Korean American community, see Kim 1987: 236.

269. Asian Pacific American Legal Center 1988: 9–11; Passel and Woodrow 1984: 642.

270. Asian Pacific American Legal Center 1988: 12–14. Fear and distrust of the INS and the government in general (because of experiences discussed in Chapter 2) were cited by Asians as a major reason those eligible among them did not apply for legalization.

271. The applicants included 4,439 Koreans, 3,101 Indians, and 1,026 Japanese. There were also many Pakistani (3,732), Thai (3,679), and Tongan (1,696) applicants (Asian Pacific American Legal Center 1988: 14).

272. *1970 INS Annual Report*, table 27B, p. 95.

273. *1982 INS Statistical Yearbook*, table ENF 1.2, p. 165.

274. Based on *1982 INS Statistical Yearbook*, table ENF 1.2, p. 165; *1988 INS Statistical Yearbook*, table 61, p. 110.

275. Passel and Woodrow 1984: 642.

276. Based on *1982 INS Statistical Yearbook*, table ENF 2.1, p. 165.

277. Based on *1970 INS Annual Report*, table 27B, p. 95.

278. I have learned that many Filipino nonimmigrants travel to the United

States to get a divorce because in the Philippines the Catholic philosophy dictates strict marriage and divorce laws. In the 1970's, I represented many Filipinos in deportation proceedings who had traveled to the United States, obtained a divorce, married a citizen, obtained lawful resident status, divorced again, then attempted to remarry the first spouse to help him or her immigrate. This pattern did not necessarily involve sham marriages, but immigration officials filed deportation charges because of the appearance of sham.

279. Mangiafico 1988: 46–47.

280. Ibid.

281. See generally Hing 1979: 292–308; Hing 1983: 22–24; see also National Lawyers Guild 1980: §§4.10, 4.16.

282. See U.S. Commission on Civil Rights 1979: 205 (testimony of the Honorable Leonel Castillo, commissioner, U.S. Immigration and Naturalization Service).

283. *Matter of Blas*, 15 I.&N. Dec. 626, 633 (BIA 1976).

284. "Green Card Asians on SSI Face Exclusion," *East/West*, Feb. 21, 1979, p. 3; National Lawyers Guild 1980: §5.2. I first discovered these cases when I was a legal services attorney working in San Francisco Chinatown. I represented more than a dozen and was in contact with legal services attorneys in other parts of the United States who were handling others.

285. "Green Card Asians on SSI Face Exclusion," p. 3; D. Schwenke, "Immigration Lowers the Boom on 81-year-old Isle Widow," *Honolulu Advertiser*, June 7, 1979, p. A-3.

286. *U.S. Code* 42: §1381 (1992 ed.); *Code of Federal Regulations* 20: §416.202 (1990).

287. D. Schwenke, "Immigration Lowers the Boom," *Honolulu Advertiser*, June 7, 979, p. A-3.

288. *U.S. Code* 8: §1182(a)(4) (1992 ed.).

289. "INS Guidelines for SSI Takers," *Philippine News*, June 16–22, 1979, p. 1.

290. See R. Glauberman, "Alien Residents' Legal Rights Upheld," *Honolulu Star-Bulletin*, Dec. 6, 1979, A-7.

291. See Gordon and Mailman 1991: §§2.3e, 2.4a, 2.19.

292. See Hing 1979: 293–94; Hing 1983: 26–28.

293. "Moratorium Sought on Honolulu SSI Cases," *Ang Katipunan*, Aug. 15–31, 1979, p. 9.

294. "Moratorium Sought," p. 9; D. Schwenke, "Immigration Lowers the Boom," p. A-3; R. Glauberman, "Alien Residents," p. A-7. In fact, representatives of the Social Security Administration eventually helped to convince INS that its actions were unfair.

295. The deportation provision provides that "[a]n alienn... shall... be deported who... has within five years of entry become a public charge from causes not affirmatively shown to have arisen after entry" [*U.S. Code* 8: 1251(a)(5) (1992 ed.)]. In order to be deported under this section, a demand for repayment

and a failure to repay must occur before deportability can be established [*Matter of B*, 3 I.&N. Dec. 323, 324 (BIA 1948)]. However, SSI rules contain no provisions for such repayment demands.

296. Social Security Act, *U.S. Code* 42: §1611(f) (1992 ed.).

297. See "INS Guidelines for SSI Takers," *Philippine News*, June 16–22, 1979, p. 1; National Lawyers Guild 1980: 5.

298. "Matter of Atanacio," *Interpreter Releases*, 56: 43 (1979).

299. See A. Bone, "Disagreement Over Whether Ruling Can Help Aliens' Reentry Problems," *Star-Bulletin Advertiser*, Dec. 9, 1979, p. H-6.

300. "Matsui Investigating Harassment Charges," *Koreatown Weekly*, Feb. 11, 1980, p. 3; Hing 1979: 293–94.

301. See A. Bone, "Disagreement," p. H-6.; D. Schwenke, "Immigration Lowers the Boom," p. A-3; R. Glauberman, "Alien Residents," p. A-7.

302. *Visa Bulletin*, vol. VI, no. 39, Dept. of State, Bureau of Consular Affairs, Oct. 1990. Mexico second preference was worse; it was backlogged over 11 years.

303. Until 1976 the sibling category permitted a citizen, regardless of age, to petition for a sibling. After 1976, the law required the petitioning citizen to be at least 21 years old (Act of Oct. 20, 1976, Public Law 94-571, *Statutes at Large* 90: 2703, §2.27f).

304. The sibling category for Mexicans is backlogged about 12 years.

305. *Visa Bulletin*, vol. V, no. 93, Dept. of State, Bureau of Consular Affairs, Oct. 1986; vol. VI, no. 27, Oct. 1989; vol. VI, no. 45, Apr. 1991.

306. National Lawyers Guild 1980: §§4.10, 4.11, 4.16–4.18.

307. Ibid., §§4.19–4.20.

308. Matter of Cheung, 17 I.&N. Dec. 365, 366 (1980).

309. See generally Hing 1979: 299–300; conversation with Jackson Wong, Dec. 18, 1990.

310. Dept. of Commerce 1991: table 1.

311. Bennett 1992: 10–11. Early calculations for the 1990 census showed that Asian American households in California had a lower income ($47,974) than that of white households ($49,103). S. Johnson, "Minorities' Income Higher in South Bay," *San Jose Mercury News*, May 13, 1992, p. 1A.

312. The 1990 census will likely reveal this same pattern found in 1980. Initial reports on the 1990 data show that in California per capita Asian American income ($13,733) is lower than that of whites ($19,028) (S. Johnson, "Minorities' Income Higher in South Bay," *San Jose Mercury News*, May 13, 1992, p. 1A). Nationwide per capita Asian American income ($13,420) is also lower than for whites ($15,560) (Bennett 1992:11).

313. D. Waugh, "Asian American Businesses See Explosive Growth in State," *San Francisco Examiner*, Aug. 2, 1991, p. A-16.

314. Although 10,000 visas have been set aside for the new investor (employment creation) category, in its first year of operation (1992) fewer than 200 applications will be filed, in part because of rigorous application requirements.

But once these requirements become more familiar and refined, I suspect that Asians will take advantage of this opportunity.

## CHAPTER FOUR

1. U.S. Department of Commerce 1991: table 1.

2. Joint Commission on the Judiciary, 97th Cong., 1st sess., *U.S. Immigration Policy and the Nat'l Interest* 1981: 88; Flexner 1974: 80.

3. Lyman 1977: 85–87.

4. Kim 1971: 3.

5. Kim 1971: 4, 23.

6. Hess 1976: 417.

7. Public Law 80-774, *United States Statutes at Large* 62: 1009, amended by Act of June 16, 1950, Public Law 81-555, chap. 262, *Statutes at Large* 64: 219; Select Commission on Immigration and Refugee Policy 1981: 154.

8. Public Law 82-203, *Statutes at Large* 76: 400 (1953), amended by the Act of Aug. 31, 1954, Public Law 83-751, *Statutes at Large* 68: 1044; Nee and Nee 1973: 410.

9. Public Law 80-774, *Statutes at Large* 62: 1009, amended by the Act of June 16, 1950, Public Law 81-555, chap. 262, *Statutes at Large* 64: 219. The roots of current refugee laws can be traced to the 1946 Constitution of the International Refugee Organization. *Statutes at Large* 62: 3037; see also Immigration and Naturalization Service v. Stevic, 467 U.S. 407, 415 (1984); Rosenberg v. Yee Chien Woo, 402 U.S. 49, 52 (1971). The IRO defined refugees as persons who expressed "valid objections" to returning to their country of nationality, including "persecution, or fear, based on reasonable grounds of persecution because of race, religion, nationality or political opinion" [International Refugee Organization Constitution, §C, subsection 1(a)(i)].

10. Select Commission on Immigration and Refugee Policy 1981: 155 (citing congressional policy statement on passage of Refugee Act of 1980).

11. Ibid., 154; Kitano and Daniels 1988: 13–14.

12. Blum 1976: 175–76.

13. Fuchs 1983: 434.

14. Laufman 1986: 508; Helton 1983–84: 243.

15. *Statutes at Large* 66: 163; *United States Code* 8: §1182(d)(5) (1956).

16. Anker and Posner 1981:15.

17. See the Fair Share Law of 1960, Public Law 86-648, *Statutes at Large* 74: 504 (1960).

18. Schwartz 1968: 139–40; Chinn et al. 1969: 29.

19. By the mid-1960's more than 3,000 Cubans were admitted each month (*1966 INS Annual Report*, p. 6). By 1976, 145,000 Cubans were paroled into the United States [Silva v. Bell, 605 F.2d 978 (7th Cir. 1979)].

20. Gordon 1987: 156.

21. Laufman 1986: 504.

22. Until the Act of Oct. 20, 1976, Public Law 94-571, *Statutes at Large* 90: 2703, the preference system established under the 1965 amendments was not applicable to the countries of the Western Hemisphere.

23. *1972–1978 INS Annual Reports*, table 7A; *1977 INS Annual Report*, table 6E.

24. *United States Treaties* 19: 6223.

25. *United Nations Treaty Series* 189: 150 (July 28, 1951); see Immigration and Naturalization Service v. Cardoza-Fonseca, 480 U.S. 241 (1987).

26. H.R. Rept. 608, 96th Cong., 1st sess., 2 (1979).

27. Strand and Jones 1985: 32.

28. Ibid.

29. Gardner et al. 1985: 9.

30. In early 1979 the United States had committed itself to accept seven thousand refugees monthly, but the figure was doubled by summer in response to the desperate conditions in the refugee camps (Gordon 1987: 155).

31. Gordon 1987: 155; Meinhardt et al. 1984: 5.

32. Gordon 1987: 155.

33. Anker and Posner 1981: 30–33; see also *Congressional Record* 125: S. 3037 (1979).

34. Some felt that the parole authority had been misused and were dissatisfied with the inconsistent treatment for refugees, which resulted in some being granted parole while others received "indefinite voluntary departure" [S. Rept. 256, 96th Cong., 1st sess., 9 (1979)]. Indefinite or extended voluntary departure is a type of group temporary safe haven that the attorney general continues to have administrative authority to grant to nationals of particular countries. See Hotel & Restaurant Employees Union Local 25 v. Attorney Gen., 804 F.2d 1256 (D.C. Cir. 1986); see also Yassini v. Crosland, 613 F.2d 219 (9th Cir. 1980). Extended voluntary departure has been granted to nationals of Nicaragua, Poland, Afghanistan, Ethiopia, and Uganda (Hing 1985: §6.36). The failure of the attorney general to grant extended voluntary departure to nationals of El Salvador and mainland China (after the Tiananmen Square massacre) became the subject of congressional debate. President Bush eventually ordered administrative protections for Chinese students. Temporary protection for Salvadorans was mandated by provisions in the Immigration Act of 1990, Public Law 101-649, *Statutes at Large* 104: 4978, §§302, 303, *U.S. Code* 8: §244A (1992).

35. Public Law 96-212, *Statutes at Large* 94: 107 (1980).

36. Select Commission on Immigration and Refugee Policy 1981: 157 (statement of Senator Edward Kennedy to the commission).

37. Statements of Senator Alan Simpson and Senator Strom Thurman during floor debates.

38. *U.S. Code* 8: §§1101(a)(42), 1157(a) (1982 ed.).

39. *U.S. Code* 8: §1182(d)(5)(B) (1982 ed.). The new refugee law also lessened the burden of proof placed on asylum applicants who seek refuge in the United States after gaining entry, usually as a nonimmigrant or without inspection. See Immigration and Naturalization Service v. Cardoza-Fonseca, 480 U.S. 421 (1987). However, the asylum provision has little impact on Southeast Asians who have a well-founded fear of persecution at entry. Only about 6,000 to 7,000 people are granted asylum per year (*1989 INS Statistical Yearbook*, table 32, p. 58).

40. Gallagher et al. 1985: 27–30.

41. D. Brough, "Political Asylum Study Provokes Criticism of U.S. Policy," *Reuters News Service*, Mar. 9, 1987; M. Benanti, "INS Removing Politics for Decisions on Asylum Requests," *Gannett News Service*, Apr. 2, 1991.

42. "Administration Proposes Admitting 144,000 Refugees This Fiscal Year," *Interpreter Releases* 68, no. 38 (Oct. 7, 1991), pp. 1290–92. Thus, in practice, the 1980 refugee law has been applied in an ideologically biased fashion, no different than under the pre-1980 framework (see also Laufman 1986: 495). In 1984, for example, Cubans were the only refugees from Latin America admitted in spite of the civil strife occurring in El Salvador and Guatemala.

43. Act of January 25, 1982; Public Law 97-359 (Act of Oct. 22, 1982); Amerasian Homecoming Act, Public Law 100-202 (Act of Dec. 21, 1987).

44. *U.S. Code* 8: §1154(g).

45. Ibid.

46. Interview with Pam Lewis, Congressional Liaison, Bureau for Refugee Programs, State Department, June 5, 1992. Most entered after the Amerasian Homecoming Act took effect in March 1988.

47. S. Mydans, "Vietnamese Find No Home in Their Fathers' Land," *New York Times*, May 28, 1991, p. 1A.

48. Forbes 1984: 2–7.

49. Strand and Jones 1985: 46; Marsh 1980: 12–13. Of the 130,000 refugees who entered in 1975, it was estimated that 45,000 would enter the job market. This was not an unmanageable number to absorb, since the national work force was about 95 million at the time (Gordon 1987: 163).

50. Dept. of Health, Education and Welfare 1977: 13. HEW was later divided into the Department of Education and the Department of Health and Human Services. The IATF was created as a temporary agency to handle the refugee resettlement program until a coordinated program for the long term could be established (U.S. Senate Committee on the Judiciary 1974: 114).

51. Interview with Vu Duc Vuong, director of Center for Southeast Asian Refugee Resettlement, Apr. 18, 1986.

52. Liu et al. 1979: 162.

53. Ibid., p. 163.

54. Forbes 1984: 7.

55. Although early Chinese moved to Chinatowns for sanctuary and camaraderie after exclusion efforts and violence reached fever pitch, many exclusionists were probably happy to have them all in one place where they could be watched and perhaps managed more easily (see, e.g., Wunder 1989: 141). (Discussed more fully in Chap. 2.)

56. Gordon 1987: 163; Baker and North 1984: 55–58.

57. "The Vietnamese concentration in New Orleans, if it sustains itself, is in essence a return to Vietnamese Catholic village structures" (Kelly 1977: 202).

58. Strand and Jones 1985: 40.

59. Dept. of State 1975: 2.

60. Sponsors agreed to provide shelter and cooking utensils (International Rescue Committee, sponsor information sheet, July 1978).

61. Cohen and Grossnickle 1983: 72; Montero 1979: 28.

62. Montero 1979: 28; Marsh 1980: 12–13.

63. Nhu 1976: 60.

64. Strand and Jones 1985: 32. The government had initially feared employment problems if large numbers of refugees concentrated in certain areas and competed for jobs in a limited market, especially since unemployment and inflation were high at the time (Dept. of State 1975: 2).

65. Gordon 1987: 165; Baker and North 1984: 59.

66. In a survey conducted in San Diego, the most frequently cited reasons for secondary migration were family reunification, employment considerations, climate, and difficulty with sponsors and the community (Strand and Jones 1985: 81; Forbes 1984: 16).

67. Gordon 1987: 163–64.

68. The ethnic Chinese in Vietnam retained their own set of institutions, refusing to be assimilated, even though their immigration extended back over 2,000 years. This caused tensions, as they became wealthy as middlemen and moneylenders. Much of the repressive measures taken against ethnic Chinese in the region was an effort to break their economic control over trade and retail businesses (Strand and Jones 1985: 28–29). An attempt by the Vietnamese government to forcibly integrate the Chinese failed. Persecution followed. By July 1978, 160,000 ethnic Chinese fled to China. Eighty-five percent of the 1978 boat people were ethnic Chinese. By 1980, 400,000 had fled by boat. Half of them died. The Chinese population in Vietnam is virtually nonexistent at this point (Strand and Jones 1985: 30–31).

69. Liu et al. 1979: 61; St. Cartmail 1983: 270.

70. Coro Foundation Public Affairs Leadership Training Program 1985: 15–16.

71. "Trouble for America's Model Minority," *U.S. News & World Report,* Feb. 23, 1987, pp. 18–19 (citing Professor Peter Rose of Smith College).

72. Also created was the Office of Refugee Resettlement within the Department of Health and Human Services. In 1981 the refugee resettlement

program was moved to state agencies. Federal government reimbursed the states 100 percent, but with a time limitation to prevent a "welfare mentality" among the refugees and to provide attempts to make refugees self-sufficient.

73. Forbes 1984: 21–24.

74. Ibid.; Gordon 1987: 169.

75. Desbarats and Holland 1983: 23–24; Dept. of Health and Human Services 1982: 22.

76. Select Commission on Immigration and Refugee Policy 1981: 185.

77. Gordon 1987: 164.

78. Dept. of Health and Human Services 1982: 22. The sites were eventually located in ten states: Arizona, Florida, Georgia, Illinois, Massachusetts, New York, North Carolina, Ohio, Texas, and Virginia (Gordon 1987: 164).

79. Ibid., pp. 165–66.

80. Sherman 1986; Forbes 1984: 30; see also F. Moritz, " 'California Dream' Beckons Asian Refugees to Resettle," *Christian Science Monitor*, July 28, 1983.

81. D. Waugh, "Luring Asians off State Welfare Rolls," *San Francisco Examiner*, Dec. 21, 1986, p. B-1.

82. Ibid.

83. Gordon 1987: 165–66.

84. Ibid., pp. 163–65. Nearly 33 percent reside in nine additional states, with 7.2 percent in Texas and 4.6 percent in Washington state. Yet the refugees from Southeast Asia remain more dispersed than other immigrant populations.

85. Dept. of Health and Human Services 1987: 91–92. Urban centers in the East and Midwest, such as Boston, Providence, and St. Paul, have become magnets for second-wave refugees from Laos and Cambodia.

86. Southeast Asian refugees presently live in most states. Of those entering in 1978, California, Texas, and Oregon were favorite secondary migration destinations (see table V-1, p. 187, of Select Commission). But as of 1987 New York became home to nearly 30,000 refugees; Illinois, Pennsylvania, Massachusetts, and Minnesota to over 26,000; Virginia and Oregon to approximately 20,000 apiece (Dept. of State 1987: 96).

87. The Japanese proportions are as follows: South, 7.9 percent; Northeast, 8.8 percent; and Midwest, 7.5 percent. For Filipinos, the figures were: South, 11.3 percent; Northeast, 10.2 percent; and Midwest, 8.1 percent (Dept. of Commerce 1991: table 3C).

88. Ibid., table 5B.

89. Kelly 1977: 155.

90. Ibid., p. 153. Of course the presence in California of most Vietnamese helped to make it an attractive place to settle as well.

91. Ibid., p. 155.

92. Strand and Jones 1985: 62.

93. Kelly 1977: 153.

94. Based on Dept. of Commerce 1988a: table 1, p. 1.

95. Approximately 48,000 Vietnamese resided in the Los Angeles–Long Beach–Anaheim area, and more than 22,000 in the San Francisco–Oakland– San Jose region (Dept. of Commerce 1983b: table 248).

96. Strand and Jones 1985: 50–51. The city of Santa Ana in Orange County has the highest ratio of refugees in the country.

97. Kelly 1977: 108; see Gordon 1987: 165; Baker and North 1984: 59; Montero 1979: 61.

98. D. Waugh, "Tenderloin's Changes: Seamy to Substantial," *San Francisco Examiner*, Oct. 29, 1988, p. A1; "New Terror for Asians: The Quake," *New York Times*, Oct. 31, 1989, p. A8. Two-thirds of a nonprofit housing development building in the area is occupied by Vietnamese, and the rest by other Southeast Asian refugees.

99. J. Woo, "Toy Town: Bustling Wholesale District Springs up Amid Squalor of Skid Row," *Los Angeles Times*, Oct. 15, 1991, p. B1; D. Waugh, "Tenderloin's Changes," *San Francisco Examiner*, Aug. 29, 1988; B. Ayres, "Prosperity Threatens Refugees of Vietnam," *New York Times*, national ed., Sept. 26, 1989, p. A10; see also Strand and Jones 1985: 131. The most visible Little Saigon may be in the Westminister section of Santa Ana, Orange County. Along the Bolsa strip, a bustling quarter of Vietnamese-owned retail shops and restaurants can be found. The Vietnamese community generates more than $300 million in sales per year in this area ("Little Saigon in Orange County," *San Francisco Chronicle*, Oct. 14, 1984, p. B-1; "Refugees: 50,000 a Year Find Both Heaven and Pain in the U.S.," *Los Angeles Times*, May 5, 1985, p. A-1).

100. Dept. of Commerce 1991: table 1.

101. Gordon 1987: 154–56.

102. Dept. of State 1987: 92.

103. *1988 INS Statistical Yearbook*, table 26, p. 50.

104. Interview with Pam Lewis, Congressional Liaison, Bureau for Refugee Programs, State Department, June 5, 1992.

105. Estimate based on Gardner et al. 1985: 5.

106. See Appendix B for an explanation of the family preference categories.

107. With some exceptions, most Vietnamese refugees must obtain lawful permanent resident status and live in the United States for five years to apply for naturalization (Hing 1985: chap. 10).

108. The rate for all 1975 immigrants was 29 percent (Davidson 1985: tables 1, 3, and 4). In 1980 an estimated 60,000 Vietnamese petitioned for citizenship (Marsh 1980: 11). Chinese, Korean, Filipino, and Asian Indian immigrants consistently apply for naturalization at a rate higher than that of non-Asian immigrants (Barkan 1983: table 6, p. 48).

109. From 1980 to 1985 about 67,000 former Southeast Asian refugees became citizens; this represents about 16 percent of those eligible for naturalization at the time (Dept. of State 1987: 129).

110. Based on *1988 INS Statistical Yearbook*, table 7, p. 16.

111. Based on information from Gordon 1987: 154–55; *1985 INS Statistical Yearbook*, tables IMM 2.1, p. 16, and REF 2.2, p. 71; *1988 and 1989 INS Statistical Yearbooks*, table 7; INS Statistical Branch, Detail Run 401—Fiscal Year 1990.

112. Gordon 1987: 170. Some progress on that issue has been made through ongoing negotiations (see, e.g., "Vietnam Will Allow Ex-Political Inmates to Leave for the U.S.," *New York Times*, July 18, 1988, p. A-4).

113. Gordon 1987: 170.

114. I suspect that restrictionists like Senator Simpson are well aware of these backlogs when they call for an end to permissive refugee policy and promote admissions for Southeast Asians through family reunification categories only.

115. The median age of the general population was 30. The median ages for other Asian Americans in 1980 were: Japanese 33.5, Asian Indians 30.1, Chinese 29.6, Filipinos 28.5, and Koreans 26 (Gardner et al. 1985: 13).

116. Gardner et al. 1985: 12.

117. Dept. of State 1984: 10–11; Dept. of State 1986: 10–11.

118. From Dept. of Commerce 1988: table 48. But the Vietnamese American population is aging. For example, although incoming refugees are still young (20), in 1980, the median age for all foreign-born Vietnamese (while still much lower than that of the general population) was a higher 23.1. And in 1986 the median age for all Southeast Asian Americans was 25 (Dept. of State 1986).

119. Based on Dept. of Commerce 1988a: table 48.

120. Liu et al. 1979: 43–46.

121. Dept. of Health and Human Services 1985: 10; Dept. of State 1987: 10.

122. Coro Foundation Public Affairs Leadership Program 1985: 15.

123. Strand and Jones 1985: 84–85.

124. Ibid.

125. "A 'Vietnamboom' in S.F.," *San Francisco Chronicle*, July 5, 1984, p. A-1. Members of older Chinese communities have also helped some Vietnamese of Chinese ethnicity (D. Waugh, "Tenderloin's Changes," *San Francisco Examiner*, Aug. 29, 1988, p. A-1).

126. Nationally they grew from 4,989 to 25,671 businesses (D. Waugh, "Asian American Businesses See Explosive Growth in State," *San Francisco Examiner*, Aug. 2, 1991, p. A-16).

127. Based on Xenos et al. 1987: table 11.12, pp. 274–75.

128. Ibid.

129. The entire U.S. population grew only 9.8 percent in the same decade (Dept. of Commerce 1991: table 1).

130. Dept. of State 1987: 105–10.

131. Ibid., p. 112–13.

132. Gardner et al. 1985: 35. But a 1984 survey in California's Santa Clara County, for example, found that 46 percent of the Vietnamese received public assistance. Seventy-seven percent of the Cambodians were receiving public

assistance. Nonrefugee Chinese had a median annual income of $35,000, an unemployment rate of 16 percent, and less than 1 percent received public assistance (Meinhardt et al. 1984: 15).

133. "Trouble for America's 'Model' Minority," *U.S. News & World Report,* Feb. 23, 1987, p. 18.

134. Coro Foundation Public Affairs Leadership Program 1985: 17.

135. U.S. Senate Judiciary Committee 1985: 7.

136. Coro Foundation Public Affairs Leadership Program 1985: 25.

137. Strand and Jones 1985: 38–39. Initial responsibility for resettlement was given to the volags. Refugee officials provided contractual funding to the volags—initially $500 per refugee processed.

138. *Federal Register* 47: 10841; *Code of Federal Regulations* 45: §400.203 (1983). On Oct. 19, 1987, a proposed rule was published that would reduce the period to 12 months (*Federal Register* 52: 28795). The time limitation policy resulted from an interpretation of the high refugee dependence rate as an indication of a lack of incentive for self-sufficiency. But this perception was distorted because earlier arrivals—who participated in the labor force more frequently than the general population—were removed from the calculations (Gordon 1987: 143).

139. See generally Joint Committee on Refugee Resettlement 1985–86. A 1982 survey by the Office of Refugee Resettlement of Southeast Asian refugees found that on arrival two-thirds of adults could speak no English and 17 percent had only "some proficiency." To make up for this handicap 40 percent of all adults were found to be attending classes in English as a second language (ESL) and two-thirds of all adults had had "substantial ESL instruction" (Xenos et al. 1987: 279).

140. See, e.g., D. Waugh, "Luring Asians off State Welfare Rolls," *San Francisco Examiner,* Dec. 21, 1986, p. B-1.

141. This helps to explain why the Southeast Asian unemployment rate of 86 percent upon arrival was reduced to 30 percent after four years (Xenos et al. 1987: 280).

142. Some have had to adopt their own strategies for survival, including working in an underground economy (M. Arax, "Refugees For Survival: Lure of the Underground Economy," *Los Angeles Times,* Feb. 9, 1987; M. Arax, "Refugees Called Victims and Perpetrators of Fraud," *Los Angeles Times,* Feb. 10, 1987, p. 1).

143. This contrasts with 7 percent of white American families. Other Asian American families are below the poverty line as follows: Japanese 4.2 percent, Filipinos 6.2 percent, Asian Indians 7.4 percent, Chinese 10.5 percent, and Koreans 13.1 percent (Gardner et al. 1985: 34).

144. In 1982 the Office of Refugee Resettlement reports found that two-thirds of all households were below the poverty level after one year; after four years of residence, the figure declined to 30 percent. Xenos et al. 1987: 278–79.

145. Dept. of Commerce 1988a: table 50; Gardner et al. 1985: table 14, p. 34.

Preliminary data from the 1990 census show the per capita income for all Asian Americans ($13,420) is lower than that of white Americans ($15,260) (Bennett 1992: 11).

146. Dept. of Commerce 1988a: table 53.

147. Dept. of State 1984: 121–26.

148. Gordon 1987: 166–67.

## CHAPTER FIVE

1. See, e.g., D. Brand, "The New Whiz Kids," *Time*, Aug. 31, 1987, p. 42 (cover story); "60 Minutes: The Model Minority," CBS television broadcast, Feb. 1, 1987; A. Ramirez, "America's Super Minority," *Fortune*, Nov. 24, 1986, p. 148; Bell 1985: 30; W. R. Doerner, "Asians: To America with Skills," *Time*, July 8, 1985, p. 48.

2. See, e.g., Salholz, "Do Colleges Set Asian Quotas?" *Newsweek*, Feb. 9, 1987, p. 60; R. Lindsey, "Colleges Accused of Bias to Stem Asians Gains," *New York Times*, Jan. 19, 1987, p. 8; R. Oxnam, "Why Asians Succeed Here," *New York Times Magazine*, Nov. 30, 1986, p. 72; S. McBee, "Asian-Americans: Are They Making the Grade?" *U.S. News & World Report*, Apr. 2, 1984, p. 41. In addition to Chinese, Japanese, and Korean Americans, the popular media prominently features Vietnamese, Filipinos, and Asian Indians in its reports on "superstar" Asian Americans (see A. Ramirez, "America's Super Minority," p. 148; F. Butterfield, "Why They Excel," *Parade Magazine*, Jan. 21, 1990, p. 4). In contrast, when African American or Latino students do well, the individuals involved are identified as being quite rare (see, e.g., "At Decaying School Top College Finds Rare Well of Talent," *New York Times*, Apr. 6, 1992, p. A7).

3. Miller 1969: 191–200; Saxton 1971: 103. In other words, Chinese were believed to lack morality and could not assimilate, even though they were thrifty, obedient, and hardworking (Tsai 1986: 45–48). Japanese, Koreans, and Filipinos were subject to similar stereotypes and nativist sentiment (Penrose 1973: 1–23; Saxton 1971: 247–48, 251–52; DeWitt 1976: chap. 2).

4. Hutchinson 1981: 161.

5. Miller 1969: 191–200; Saxton 1971: 103.

6. The Chinese Exclusion Case, Chae Chan Ping v. United States, 130 U.S. 581 (1889); see Appendix C.

7. Chan 1991a: 121 (citing Isaacs 1972: xviii–xix).

8. Ramirez, "America's Super Minority," p. 149; Brand, "The New Whiz Kids," p.42.

9. Commission on Minority Participation in Education and American Life 1988: 14 (acknowledging only casually that "nevertheless, some segments of the

Asian American population experience problems similar to those of other minority groups").

10. Haycock and Navarro 1988: 14.

11. McLeod 1986: 51; "Asian Enrollment up at Stanford," *Asian Week*, May 13, 1988, p. 32; Doerner, "Asians: To America with Skills," p. 42.

12. Gardner et al. 1985: 24–27. According to 1990 census data, 38 percent completed college compared to 2.2 percent of whites (Bennett 1992: 11).

13. Asian Americans had the highest average SAT math score followed by whites, Latinos, and blacks ["1989 Profile of SAT and Achievement Test Takers," *The College Board, National Report*, table B (1989), p. iv].

14. "Asians 3 of 10 Top Westinghouse Science Winners," *Asian Week*, Mar. 4, 1988, p. 5; A. Ramirez, "America's Super Minority," p. 149; "Asians Win 4 of 10 Science Awards," *Asian Week*, Mar. 6, 1987, p. 1; D. Brand, "The New Whiz Kids," p. 42. The Asian American winners in the last few years have included Chinese, Asian Indians, Vietnamese, and Japanese Americans.

15. Bell 1985: 22; Moon 1986: 144; B. McLeod, "The Oriental Express," p. 50; Okimoto 1971: 150. A telephone survey revealed the following information. In the 1989–90 academic year, the University of California at San Francisco (UCSF) Medical School had 597 medical students; 119 were Asian Americans. In the pharmacy school at UCSF, 242 out of 502 students were Asian Americans. At the University of California at Berkeley College of Engineering during the spring of 1990, 1,058 Asian American students were enrolled in the undergraduate college of 2,167. In the graduate school 186 of 1,443 students were Asian American.

16. Rosen 1959: 48; R. Oxnam, "Why Asians Succeed Here," *New York Times Magazine*, Nov. 30, 1986, p. 70.

17. Sowell 1981: 135; Kitano 1969: 8, 97, 101; Sung 1967: 124–25.

18. M. W. Browne, "A Look at Success of Young Asians," *New York Times*, Mar. 25, 1986, p. A31.

19. Lee and Rong 1988: 550; S. Graubard, "Why do Asian Pupils Win Those Prizes?" *New York Times*, Jan. 29, 1988, p. A35; M. Kasindorf, "Asian-Americans: A 'Model Minority,' " *Newsweek*, Dec.6, 1982, p. 39.

20. See Divoky 1988: 219, 221; Sung 1979: 59.

21. See Tsuang 1989: 660–61; Nakanishi 1989: 39–47; W. Raspberry, "Asian Americans—Too Successful?" *Washington Post*, Feb. 10, 1990, p. A23; M. Harris, "How Asians Fare in UC Admissions," *San Francisco Examiner*, Oct. 8, 1987, p. A2; "Asian Freshmen down, Other Minorities Rise at Stanford," *Asian Week*, June 19, 1987, p. 1; A. Nakao, "Checking Possibility of Anti-Asian Bias in Colleges," *San Francisco Examiner*, June 1, 1987, p. B-1; A. Nakao, "Thorny Debate Over U.C.: Too Many Brainy Asians?" *The San Francisco Examiner*, May 3, 1987, p. A-1; S. Hickey, "Unequal Opportunity—Does UC Berkeley's Language Requirement Subtly Discriminate Against Asians?" *San Francisco*

*Focus*, Sept. 1987, p. 38; R. Springer, "Study Shows Asians Have Lowest Rate of Admissions to UC Graduate Programs," *East West News*, July 30, 1987, p. 1; see also K. Seligman, "Parents Irked at Lowell High Limit on Chinese," *San Francisco Examiner*, June 19, 1987, p. A-1.

22. Hune 1989: 62. In fund-raising, community agencies in Asian American communities "tend to be hampered by the 'model minority' fallacy, implying that [Asian Americans] have less of the problems faced by non-Asian minority groups" (Siao, "L.A. Study: $2.42 Billion in Foundation Grants, But Only 0.17% Goes To Asians," *Asian Week*, Apr. 6, 1990, p. 1).

23. J. Walsh, "School Colors: White Students at the University of California at Berkeley Search for Identity on a Campus Where Social and Political Life Is Increasingly Defined by Color," *San Francisco Examiner, This World* section, Feb. 4, 1990, p. 10. "Some students say if they see too many Asians in a class, they are not going to take it because the [grading] curve will be too high" (Hsia 1988: 96). A Yale sophomore was quoted: "If you are weak in math or science and find yourself assigned to a class with a majority of Asian kids, the only thing to do is transfer to a different section" (D. Brand, "The New Whiz Kids," p. 46). "With mix of awe and animosity, students in the Boston area joke that MIT stands for Made in Taiwan [and at] UCLA, where Asians make up upwards of 18 percent of the student body, Anglo students joke that the school's initials really stand for 'United Caucasians Lost Among Asians'" (Salholtz, "Do Colleges Set Asian Quotas?" *Newsweek*, Feb. 22, 1988, pp. 46, 58). Typically, Asians are regarded as "grade-busters" (Greene 1987: 1, A38–A39).

24. I found most of these works through the Educational Resources Information Center (ERIC) available at the Department of Education Library of Stanford University, and others with the aid of the exceptional Stanford Law Library staff using University Microfilms International, a dissertation information service.

25. Peng 1988: 8.

26. Ibid.

27. Ibid.

28. The average SAT verbal score for Asian Americans in 1989 was 409, compared to 446 for whites ("1989 Profile of SAT and Achievement Test Takers," *The College Board, National Report*, 1989, table B, p. iv).

29. Olsen 1988: 86.

30. A. Nakao, "Asian Students Paying a Price for Success," *San Francisco Examiner*, Dec. 6, 1986, p. A-1.

31. The late An Wang, computer giant and founder of Wang Laboratories, India-born Sirjang Tandon, developer of computer disk drives, and Filipino American engineer David Chavez have been prominently featured in the national media (see, e.g., A. Ramirez, "America's Super Minority," *Fortune*, Nov. 24, 1986, pp. 149–50; Hevesi, "An Wang, 70, Is Dead of Cancer; Inventor and Maker of Computers," *New York Times*, Mar. 25, 1990, p. 22; Stein,

"Computer Pioneer Wang Dies," *San Francisco Examiner*, Mar. 25, 1990, p. B–7). In addition to the publicity over Asian American students who have won national science awards, we are reminded that many Asian Americans are teaching assistants in mathematics, engineering, and the sciences, and that four Chinese Americans and an Asian Indian have won Nobel awards in scientific fields (Lee and Rong 1988: 546; S. B. Woo, "Voices—Lest We Forget," *Asian Week*, Aug. 28, 1987, p. 2).

32. Haycock and Navarro 1988: 14; Rumbaut and Ima 1987: 26–27. In 1986–87 the dropout rate in San Francisco public schools was 5.5 percent. The rates for Chinese (2.3 percent) and Japanese Americans (2.4 percent) were lower, but higher for Koreans (5.6 percent) and Filipinos (6.1 percent) (R. Harrington, "86–87 Dropout Report," memorandum to Board of Education members of the San Francisco Unified School District, July 10, 1987, p. 1). In San Mateo County, California, the dropout rate among Filipino students in 1988 was 4.1 percent, compared to 2 percent for all Asians (S. Chin, "Filipino Teens Top Asian Dropout Rate," *San Francisco Examiner*, Sept. 18, 1989, p. 1). Hong Kong school officials feel that "if it were not for the compulsory education system, the number of school drop-outs [in Hong Kong] would be mindboggling" ("Factors That Add Up to Educational Deprivation," *South Morning Post*, Jan. 21, 1990, p. 15).

33. Rumbaut and Ima 1987: 55–56.

34. Gardner et al. 1985: table 11, p. 27.

35. Ibid., pp. 24–25. The 1990 census shows that 20 percent of adult Asian Americans do not have a high school degree, compared to 19 percent of Latinos (data provided by Linda Cummings of Communications Consortium, Washington, D.C., Nov. 9, 1992).

36. Based on Dept. of Commerce 1988a: tables 16, 22, 28, 34, 40, 46, 52; and Gardner et al. 1985: 24–25, table 11.

37. Dolly et al. 1988: 10, table 2.

38. Rumbaut and Ima 1987: 26–27.

39. Ibid., 27–28. The Hmong also had a smaller proportion of students with GPAs below 2.0 than any other Asian group (4.3 percent).

40. Rumbaut and Ima 1987: 27–28 and table 3-1.

41. Olsen 1988: 86.

42. F. Butterfield, "Why Asians Are Going to the Head of the Class," *New York Times*, Aug. 3, 1986, p. 18.

43. Dornbusch et al. 1987a: 3, 14.

44. Montero and Tsukashima 1977: 499.

45. In the 1988 study of Hawaiian high school students, females had significantly higher GPAs, and socioeconomic status was significantly correlated to SAT scores (Dolly et al. 1988: 3). Also, in a 1984 study of Seattle Public Schools, when ethnicity was paired with economic status of Asian American students, those in the higher economic group were more likely to get better grades (Mizokawa and Ryckman 1988: 14–15).

46. Sue and Zane 1985: 574.

47. Kwong 1987: 73–74.

48. Sue and Zane 1985: 574.

49. See, e.g., Commission on Minority Participation in Education and American Life 1988: 3, 11–13; Hsia 1987: 94.

50. For example, the median years of schooling for foreign-born Filipino, Japanese, Asian Indian, and Korean Americans is higher than that of their American-born counterparts (Dept. of Commerce 1988a: tables 28, 34, 40, and 46). In comparing years of schooling completed for Asian immigrants with those of native-born Asian Americans, two groups of researchers fail to consider the impact of the 1965 amendments on the data even though they considered the profile of those entering over various periods of immigration (Moon 1986: 143–44; Xenos et al. 1987: 267–69).

51. Hirschman and Wong 1981: 504–5, table 3. In 1940 the mean for Chinese was 5.5 years (Hess 1976: 419; Dept. of Commerce 1988a: table 22, p. 268). For women, the median was 13.1 years.

52. Hirschman and Wong 1981: 504–5, table 3; Dept. of Commerce 1988a: table 28, p. 344. For adult women, the median was 14.6 years.

53. Hirschman and Wong 1981: 504–5, table 3; Dept. of Commerce 1988a: table 34, p. 413. For adult women, the median was 12.2 years.

54. Hess 1976: 419; Dept. of Commerce 1988a: table 40, p. 472.

55. In 1980 the median years of schooling for adult foreign-born Koreans (13.6 years) was also higher than that of whites (Dept. of Commerce 1988a: 531, table 46). In 1960 the white population had 10.4 mean years of school, significantly higher than Chinese and Filipinos at the time; but the mean only increased to 12.5 in 1980 (Hirschman and Wong 1981: 504–5, table 3; Dept. of Commerce 1980: table 160 and table 16). On the other hand, the median level of education for Vietnamese Americans has declined since the arrival of the first wave, whose median level was 9.5 years, with only 14 percent speaking no English. Those in the second wave (1978–83) had an average 6.3 years of education with 43 percent unable to speak any English (National Coalition of Advocates for Students Research and Policy Report 1988: 7).

56. F. Butterfield, "Why Asians Are Going to the Head of the Class," *New York Times*, Aug. 3, 1986, p. 18.

57. See, e.g., Kwong 1987: 71; F. Viviano, "When Success Is a Family Prize," *San Francisco Examiner, This World* section, Oct. 1989, p. 8.

58. Caplan et al. 1992: 38–40; Rumbaut and Ima 1987: 38, 86.

59. B. Diamond, "Are Asian American Kids Really Smarter?" *Seventeen Magazine*, May 1988, p. 206; F. Butterfield, "Why They Excel," *Parade Magazine*, Jan. 27, 1990, p. 6.

60. Chinn and Plata 1986: 23.

61. Vernon 1982: 273–74; see also Yee 1990: 17, 19.

62. Sociologist Stephen Steinberg poses this question as well (Steinberg 1989: 272).

63. See, e.g., Hsia 1987; Mordkowitz and Ginsburg 1986.

64. Peng 1988: 3, 10.

65. Hsia 1987: 94.

66. Caplan et al. 1992: 42.

67. National Coalition of Advocates for Students 1988: 79.

68. Olsen 1988: 81; Sung 1979: 139–40, 154–55.

69. In northern California 55 percent of the "at risk" (truancy or disciplinary problem) Southeast Asian students do not live with their parents (B. Lee, "Southeast Asian Teens Carry Scars of Horror," *Asian Week*, July 24, 1987, p. 9).

70. Olsen 1988: 88.

71. Dornbusch 1987a: 2; Kitano 1969: 8; Stevenson 1987: 29–30.

72. Researchers have found that authoritarian parenting is negatively correlated to grades for all other groups (see Dornbusch et al. 1987b: 1249). Authoritarian parenting is contrasted with authoritative parenting, where parents expect mature behavior from the child, set standards, enforce rules, but encourage the child's independence and individuality, and open communication, and permissive parenting, where they are tolerant, make few demands for mature behavior, and allow considerable self-regulation by the child. Both authoritarian and permissive parenting are generally associated with lower grades. Authoritative parenting is generally associated with higher grades. Asians failed to fit within this typology; even those whose parents were authoritarian often get good grades (Dornbusch et al. 1987b: 1248–56; Dornbusch et al. 1987a: 5, 9; Sam Chan 1986: 42). A 1979 survey of Chinese children in New York City found that many parents had to work long hours and were away from home—"82 percent lived with both mother and father, but 32 percent did not see their fathers from one day to the next and 21 percent never even caught a glimpse of their mothers" (Sung 1979: 151).

73. Olsen 1988: 88.

74. J. Rigdon, "Asian-American Youth Suffer a Rising Toll from Heavy Pressures: Suicides and Distress Increase as They Face Stereotypes and Parents' Expectations," *Wall Street Journal*, July 10, 1991, p. A1.

75. Rumbaut and Ima 1987: 52; Olsen 1988: 88.

76. Mizokawa and Ryckman 1988: 8, fig. 1.

77. Rumbaut and Ima 1987.

78. Steinberg 1989: 132.

79. Ibid., 275.

80. See Hirschman and Wong 1986: 22–23; Steinberg 1989: 273.

81. Hirschman and Wong 1986: 2–3; Sung 1967: 171.

82. Hmong students, who come from a poor economic class, have performed well in San Diego and Minneapolis (see Rumbaut and Ima 1987: 1; Walker 1988: 8–10).

83. See, e.g., Takahashi 1980: 339; see also Smith 1988: 107–12.

84. See, e.g., Jo 1984: 600–601.

85. See, e.g., Okimoto 1971: 151–53; Tachibana 1986: 540 (citing University of California Regent Yori Wada).

86. See, e.g., Mizokawa and Ryckman 1988.

87. See, e.g., Lee and Rong 1988.

88. Ibid., pp. 549–50.

89. Ibid., p. 550. Hirschman and Wong provide a thoughtful analysis of the middleman explanation for Asian American accomplishment, concluding that "changes in the occupational structure of the Asian-American population and a somewhat positive rate of occupational returns to education appear to be plausible explanations for Asian-American gains" (1986: 1). Yet they too withdraw to the popular image and resolve that these "patterns may have provided critical reinforcement to the Asian-American cultural emphasis on education as a way to get ahead" (p. 22).

90. Recall the earlier discussion on variations in scores between groups reported on the California Assessment Program achievement test.

91. Observers have noticed that almost all Asian students are the victims of harassment, name-calling, racial violence, or other forms of racism (see, e.g., Rumbaut and Ima 1987: 96; Olsen 1988: 7).

> While some react passively with tearful hurt feelings, others respond with physical violence. We heard a Chinese-born girl speak with tears in her eyes at a public hearing about the violence, harassment and hostility she experienced in her first few years in U.S. schools. . . . "I am not even Chinese and they call me Chink. It gets me so mad. Some of my friends just walk away, but I cannot. I am a troublemaker when that happens. I fight back hard. My fathers says not to fight. But I feel ashamed to just turn my back." 10th-grade Vietnamese boy, immigrated at age 11. (Olson 1988: 7, 38)

92. Lee 1960: 178. In 1969 Japanese American sociologist Harry Kitano regarded Japanese Americans as an "apolitical population" (Kitano 1969: 138).

93. J. Jacobs, "Asian-American Political Muscle," *Wall Street Journal,* Dec. 27, 1985, p. 8.

94. Wilke and Mohan 1984: 63.

95. The Asian American community has been described as "politically ambiguous" ("Asian Americans Torn Between Two Parties," *Washington Post,* June 2, 1984, p. A1; see also Massey 1986: 25–26; J. Jacobs, "Asian-American Political Muscle," *Wall Street Journal,* Dec. 27, 1985, p. 8).

96. See, e.g., L. May, "Asian-Americans Seek to Join Power Structure," *Los*

*Angeles Times*, Feb. 17, 1987, p. A-15 (citing San Francisco Supervisor Thomas Hsieh); Okimoto 1971: 149–53.

97. Lee 1960: 140.

98. Jo 1984: 592; "An Interview with S. I. Hayakawa" in Tachiki et al. 1971: 20.

99. Okimoto 1971: 151–52; Uyematsu 1971: 10–12.

100. Lee 1960: 179; Li 1982: 316.

101. Song 1966: 402.

102. Bell 1985: 30.

103. Tachibana 1986: 536; Massey 1986: 24. Wealthy Asians are seen as "patsies" by some politicians (W. Wong, "Asian Americans and Political Power," *East West News*, Sept. 3, 1987, p. 4).

104. In 1984 the Democratic National Committee established an Asian Pacific American caucus to generate more political participation among Asian Americans. But in February 1985 newly elected Democratic National Committee Chair Paul Kirk said that caucuses within the DNC (representing African Americans, Latinos, Asian Americans, women, and gays) were "political nonsense" and proposed to abolish them (Omi and Winant 1986: 132; L. May, "Asian-Americans Seek to Join Power Structure," *Los Angeles Times*, Feb. 17, 1987, p. A-15). But while the Asian caucus lost its official status, the caucuses for blacks, Latinos, and women remained in the party's bylaws (J. Jacobs, "Asian-American Political Muscle," p. 8).

105. See, e.g., J. Jacobs, "Asian-American Political Muscle," p. 8; Bell 1985: 30.

106. See, e.g., "Group Seeks to Reverse Voter Apathy by Asians," *Los Angeles Times*, Mar. 3, 1986, Metro, p. 1; J. Mathews, "Ethnic Asians Favor GOP in Poll," *Washington Post*, Nov. 10, 1985, p. A4.

107. The literature on differences in black and white participation include: R. Bush, "Black Enfranchisement, Jesse Jackson and Beyond," in R. Bush, ed. *The New Black Vote* (San Francisco: Synthesis Publishing, 1984); M. B. Preston et al., *The New Black Politics: The Search for Political Power*, 2d ed. (New York: Longman, 1987); D. McAdams, *Political Process and the Development of Black Insurgency 1930–1970* (1982); M. D. Morris, *Politics of Black America* (New York: Harper & Row, 1975); H. Walton, *Invisible Politics: Black Political Behaviour* (Albany: State Univ. of N.Y. Press, 1985); D. R. Matthews and J. W. Prothro, *Negroes and the New Southern Politics* (New York: Harcourt, Brace & World, 1966); Orum, "A Reappraisal of the Social and Political Participation of Negroes," *American Journal of Sociology* 72 (July 1966), pp. 32–46; M. E. Olsen, "Social and Political Participation of Blacks," *American Sociological Rev.* 35 (1970), pp. 682–96; S. Verba and N. H. Nie, *Participation in America: Political Democracy and Social Equality* (1972); Danigelis, "Race, Class and Political Involvement in the U.S.," *Social Forces* 61 (1982), pp. 532–50; R. D. Shingles, "Black Consciousness and Political Participation: The Missing Link," *American Political Science Rev.* 75 (1981), pp. 76–91; Miller et al., "Group Consciousness

and Political Participation," *American Journal of Political Science* 25 (Aug. 1981), pp. 494–511; S. Welch and P. Secret, "Sex, Race and Political Participation," *Western Political Quarterly* 34 (Mar. 1981), pp. 5–16; Brown et al., "Racial Consciousness and Political Mobilization of Black Americans," paper prepared for the 1982 annual meeting of the American Political Science Association, Denver, Colo.; K. Miller, "The Impact of Organizational Activity on Black Political Participation," *Social Science Quarterly* 62 (1982), pp. 83–98; T. M. Guterbock and B. London, "Race, Political Orientation, and Participation: An Empirical Test of Four Competing Theories," *American Sociological Rev.* 48 (1983), pp. 439–53. The literature on Latino electoral activity includes A. Portes and R. Mozo, "The Political Adaptation Process of Cubans and Other Ethnic Minorities in the United States: A Preliminary Analysis," *International Migration Rev.* 19, no. 1, pp. 35–62; M. Vigil, *Chicano Politics* (1978); J. A. Garcia, "The Political Integration of Mexican Immigrants: Examining Some Political Orientations," *International Migration Rev.* 21, no. 2, pp. 372–405; Welch et al., "Ethnic Differences in Social and Political Participation: A Comparison of Some Anglo and Mexican Americans," *Pacific Sociological Rev.* 18 (July 1975), pp. 361–82; Antunes and Gaitz, "Ethnicity and Participation: A Study of Mexican-Americans, Blacks and Whites," *American Journal of Sociology* 80 (Mar. 1975), pp. 1192–211; L. P. Lovrich and O. Marenin, "A Comparison of Black and Mexican American Voters in Denver: Assertive Versus Acquiescent Political Orientations and Voting Behavior in an Urban Electorate," *Western Political Quarterly* 29 (June 1976), pp. 284–94; Welch, "Identity in the Ethnic Community and Political Behavior," *Ethnicity* 4 (Sept. 1977), pp. 216–25; R. C. Guzman, *The Political Socialization of the Mexican American People* (1976); Buehler, "Voter Turnout and Political Efficacy Among Mexican-Americans in Michigan," *Sociological Quarterly* 18 (Autumn 1977), pp. 504–17; Brischetto and de la Garza, "The Mexican American Electorate: Political Participation and Ideology," Mexican American Electorate Series, Occasional Paper no. 3 (Austin: Center for Mexican American Studies, University of Texas, 1983); de la Garza and Weaver, "The Mexican American Electorate: An Explanation of Their Opinions and Behavior," Mexican American Electorate Series, Occasional Paper no. 4 (Austin: Center for Mexican American Studies, University of Texas, 1984).

108. Din 1984: 41.

109. Nakanishi 1986; see also Nakanishi 1985–86.

110. Uhlaner et al. 1989; Cain et al. 1986.

111. California Dept. of Finance, "California Statistical Abstract," 1987, pp. 228–29.

112. Din 1984: 79, 85.

113. Nakanishi 1986: 21.

114. See, e.g., M. Arax, "Group Seeks to Reverse Voter Apathy by Asians," *Los Angeles Times*, Mar. 3, 1986, Metro, p. 1.

115. Uhlaner et al. 1989: 199.

116. Uhlaner et al. 1989: table 1, p. 38.

117. Unpublished data supplied by Carole Uhlaner, University of California at Irvine.

118. Interview with Harold Yee, executive director, Asian Inc., San Francisco, Dec. 14, 1989.

119. Uhlaner et al. 1989: 203–4.

120. Cain et al. 1986: 34 (table I-4). African Americans had a level of participation in these activities that was quite comparable to whites.

121. Unpublished data supplied by Carole Uhlaner, University of California at Irvine.

122. Cain et al. 1986: 19–20. In 1986 in California 50.8 percent were registered Democratic, 38.3 percent Republican, and only 8.7 percent declined to state a party (California Dept. of Finance 1987: 226–27). The comparative figures for African Americans were 89 percent Democrats, 6 percent Republicans, and 6 percent who declined to state. As for Latinos 75 percent were Democrats, 17 percent Republicans, and 9 percent declined to state (Cain et al. 1986: 18–19).

123. Nakanishi 1985–86: table 2b, p. 15.

124. Nakanishi 1987: 42–52. In an informal survey conducted by the *San Jose Mercury News* in 1987, 53 percent of the Vietnamese Americans in Santa Clara County were registered Republicans and 21 percent Democrats (Trounstine, "Most Vietnamese Voters in County are Republican," *San Jose Mercury News,* Aug. 17, 1987, p. 1A; L. Harrison, "No One Dares to Disagree," *Asian Week,* Aug. 21, 1987, p. 5).

125. Din 1984: tables 3-11, 3-8, and 3-9 (Japanese figure is based on weighted average), pp. 8–9.

126. Cain et al. 1986: table I-1.

127. Ibid., p. 14. There is little beyond the California study from which to draw on regarding attitudinal differences between groups. A separate study on a group of "highly educated" Asian Indians from New York showed that 43.5 percent regarded themselves as liberal, 1 in 6 as highly conservative, and one-third as independent or middle-of-the-road ("Center for Management at Baruch College of CUNY," *India West,* Apr. 15, 1988, p. 30).

128. In Northern California, Chinese were split between Clinton and Bush 47–46 percent. Filipinos leaned heavily to Clinton (61–34 percent), as did Japanese (74–25 percent) (S. A. Chin, "Bay Area Asians Backed Clinton by Big Margin," *San Francisco Examiner,* Nov. 6, 1992, p. A-20; L. I. Barrett, "A New Coalition for the 1990s," *Time,* Nov. 16, 1992, p. 47). In 1984 Californians favored Reagan over Mondale 57.5 to 41.3 percent (James Fay, Sr., ed., *California Almanac,* 3d ed. [1987], p. 265). In 1992 they voted 47 percent for Clinton, 32 percent for Bush, and 21 percent for Perot ("How Californians Voted in the Presidential Race," *San Francisco Examiner,* Nov. 4, 1992, p. A-11).

129. "Polls: Asians Sensitive on Ethnic Issues," *Asian Week,* Nov. 14, 1986, pp. 1, 11.

130. Cain et al. 1986: 19–20; Tachibana 1986: 536; Aoki 1986: 546.

131. Cain et al. 1986: 18–19. In 1992 California African Americans voted 83 percent Clinton, 9 percent Perot, and 8 percent Bush. Latinos voted 65 percent Clinton, 21 percent Bush, and 14 percent Perot ("How Californians Voted in the Presidential Race," *San Francisco Examiner,* Nov. 4, 1992, p. A-11). The figures were similar nationwide (L. I. Barrett, "A New Coalition for the 1990s," *Time,* Nov. 16, 1992, p. 47).

132. Maykovich 1972: 76–82; Jo 1984: 586–87; see also the information on Japan in Chap. 2.

133. Brown 1948; Hess 1976: 417; Kitano and Daniels 1988: 92.

134. Wakeman 1974: 28; Tong 1973–74: 184; Tong 1971: 1.

135. See, e.g., Takahashi 1980: 329; Parillo 1982: 90; Jo 1984: 595–98; Uhlaner et al. 1989: 218–19; Uyematsu 1971: 10; Massey 1986: 22.

136. Omi and Winant 1986: 74.

137. Uyematsu 1971: 10.

138. Massey 1986: 22.

139. Surh 1973–74: 170; see also Lyman 1977: 43–57; Wong 1971: 132.

140. Almirol 1985: 156.

141. Tong 1973–75: 179.

142. See, e.g., Parillo 1982.

143. A portrait of Chiang Kai-Shek remains in the living room of my parents' old home in Arizona. I was born in 1949, and I recall my father purchasing thousands of dollars of Republic of China war bonds while I was growing up in support of Chiang's efforts to reclaim mainland China.

144. Kitano and Daniels 1988: 92; Hess 1976: 417–18.

145. L. May, "Asian-Americans Seek to Join Power Structure," *Los Angeles Times,* Feb. 17, 1987, p. 15 (citing Congressman Norman Mineta).

146. Tachibana 1986: 540; Okimoto 1971: 150–52.

147. Jo 1984: 583. Encouraged by ostensible acceptance, even admiration, from the white majority as a "model minority," Asian Americans may reject a militant approach toward minority rights for a more compliant one in hopes of being embraced by the majority. Jo further argues that later, when it becomes obvious that they will never be accepted as full members of society by the mainstream, Asian Americans continue their compliant attitudes out of fear that if they tried a more assertive approach, the mainstream will retaliate and take away their limited success.

148. Including contacting elected officials within *electoral* activities might be challenged by some. Researchers in the California survey classified "contacting elected officials" as a nonelectoral activity (Uhlaner et al. 1989: 198).

149. The chief researcher in the Los Angeles County study, Don Nakanishi,

notes: "Electoral politics is only one activity pursued in order to protect and advance [Asian Americans'] interests. The study of nonelectoral activity shows how the Asian American experience differs from that of other immigrant and minority groups" (1985–86: 3). The California researchers, Carole Uhlaner, Bruce Cain, and Rod Kiewiet, included specific nonelectoral questions on "contacting the media" and "working with a group to solve a community problem" (Uhlaner et al. 1989: 189–91; Cain et al. 1986: 23–25).

150. Though lacking a careful empirical study on registration and voting, Professor Nakanishi did note in closing that "Asian Americans have also been long involved with political activities which transcend internal community politics, and yet fall short of being considered a form of protest, or a straightforward example of electoral politics. . . . Electoral politics is a vital part of our lives, and yet it must be understood within broader contexts. By not doing so, we will provide electoral politics with a mandate, which it neither deserves nor has gained in relation to other campaigns" (1985–86: 19–21).

151. Piven and Cloward 1988; Piven and Cloward 1977.

152. The Unemployed Workers' Movement, the Industrial Workers' Movement, the Civil Rights Movement, and the Welfare Rights Movement are primary subjects (Piven and Cloward 1977: chaps. 2–5; Jo 1984: 592–93).

153. Sandmeyer 1939: 51–63. The plaited queue was a badge of Chinese citizenship and a mark of subjection to the Manchu rulers of the Qing dynasty; the queue was required of all Chinese subjects beginning in 1645 (Lyman 1970: 11; Fairbank and Reischauer 1973: 364). To cut off one's queue was a sign of rebellion against the government, and fatal consequences awaited a man who returned to China without it (see also Dong 1974: 367–70). For examples of Chinese American lobbying in the nineteenth century, see generally McClain 1984: 529. Chinese in the nineteenth century also used the courts to challenge offensive statutes and ordinances (see Dong 1974; McClain 1984; Salyer 1989).

154. DeWitt 1978: 1–22. The famous United Farm Workers strike of 1965 began when Filipinos represented by the Agricultural Workers Organizing Committee walked out of the fields. Mexican workers organized by Cesar Chavez joined them two weeks later.

155. Hartman 1978: 47–58; "International Hotel," in Tachiki et al. 1971: 310–11; "Demonstration Marks Anniversary of International Hotel Eviction," *San Francisco Examiner*, Aug. 5, 1978, p. 14; "S.F. Hotel Tenants Near Victory on Battle Against Eviction," *San Francisco Examiner*, Nov. 16, 1976, p. 19.

156. J. Mathews, "Quiet Minority Shifts Tactics in California—Appointee Battle Reflects Asian Americans' Power," *Washington Post*, Feb. 25, 1988, p. A3.

157. See Lee 1960: 147–52; Parillo 1982: 90–92; Wilke and Mohan 1984: 45; Lyman 1977: 87. The Chinese Six Companies is credited with influencing important antidiscrimination provisions of the Civil Rights Act of 1870. Runyon v. McCrary, 427 U.S. 160, 192 (1976) (White, J., dissenting); McClain 1984: 564–67.

158. F. Chuman 1976: 165–71; Wilke and Mohan 1984: 50–53; Parillo 1982: 97–98.

159. Chan 1991a: 78.

160. L. Pike, "Church Fills Spiritual Needs with a Cultural and Social Blend," *Los Angeles Times*, Sept. 1, 1990, p. F-18; "Dissident Vietnamese Catholics Who Have Occupied San Jose Church Since 1986 Purchase Building from Diocese of San Jose and Plan to Ask Pope to Declare It a Shrine," *San Jose Mercury News*, Dec. 7, 1988, p. A6.

161. The concerns I express here about disenfranchisement in Asian American politics may apply with even more force to Japanese American internment.

162. Tachibana 1986: 535; R. Lindsey, "Asian-Americans Press to Gain Political Power," *New York Times*, Nov. 10, 1986, p. B-6.

163. H. M. Koo, "What We Must Do!" *Koreatown*, Oct. 20, 1979, p. 5.

164. Address by University of California Chancellor Chang-Lin Tien at a dinner in his honor sponsored by the Chinese Consolidated Benevolent Association and the U.C. Chinese Alumni Chapter, San Francisco, May 22, 1991.

165. "Today the term Oriental is definitely out. . . . Some consider Oriental offensive. . . . It is considered to be in the same class as 'colored' is in reference to blacks." . . . "The problem with 'Oriental' is it is a word used in colonialization. It is an English concept that doesn't account for the people. . . . It is a design or a rug, not a person" (E. Gant, "Which Term Do Asians Prefer?" *Gannett News Service*, Apr. 22, 1991, citing Glenda Joe of the Council of Asian American Organizations in Houston and Tommy Lee Woon, associate dean and director of the Third World Center at Brown University).

166. Omi and Winant 1986: 105; Almirol 1985: 159.

167. Joane Nagel explains:

> Historically "Indian" has been a content-free, ascriptive designation that has always included religiously, culturally, and linguistically diverse and historically separate and factious groups. The several hundred remaining American Indian tribes in the U.S. represent dozens of distinct language groups and are geographically dispersed across the continent. In light of this heterogeneity, Guillemin has described the designation of "Indian" as racist in recognition of its purely external character—a label applied to religiously and culturally varied peoples for the convenience of an outside group. (1982: 37)

The term Hispanic was adopted during the Nixon administration. "Through an ingenious political stroke, the Nixon administration hit on a word that includes all of the so-called Spanish speaking minorities. . . . The term has been embraced by some, but to purists, it rejects the Mexican's Indian heritage and the Puerto Rican's African roots" (R. Acuña, "Hispanic Label—Gringo's Revenge," *Pacific News Service*, Feb. 15–21, 1988, pp. 9–10). " 'Latino' (from Latin American) is a more inclusive denomination accounting for those who come from, or descend from, a specific geographical area where the Spanish and Portuguese legacy is dominant but not exclusive" (Totti 1987: 537–42).

168. Omi and Winant 1986: 84.

169. Omi and Winant 1986: 105; E. Gant, "Which Term Do Asians Prefer?" *Gannett News Service,* Apr. 22, 1991.

170. This might even include what is viewed as the common experience of being an immigrant from Asia.

171. The radicalization of college students at the time of the Vietnam War included Asian Americans. Many viewed the war as a racist one in which Asian life was "cheap" (Omi and Winant, p. 105, citing Paul Wong: "The most widely accepted slogans in the white antiwar movement have been 'Give peace a chance' and 'Bring the GIs home.' The Asian-American movement, in contrast, emphasized the *racist* nature of the war, using such slogans as 'Stop killing *our* Asian brothers and sisters,' and 'We don't want *your* racist war'" [Wong 1972: 35–36]).

172. E. Iwata, "Race Without Face," *San Francisco Focus,* May 1991, p. 132.

173. Vincent Chin was a Chinese American who was fatally beaten with a baseball bat by unemployed Detroit autoworkers who thought Chin was Japanese and blamed him for layoffs in the industry. The defendants pled guilty to manslaughter and were sentenced in state court to three years' probation and fined $3,780 each. Incensed by the lenient sentences, a coalition of Asian Americans protested to the U.S. Department of Justice, and federal civil rights indictments were brought against the defendants. The federal court found one defendant guilty and sentenced him to 25 years in prison, but a court of appeals eventually reversed the conviction on technical grounds. On retrial, the remaining defendant was acquitted. U.S. Commission on Civil Rights 1992: 25–26; American Citizens for Justice, *The Case for Vincent Chin: A Tragedy in American Justice,* Oak Park, Mich., May 1, 1983; American Friends Service Committee, New England Regional Office, "The Case for Vincent Chin: A Tragedy in American Justice," *Outlook on Justice* 1, no. 8 (Feb. 1984); U.S. Commission on Civil Rights 1986: 43.

174. These diverse groups have come together to protest the resurgence in anti-Asian violence generally. One of their first chances to do so was at a conference called Break the Silence on May 10, 1986, at U.C. Berkeley.

175. J. Mathews, "Quiet Minority Shifts Tactics in California; Appointee Battle Reflects Asian Americans' Power," *Washington Post,* Feb. 25, 1988, p. A3.

176. K. Lew, "Rolling Stone Concedes to 3 Korean Demands," *Asian Week,* Mar. 18, 1988, p. 1; W. Wong, "Asian Americans Shake Off Stereotypes, Increases Clout as Political Activism Grows," *Los Angeles Times,* Feb. 23, 1988, p. B-7.

177. A. Lew, "History in the Making: Nikkei, Koreans Join Hands," *Asian Week,* Sept. 4, 1987, p. 12. Consider the following lead sentence in another story: "SACRAMENTO—Speaking for the first time as a united voice, Asian American health providers from around California descended on the state Capitol to demand that legislators start addressing the needs of their rapidly

growing communities" (S. Chin, "Asian American Health Providers Seek State Aid," *San Francisco Examiner*, May 22, 1991, p. A-6).

178. See, e.g., M. Tom, "Capitol Watch," *Asian Week*, May 20, 1988, p. 6.

179. Wong 1972: 37.

180. Even within the foreign-born segment of a community, differences can be found, as with dissimilarities between generations. Immigrants from the same nation who entered in different eras are likely to have dissimilar cultural, social, and political habits. We have already seen that the changes in the law have given rise to class differences within (as well as between) each community, which are often but not always reflected in comparisons between earlier immigrants from the working class and more recent ones from a more educated class. For example, the values and attitudes of Filipinos who entered as agricultural workers or even as students in the 1920's are certainly not interchangeable with those of the young urban professionals entering from Manila today. Interest in electoral versus nonelectoral politics has been found to vary between postwar Filipinos and earlier Filipino immigrants (Almirol 1985: 152). In Chinatown, debates over land use between new entrepreneurs and those who would preserve smaller stores have intensified (D. Waugh, "Glitzy Electronics, Camera Shops Make Chinatown Shudder," *San Francisco Examiner*, June 5, 1988, p. B-3).

181. In the Filipino community distinctive Tagalog and Ilocano languages can both be found. And in the Chinese American community (with potentially hundreds of dialects), Mandarin and Cantonese are so different that a Mandarin speaker (from Taiwan or Beijing) cannot understand a Cantonese speaker (from Hong Kong or Canton)—much less Toishan or any other rural Cantonese dialect (see, e.g., Tsai 1980: 336–37). Before 1965 over 90 percent of the Chinese immigrants came from the Canton delta area (Sung 1979: 16).

182. See, e.g., Fujitomi and Wong 1973.

183. In the battle over the rights of elderly Filipino and Chinese tenants of the International Hotel in San Francisco Chinatown in the 1970's, the building was owned during much of the fight by a Hong Kong company.

184. Tachibana 1986: 542; see also W. Wong, "Asian Americans & Political Power," *East West News*, Sept. 3, 1987, p. 4.

185. Perhaps one reason is that because of their economic displacement and dependency on public benefits, Vietnamese have been influenced by the Democratic party's general pro-social services orientation.

> In Santa Clara County, for example, Democrats have been working with that county's large Southeast Asian population on social-service issues. County Democratic Chairman Scott Strickland says the immigrants are fairly conservative by American standards, being stridently anti-Communist. So when you have a Republican Party rattling sabers, that plays very well in this community. On the other hand, much of the emerging leadership of the Southeast Asian community

found it comfortable to work with government and elected officials. In our county most of the elected officials are Democrats. (Aoki 1986: 545–46)

186. Some 89 percent of African Americans and 75 percent of the Latinos in California are registered Democrats (Cain et al. 1986: 18–19).

187. Sue and Sue 1973: 111–24. These psychologists attach the Asian American personality label to those who sense that Asians have been subordinated in the United States and feel that a new identity must be formed, mixing traditional Asian heritage with American social and political elements to break into the American structure. In her book *Chinatown* Gwen Kinkead scolds traditionalists ("they can't have it both ways—they cannot charge mistreatment and racism and, at the same time, refuse to talk to outsiders, or vote, or lend a cup of sugar to their neighbor") and highlights an elderly man who has lived in Chinatown for 60 years and "has never spoken to a white person" (1992: x, 204)

188. Ibid. Rumbaut and Ima observed this among some Indochinese refugees: "During a recent public session on Khmer youth, the son of a pre–Pol Pot leader, an Americanized Khmer, admitted that he along with other pre–Pol Pot Cambodian refugees avoided contact with the post–Pol Pot refugees because they were embarrassed by their accents and non-American ways" (1987: 99).

189. Sue 1973: 140–47. How the confluence of pressures, external and internal, and the disparity in environmental influences come together are partially illustrated in the following two examples: "'I don't know who I am. Am I the good Chinese daughter? Am I an American teenager? I always feel I am letting my parents down when I am with my friends because I act so American, but I also feel that I will never really be an American. I never feel comfortable with myself anymore.' 10th-grade Chinese girl, immigrated at age 12" (Olsen 1988: 30). "A Chinese American manager at Westinghouse was quoted in *The Wall Street Journal* a few years ago saying he socialized mainly with ethnic Chinese. He said he considered his career opportunities limited and envisions himself rising only one more level. To go higher, he said, he would 'have to attend cocktail parties and play golf'" (W. Wong, "The 'Glass Ceiling' Isn't a Yuppie Home Decor," *East West News*, June 9, 1988, p. 4).

190. See Surh 1973–74: 156–71; Tong 1973–74: 178–202. Professor Jerry Surh points out that

> Assimilation in a racist society inverts the normal relation among members of the rejected minority, replacing trust with mistrust and fellow-feeling with hostility. . . . Identity is therefore not *the* problem of Asian Americans, and it is not one that is solvable in personal terms. The problem stems from the historical choice Asian Americans made to live in this society, from their necessary involvement with it, and from the racism they encounter from its institutions and its inhabitants. . . . Identities imposed and chosen in racist circumstances must be transcended to be seen for what they are. (1973–74: 163, 171)

Ben Tong notes:

> Locked out of legitimate economic enterprise by white law, the Chinamen invented *fake Chinese culture* to survive. . . . An implicit contract for intergroup harmony emerged between the races. It was considered violated if Chinamen were ever to stop "preserving" the "superior culture" baloney or, worse yet, if they were to lower the facade of blunted masculinity. . . . The message was clear. Stay transcendentally frozen out of the country's history and affairs, act forever homesick for the Orient, settle for shit work, and lay off white women. (1973–74: 190–92)

See also Jo 1984.

191. The issue of bilingual education would likely engender strong disagreement between extreme personalities (one willing to be stripped of culture and the other fighting to preserve it). Not only are there disagreements over bilingual education, but we have also seen evidence of an apparently deep split among Asian Americans over the related "English only" issue.

192. Sue and Sue 1973: 115; Surh 1973–74: 162–63.

193. It is not uncommon to hear some Asian Americans referred to as "bananas"—yellow on the outside, white on the inside.

194. Because group action is not the only way of expressing oneself politically, the traditionalist's withdrawal and isolation from society may be a complicated form of political expression.

195. In spite of the presence of an Asian American fraternity and sorority at Berkeley, while I was there from 1967 to 1971, the Chinese Students Assocation (for foreign-born Chinese Americans), the Chinese Students Club (for American-born Chinese Americans), and the Nisei Students Club (for Japanese American students) were quite active. In my conversations with students from the 1970's and 1980's, various forms of these organizations have continued to exist, along with clubs for Korean, Vietnamese, Asian Indian, and Filipino students.

196. See, e.g., M. Cha, "Koreans Must Build a Political Base," *Koreatown*, Apr. 6, 1981, p. 3; H. Yee, "Ethnicity—Enuff?" *Asian Week*, Mar. 21, 1986, p. 2 (discussing representation for the Chinese American community).

197. See, e.g., K. Hwangbo, "It's Martha Choe: First Korean American Councilwoman in U.S.," *Korea Times*, Nov. 11, 1991, p. 1. I attended a small dinner meeting in San Francisco Chinatown on May 15, 1991, where Chinese community leaders were asked to meet with a prospective U.S. congressional candidate from Houston. Much of her speech, which was greeted warmly by some in attendance (who were willing to overlook her lack of political sophistication), was that it was important to have a Chinese American in Congress, and if elected, she would become the Chinese American spokesperson.

198. Nagel 1984: 426.

199. Horowitz 1975: 111–15.

200. See, e.g., Nagel 1982.

201. See Saran 1985: 8; Wolfinger 1965: 896; Parenti 1967: 717. Parenti distinguishes between acculturation (the adoption of another group's styles and values) and assimilation (the integration into the social matrix of another group through primary ties like marriage). He argues that ethnic politics persists because ethnic groups in America have achieved acculturation but not assimilation.

202. Amalgamation and incorporation involve the widening of ethnicity or group boundaries, though they can narrow as well.

> *Differentiation* is the narrowing of boundaries by the creation of additional groups. A group may separate into its component parts. . . . This is *division.* . . . On the other hand, there is the possibility of *proliferation:* a new group comes into existence without its "parent group" (or groups) losing its (or their) identity. . . . Despite the manifold possibilities for changes in group identity, some groups seem able to retain their traditional identity more or less intact over long periods of time. . . . Other groups are simply new. . . . Generally, two types of variables seem to be most influential in shaping and altering group boundaries. The first is contact with ethnic strangers perceived as possessing varying degrees of likeness and difference. The second is the size and importance of the political unit in which groups find themselves. (Horowitz 1975: 115–16)

203. Saran 1985: 7; Yinger: 1978; Esman 1977; Cohen: 1974; Dahl 1961; see also Fuchs 1968. Yinger, Moynihan and Glazer, and Esman recognize, however, that there is more involved than merely common background.

204. Nagel and Olzak 1982: 127; Garcia 1987: 376–77; see also Gans 1962.

205. Horowitz 1975: 116; Saran 1985: 4–5. Cynthia Enloe submits that because of its enforcement policies, the Immigration and Naturalization Service "has become a stimulus for Chicano (and other Hispanic group) mobilization" (1981: 133).

206. Saran 1985: 5; Nagel 1984: 421–24; Omi and Winant 1986: 84.

207. Wong 1972: 36.

208. "'For (some) Asians to consider that they have something in common with others in another culture is difficult for them to accept.' . . . This is especially true of new immigrants, such as the Vietnamese and Cambodians, who still have strong ties to their homeland and might have cultural clashes with others" (E. Gant, "Which Term Do Asians Prefer?" *Gannett News Service,* Apr. 22, 1991).

209. "Asian Victory: Census Bureau Drops 1990 Plan," *Asian Week,* Mar. 18, 1988, p. 1. Of course one could say that the plan to lump Asian Americans together prompted united mobilization to oppose it.

210. Nagel and Olzak 1982: 129; Omi and Winant 1986: 84.

211. Nagel and Olzak 1986: 129; Saran 1985: 5.

212. Omi and Winant 1986: 74.

213. Interview with Rose Matsui Ochi, Jan. 10, 1992.

214. When California legislator Tom Hayden, a peace activist during the Vietnam War, was scheduled to speak at a college in San Jose, Vietnamese American students and residents protested and threatened a demonstration. The speech was canceled (K. Bishop, "Despite Gains, Many Vietnamese Refugees Are Refusing to Let War End," *New York Times*, Aug. 3, 1987, late city ed., sec. 8, p. 12; "College That Canceled Hayden Speech After Threats Honors Him," *Los Angeles Times*, June 7, 1987, home ed., p. 39).

215. S. Chin, "Innocence Lost: L.A.'s Koreans Fight to be Heard," *San Francisco Examiner*, May 9, 1992, p. A1; L. Chung, "Asian Americans Frustrated Trying to Respond to Rioting," *San Francisco Chronicle*, May 6, 1992, p. A4; D. Freed and C. Jones, "Blacks, Koreans Seek Conciliation," *Los Angeles Times*, May 26, 1992, p. B5.

216. Of course there is some overlap here with the utilitarian model.

217. Saran 1985: 8; see generally Erikson 1968.

218. *Time* wrote of the new Asian American novels "of the immigrant's life" and the "enthusiasm among publishers for Asian-American writing." The four new talents mentioned were all Chinese American—Gish Jen, David Wong Louie, Gus Lee, and Amy Tan (J. Simpson, "Fresh Voices Above the Noisy Din," *Time*, June 3, 1991, pp. 66–67). Two other highly acclaimed Asian American writers are Wayne Wang, a filmmaker and a Chinese American, and Phil Gotanda, a playwright and Japanese American. Chinese American novelists Maxine Hong Kingston and Frank Chin are regarded as the matriarch and patriarch of Asian American writers.

219. The two most prominent histories of Asian Americans have been written by Chinese American professor Sucheng Chan (Chan 1991a) and Japanese American professor Ronald Takaki (Takaki 1989).

220. This writer seems to receive similar signals: "Growing up in white America as an Asian American has not, is not, and will not be easy. Though today we do not face nearly as much prejudice as we have in the past, it is still there—in the mainly white male work world, in the college acceptance quotas, in the look on people's faces when they meet you for the first time and find out that you are Asian" (H. Woo, "Growing Up in White America," *Asian Week*, Aug. 3, 1990, p. 16). Perhaps the reason is that "Asian Americans are not perceived as Americans, but rather as foreigners" (E. Gant, "Which Term Do Asians Prefer?" *Gannett*, Apr. 22, 1991, quoting Valerie Decruc, director of Asian American Affairs at Oberlin College in Ohio).

221. Oral interviews conducted by Dorothy Liu, Elan Nguyen, and Bill Ong Hing, May 1–30, 1991.

222. E. Tsao, "What's Wrong with Calling Myself Oriental?" *San Francisco Chronicle*, Sept. 10, 1991, p. A17.

223. The costs of flexibility in multilevel mobilization have been observed in the Native American movement. Conflicts among members "regarding interests and strategies that such multi-level mobilization" fosters is inevitable (Nagel 1982: 44).

224. Americanization (also popularly referred to as assimilation) is commonly divided into three categories: melting pot, Anglo-conformity, and cultural pluralism (see Gordon 1961). The melting pot notion blends races and cultures. It motivated some American opinion leaders before the arrival of the Chinese (albeit Native Americans and African Americans were already excluded) (Miller 1979: 191–200; Saxton 1971: 103). However, restrictionists were adamantly opposed to the melting pot, and many embraced stripping the immigrant of homeland culture and making "[the person] over into an American along Anglo-Saxon lines" (Bouvier and Gardner 1986: 32). This movement was evident as far back as colonial times and was fueled by sentiments such as those expressed by President Woodrow Wilson in 1917: "A man who thinks of himself as belonging to a particular national group in America has not yet become an American" (Adams 1983: 110–11). Liberal intellectuals challenged the Anglo-conformity approach. They offered a model of cultural pluralism, arguing that the nation should "consciously allow and encourage its ethnic groups to develop democratically, each emphasizing its particular cultural heritage" (Kallen 1915; Kallen 1924).

225. In evaluating Americanization, sociologist Milton Gordon established an intellectual framework by dividing the process into acculturation (or behavioral assimilation) and structural assimilation (or social assimilation). Acculturation referred to the change in the cultural patterns of immigrants to those of the host society, while social or structural assimilation referred to the large-scale entrance of immigrants into the general civic life of the receiving society, such as through social cliques, clubs, and institutions on the primary group level. But unlike acculturation, social assimilation requires acceptance of the immigrant group by the dominant group. Gordon concluded that while considerable acculturation had occurred for most immigrants, structural assimilation had not been extensive. He felt that this was particularly true for newer immigrants and racial minorities such as Italians, Poles, Mexicans, African Americans, and Puerto Ricans largely because of religious and racial differences. In his view the mainstream simply did not intend to open up "primary group life to entrance by these hordes of alien newcomers." Any indication the dominant group might invite old immigrant groups into the social structure was simply a sham or a "mirage"; as for "racial minorities, there was not even the pretense of an invitation." But Gordon also sensed a "complementary standoff" because some immigrant groups may not prefer structural assimilation that might lead to intermarriage or a failure to perpetuate religious ideology (Gordon 1961: 280–83).

226. Admittedly, the racial identification index is not uniform for all Asian Americans, given complicated racial histories in the Philippines and India, and interracial marriages in the United States. Racial identification among all Asian Americans would probably be necessary for a totally collective response. But because some immigrants actively seek to strip themselves of their cultural her-

itage and because others enjoy the materialistic side of acculturation and are apathetic toward ethnic politics, it seems unlikely that short of another catastrophe like internment Asian Americans would not unify along racial lines. Of course young Asian professionals might come to realize that a glass ceiling prevents them from promotions to executive positions, fueling a pan-Asian response.

## EPILOGUE

1. Figures do not include those who obtained immigrant status in 1990 under the amnesty provisions of the Immigration Reform and Control Act of 1986 (Detail Run 401—Total, Fiscal Year 1990, INS Statistical Branch).

# Bibliography

Adams, W. 1983. "A Dubious Host." *Wilson Quarterly* (Jan.): 110–11.

Adeva, M. A. 1932. "Filipino Students in the United States." *Mid Pacific Magazine* 44 (Aug.): 119–23.

Akagi, R. 1936. *Japan's Foreign Relations, 1524–1936.* Tokyo: The Hokuseido Press.

Allen, L. 1971. *Japan: The Years of Triumph.* London: BPC Unit.

Almirol, E. B. 1985. *Ethnic Identity and Social Negotiation.* New York: AMS Press.

Anker, D. E., and M. H. Posner. 1981. "The Forty Year Crisis: A Legislative History of the Refugee Act of 1980." *San Diego Law Review* 19, no. 1: 9–89.

Antunes, G., and C. H. Gaitz. 1975. "Ethnicity and Participation: A Study of Mexican-Americans, Blacks and Whites." *American Journal of Sociology* 80 (Mar.): 1192–211.

Aoki, E. 1986. "Which Party Will Harvest the New Asian Votes?" *California Journal* (Nov.): 545–46.

Asian Pacific American Legal Center. 1988. *Asian Pacifics and U.S. Immigration Policy: IRCA Legalization, Phase I.* Los Angeles: The Center.

Bach, R., and D. Meissner. 1989. *America's Economy in the 1990's: What Role Should Immigration Play?* Carnegie Endowment for International Peace.

Bailey, T. 1934. *Theodore Roosevelt and the Japanese-American Crisis.* Stanford, Calif.: Stanford University Press.

Baker, R. P., and D. S. North. 1984. *The 1975 Refugees: Their First Five Years in America.* Washington, D.C.: New TransCentury Foundation.

Barkan, E. R. 1983. "Whom Shall We Integrate?: A Comparative Analysis of the Immigration Trends of Asians Before and After the 1965 Immigration Act (1951–1978)." *Journal of American Ethnic History* (Fall): 29–57.

Barth, G. 1964. *Bitter Strength.* Cambridge, Mass.: Harvard University Press.

Bell, D. 1985. "The Triumph of Asian Americans." *New Republic* (July 15–22): 30.

Bennet, M. T. 1963. *American Immigration Policies*. Public Affairs Press.

Bennett, C. E. 1992. *The Asian and Pacific Islander Population in the United States*. Washington, D. C.: Bureau of the Census.

Bernstein, B. J., and A. J. Matusow. 1966. *The Truman Administration: A Documentary History*. New York: Harper and Row.

Blalock, H. 1967. *Toward a Theory of Minority Group Relations*. New York: Wiley.

Blum, J. M. 1976. *V Was for Victory: Politics and American Culture During WWII*. New York: Harcourt, Brace, Jovanovich.

Bogardus, E. S. 1929. "American Attitudes Towards Filipinos." *Sociology and Social Research* 14, no.1 (Sept.–Oct.): 59–69.

———. 1930. "Anti-Filipino Race Riots." Report made to the Ingram Institute of Social Science of San Diego, May 15.

Bonacich, E. 1972. "A Theory of Ethnic Antagonism: The Split Labor Market." *American Sociological Review* 37: 547–49.

Bonacich, E., I. Light, and C. C. Wong. 1988. "Korean Immigrant: Small Business in Los Angeles." In R. Bryce-Laporte, ed., *Sourcebook on the New Immigration*, pp. 167–84.

Borjas, G. 1986. "Immigrants and the U.S. Labor Market." In S. Pozo, ed., *Essays on Legal and Illegal Immigration*, pp. 7–20. Kalamazoo, Mich.: Upjohn Institute for Employment Research.

Bouvier, L., and R. Gardner. 1986. "Immigration to the United States: The Unfinished Story." *Population Bulletin* 41, no. 4.

Boyd, M. 1971. "Oriental Immigration: The Experience of the Chinese, Japanese and Filipino Population in the United States." *International Migration Review* 5, no. 1 (Spring).

———. 1974. "The Changing Nature of Central and Southeast Asian Immigration to the United States: 1961–1972." *International Migration Review* 8, no. 4 (Winter): 507–19.

Briggs, V. 1986. "The Imperative of Immigration Reform." In S. Pozo, ed., *Essays on Legal and Illegal Immigration*, pp. 43–71. Kalamazoo, Mich.: Upjohn Institute.

Brischetto, R., and R. de la Garza. 1983. *The Mexican American Electorate: Political Participation and Ideology*. Austin: Center for Mexican American Studies, University of Texas.

Brown, G. T. 1948. "The Hindu Conspiracy, 1914–1917." *Pacific Historical Review* 15, no. 2: 299–310.

Brown, K. 1982. "Racial Consciousness and Political Mobilization of Black Americans." Paper prepared for the 1982 annual meeting of the American Political Science Association, Denver, Colo.

Bryce-Laporte, R., ed. 1980. *Sourcebook on the New Immigration*. New Brunswick, N.J.: Transaction Books.

Buehler, M. H. 1977. "Voter Turnout and Political Efficacy Among Mexican-Americans in Michigan." *Sociological Quarterly* 18 (Autumn): 504–17.

Bunge, F., ed. 1982. *South Korea: A Country Study.* Washington, D.C.: Dept. of the Army.

———. 1984. *The Philippines: A Country Study.* Washington, D.C.: American University.

Burks, A. 1964. *The Government of Japan.* 2d ed. New York: Thomas Y. Crowell.

Bush, R. 1984. "Black Enfranchisement, Jesse Jackson and Beyond." In R. Bush, ed., *The New Black Vote,* pp. 13–51. San Francisco: Synthesis.

Buss, F. L. 1985. *Dignity.* Ann Arbor: University of Michigan Press.

Cain, B. E., D. R. Kiewiet, and C. Uhlaner. 1986. "The Political Impact of California's Minorities." Paper prepared for the Western Political Science Association, Eugene, Ore., March 22.

California Board of Control. 1920. *California and the Oriental: Japanese, Chinese and Hindus.* Sacramento, Calif.: State Printing Office.

Caplan, N., M. H. Choy, and J. K. Whitmore. 1992. "Indochinese Refugee Families and Academic Achievement." *Scientific American* 266, no. 2 (Feb.): 36–42.

Cariño, B. V. 1987. "The Philippines and Southeast Asia: Historical and Contemporary Linkages." In J. T. Fawcett and B. V. Cariño, eds., *Pacific Bridges,* pp. 305–25.

Catapusan, B. 1934. "The Filipino Occupational and Recreational Activities in Los Angeles." Ph.D. diss., University of Southern California.

———. 1940. "The Social Adjustment of Filipinos in the United States." Ph.D. diss., University of Southern California.

Chan, Sam. 1986. "Parents of Exceptional Asian Children." In M. Kitano and P. Chinn, eds., *Exceptional Asian Children and Youth,* pp. 36–53. Reston, Va.: Council for Exceptional Children.

Chan, Sucheng. 1986. *Bittersweet Soil.* Berkeley: University of California Press.

———. 1990. "Strangers from a Different Shore as History and Historiography." *Amerasia Journal* 16, no. 2: 81–100.

———. 1991a. *Asian Americans: An Interpretive History.* Boston: Twayne.

———. 1991b. "The Exclusion of Chinese Women, 1870–1943." In S. Chan, ed., *Entry Denied: Exclusion and the Chinese Community in America, 1882–1943,* 94–146. Philadelphia: Temple University Press.

Chan, W. 1986. "Media Stereotyping and the Rise in Anti-Asian Violence." From the proceedings of Break the Silence—A Conference on Anti-Asian Violence, May 10. Berkeley, Calif.

Chatters, B. 1966. *Modern Japan—A Short History.*

Chen, J. 1980. *The Chinese of America.* San Francisco: Harper and Row.

Cheng, J. 1984. *Hong Kong: In Search of a Future.* Hong Kong: Oxford University Press.

Cheng, L., and E. Bonacich, eds. 1984. *Labor Immigration Under Capitalism:*

*Asian Workers in the United States Before World War II.* Berkeley: University of California Press.

Chinese for Affirmative Action. 1989. "The Broken Ladder '89." San Francisco: Chinese for Affirmative Action.

Chinn, P., and Plata, M. 1986. "Perspectives and Educational Implications of Southeast Asian Students." In M. Kitano and P. Chinn, eds., *Exceptional Asian Children and Youth*, pp. 12–28. Reston, Va.: Council for Exceptional Children.

Chinn, T., H. Lai, and P. Choy. 1969. *A History of the Chinese in California: A Syllabus.* San Francisco: Chinese Historical Society.

Chiswick, B. 1978. "The Effects of Americanization on the Earnings of Foreign-Born Men." *Journal of Political Economy* 86: 897–921.

———. 1980. "Immigrant Earnings: Patterns by Sex, Race, and Ethnic Grouping." *Monthly Labor Review* 22 (Oct.): 22–25.

———. 1982. "The Economic Progress of Immigrants: Some Apparently Universal Patterns." In B. Chiswick, ed., *The Gateway: U.S. Immigration Issues and Policies*, pp. 119–58. Washington, D.C.: American Institute for Public Policy Research.

Choy, B. 1979. *Koreans in America.* Chicago: Nelson Hall.

Chuman, D. 1976. "Little Tokyo." *Civil Rights Digest* 9, no. 1 (Fall): 36–38.

Chuman, F. 1976. *The Bamboo People: The Law and Japanese-Americans.* Del Mar, Calif.: Publisher's Inc.

Clark, P. F. 1980. "Those Other Camps: An Oral History Analysis of Japanese Alien Enemy Internment During World War II." Master's thesis, California State University, Fullerton.

Clifford, B. 1976. "The Hawaiian Sugar Planters Association and Filipino Exclusion." In *Letters in Exile: An Introductory Reader on the History of Filipinos in America.* Los Angeles: UCLA Asian American Studies Center.

Coates, A. 1978. *Macao Narrative.* Hong Kong: Heinemann.

Cohen, A., ed. 1974. *Urban Ethnicity.* London: Tavistock.

Cohen, L. M., and M. A. Grossnickle. 1983. *Immigrants and Refugees in a Changing Nation.* Washington, D.C.: Catholic University of America, Dept. of Anthropology.

Cole, D. 1990. "McCarran-Walter." *Constitution* 2, no. 1 (Winter): 51–59.

Commission on Minority Participation in Education and American Life. 1988. "One-Third of a Nation." Washington, D.C.: American Council on Education.

Conwell, R. H. 1871. *Why and How.* Boston: Lee and Shephard.

Coolidge, M. 1909. *Chinese Immigration.* New York: Arno Press.

Coro Foundation Public Affairs Leadership Training Program. 1985. "Refugee Assistance Programs and the Refugee Communities: Case Study." San Francisco: Coro Foundation.

Crow, C. 1913. "What About the Filipinos?" *World's Work* (Sept.).

Dahl, R. 1961. *Who Governs?* New Haven, Conn.: Yale University Press.

Dandekar, V. M. 1968. "India." In W. Adams, ed., *The Brain Drain.* New York: Macmillan.

Daniels, R. 1962. *The Politics of Prejudice.* Berkeley: University of California Press.

———. 1981. *Concentration Camps: North America.* Malabar, Fla.: R. E. Krieger.

———. 1988. *Asian America.* Seattle: University of Washington Press.

Danigelis, N. L. 1982. "Race, Class and Political Involvement in the U.S." *Social Forces* 61, no. 2: 532–50.

Davidson, C. 1985. *Naturalization Rates of Vietnamese and Kampuchean Refugees.* Washington, D.C.: Immigration and Naturalization Service Statistical Branch.

De la Garza, R., and J. Weaver. 1984. *The Mexican American Electorate: An Explanation of Their Opinions and Behavior.* Austin: Center for Mexican American Studies, University of Texas.

Desbarats, J., and L. Holland. 1983. "Indochinese Settlement Patterns in Orange County." *Amerasia Journal* 10 (Spring/Summer): 23–24.

De Witt, H. A. 1976. *Anti-Filipino Movements in California: A History, Bibliography, and Study Guide.* San Francisco: R&E Research Associates.

———. 1978. "The Filipino Labor Union: The Salinas Lettuce Strike of 1934." *Amerasia Journal* 5, no. 2: 1–22.

Din, G. 1984. "An Analysis of Asian/Pacific American Registration and Voting Patterns in San Francisco." Master's thesis, Claremont Graduate School, Los Angeles.

Divoky, D. 1988. "The Model Minority Goes to School." *Phi Delta Kappan* (Nov.): 219–22.

Dolly, J., D. Blaine, and K. Power. 1988. "Performance of Educationally-at-risk Pacific and Asian Students in a Traditional Academic Program." Paper presented at the annual meeting of the American Educational Research Association, New Orleans, Apr. 5–9.

Dong, N. 1974. "The Chinese and the Anti-Chinese Movement: The Judicial Response in California, 1850–1886." Seminar paper, Yale Law School.

Dornbusch, S. M., B. L. Prescott, and P. L. Ritter. 1987a. "The Relation of High School Academic Performance and Student Effort to Language Use and Recency of Migration Among Asian and Pacific Americans." Paper presented to the annual meeting of the American Educational Research Association. Washington, D.C., Apr. 20–24.

Dornbusch, S. M., P. L. Ritter, P. H. Leidermann, D. F. Roberts, and M. Fraleigh. 1987b. "The Relation of Parenting Style to Adolescent School Performance." *Child Development* 58: 1244–57.

Dutta, M. 1982. "Asian Indian Americans: Search for an Economic Profile." In S. Chandrasekhar, ed., *From India to America,* pp. 76–85. La Jolla, Calif.: Population Review Books.

Dworkin, A. G., and R. J. Dworkin. 1982. *The Minority Report.* New York: Holt, Rinehart and Winston.

Enloe, C. 1981. "The Growth of the State and Ethnic Mobilization: The American Experience." *Ethnic and Racial Studies* 4 (Apr.): 123–36.

Erikson, E. H. 1968. *Identity: Youth and Crisis.* New York: Norton.

Esman, M. H., ed. 1977. *Ethnic Conflict in the Western World.* Ithaca, N.Y.: Cornell University Press.

Espina, M. 1988. *Filipinos in Louisiana.* New Orleans: A. F. Laborde.

Esthus, R. 1969. *Theodore Roosevelt and Japan.* Seattle: University of Washington Press.

*The Europa World Year Book.* London: Europa.

Fairbank, J. K., and E. Reischauer. 1973. *East Asia: Tradition and Transformation.* Boston: Houghton Mifflin.

Fawcett, J. T., and B. V. Cariño, eds. 1987. *Pacific Bridges.* Staten Island, N.Y.: Center for Migration Studies.

First, J. M. 1988. *New Voices: Immigrant Students in U.S. Public Schools.* Boston: National Coalition of Advocates for Students.

Flexner, J. T. 1974. *Washington: The Indispensable Man.* Boston: Little, Brown.

Forbes, S. 1984. "Residency Patterns and Secondary Migration of Refugees." Washington, D.C.: Refugee Policy Group.

Fuchs, L. 1968. *American Ethnic Politics.* New York: Harper & Row.

———. 1983. "Directions for U.S. Immigration Policy: Immigration Policy and the Rule of Law." *University of Pittsburgh Law Review* 44 (Winter): 443–46.

Fujitomi, I., and D. Wong. 1973. "The New Asian-American Woman." In S. Sue and N. Wagner, eds., *Asian-Americans: Psychological Perspectives,* pp. 252–63. Ben Lomond, Calif.: Science and Behavior Books.

Gallagher, D., S. Forbes, and P. W. Fagen. 1985. *Of Special Humanitarian Concern: U.S. Refugee Admissions Since Passage of the Refugee Act.* Washington, D.C.: Refugee Policy Group.

Gans, H. J. 1962. *The Urban Villagers: Groups and Class in the Lives of Italian Americans.* New York: Free Press.

Garcia, J. A. 1987. "The Political Integration of Mexican Immigrants: Examining Some Political Orientations." *International Migration Review* 21, no. 2: 372–89.

Gardner, R., B. Robey, and P. Smith. 1985. "Asian Americans: Growth, Change, and Diversity." *Population Bulletin* 40, no. 4 (Oct.).

Glenn, E. N. 1986. *Issei, Nisei, War Bride.* Philadelphia: Temple University Press.

Gonzales, J. 1986. "Asian Indian Immigration Patterns: The Origins of the Sikh Community in California." *International Migration Review* 20, no. 1 (Spring): 40–54.

Gordon, C. 1943. "Our Wall of Exclusion Against China." *Lawyers Guild Review* (aka *National Lawyers Guild Practitioner*) 3, no. 6: 7–19.

Gordon, C., and S. Mailman. 1991. *Immigration Law and Procedure.* New York: Matthew Bender.

Gordon, L. 1987. "Southeast Asian Refugee Migration to the United States." In J. T. Fawcett and B. V. Cariño, eds., *Pacific Bridges,* pp. 153–73.

Gordon, M. 1961. "Assimilation in America: Theory and Reality." *Daedalus* 90 (Spring): 263–85.

Greene, D. 1987. "Asian-Americans Find U.S. Colleges Insensitive, Form Campus Organizations to Fight Bias." *Chronicle of Higher Education* (Nov. 18): 1, A38–39.

Guterbock, T. M., and B. London. 1983. "Race, Political Orientation, and Participation: An Empirical Test of Four Competing Theories." *American Sociological Review* 48, no. 4 (Aug.): 439–53.

Guzman, R. 1975. *The Political Socialization of the Mexican American People.* Ann Arbor, Mich.: University Microfilms.

Hall, J. 1970. *Japan.* New York: Delacorte Press.

Hartman, S. 1978. "San Francisco's International Hotel: Case Study of a Turf Struggle." *Radical America* 12, no. 3 (May–June): 47–58.

Hata, D. 1977. *Japanese in America Prior to 1893.* Ann Arbor, Mich.: University Microfilms.

Haycock, K., and Navarro, M. S. 1988. *Unfinished Business—Fulfilling Our Children's Promise.* Oakland, Calif.: Achievement Council.

Heizer, R., and A. Almquist. 1971. *The Other Californians.* Berkeley and Los Angeles: University of California Press.

Helton, A. 1983–84. "Political Asylum Under the 1980 Refugee Act: An Unfulfilled Promise." *University of Michigan Journal of Law Reform* 17: 243–64.

Hemp, M. K. 1986. *Cannery Row: History of Old Oceanview Avenue.* Monterey, Calif.: History Company.

Hess, G. 1976. "The Forgotten Asian Americans: The East Indian Community in the United States." In E. Gee, ed., *Counterpoint: Perspectives on Asian Americans,* pp. 413–22. Los Angeles: UCLA Asian American Studies Center.

———. 1986. "The Asian Indian Immigrants in the U.S.: The Early Phase, 1900–1965." In S. Chandrasekhar, ed., *From India to America,* pp. 29–34. La Jolla, Calif.: Population Review Books.

Higham, J. 1963. *Strangers in the Land.* New Brunswick, N.J.: Rutgers University Press.

Hing, B. 1979. "An Overview of Federal Immigration Policies and Their Effects on Asian and Pacific Americans." *Civil Rights Issues of Asian and Pacific Americans: Myths and Realities.* U.S. Commission on Civil Rights.

———. 1983. "Racial Disparity: The Unaddressed Issues of the Simpson-Mazzoli Bill." *La Raza Law Journal* 1, no. 1 (Spring): 21–52.

———. 1985 [1992 supp.]. *Handling Immigration Cases.* New York: Wiley.

Hirschman, C., and M. G. Wong. 1981. "Trends in Socioeconomic Achievement Among Immigrant and Native-Born Asian-Americans, 1960–1976." *Sociological Quarterly* 22 (Autumn): 495–513.

———. 1981. "Trends in Socioeconomic Achievement Among Immigrant and Native-Born Asian Americans, 1960–1976." *Sociological Quarterly* 22, no. 4 (Autumn): 495–513.

———. 1986. "The Extraordinary Educational Attainment of Asian-Americans: A Search for Historical Evidence and Explanations." *Social Forces* 65 (Sept.): 1–27.

Hong Kong Census and Statistics Department. 1972. *Hong Kong Population and Housing Census.* Hong Kong.

———. *Hong Kong Social and Economic Trends 1968–1972.* Hong Kong.

Horowitz, D. 1975. "Ethnic Identity." In N. Glazer and D. Moynihan, eds., *Ethnicity*, pp. 111–40. Cambridge, Mass.: Harvard University Press.

Hosokawa, B. 1969. *Nisei, the Quiet Americans.* New York: William Morrow.

Houchins, L., and C. Houchins. 1974. "The Korean Experience in America, 1903–1924." *Pacific Historical Review* 43, no. 4 (Nov.): 548–75.

Hoyt, E. 1974. *Asians in the West.* New York: Thomas Nelson.

Hsia, J. 1987. "Asian Americans Fight the Myth of the Super Student." *Educational Record* 68, no. 4 (Fall): 94–97.

Hsu, I. 1970. *The Rise of Modern China.* New York: Oxford University Press.

Hune, S. 1989. "Opening the American Mind and Body." *Change* (Nov./Dec.): 56–63.

Hutchinson, E. 1981. *Legislative History of American Immigration Policy 1798–1965.* Philadelphia: University of Pennsylvania Press.

Ichihashi, Y. 1915. *Japanese Immigration: Its Status in California.* San Francisco: Marshall Press.

———. 1932. *Japanese in the United States.* Stanford, Calif.: Stanford University Press.

Ichioka, Y. 1988. *The Issei.* New York: Free Press.

Inui. 1926. "The Gentlemen's Agreement: How It Has Functioned." *Japanese Exclusion Act.* 42 Pamphlets 1913–27. Widener Library Collection, Harvard University.

Irons, P. 1983. *Justice at War.* New York: Oxford University Press.

Isaacs, H. 1958. *Scratches on Our Minds.* New York: J. Day.

———. 1972. *Images of Asia: American Views of China and India.* New York: Harper and Row.

Jansen, M. B. 1968. "Modernization and Foreign Policy in Meiji Japan." In R. E. Ward, ed., *Political Development in Modern Japan*, pp. 149–88. Princeton, N.J.: Princeton University Press.

Jensen, J. 1988. *Passage From India.* New Haven, Conn.: Yale University Press.

Jensen, J. M. 1969. "Apartheid: Pacific Coast Style." *Pacific Historical Review* 38: 335–40.

Jo, M. H. 1984. "The Putative Political Complacency of Asian Americans." *Political Psychology* 5, no. 4: 583–605.

Joint Committee on Refugee Resettlement and Immigration. 1983–84. *Annual Report.* Sacramento: California Legislature.

Kallen, H. M. 1915. "Democracy Versus the Melting Pot." *The Nation* (Feb. 18–25): 190–94.

——. 1924. *Culture and Democracy in the United States.* New York: Boni and Liveright.

Kawakami, K. 1921. *What Japan Thinks.* New York: Macmillan.

Keely, C. B. 1971. "Effects of the Immigration Act of 1965 on Selected Population Characteristics of Immigrants to the United States." *Demography* 8, no. 2 (May): 157–69.

——. 1974. "The Demographic Effects of Immigration Legislation and Procedures." *Interpreter Releases* 51 (Apr. 8): 89–93.

——. 1975. "Effects of U.S. Immigration Law on Manpower Characteristics of Immigrants." *Demography* 12, no. 2 (May): 179–91.

Kellogg, J. 1988. "Forces of Change." *Phi Delta Kappan* (Nov.): 199–204.

Kelly, G. P. 1977. *From Vietnam to America: A Chronicle of the Vietnamese Immigration to the United States.* Boulder, Colo.: Westview Press.

Kennedy, E. 1966. "The Immigration Act of 1965." *Annals of the American Academy* 367: 137–49.

Kennedy, J. F. 1964. *Nation of Immigrants.* New York: Harper and Row.

Kihl, Y. W. 1984. *Politics and Policies in Divided Korea: Regimes in Contest.* Boulder, Colo.: Westview Press.

Kim, B. 1978. *The Asian Americans: Changing Patterns, Changing Needs.* Nashville, Tenn.: Association of Korean Christian Scholars.

Kim, B. C. 1976. "Korean Americans." *Civil Rights Digest* 9 (Fall): 40: 39–41.

Kim, H. 1974. "Some Aspects of Social Demography of Korean Americans." *International Migration Review* 8, no. 1 (Spring): 23–42.

Kim, I. 1981. *Urban Immigrants: The Korean Community in New York.* Princeton, N.J.: Princeton University Press.

——. 1987. "The Koreans: Small Business in an Urban Frontier." In N. Foner, ed., *New Immigrants in New York.* New York: Columbia University Press.

Kim, W. Y. 1971. *Koreans in America.* Seoul: Po Chin Chai.

Kimura, Y. 1988. *Issei.* Honolulu: University of Hawaii Press.

Kinkead, G. 1992. *Chinatown.* New York: Harper Collins.

Kitano, H. 1969. *Japanese Americans: The Evolution of a Subculture.* Englewood Cliffs, N.J.: Prentice Hall.

——. 1974. "Japanese Americans: The Development of a Middleman Minority." *Pacific Historical Review* 43, no. 4 (Nov.): 500–519.

Kitano, H., and R. Daniels. 1988. *Asian Americans: Emerging Minorities.* Englewood Cliffs, N.J.: Prentice Hall.

Knoll, T. 1982. *Becoming Americans: Asian Sojourners, Immigrants and Refugees in the Western United States.* Portland, Ore.: Coast to Coast Books.

Konvitz, M. 1946. *The Alien and the Asiatic in American Law.* Ithaca, N.Y.: Cornell University Press.

Kwong, P. 1987. *The New Chinatown.* New York: Hill and Wang.

La Brack, B., and K. Leonard. 1984. "Conflict and Compatibility in Punjabi-Mexican Immigrant Marriages in Rural California, 1915–1965." *Journal of Marriage and the Family* 46: 527–37.

Lai, H. M., G. Lim, and J. Yung, eds. 1980. *Island: Poetry and History of Chinese Immigrants on Angel Island 1910–1940.* San Francisco: Hoi Poi.

Landa, J. 1978. "The Economics of the Ethnically Homogeneous Middleman Group: A Property Rights Public Choice Approach." Ph.D. diss., Virginia Institute and State University.

Lasker, B. 1931. *Filipino Migration to the Continental United States and Hawaii.* Chicago: University of Chicago Press.

Laufman, D. H. 1986. "Political Bias in United States Refugee Policy Since the Refugee Act of 1980." *Georgetown Immigration Law Journal* 1, no. 3: 495–580.

Lee, R. H. 1960. *The Chinese in the United States of America.* Hong Kong: Hong Kong University Press.

Lee, E. S., and X. Rong. 1988. "The Educational and Economic Achievement of Asian-Americans." *Elementary School Journal* 88, no. 5 (May): 545–60.

Leibowitz, A. 1983. *Immigration and Refugee Policy.* New York: Matthew Bender.

Leonard, K. 1986. "Marriage and Family Life Among Early Asian Indian Immigrants." In S. Chandrasekhar, ed., *From India to America*, pp. 67–75. La Jolla, Calif.: Population Review Books.

Li, W. L. 1982. "Chinese Americans: Exclusion from the Melting Pot." In A. G. Dworkin and R. J. Dworkin, eds., *The Minority Report*, pp. 303–28.

Li, T. 1987. *Congressional Policy of California Immigration.* New York: Arno Press.

Little Tokyo Anti-Eviction Task Force. 1976. "Redevelopment in Los Angeles' Little Tokyo." In E. Gee, ed., *Counterpoint*, pp. 327–33. Los Angeles: UCLA Asian American Studies Center.

Liu, W. T., M. Lamanna, and A. Murata. 1979. *Transition to Nowhere: Vietnam Refugees in America.* Nashville, Tenn.: Charter House.

López, G. P. 1981. "Undocumented Mexican Migration: In Search of a Just Immigration Law and Policy." *UCLA Law Review* 28, no. 4 (Apr.): 641–72.

Lovrich, N. P., and O. Marenin. 1976. "A Comparison of Black and Mexican American Voters in Denver: Assertive Versus Acquiescent Political Orientations and Voting Behavior in an Urban Electorate." *Western Political Quarterly* 29 (June): 284–94.

Lowenstein, E. 1960. "Chinese Confession Program of the Immigration and Naturalization Service." *Interpreter Releases* 37, no. 2 (Jan. 15): 6–10.

Lyman, S. M. 1974. *Chinese Americans*. New York: Random House.

——, ed. 1977. *The Asian in North America*. Santa Barbara, Calif.: Clio Books.

——. 1970. *The Asian in the West*. Reno: Western Studies Center, University of Nevada.

McAdams, D. 1982. *Political Process and the Development of Black Insurgency 1930–1970*. Chicago: University of Chicago Press.

McClain, C. 1984. "The Chinese Struggle for Civil Rights in Nineteenth Century America: The First Phase, 1850–1870." *California Law Review* 72: 529–31.

McGovney, J. 1947. "The Anti-Japanese Land Laws of California and Ten Other States." *California Law Review* 35: 7.

McLeod, B. 1986. "The Oriental Express." *Psychology Today* 20, no. 7 (July): 48–52.

Mangiafico, L. 1988. *Contemporary American Immigrants*. New York: Praeger.

Manning, W., and W. O'Hare. 1988. "The Best Metros for Asian-American Businesses." *American Demographics* 10, no. 8 (Aug.): 35–36.

Mar, D. 1985. "Chinese Immigrants and the Ethnic Labor Market." Unpublished diss., Dept. of Economics, University of California, Berkeley.

Marsh, R. 1980. "Socioeconomic Status of Indochinese Refugees in the United States: Progress and Problems." *Social Security Bulletin* 43, no. 10: 11–20.

Massey, T. 1986. "The Wrong Way to Court Ethnics." *Washington Monthly* (May): 21–26.

Matthews, D. R., and J. W. Prothro. 1966. *Negroes and the New Southern Politics*. New York: Harcourt, Brace & World.

Maykovich, M. K. 1972. *Japanese American Identity Dilemma*. Tokyo: Waseda University.

Meinhardt, K., S. Tom, P. Tse, and C. Y. Yu. 1984. *Asian Health Assessment Project*. San Jose, Calif.: Santa Clara County Health Department.

Melendy, H. B. 1972. *The Oriental Americans*. New York: Hippocrene Books.

——. 1974. "Filipinos in the United States." *Pacific Historical Review* 43: 526–27.

——. 1977. *Asians in America: Filipinos, Koreans, and East Indians*. Boston: Twayne.

Miller, A. H. 1981. "Group Consciousness and Political Participation." *American Journal of Political Science* 25, no. 3 (Aug.): 494–511.

Miller, P. L. 1982. "The Impact of Organizational Activity on Black Political Participation." *Social Science Quarterly* 62: 83–98.

Miller, S. 1969. *The Unwelcome Immigrant*. Berkeley: University of California Press.

Min, P. G. 1984. "From White-Collar Occupations to Small Business: Korean Immigrants' Occupational Adjustment." *Sociological Quarterly* 25: 333–52.

Minocha, U. 1987. "South Asian Immigrants: Trends and Impacts on the Sending and Receiving Societies," pp. 347–73. In J. T. Fawcett and B. V. Cariño, eds., *Pacific Bridges*, pp. 347–73.

Mirandé, A. 1987. *Gringo Justice*. Notre Dame, Ind.: University of Notre Dame Press.

Miyamoto, F. 1939. *Social Solidarity Among the Japanese in Seattle*. Seattle: University of Washington.

Mizokawa, D., and D. Ryckman. 1988. "Attributions of Academic Success and Failure to Effort or Ability: A Comparison of Six Asian American Ethnic Groups." Paper presented at the American Educational Research Association annual meeting, New Orleans, Apr.

Montero, D. 1979. *Vietnamese Americans: Patterns of Resettlement and Socio-economic Adaptation in the United States*. Boulder, Colo.: Westview Press.

Montero, D., and R. Tsukashima. 1977. "Assimilation and Educational Achievement: The Case of the Second Generation Japanese-American." *Sociological Quarterly* 18 (Autumn): 490–503.

Moon, C. 1986. "Year of Immigration and Socioeconomic Status: Comparative Study of Three Asian Populations in California." *Social Indicators Research* 18: no. 2 (May): 129–52.

Mooney, R. J. 1984. "Matthew Keady and the Federal Judicial Response to Racism in the Early West." *Oregon Law Review* 63: 561–637.

Morales, R. F. 1976. "Pilipino Americans." *Civil Rights Digest* 9, no. 1 (Fall): 30–32.

Mordkowitz, E., and H. Ginsburg. 1986. "The Academic Socialization of Successful Asian-American College Students." Paper presented at the Annual Meeting of the American Educational Research Association, ERIC no. 273 219, San Francisco, Apr. 20.

Morris, M. 1975. *The Politics of Black America*. New York: Harper & Row.

Nagel, J. 1984. "The Ethnic Revolution: The Emergence of Ethnic Nationalism in Modern States." *Sociology and Social Research* 68, no. 4 (July): 417–34.

———. 1982. "The Political Mobilization of Native Americans." *Social Science Journal* 19, no. 3 (July): 37–45.

Nagel, J., and S. Olzak. 1982. "Ethnic Mobilization in New and Old States: An Extension of the Competition Model." *Social Problems* 30, no. 2 (Dec.): 127–43.

Nakanishi, D. 1989. "A Quota on Excellence? The Asian American Admissions Debate." *Change* (Nov./Dec.): 39–47.

———. 1986. *The UCLA Asian Pacific American Voter Registration Study*. Report sponsored by the Asian Pacific American Legal Center of Los Angeles, UCLA Graduate School of Education.

———. 1985–86. "Asian American Politics: An Agenda for Research." *Amerasia Journal* 12, no. 2: 1–27.

National Coalition of Advocates for Students. 1988. "New Voices—Immigrant Students in U.S. Public Schools." Boston: National Coalition of Advocates for Students Research and Policy Report.

National Lawyers Guild. 1980. *Immigration Law and Defense.* New York: C. Boardman.

Nee, V., and B. Nee. 1973. *Longtime Californ': A Documentary Study of an American Chinatown.* New York: Pantheon Press.

Ng, W. 1977. "An Evaluation of the Labor Market Status of Chinese Americans." *Amerasia Journal* 4, no. 2: 101–22.

Nhu, T. T. 1976. "The Trauma of Exile: Vietnamese Refugees." *Civil Rights Digest* 9, no. 1 (Fall): 59–62.

Okimoto, D. I. 1971. *Americans in Disguise.* New York: Weatherhill.

Olsen, L. 1988. *Crossing the Schoolhouse Border: Immigrant Students and the California Public Schools.* San Francisco: California Tomorrow.

Olsen, M. E. 1970. "Social and Political Participation of Blacks." *American Sociological Review* 35, no. 4: 682–97.

Omi, M., and H. Winant. 1986. *Racial Formation in the United States From the 1960's to the 1980's.* New York: Routledge and Kegan Paul.

Orum, A. M. 1966. "A Reappraisal of the Social and Political Participation of Negroes." *American Journal of Sociology* 72 (July): 32–46.

Otsuka, S. 1969. "Japan's Early Encounter with the Concept of the Law of Nations." *Japanese Annual of Immigration Law* 13: 35.

Parenti, M. 1967. "Ethnic Politics and the Persistence of Ethnic Identification." *American Political Science Review* 61, no. 3: 717–26.

Parillo, V. 1982. "Asian Americans in American Politics." In J. Roucek and B. Eisenberg, eds., *America's Ethnic Politics,* 89–112. Westport, Conn.: Greenwood Press.

Passel, J. S., and K. A. Woodrow. 1984. "Geographic Distribution of Undocumented Immigrants: Estimates of Undocumented Aliens Counted in the 1980 Census by State." *International Migration Review* 18, no.3 (Fall): 642–71.

Patterson, J. T. 1983. *America in the Twentieth Century.* New York: Knopf.

Patterson, W. 1988. *The Korean Frontier in America.* Honolulu: University of Hawaii Press.

Paul, R. 1978. "The Abrogation of the Gentlemen's Agreement." In R. Daniels, ed., *Three Short Works on Japanese Americans,* part 3: 1–117. New York: Arno Press.

Peffer, G. A. 1986. "Forbidden Families: Emigration Experiences of Chinese Women Under the Page Law, 1875–1882." *Journal of American Ethnic History* 6: 28–46.

Pei, C. H. 1987. "Research Report." Study funded by the United Chinese Restaurants Association (Dec.).

Peng, S. S. 1988. "Attainment Status of Asian Americans in Higher Education." Paper presented at the Conference of the National Association for Asian and Pacific American Education, Denver, Apr. 7–9.

Penrose, E. R. 1973. *California Nativism: Organized Opposition to the Japanese 1890–1913.* San Francisco: R&E Research Associates.

Petersen, W. 1971. *Japanese Americans.* New York: Random House.

Piore, M. 1979. *Birds of Passage, Migrant Labor and Industrial Societies.* Cambridge, Eng.: Cambridge University Press.

Piven, F., and R. Cloward. 1988. *Why Americans Don't Vote.* New York: Pantheon Books.

———. 1977. *Poor People's Movements: Why They Succeed, How They Fail.* New York: Pantheon Books.

Portes, A., and R. Bach. 1985. *Latin Journey: Cuban and Mexican Immigrants in the United States.* Berkeley: University of California Press.

Portes, A., and R. Mozo. 1985. "The Political Adaptation Process of Cubans and Other Ethnic Minorities in the United States: A Preliminary Analysis." *International Migration Review* 19, no. 1 (Spring): 35–61.

Powell, T. R. 1924. "Alien Land Law Cases in the United States Supreme Court." *California Law Review* 12, no. 4: 259–82.

Preston, M., L. Henderson, Jr., and P. Puryear, eds. 1987. *The New Black Politics: The Search For Political Power.* New York: Longman.

Reimers, D. 1982. "Recent Immigration Policy: An Analysis." In B. Chiswick, ed., *The Gateway: U.S. Immigration Issues and Policies*, pp. 13–53. Washington, D.C.: American Enterprise Institute for Public Policy Research.

Reischauer, H. 1986. *Samurai and Silk.* Cambridge, Mass.: Belknap Press of Harvard University.

Ringer, B. 1983. *"We the People" and Others.* London: Tavistock.

Rosen, B. 1959. "Race, Ethnicity, and the Achievement Syndrome." *American Sociological Review* 24: 47–70.

Roucek, J. S., and B. Eisenberg. 1982. *America's Ethnic Politics.* Westport, Conn.: Greenwood Press.

Rumbaut, R., and K. Ima. 1987. *The Adaptation of Southeast Asian Refugee Youth: A Comparative Study.* Final report to the Office of Refugee Resettlement. San Diego, Calif.: San Diego State University, Dept. of Sociology.

St. Cartmail, K. 1983. *Exodus Indochina.* Auckland, New Zealand: Heineman.

Salyer, L. 1989. "Captives of Law: Judicial Enforcement of the Chinese Exclusion Laws, 1891–1905." *Journal of American History* 76, no. 1 (June): 91–117.

Sandmeyer, E. 1939. *The Anti-Chinese Movement in California.* Urbana: University of Illinois Press.

Saran, P. 1985. *The Asian Indian Experience in the United States.* Cambridge, Mass.: Schenkman.

Saxton, A. 1971. *The Indispensable Enemy.* Berkeley: University of California Press.

Schoenman, T., ed. 1979. *The Father of California Wine—Agoston Haraszthy.* Santa Barbara, Calif.: Capra Press.

Schwartz, A. 1968. *The Open Society.* New York: William Morrow.

Scully, T. J. 1966. "Is the Door Open Again? A Survey of Our New Immigration Law." *UCLA Law Review* 13: 227–49.

Select Commission on Immigration and Refugee Policy. 1981. *U.S. Immigration Policy and the National Interest.* Washington, D.C.: Government Printing Office.

Sherman, S. 1986. "When Cultures Collide." *California Lawyer* 6, no. 1 (Jan.): 32–36, 60.

Shingles, R. D. 1981. "Black Consciousness and Political Participation: The Missing Link." *American Political Science Review* 75, no. 1: 76–91.

Shin, L. 1971. "Koreans in America: 1903–1945." In A. Tachiki, E. Wong, F. Odo, and B. Wong, eds., *Roots: An Asian American Reader,* pp. 200–206. Los Angeles: Continental Graphics.

Smith, P. 1976. "The Social Demography of Filipino Migrations Abroad." *International Migration Review* 10, no. 3 (Fall): 307–53.

Smith, S. 1988. *The Power Game.* New York: Random House.

Song, A. 1966. "Politics and Policies of the Oriental Community." In E. P. Dvorin and A. J. Misner, eds., *California Politics and Policies,* 387–411. Reading, Mass.: Addison-Wesley.

Sowell, T. 1981. *Ethnic America: A History.* New York: Basic Books.

Statistical Office of the United Nations. 1971. *1970 Demographic Yearbook.* New York: Dept. of Economic and Social Affairs, United Nations.

Steinberg, D. 1982. *The Philippines: A Singular and a Plural Place.* Boulder, Colo.: Westview Press.

Steinberg, S. 1989. *The Ethnic Myth: Race, Ethnicity, and Class in America.* New York: Atheneum.

Steiner, J. 1917. *The Japanese Invasion.* Chicago: McClurg.

Stevenson, H. 1987. "The Asian Advantage: The Case of Mathematics." *American Educator* (Summer): 26–47.

Strand, P. J., and W. Jones, Jr. 1985. *Indochinese Refugees in America: Problems of Adaptation and Assimilation.* Durham, N.C.: Duke University Press.

Strong, E. 1933. *Vocational Aptitudes of Second-Generation Japanese in the United States.* Stanford, Calif.: Stanford University Press.

Sue, D. 1973. "Ethnic Identity: The Impact of Two Cultures on the Psychological Development of Asians in America." In S. Sue and N. Wagner, eds., *Asian-Americans: Psychological Perspectives,* pp. 140–49. Ben Lomond, Calif.: Science and Behavior Books.

Sue, S., and D. Sue. 1973. "Chinese-American Personality and Mental Health." In S. Sue and N. Wagner, eds., *Asian-Americans: Psychological Perspectives,* pp. 111–24.

Sue, S., and N. Zane. 1985. "Academic Achievement and Socioemotional Adjustment Among Chinese University Students." *Journal of Counseling Psychology* 32, no. 4 (Oct.): 570–79.

Sung, B. L. 1967. *Mountain of Gold: The Story of the Chinese in America.* New York: Macmillan.

———. 1972. *The Chinese in America.* New York: Macmillan.

———. 1976. *A Survey of Chinese-American Manpower and Employment.* New York: Praeger.

———. 1978. *Statistical Profile of the Chinese in the United States: 1970 Census.* New York: Arno Press.

———. 1979. *Transplanted Chinese Children.* Washington, D.C.: U.S. Dept. of Health, Education and Welfare.

———. 1980. "Polarity in the Makeup of Chinese Immigrants." In R. Bryce-LaPorte, ed., *Sourcebook on the New Immigration,* pp. 37–49.

Surh, J. 1973–74. "Asian American Identity and Politics." *Amerasia Journal* 2: 158–71.

Tachibana, J. 1986. "California's Asians: Power from a Growing Population." *California Journal* (Nov.): 535–43.

Tachiki, A., E. Wong, F. Odo, and B. Wong, eds. 1971. *Roots: An Asian American Reader.* Los Angeles: Continental Graphics.

Takahashi, J. H. 1980. "Changing Responses to Racial Subordination: An Exploratory Study of Japanese American Political Styles." Ph.D. diss., Dept. of Sociology, University of California, Berkeley.

Takaki, R. 1987. "Asian Immigrant Women 1850–1940." *Chinese Historical Society* (Sept. 18).

———. 1989. *Strangers from a Different Shore.* Boston: Little, Brown.

Tambs-Lyche, H. 1980. *London Patidars.* London: Routledge and Kegan Paul.

Tewari, S. C. 1977. *Indo-U.S. Relations: 1947–1976.* New Delhi, India: Radiant.

Thernstrom, S., ed. 1980. *Harvard Encyclopedia of American Ethnic Groups.* Cambridge, Mass.: Belknap Press of Harvard University.

Thompson, J., P. Stanley, and J. Perry. 1981. *Sentimental Imperialists.* New York: Harper and Row.

Thompson, R. 1978. *The Yellow Peril 1890–1924.* New York: Arno Press.

Todaro, M. P. 1985. *Economic Development in the Third World.* New York: Longman.

Tong, B. 1971. "Ghetto of the Mind: Notes on the Historical Psychology of Chinese Americans." *Amerasia Journal* 1, no. 3: 1–31.

———. 1973–74. "A Living Death Defended as the Legacy of a Superior Culture." *Amerasia Journal:* 2, 186–87.

Totti, X. 1987. "The Making of a Latino Ethnic Identity." *Dissent* 34, no. 1 (Fall): 537–42.

Tsai, F. W. 1980. "Diversity and Conflict Between Old and New Chinese

Immigrants in the United States." In R. Bryce-LaPorte, ed., *Sourcebook on the New Immigration*, pp. 329–37.

Tsai, S. H. 1986. *The Chinese Experience in America*. Bloomington: Indiana University Press.

Tsuang, G. W. 1989. "Assuring Equal Access of Asian Americans to Highly Selective Universities." *Yale Law Journal* 98: 659–78.

Uhlaner, C., B. E. Cain, and D. R. Kiewiet. 1989. "Political Participation of Ethnic Minorities in the 1980's." *Political Behavior* 11, no. 3 (Sept.): 195–231.

United Nations. 1983. *International Migration: Policies and Programs*. New York: United Nations.

U.S. Commission on Civil Rights. 1992. *Civil Rights Issues Facing Asian Americans in the 1990's* (Feb.).

———. 1979. *Civil Rights Issues of Asian and Pacific Americans: Myths and Realities*. Consultation sponsored by the U.S. Commission on Civil Rights (May 8–9).

———. 1986. *Recent Activities Against Citizens and Residents of Asian Descent*. Clearinghouse Publication No. 88.

U.S. Department of Commerce. 1975a. *Statistical Abstract of the United States*. Washington, D.C.: Bureau of the Census.

———. 1975b. *Historical Statistics of the United States: Colonial Times to 1970*, part 1. Washington, D.C.: Bureau of the Census.

———. 1983a. *Asian and Pacific Islander Population by State: 1980*. PC80-S1-12. Washington, D.C.: Bureau of the Census.

———. 1983b. *General Social and Economic Characteristics*. PC80-1-C1. Washington, D.C.: Bureau of the Census (Dec.).

———. 1988a. *Asian and Pacific Islander Population in the United States, 1980*. PC80-2-1E. Washington, D.C.: Bureau of the Census (Jan.).

———. 1988b. *We, the Asian and Pacific Islander Americans*. Washington, D.C.: Bureau of the Census (Sept.).

———. 1991. "Release CB91-215." *U.S. Department of Commerce News*. Washington, D.C.: Bureau of the Census (June 12).

U.S. Department of Health and Human Services. 1982. *Refugee Resettlement Program*. Report to Congress by the Social Security Administration, Office of Refugee Resettlement. Washington, D.C.: Government Printing Office.

———. 1984–87. *Refugee Resettlement Program*. Report to Congress by the Social Security Administration, Office of Refugee Resettlement. Washington, D.C.: Government Printing Office.

U.S. Department of Health, Education and Welfare. 1977. *Refugee Task Force, Report to the Congress*. Washington, D.C.: Government Printing Office (Dec. 31).

U.S. Department of State. 1975. *Indochina Refugee Resettlement Program*. Special Report no. 21. Washington, D.C.: Bureau of Public Affairs (Sept.)

U.S. Immigration Commission. 1911. *Dictionary of Races or Peoples.* Washington, D.C.: Government Printing Office.

U.S. Senate Judiciary Committee. 1985. *Report, Refugee Assistance Act of 1985.* Washington, D.C.: Government Printing Office (Apr. 30).

U.S. Treasury Department. 1903. *Immigration into the United States, 1820–1903.* Washington, D.C.: Bureau of Statistics.

Uyematsu, A. 1971. "The Emergence of Yellow Power in America." In A. Tachiki, E. Wong, F. Odo, and B. Wong, eds., *Roots: An Asian American Reader,* pp. 9–13. Los Angeles: Continental Graphics.

Verba, S., and N. Nie. 1972. *Participation in America: Political Democracy and Social Equality.* New York: Harper and Row.

Vernon, P. E. 1982. *The Abilities and Achievements of Orientals in North America.* New York: Academic Press.

Vialet, J. 1980. *A Brief History of U.S. Immigration Policy.* Washington, D.C.: Congressional Research Service, Library of Congress.

Vigil, M. 1978. *Chicano Politics.* Washington, D.C.: University Press of America.

Vreeland, N. 1976. *Area Handbook For the Philippines.* Washington, D.C.: Government Printing Office.

Wakeman, F. E. 1974. *Strangers at the Gate: Social Disorder in South China, 1838–1861.* Berkeley: University of California Press.

Walker, W. 1988. "The Other Side of the Asian Academic Success Myth: The Hmong Story." Qualifying paper for the doctorate in education, Harvard Graduate School of Education. ERIC no. ED 302 609 (Dec.).

Waller, C., and L. M. Hoffman. 1989. "United States Immigration Law as a Foreign Policy Tool: The Beijing Crisis and the United States Response." *Georgetown Immigration Law Journal* 3, no. 3 (Fall): 313–59.

Walton, H. 1985. *Invisible Politics: Black Political Behavior.* Albany: State University of New York Press.

Wasserman, J. 1979. *Immigration Law and Practice.* Philadelphia: Joint Committee on Continuing Legal Education of the American Law Institute and the American Bar Association.

Welch, S., and P. Secret. 1981. "Sex, Race, and Political Participation." *Western Political Quarterly* 34, no. 1 (Mar.): 5–16.

Welch, S. 1975. "Ethnic Differences in Social and Political Participation: A Comparison of Some Anglo and Mexican Americans." *Pacific Sociological Review* 18, no. 3 (July): 361–82.

Welch, S. 1977. "Identity With the Ethnic Community and Political Behavior." *Ethnicity* 4, no. 3 (Sept.): 216–25.

Wesley-Smith, P. 1980. *Unequal Treaty 1898–1997.* Hong Kong: Oxford University Press.

Whitney, J. 1888. *The Chinese and the Chinese Question.* New York: Thompson & Morean.

Wilke, A. S., and R. P. Mohan. 1984. "The Politics of Asian Americans: An Assessment." *International Journal of Contemporary Sociology* 21 (July and Oct.): 29–71.

Wolfinger, R. E. 1965. "The Development and Persistence of Ethnic Voting." *American Political Science Review* 59, no. 4: 896–908.

Wollenberg, C. 1976. *All Deliberate Speed*. Berkeley: University of California Press.

Wong, B. 1971. "Introduction: Asian Americans and the Apotheosis of American Democracy." In A. Tachiki, ed., *Roots: An Asian American Reader*, pp. 131–33. Los Angeles: Continental Graphics.

Wong, M. G. 1980. "Changes in Socioeconomic Status of Chinese Male Population in the United States from 1960 to 1970." *International Migration Review* 14, no. 4: 511–24.

Wong, P. 1972. "The Emergence of the Asian-American Movement." *Bridge* 2, no. 1 (Sept./Oct.): 33–39.

Woolsey. 1921. "The California-Japanese Question: An Editorial Comment from the Annual Meeting of the American Society of International Law." *American Journal of International Law* 15: 58.

World Bank. 1988. *World Development Report*. New York: Oxford University Press.

Wunder, J. R. 1989. "Law and the Chinese on the Southwest Frontier, 1850–1902." *Western Legal History* 2, no. 2 (Summer/Fall): 139–58.

Wynne, R. 1966. "Labor Leaders and the Vancouver Anti-Oriental Riot." *Pacific Northwest Quarterly* 67: 172–79.

———. 1978. *Reaction to the Chinese in the Pacific Northwest and British Columbia, 1850 to 1910*. New York: Arno Press.

Xenos, P., R. Gardner, H. Barringer, and M. Levin. 1987. "Asian Americans: Growth and Change in the 1970's." In J. Fawcett and B. Cariño, eds., *Pacific Bridges*, pp. 249–84.

Yamamoto, E. 1990. "Efficiency Threat to the Value of Accessible Courts for Minorities." *Harvard Civil Rights Civil Liberties Law Review* 2, no. 2 (Summer): 341–429.

Yanagisako, S. 1985. *Transforming the Past*. Stanford, Calif.: Stanford University Press.

Yee, A. H. 1990. "Asian Students as Stereotypes." Unpublished paper, National University of Singapore (Feb. 7).

Yinger, J. M. 1978. "Ethnicity in Complex Societies: Structural, Cultural and Characterological Factors." In L. A. Coser and O. N. Larsen, eds., *The Uses of Controversy in Sociology*. New York: Free Press.

Yu, E. 1980. "Filipino Migration and Community Organizations in the United States." *California Sociologist* 3, no. 2 (Summer): 76–102.

# Index

In this index an "f" after a number indicates a separate reference on the next page, and an "ff" indicates separate references on the next two pages. A continuous discussion over two or more pages is indicated by a span of page numbers, e.g., "pp. 57–58." *Passim* is used for a cluster of references in close but not consecutive sequence.